Marveling Religion

Religion and Science as a Critical Discourse

Series Editors: Lisa Stenmark, San Jose State University, and Whitney Bauman, Florida International University

Understanding religion and science as a critical discourse means building on theoretical issues and concerns to address social transformation, and issues of justice and global concerns. Contributions to this series will employ multiple perspectives upon the process of doing and thinking "science and religion" together, but ultimately see the relationship of religion and science as creating space for a kind of critical discourse. This might mean: exploring disagreements between two authoritative disciplines that challenge one another; incorporating critical theories and discourses (understood narrowly as the Frankfort School, and, more broadly, as critical race theory and feminist, postcolonial, and queer approaches within the social sciences, natural sciences, or humanities); or a focus on voices from outside the dominant discourse, which in the case of this series means people from outside of the western academy. In each case, the goal is to shake up assumptions, challenge givens, and open up space for new questions and new perspectives so we can think about pressing problems in a more productive and inclusive way.

Recent Titles in Series
Marveling Religion: Critical Discourses, Religion, and the Marvel Cinematic Universe, edited by Jennifer Baldwin and Daniel White Hodge

Religious Transhumanism and Its Critics, edited by Arwin M. Gouw, Brian Patrick Green, and Ted Peters

Amor Mundi and Overcoming Modern World Alienation, by Justin Pack

Navigating Post-Truth and Alternative Facts: Religion and Science as Political Theology, edited by Jennifer Baldwin

Unsettling Science and Religion: Contributions and Questions from Queer Studies, edited by Lisa Stenmark and Whitney Bauman

Marveling Religion

Critical Discourses, Religion, and the Marvel Cinematic Universe

Edited by
Jennifer Baldwin and Daniel White Hodge

LEXINGTON BOOKS
Lanham • Boulder • New York • London

Published by Lexington Books
An imprint of The Rowman & Littlefield Publishing Group, Inc.
4501 Forbes Boulevard, Suite 200, Lanham, Maryland 20706
www.rowman.com

86-90 Paul Street, London EC2A 4NE

Copyright © 2022 by The Rowman & Littlefield Publishing Group, Inc.

All rights reserved. No part of this book may be reproduced in any form or by any electronic or mechanical means, including information storage and retrieval systems, without written permission from the publisher, except by a reviewer who may quote passages in a review.

British Library Cataloguing in Publication information available

Library of Congress Cataloging-in-Publication Data

Names: Baldwin, Jennifer, editor. | Hodge, Daniel White, 1974- editor.
Title: Marveling religion : critical discourses, religion, and the Marvel cinematic universe / edited by Jennifer Baldwin and Daniel White Hodge.
Description: Lanham : Lexington Books, [2022] | Series: Religion and science as a critical discourse | Includes bibliographical references and index.
Identifiers: LCCN 2022024484 (print) | LCCN 2022024485 (ebook) | ISBN 9781793621382 (cloth) | ISBN 9781793621405 (paperback) | ISBN 9781793621399 (epub)
Subjects: LCSH: Religion in motion pictures. | Motion pictures and comic books. | Motion pictures—Religious aspects. | Superhero films—History and criticism. | Marvel Studios. | LCGFT: Film criticism.
Classification: LCC PN1995.9.R4 M376 2022 (print) | LCC PN1995.9.R4 (ebook) | DDC 607/.04—dc29
LC record available at https://lccn.loc.gov/2022024484
LC ebook record available at https://lccn.loc.gov/2022024485

Contents

Preface: Marveling Religion: Visual Culture as a Common Tongue   vii
   Daniel White Hodge and Jennifer Baldwin

PART I: TECHNOLOGY, VIOLENCE, AND SACRIFICE

1. "I See a Suit of Armor around the World": Tony Stark's Techno-Idolatry and Self-Sacrificial Love   3
   George A. Dunn and Jason T. Eberl

2. Mimesis, Conflict, and Sacrificial Crisis in Black Panther   19
   Matthew Brake

3. Bulletproof Love: *Luke Cage*, Race, and Religion   33
   Ken Derry, Daniel White Hodge, Laurel Zweissler, Stanley Talbert, Matthew J Cressler, and Jon Ivan Gill

PART II: POWER, WORTH, AND SOCIETY

4. Old Gods in New Films: History, Culture, and Religion in *Black Panther*, *Doctor Strange*, and *Thor: Ragnarok*   67
   Rhiannon Grant and Jo Henderson-Merrygold

5. The Worthiness of Thor   87
   Adam Barkman and Bennet Soenen

6. "Who Are You?": René Girard, W. E. B. Du Bois, and Black Panther   101
   Ryan Smock

7   The Failure of a God: Thor, the Snap, and Post-Holocaust
    Political Theology   113
    Andrew T. Vink

8   Mysterio as Antichrist in *Spider-Man: Far From Home*   127
    George Tsakiridis

PART III: DECONSTRUCTING NORMS, IMAGINING THE NEW

9   Science and the Marvel Cinematic Universe: Deconstructing the
    Boundary between Science, Technology, and Religion   143
    Lisa Stenmark

10 Religion, Science, and the Marvel Universe: Reimagining
    Human–Earth Relations   159
    Whitney Bauman and Imran Khan

11 "Open Your Eye": Psychedelics, Spirituality,
    and Trauma Resolution   179
    Jennifer Baldwin

PART IV: FORMING IDENTITY

12 Marveling at Captain Danvers, Or, What Is So Super about Our
    Heroes? Contesting the Identity Politics of Self-Other   197
    John C. McDowell

13 The Supermuslim and the Marvel Cinematic Universe:
    A Complicated Trajectory of Fantasy and Agency   217
    Dilyana Mincheva

14 Bad Girls Turned Superwomen: A Critical Appraisal of the MCU
    Archetype for Superheroines   239
    Will Abney

Index   257

About the Contributors   261

Preface

Marveling Religion: Visual Culture as a Common Tongue

Daniel White Hodge and Jennifer Baldwin

So, can we keep it real here? I mean, let me be honest, the year that this text is being written is one of the most difficult years we have had in the contemporary Western world. A pandemic. A president that is anything but normal. A racial reckoning in the United States. The loss of truth as a common baseline and the rise of "fake-news." I mean, there is no part of me, Hodge, that feels like a superhero. Most of this feels like the ending of *Infinity War* (2018), when people start to fade away into small pieces of matter; in fact, that is quite reminiscent of what Covid-19 is doing to so many. Except the reality is we do not have a Stark-created time machine that can bring those who have fallen to the Coronavirus back. So, we are left with a void. These are dark times, at least for me, Hodge. It has taken me so much just to scribble out an introduction to such a great book like this; if anything, I feel so much of the weight of being Black and entombed in the four walls of my house that any form of creativity goes to, well, remodeling the bathroom. Religiously speaking, there could be a lot to interpret from this. Is it the end of the world? Are we witnessing the "wrath of God?" I am not so sure or convinced on either of those thought processes. But here we are; in it. I only wish I could have a spaceship like Peter Quill that could take us out of this mess and find a new planet. Yet, so much of what is happening feels like some type of Thanos snapped their fingers and, here we are with no escape. I know, I know, there are a lot of folks that have it much worse; I get that. It just bears noting that a book dealing with superheroes and religion seems a bit odd and out of sorts, right? Or is it?

I mean, it is interesting, is it not? The notion that a comic book series could generate such a response. I mean, something that was once looked at as a child's way of escape into fantasy is now front and center of so many conversations, and look, now we have a book dealing with the religion of it all! Amazing. What a time to be alive, right? Well, let us ponder that and the significance of religion within the Marvel Comic Universe (MCU). I, Hodge, grew up in a strict and rigid religious household; often anything that did not have an explicit "Jesus" sticker on it was proxy to being "secular" or "of the world." So, comic books were of course not exactly a "spiritual" oasis that my family would approve of as "biblical." Still, I was able to sneak a few in and, can I just be honest here? I was not impressed—it did not make sense to me! It was difficult, for me, to get into the story. My entry into the MCU would not come until years later when I was an adult and had attended academic panels on comic books. But, in that time something else had developed in me, a sense of story and the critical inquiry of it through popular culture. I was now fascinated with how religion and theology show up in the complex narratives of characters within the film. Christopher Nolan's *The Dark Knight* (2008) gave a visual tale of a multifaceted hero in Batman and the dystopian space The Joker took up was scene stealing. Yes, I realize that is from the D.C. universe, but my point here is that there is a lot to unpack with "superheroes." It is not a simple cut-and-paste heroism. Growing up superheroes were perfect, pure, always able to overcome. The narratives of those who "help us mortals" did not always resonate with me. As a racially Black man, there were very few superheroes I could identify with and my idealization of White cis male heroes wearing capes to "save all" was all but vanished by my early teens. So, an all-encompassing hero to make things right was not present for me. Until I was introduced in a better manner, to the MCU and its complexity and multi-layered characters—they were not perfect! Genius in some sense like Bruce Banner or Tony Stark, but wrought with rage, trauma, angst, dysfunctional pride, and even depression. These are not traits typically seen in what we conceptualize as superheroes.

More importantly, in a culture that appears to desire more of the authentic human experience, it would seem a scrappy crew of Avengers is exactly what we need now. Not a polished embodied perfected superhero that only has one or two hang-ups. No. We need something that is a little messy; I love the line from Talos in *Captain Marvel* (2019) in that we all have our hands dirty from war. So true.

And what do we make of deity in all this? Thanos, in many ways, could be a version of the Old Testament God situated clearly in the Christian faith. God, being all powerful and in control of a lot of the elements, can cause plagues, massive floods, planetary extinctions, and even nuke cities at their own will. Sounds like a Thanos to me. And the jargon that Thanos's team uses such as cleansing, and sacrifice; wow. That is eerily similar to Old Testament language; Ebony Maw could be Elijah or even Joshua for that matter, with his zealous fundamentalism for his master. And doesn't Thanos have a stimulating point to make about resources, population increases, and social capital? It is something that the God of the Old Testament refers to when people would stray too far from God's "plan." Most of the time, humans were at the whim of God's power much like so many civilizations were to Thanos. Thanos is so strong; it took the entire combined power of the Avengers to defeat him and that is including Captain Marvel and Hulk. That is something to consider.

What about the technology that is covered in connection to religion? I, Hodge, have long contended that the God and Jesus deities in the Christian faith are simply Type IV civilizations whose technological advancements look like nothing more than magic to their creations. They are the original organic architects who, in some way, could have owned an Infinity Stone or created a world in which their creations would serve them—they would not have much of a choice. In many ways, the language used in the Christian Canon reflects that of Quantum language and Metaphysics to describe a God or just a technological being far beyond our understanding. Could God just be another cog in the wheel of the universe attempting to conquer worlds like Thanos and we, their servants, are left "worshipping" God only because their technology outreaches us and we surmise that technology down to religion? You have to remember; Stark was quite the humanist until he met Thor—even though he tried to fight him with his own technology. Further, Thor was, in fact, a God to humans; it is part of what made him so arrogant in that people worshiped him. Loki had another good point in *The Avengers* (2012) in that humans needed to be ruled; that we looked for someone to lead us. Wow. A true statement—especially in times of peril or danger. Loki figured we, humans, were an easy group to rule given our lack of technological achievement. God from the Old Testament could fit right into this and Jesus could have been a Thor-like character who wanted to run interference between us and his parents.

VISUAL CULTURE AND SACRED TEXTS

It is no doubt that visual and social media culture is making an indelible mark on the cultural language of the twenty-first century. From Facebook, Instagram, Twitter, and TikTok to YouTube, streaming services like Hulu and Netflix, and cinema franchises that span platforms, our cultures' primary means of social communication is through visual media. Print media like physical newspapers and books are waning in their capacity to provide the shared language of our culture, for better or worse. Consequently, if academic pursuits desire to remain relevant and believe that there is a significant common benefit offered by careful analysis and rigorous theory construction, scholars would be wise to engage with the visual media that often captures popular awareness and speaks to the shared affect of the times. The idea that popular forms of visual media function as a common language is not new. In fact, the stained glass windows in houses of worship often functioned as a sacred text for populations prior to widespread literacy. Social images have always been a common language that functioned both prescriptively and descriptively—showing us who we can aspire to be and who we are in both our fears and gifts. The primary element that changes over time as a consequence of the growth in technological complexity is the form of our visual media and the range of affect, imagination, and complexity it is able to convey. Graphic novels are more complex, responsive, reflective, and complete than stained glass windows. Virtual reality is more complex and immersive than cinema. In our current technotemporal age (especially in the age of covid), cinema via streaming platforms and social media is the most prolific and best primed to contribute to cultural discourse and mirror social affect.

The Marvel Cinematic Universe (MCU) and its streaming and televised offspring (2008–ongoing) provide a critical lens through which to examine dominant trends in our shared life precisely due to its longevity, diversity, and internal continuity. While the historical and cultural vision of the MCU is truncated in comparison to its comic source materials, the MCU's global distribution via film and television grants it a popular cultural awareness, fandom, and currency that dwarfs the comic books. Since 2008's introduced the wider populace to Tony Stark with his concluding pronouncement "I am . . . Iron Man," the visual world crafted through the MCU, television, and streaming has developed alongside the prevailing cultural currents. The critiques of capitalism, toxic masculinity, and armament that were central to the opening film grew into a recognition of the importance of representation and diversity. As the MCU moved toward greater representation in phase three, it aptly shifted the "heroes journey" to reflect societal challenges faced by our heroes and heroines including patriarchy, global responsibility, repatriations, climate change, genocide, and colonialism. The depth of representation cultivated in the course of the first three phases of the MCU, while remaining vastly insufficient, provides fruitful soil to explore shifts in our cultural norms over the course of twelve years (2008–2019)—to look at who we have been, who we are, and who we want to be.

As a field ripe with popular currency and of societal reflection, the MCU can be a prism through which scholars can world-reflect and world-build. What are the themes present in the media? How do they illuminate or conceal components of our shared cultural and religious life? How do they creatively reflect to us our generativity and our limitations? What hermeneutical lenses are most effective in cinematic exegesis? As an academically inclined person (Baldwin) who is married to a nonacademic comic lover, we have very different interests with regard to the MCU and the place of analysis and post-viewing commentary. For my partner, he is primarily interested in seeing how filmmakers bring characters and storylines to life on the screen. The visual media is an end unto itself. For me, these films are a beginning of the conversation that is most vitalizing when it can inform or illuminate patterns in our current culture and historical context. This type of book is the next layer of fun for me; for others, it is an unnecessary complication of something meant just to entertain and provide an escape from the demands of daily life. For those of us burdened with a desire to glean additional meaning and depth from the artistic work of others, questions of how we go about that work and toward what end will orient the path we travel and how we identify ourselves within the visual media. Do we identify ourselves and those who agree with us as the hero? (Spoiler alert: most of us will.) To what degree are we willing to demonize the other in order to solidify that belief regardless of historical or ethical analysis? Identification without a guiding hermeneutic can become dangerous as the sacred becomes at risk of turning to the demonic.

Religion and Assembling the Avengers

Religion, in broad conceptualization, are the practices that members of a community enact and perform together for the purpose of connecting to and exploring the sacred. As distinct from spirituality as the set of our personal practices of connection to the divine presence, faith as a Tillichian concept of centering one's life, and theology as the linguistic and conceptual articulation of spirituality, faith, and religion, religion itself includes the symbolic, ritual, and embodied acts that tie us together as a community of faith. The content of our shared faith can range from political parties, nationalities, sports teams, or even religions more commonly understood but all include symbols of meaning, rituals of inclusion/exclusion, and practices that enhance intergroup connections. As a set of embodied practices that tie members of a community together, religion is assembling with a shared mission. When religion enjoins toward the sacred, as in our most common understanding, we share songs of praise, confessions of faith, gestures of devotion, and rites of life passage and community inclusion. When religion binds our citizenry, we sing anthems, recite pledges, salute, and vote. If we happen to be a superhero in the Marvel Universe, we show up to the fight, protect our friends, complete the mission, leave no one behind, and when the time comes, assemble. The internal codes that uniquely guide all communities and their members are also present and equally malleable for the Avengers.

Within the MCU, the journey of assembly begins, in a sense, with Tony Stark's disclosure "I am . . . Iron Man." Echoing the self-identification of YHWH to Moses as "I am," Tony points to himself as the centralizing god of this universe—at least until Thor shows up. However, Tony's godship isn't through a distinction of being; rather it is through his creative technological ability. His capacity to create from the chaos of the caves a supertechnosapien. Tony is not divine. He is a super co-creator. The task of assembling builds through the first three phases as we are introduced to more characters. As our heroes increase in number, they expand our awareness of the scope of the universe—its mysteries, gifts, and challenges expand geographically, temporally, dimensionally, and mystically. Not only do we depart from Earth as THE central location and get a glimpse of it as Midgard for the Asgardians and as C-53 through the naming system of the Kree, though it remains a common location, we also travel throughout the universe, into the quantum realm and the dark dimension, and through time. As the scope of our awareness grows, so does our awareness of human and Earth vulnerability. Human beings are not only not the only living beings in the universe; we are not even the most technologically, intellectually, or physically advanced. If Copernicus and Galileo were a significant threat to the centrality of Earth and humanity by advancing heliocentrism, what does the idea that we are designated as C-53 say about human centrality and dominance? Talk about a center that cannot hold. However, it is precisely threats from a greater power wielding the power of the creation of the universe that leads to our Avengers assembling in their fullness, cohesion, and strength. Teased in the final seconds of *Age of Ultron*, viewers are rewarded with Captain America's call "Avengers assemble" as all of the heroes emerge through portals to battle 2014 Thanos and crew. Decentralization from the centers of American wealth, technology, and militarization that characterized Iron Man, Hulk, and Captain America materialize into a universally diverse ensemble capable of matching and defeating a universal threat.

The inquiry of what makes one human super or divine only becomes more complex as the viewer moves through the phases calling us to both expand and refine what it means to be a god/God. As Hodge invites us to consider in the opening section, the question of humanity and our relation to divinity is ripe soil in the MCU. What does it mean to be a god/God? What happens to the collective theology of monotheistic traditions when Thor shows up? What about when Thor gets his butt kicked? Or when half of all life in the universe goes up in a puff of ash, reminding us of Ash Wednesday, Shoah, and our creation from chaos clay, and YHWH still doesn't show up? What if being a god isn't ultimately about controlling power and directing universal events? While these are evocative theological questions, terrifying or enraging some and exciting others, they are not questions at the center of concern within the

MCU. The larger arch in this universe, thus far, is about personal identity formation, overcoming adversity in a wide variety of forms, community building, and accountability for those who wield power. They offer us, as viewers, a multitude of templates for how we could navigate these forms of questions and challenges in our lives and communities. When we face overwhelming trauma, will we face post-traumatic symptoms like Tony or escape into alcohol like Thor? When we encounter devastating loss, will we return to our ancestral homes and build a community like T'Challa or stoke the fires of vengeance and retribution like Killmonger/N'Jadaka—and which one holds the more just response? How do we see through the mirages of alternative facts spun by those who only seek power and fame like Mysterio in *Far From Home*?

One of the reasons this cinematic universe is so compelling is that the answers it offers are rarely easy. While Thanos was the "bad guy" of the Infinity Saga, 2018 Thanos also kinda had a good point. When particular species overrun the capacity of the ecosystem to support their life and the lives of other species, what is the ethical response? For humans on this planet, we are fairly adept at increasing hunting permissions to reduce the population size of various animals and yet are abysmal at noticing the ways in which the impact of our collective life on the planet is decimating other species and threatening the sustainable health of the planet. These forms of ethical questions permeate the films in the MCU and call us to imagine how we might respond. Ethics, like theology or religious studies, requires us to extend beyond the particularities of our personal lives to consider bigger questions. These matters are not tangential to our religious or spiritual lives. They flow from them and reflect them. How we embody our sense of connection to the divine, however we encounter and understand it, will manifest in how we care for others in our midst, utilize our power, and respond to challenging demands. Sometimes our hero/ines make a good choice and rise to the occasion. Sometimes they collapse under the weight of loss or pressure. And sometimes the "villains" surprise us with valiant ideals, hopes, and/or actions. The point is that the MCU like real life is often far more messy than it is clear—and yet, we still must respond.

In times when our visual or cinematic culture reaches further than a print media, it is worth engaging these global "texts" as offering far more than escapist entertainment. They unwittingly become our shared sacred texts offering us a catalyst to imagine alternative responses to shared challenges and an opening into difficult conversations regarding our history and hopes for a more just society and planet. In times when it may be difficult to engage in these conversations through the lens of religious devotion and affiliation or political alignment, the MCU can provide a common point of discourse. While we may not be able to come to an agreement on political parties or platforms, I imagine very few people were rooting for Red Skull in *Captain America* or Thanos. The MCU can give us a common ground from which we can then explore other themes. Additionally, *Captain America: Civil War* can show us how to have substantial disagreements within our community and even fight about it without devolving into hatred or abandoning each other when it is time to come together in the face of a bigger threat. This offering seems especially urgent at the beginning of 2021 in the United States.

Overview

Marveling Religion: Critical Discourses, Religion, and the Marvel Cinematic Universe is an edited volume that explores the critical intersection of religion and cinema through the lenses of critical discourse. The focus of the shared inquiry are various films comprising the first three phases of the MCU with reaches into streaming series on Netflix. This text explores various religious themes and how they intersect with culture through the cannon on the MCU. It is organized into four parts. The first part focuses on the themes of technology, violence, and sacrifice and how they interplay in the character development of heroes in the MCU. Part II explores how power transfers within the various cultures of the MCU, how our heroes navigate questions of worth and identity, and the role of Jesus as a model. The third part centers on deconstructing hegemonic norms within the MCU through the lenses of science fiction and altered states of consciousness. These contributions explore possibilities that emerge for newness and healing when we allow ourselves to decenter. The final section investigates how female-identified characters are portrayed in the MCU and how that portrayal could expand in future ventures. The overarching aim of the volume is to promote critical discourse utilizing the shared social medium of the MCU.

Part I, "Technology, Violence, and Sacrifice," opens with George Dunn and Jason Eberl's exploration of Tony Stark's journey from arms dealer to self-sacrifice as the only means of defeating Thanos. They wonder about the transfer from violence to sacrifice as the only true way of securing protection from threat. Matthew Brake takes up the threat of violence and sacrifice through the lens of Rene Girard's mimetic theory with an eye on the central conflict in *Black Panther*. Brake describes a "sacrificial crisis" in which the clear lines of hero and villain become blurred leading to more questions rather than clear answers. The blurred lines of hero/villain and sacrifice/scapegoat problematize the genre in ways that call viewers to expand our "easy" answers. Derry et al. also explore themes of violence centering on liberation rather than sacrifice and with a call for us to look toward complexity rather than simplicity. This chapter explores love and religion through the medium of *Luke Cage*. Holding in tension competing themes and imagery, the authors of this chapter examine Luke Cage as a Christ figure who is also deeply humanized and imperfect to make the claim that "Luke is a sacred, secular, and profane hero." Through these chapters, the authors make the overarching case that technology, violence, and sacrifice are not as monolithic and simple as a cursory viewing of films in the broader superhero genre may present. When we look more closely, a rich complexity opens up giving us creative space to navigate how we consider the role of technology in aggression/protection and the role of sacrifice and power as a remedy for violence.

The second section most directly weaves in more traditional Christian tropes and questions. This section begins with an analysis of religion and the transfer of power within various lineages of kingship. Rhiannon Grant and Jo Henderson-Merrygold compare religious and cultural frames within *Black Panther*, *Doctor Strange*, and *Thor: Ragnarok* to illuminate religious formations that deviate from the continued establishment of "white Protestant Christian hegemony." Grant and Henderson-Merrygold helpfully direct our attention to the use and inheritance of power while warning us of the risk of falling into a form of religious tourism even in the canon of the MCU. Adam Barkman and Bennet Soenen wonder about the category of worth in relation to Thor and the power of Mjolnir. They also discuss the inheritance of power through a kingship line and its connection to an assessment of worth. Worthiness for Barkman and Soenen is a potential ground for connecting Jesus and Thor as a Christ figure via their function as a sacrifice. They argue that Mjolnir, Thor's hammer, functions as an indicator of whether or not one is worthy and makes its determination based on one's willingness to sacrifice themselves for others. Ryan Smock returns our attention to Rene Girard but explores questions of identity formation, desire, and Christ as a model for nonviolent social influence. Smock turns toward *Black Panther* to elucidate connections among power, desire, and who we choose to be. He also invokes Jesus as an exemplar of the correct path counter to the Satan figure as the path of desire. However, the path toward clarifying our identity is often more complicated and multivariate. In the fourth chapter of this section, Andrew Vink investigates the intersections between the tragedy of the Holocaust, post-Shoah theological reflection, and suffering in the aftermath of the Snap. Vink utilizes points of intersection with an intention toward the quandary at the center of theodicy. He asks, "how do we make sense of an apparent failure of (a) God in light of an atrocity?" Vink hones in on Thor in *Infinity War* and *Endgame* as a lens for where we go theologically when god fails to prevent catastrophic loss and draws on post-Shoah Christian theologians Metz, Moltmann, Soelle for leads on how to navigate desolate terrain. In the final chapter of the section, George Tsakiridis guides us to the final film in phase three *Spider-Man: Far From Home*. He argues that Mysterio functions as an anti-Christ figure counter to Peter Parker. Mysterio provides Parker with an adversary that moves him from his role as a friendly neighborhood superhero into the light of a global threat. As Fury reminds him, he's been to space and can no longer hide out in the neighborhood. Drawing on Biblical and Early Church theology, Tsakiridis asserts that Mysterio as primarily an agent of deception to draw power and become the arbiter and creator of "truth" fulfills the role of the antichrist. Parker's task is then to prevail over deception and step into his true identity, role, and promise.

Part III explores the outer bounds and intentionally decenters established norms. Lisa Stenmark opens this section with an examination of the boundaries between science, technology, and religion in the MCU. Coming from a home in Science and Religion Discourse (SRD), Stenmark offers the genre of science fiction as a guide to breaking out of the questions that have bound SRD for nearly 60 years. Intersecting this larger project with the MCU, Stenmark offers science fiction and visions of utopia as a lubricant to envision new ways of being unhindered by the legacies of colonialism. She specifically offers the lenses of magic, Afrofuturism, and the multiverse as paths out of the old paradigms that have become stale or calcified and unable to carry us into a new future. Whitney Bauman and Imran Khan also delve into the intersections of science, religion, and the MCU; however, they focus their discussion on hybridity, time, and planetary care. Bauman and Khan wonder how we can "think anew our relationships to one another and to the rest of the natural worlds in which we live." In a creative transition from the MCU to the more expansive Marvel Universe, they weave in wisdom from the X-Men into the film canon that is the primary focus of this text. Ultimately, they press us to think beyond human centrality and exceptionalism to rediscover the awesome humility that comes when we release the idea that we are the center of creation. The lenses employed by Stenmark, Bauman, and Khan draw us to consider futures that require creativity and draw us into alternative awareness spaces and times. Jennifer Baldwin draws on the film *Doctor Strange* as a framework for journeying through the impacts of trauma, states of consciousness, and mystical forms of spirituality. Spanning fields of trauma psychotherapy, cinema, and theology, Baldwin highlights the growing utility of psychedelics for the treatment of trauma and depression. She argues that altered states of conscious can pull us out of our vitality in cases of traumatized dissociation or draw us into healing states of mystical connection.

The fourth and final section of *Marveling Religion* focuses on the intersections of politics, religion, and gender in the MCU. John C. McDowell starts this section with an analysis of the political and cultural underpinnings of cinema. He argues that in a post-9/11 world (where quoting Kevin Wetmore 9/11 points to a traumatizing cultural experience, "a day, an event, a period, a mindset and a cultural shift"), the primary themes of many films, including

Captain Marvel, are a means of working through the unanswered questions and challenges faced during culture-altering social events. For McDowell, these films call us to re/consider how we treat our neighbors, utilize our power, and form our collective identity. Drawing heavily on Žižek and the five marks of post-9/11-cinema, he argues that *Captain Marvel* falls clearly into the category of post-9/11 cinema. Dilyana Mincheva develops the image of the Supermuslim through real-life utilization of superhero motifs, new comic developments focusing on explicitly Muslim heroes and heroines, and various Muslim cultural responses to *Jessica Jones.* Mincheva keenly notes and expands the multidimensionality of the intersections of the MCU and the Muslim world impacting psychological, sociological, and political imagery, symbolism, affiliation, identity, and action. William Abney continues this conversation by investigating the central tropes surrounding superheroines in the MCU arguing that the dominant template exemplifying a postfeminist lens, which often feels like a return to pre-feminism ideals and expectations, is the "bad girl turned good." Abney traces the character development of five central female characters in the MCU and notes how their trajectory falls short of the complexity and nuancing of the male characters. While this general critique of the MCU is not new, Abney helps clarify key areas in need to overview and transformation as the MCU moves into phase four if they hope to craft the developmentally rich and engaging female characters.

As I, Baldwin, have been reading and organizing these rich chapters, I have also enjoyed rewatching the films from *Iron Man* through the first few episodes of *WandaVision.* Through the interweaving of viewing and reading, I have consistently found that the questions, themes, and connections exemplified in this volume have deepened and expanded what I notice as a repeat viewer. For instance, in watching *Infinity War* and *Endgame* post-reading, I can't help but wonder about and enjoy imagining a chapter on Thanos's assessment of worth. I wonder about the intentional decision to place *Captain Marvel* in the space between the dusting and Tony's rescue. I find myself fascinated anew by the decision to have Tony trapped in space in the aftermath of Thanos's violence and ultimate weapon and its parallel with Tony's time as a prisoner in the cave following a demonstration of his capacity to weld weapons of mass violence. I am also newly curious and excited by the decision to make *Far From Home* with its emphasis on fake news occupying the void and disorientation of the global populations now living with two very different experiences of time as the final chapter of Phase 3 and *WandaVision* as the Covid-era beginning of Phase 4 as a television-based (in setting and distribution) journey into, what I think will be, the psychic wounds of traumatic loss.

Popular culture media curates mass interest when it has the capacity to both reflect the dominant affect of the time and express what we may not even realize needs expressing. It grants us a shared visual culture to explore our collective wounds and hopes. And hopefully will expand our capacity for understanding and empathy for those whose stories differ from our own as the MCU expands its roster of heroes to more fully represent humanity. The stories we show and tell are important. Who we cast as hero/ine or villain will inform how we subconsciously see our neighbors. In eras when we are both more aware of those whose cultural and religious practices diverge from our lived experience and less open to pausing our own experience to learn from others from their perspective, there is greater power and responsibility to craft our shared global "texts" with care. For better or worse, the films and shows of the MCU are a global language and symbol set—what will we make of them? The collection of essays in this volume give us a community of responses to explore these films with increasing depth and connection. They also help us imagine what could be and begin the work of moving together toward a richer future.

Part I

TECHNOLOGY, VIOLENCE, AND SACRIFICE

Chapter 1

"I See a Suit of Armor around the World"

Tony Stark's Techno-Idolatry and Self-Sacrificial Love

George A. Dunn and Jason T. Eberl

The Marvel Cinematic Universe (MCU) is full of heroes who have been enhanced in various ways, whether injected with an experimental serum, accidentally exposed to gamma radiation, or integrated with a weaponized suit. Steve Rogers was selected for the super-soldier program precisely because Dr. Erskine perceived him to have the right moral qualities—he wasn't just a war-mongering fighter, but "a good man." In contrast with Captain America's relatively steady moral compass, Tony Stark follows a more circuitous route of moral maturation toward his heroic sacrifice in *Avengers: Endgame*. Initially adhering to his father's philosophy that "peace means having a bigger stick than the other guy," Tony eventually realizes that Stark Industries needs to stop manufacturing and selling offensive weapons of war. Tony's change of heart, however, does not mean he gave up on the idea of technological weapons being developed and used for *defensive* purposes— thus his creation of the first Iron Man suit as a means of immediate survival. Yet, the technology quickly gets away from him as first Obadiah Stane steals his plans and builds the Iron Monger suit in *Iron Man*, then Brody confiscates a suit in *Iron Man 2* to become Iron Patriot/War Machine. Ultimately, Tony realizes in *Iron Man 3* how much his technological endeavors have run amok after creating dozens of different armored suits and facing Aldrich Killian's Extremis-enhanced minions.

Though Tony dials back the number of suits he has invented, *Avengers: Age of Ultron* sees him and Bruce Banner making a quantum leap in technological innovation when they utilize the power of the Mind Stone in Loki's captured staff to create the artificially intelligent Ultron. Why?

Because in a vision of the future engendered by Wanda Maximoff's mental manipulation, Tony foresees the devastation that will be wrought by Thanos unless he builds "a suit of armor around the world." Tony's failures with Ultron and against Thanos in *Avengers: Infinity War* lead him to realize that he cannot simply "cut the wire" as he arrogantly told Steve Rogers, but must lay himself over the wire just as Steve threw his body on what he thought was a live grenade way back at Camp Lehigh. Old-fashioned self-sacrificial *virtue*, not technology, ultimately defeats Thanos.

Tony's prideful belief in his own technological prowess is a manifestation of the "technocratic paradigm" that both philosophers (such as Martin Heidegger in his essay "The Question Concerning Technology"[1]) and religious leaders (such as Pope Francis in his encyclical *Laudato Si'*[2]) have warned against for nearly a century. Such warnings are not anti-technology *per se*—certainly various technological apparatus, including Hank Pym's van-ensconced device for entering the quantum realm, play an essential role in defeating Thanos. Rather, they concern a certain way of being that is inevitably cultivated through our faith in technological solutions for every type of problem. Technology has its own "internal logic" that "enframes" the natural world, rendering it intelligible in mathematical terms and thus entirely at our disposal to manipulate as we see fit. Meanwhile, the technological imperative to go "higher, further, faster" becomes civilization's overriding goal to which all other moral values and ends become subservient. The Christian philosopher Jacques Ellul has gone so far as to suggest that technology has become our new "sacred."[3] Rather than being a set of neutral tools in the service of human purposes and desires, the technological system has become the overarching framework of our civilization to which human beings are forced to adapt, engendering in us new desires that would be inconceivable apart from it. Technology not only enframes the natural world, it enframes *us*. The technocratic paradigm even distorts Tony's relationship with Pepper Potts, which is why his retreat to an idyllic lake cabin after The Snap is the only way he can recover his humanity and start a family.

Is there an appropriate use of technology that can help Tony and the rest of us avoid the entrapment of the technocratic mindset? Can morally virtuous persons utilize technology for laudable ends or is technology ultimately and inevitably corrupting? Can we replace the technocratic paradigm with a new conception of our place in nature, one that no longer sacralizes technology and treats nature as mere "standing reserve," as Heidegger aptly describes it, fodder to be pressed into service to the machine? We can only hope that we can find that one way out of 14,000,605 possibilities to repair the damage to our humanity wrought by our quasi-religious faith in technology as our savior.

THE FALLEN WORLD OF TONY STARK

Tony Stark is in trouble. He is in a cave surrounded by members of the terrorist group, The Ten Rings. They have threatened to kill him unless he makes for them a weapon of mass destruction. Technologically, this presents no problem for Tony. Morally, it is not that much of a problem either as his highly lucrative business specializes in creating all sorts of destructive weapons—but only for the right customers. Instead of building a weapon, Tony constructs an armored suit—Iron Man Mark 1—to effect his escape. Assisting him is Ho Yinsen, another captive. Unlike Tony, Yinsen has no plans to escape; he is ready to join the rest of his family, who were killed by The Ten Rings. When Tony enacts his escape plan, Yinsen sacrifices himself to buy time for Tony, to whom such self-sacrifice probably seemed inconceivable. After all, other than his parents' untimely death, he has never had to face the type of hardship that most people not born into wealth and privilege experience on an almost daily basis. The lack of existential threat in Tony's life has resulted not only in his inclination toward hedonistic indulgence—liquor, women, fast cars—but also a hubristic expectation that he can control his own fate and even that of the world-at-large. Having a bomb with his name on it blow up right in front of his face was the first step in the humbling of Tony Stark. Yet, he was not immediately humbled after being victimized by his own creation. Instead, he harnessed his technical prowess to fabricate the means of his deliverance—a deliverance, it must be emphasized, that probably would not have come about if not for Yinsen's sacrifice.

The fear for his own survival that motivates Tony to build the first Iron Man suit increases exponentially when he experiences a vision of the Avengers' future defeat by Thanos, without even yet realizing that their defeat would result in half of all living beings in the universe blinking out of existence. This fear motivates Tony to build the artificially intelligent weapon Ultron. The existential threat of Thanos is to be met by the technological power of Ultron. Tony's belief that he can build a savior mechanism for the world evinces the height of his pride, his *hubris*. "Hubris" is a classical Greek term that refers to the belief that one can control one's fate by exerting control over nature. A prime exemplification of this concept is the story of Icarus. Like Tony, Icarus and his father want to say, "Yeah, I can fly." Though they lack repulsor technology, they construct wings that allow them to soar into the sky like eagles. When Icarus flies too close to the sun, however, the wax holding his wings together melts and he plummets to his death. Tony does not have that problem—though he did encounter ice build-up as he tried to break the SR-71 altitude record. Tony's hubris almost killed him in his very first flight as Iron Man; yet, his ability to eventually control his suit and make it perform exactly as he wants feeds his prideful belief that can control anything he creates. Ultron will teach him how wrong he was.

Like the fall to earth that nearly killed Tony in his first test flight of the Iron Man Mark 2 suit, the Bible recounts the mythical fall of the first humans, Adam and Eve, also the result of hubris. As the story goes in the first chapters of the Book of Genesis, God created the primordial humans on the sixth and final day of creation and immediately issued to them his prime directive: "Be fruitful and multiply, and fill the earth and subdue it; and have dominion over the fish of the sea and over the birds of the air and over every living thing that moves upon the earth" (Genesis 1:28). In the second version of the story, God placed Adam in the Garden of Eden and told him "to till it and keep it" (Genesis 2:15). Right away, it sounds as if the divine creator of the universe is privileging one among the living kinds he has created with both the capacity—intelligence and free will, according to his own "image and likeness"—and the charge to exercise technocratic control over the rest of creation. But does "dominion" mean *dominance* of the sort Thanos seeks to obtain over the universe using the Infinity Stones? Or does it mean *stewardship*? In his encyclical letter addressing present-day ecological concerns, Pope Francis affirms the latter interpretation:

> "Tilling" refers to cultivating, ploughing or working, while "keeping" means caring, protecting, overseeing and preserving. This implies a relationship of mutual responsibility between human beings and nature. Each community can take from the bounty of the earth whatever it needs for subsistence, but it also has the duty to protect the earth and to ensure its fruitfulness for coming generations.... This responsibility for God's earth means that human beings, endowed with intelligence, must respect the laws of nature and the delicate equilibria existing between the creatures of this world.[4]

The "original sin" of Adam and Eve originates in the temptation to eat of the one forbidden tree in the paradisal garden, the fruit of which will allow them to "be like God, knowing good and evil" (Genesis 3:5). Pride obscured their awareness of their own *creaturehood* and they forgot that they were not meant to "be like God"—and could not be anyway—but rather were intended to live *harmoniously*, Wakanda-like, with all other types of creatures. But neither this initial prideful fall nor the punishment it brought upon all subsequent generations, has stopped human beings from hubristically aiming to manufacture their own divinity. Another apt biblical story is that of the Tower of Babel, in which humanity, united in one language, attempts to construct a city with a tower reaching into the heavens. Interestingly, this is perceived as a *threat* to God, who muses, "this is only the beginning of what they will do; nothing that they propose to do will now be impossible for them" (Genesis 11:6). But perhaps the threat is not to God *per se*—he has already one-upped Thanos by destroying all but a handful of humans and animals in a "great flood" (Genesis 7). Rather, perhaps God foresees that such an immense technological feat will inevitably lead humans to becoming further enframed in the technocratic mindset, exacerbating their already fractured relationship with the rest of the natural world. The story concludes with God confusing their language, such that humanity can no longer so easily collaborate together and ends up scattered across various parts of the globe.

THE QUESTION CONCERNING TONY STARK

Tony Stark is motivated by a fundamental drive to maximize his own self-interest—his survival above all—and the welfare of those he loves. He also desires wealth, influence, and to belittle those he considers his intellectual inferiors, such as Justin Hammer and Senator Stern. These all-too-human imperatives lead Tony to do what he does best: harness technology to attain his goals. Little does he know that technology possesses its own imperatives. While technology can be an aid to human endeavors, it can also end up dictating those endeavors, reshaping the structure of our desires, and entrapping us, the putative "users" of technology, in a dependent relationship with the tools we have created. Tony gets an inkling of how technology can get the upper hand on its creators when he realizes how much he has become embedded in the military-industrial complex as a weapons-manufacture for the U.S. government, some of those weapons having fallen into the hands of terrorists such as The Ten Rings. In the press conference he held after returning from captivity, Tony avowed that Stark Industries will cease to produce such weapons, announcing, "I saw that I had become part of a system that is comfortable with zero accountability."

Alas, this glimmer of wisdom is overshadowed by Tony's continued infatuation with seeking technological solutions to every problem. It is obvious that he shares the conviction of his father, Howard Stark, who proclaimed, "Everything is achievable through technology." This totalizing logic blinds Tony to the potential misappropriation of his inventions. When Obadiah Stane adapts Tony's blueprints for the Mark 1 to develop the Iron Monger suit, he taunts Tony, telling him, "Trying to rid the world of weapons, you gave it its best one ever!" But contrary to what Howard and Tony believe, it is simply not true that every human problem can be solved through technology, nor is technology a dependable route to human betterment.

The twentieth-century German philosopher Martin Heidegger offers a powerful reflection on technology in his essay "The Question Concerning Technology." Presumably, so we do not mistake his question as an exploration of purely technical problems of the sort Tony grapples with when he refines his suits, Heidegger alerts us at the outset that his question concerns the *essence* of technology, not the hardware *per se* but the way in which technology has come to hold sway over our lives. We tend to identify technology with technical devices, those gadgets large and small that we encounter at every turn and that frame our every activity—from the alarm clocks that awaken us in the morning to the transportation systems that ferry us to work, from the addictive screens that transport us into us the MCU and other worlds of entertainment to the medical miracles that pull us back from the brink of death. For Tony Stark, the technological apparatus interlaced in his daily routine even include artificially intelligent assistants like Jarvis and Friday. But, for Heidegger, all of these accoutrements of technological civilization are really just surface phenomena, the outward armor of a recondite *essence* that "is by no means anything technological."[5] Just as the Iron Man suit obscures from view the flesh-and-blood human being operating it from within, so too the enthralling ensemble of technological tools and techniques within which we live our lives hides something more fundamental that makes it all possible. To grasp what really animates these machines and how they came to be, we must look beneath the armor. Heidegger warns that we will be misled if we remain fixated exclusively on the Iron Man suit's admittedly dazzling surface or become too entranced with its hot-rod paint scheme. "Technology is not equivalent to the essence of technology," he declares.[6]

What is technology, then, and what is its essence? When we examine Tony's armor, a couple of things immediately stand out. First, this product of technical ingenuity was designed to be a *means* to an end. We cannot give an adequate account of Tony's armor, let alone any of the myriad other items in the vast arsenal of high-tech weapons scattered throughout the Avengers' headquarters, without attending to the purposes to which they are put. They are tools and we do not really know what a tool *is*—be it an enchanted hammer, a vibranium shield, or an Artificially Intelligent Peacekeeping Program like Ultron—until we know what it is *for*. And that leads to the second salient aspect of Tony's armor, which also applies to tools in general. Precisely because these technological artifacts exist for a purpose, they derive their meaning from the *human activity* that posits the ends they serve. From these two considerations emerge what Heidegger calls the *anthropological* and *instrumental* definition of technology: it is a *human activity* through which we employ *means* of various degrees of sophistication and efficacy to accomplish our humanly chosen ends. In short, technology is our *instrument* and we are its *masters*. That technology can sometimes "get away" from us—cutting its strings like Ultron—and forget who is boss only underscores the urgency of reasserting our control, using technology to reign in technology, as the Avengers do in *Age of Ultron*.

Yet, regardless of whether we are battling against our own runaway technology or cautiously keeping it on a short leash, we are tyrannized by technology in ways that Heidegger believes imperil our humanity. One source of the problem is that we fail to understand our true relationship to our technology. The anthropological and instrumental definition of technology is *correct* as far as it goes, since it does indeed reflect how we usually view ourselves in relation to technology, but it misses everything *essential*. Technology is not just a set of technical means for getting the job done while leaving us free to determine what the job will be; it ineluctably shapes our ends and has even in a sense *become* our primary end, the defining project of our civilization. It is, in Heidegger's portentous language, our *destiny*, more like a fate into which we have been ensnared than an instrument we employ. Part of what Heidegger is getting at is that we are inextricably enmeshed in a technological system that shapes our lives at every turn. We work in factories such as Hammer Industries, research institutes such as Aldrich Killian's AIM, and bureaucracies such as SHIELD—all of which perpetuate and advance the technological system—only to come home and consume entertainment that has been engineered in different sorts of factories to keep our attention pleasantly occupied while we recuperate, just as Wanda retreats into classic American television sitcoms. And, like Tony, we always assume that the solution to any problems created by technology is more and better technology and approach every difficulty as a problem to be solved through technical means. We are "claimed" head to toe (or helmet to jet boots) by technology, says Heidegger. Understanding the *real* essence of technology means grasping the nature of this claim.

But first, we must first back up a bit and consider Heidegger's account of what it means to be human. Bucking the dominant philosophical tradition of the West, Heidegger does not regard human beings primarily as "rational animals," as living beings endowed with the ability to cogitate and calculate about things given in our experience. Before we can reason about the world, Heidegger reminds us, we must first and more essentially be the sort of beings for whom the world shows up as meaningful. Things acquire their meanings due to human activity. It is only because of our activities and purposes, our needs and desires, our fears and aspirations, that things present themselves to us meaningfully—as opposed to being mere sensations and behavioral triggers. Consider one of Heidegger's favorite examples, the workshop, an environment very familiar to Tony Stark. Whether in the primitive workshop in Afghanistan, where he cobbled together the Iron Man prototype, or in the high-tech workshop of his Malibu home, with its futuristic see-through monitors and the 3D interface he uses to interact with Jarvis, every item within Tony's reach has significance only in relationship to the whole ensemble of tools to which it belongs and the uses to which they are put.

Remove a mechanical claw, say, from the practical context provided by the workshop and it ceases to be a claw and becomes nothing but an oddly shaped hunk of metal—and this is no less true for any of Tony's other toys. It is a human purpose that makes them what they are. Likewise, an artifact like the "Jericho" missile has the meaning of being a dangerous weapon commanding "fear" and "respect" only because of how it relates to human concerns. The world we inhabit is textured with meaning—it is a world of things that appear as not just neutral sense data but as beings that can be menacing, dangerous, loveable, desirable, disgusting, comforting, useful, entertaining, and even boring—solely due to the fact that we are more than just bags of chemicals attached to primitive computers made of meat, but beings whose nature it is to be concerned about our existence.[7]

Human beings are thus best understood as occupants of a meaningful world that is "revealed" or brought to presence through our practical engagements with the things around us, which become what they are due to where they stand in relation to a vast range of interlocking activities through which we interpret or make sense of them. Tony Stark may think he is responding only to the practical exigencies of the moment when he aspires to encase the world in a suit of armor, but even more primordially he is answering to what Heidegger calls the "challenging claim" to "reveal" the world in *one* certain way. Technology is not just a set of hyper-efficient means to achieving our goals, nor is it just an assembly of mechanical parts fitted together to perform some task. Most essentially, technology is a particular way of interpreting and ordering the world, in which the whole of nature presents itself to us as what Heidegger calls "standing reserve"—a vast storehouse of raw materials and energy waiting to be unlocked, extracted, accumulated, transported, transformed, and commandeered by human beings. When we bow to the challenging claim of technology, all of nature becomes like the vibranium reserve underneath Wakanda, something to be plundered and recruited to various human purposes. Heidegger's term for this challenging claim is *Ge-stell*, sometimes translated as "enframing." This term captures the idea of inhabiting a world where we set upon nature to unlock its secrets and reveal the world as "standing reserve," stuff to be mastered and manipulated by us. Just as Tony taps into New York City's power grid with a modified arc reactor to power Stark Tower, so too nature as a whole becomes one vast power source, the repository of energies to be extracted, harnessed, and configured into ever-new "enframings," open to human exploitation.

It is telling that when, in *Captain America: Civil War*, Tony addresses a crowd of students at MIT and announces that they will all receive grants with "no strings, no taxes" from his newly established September Foundation, he directs them to "reframe the future," echoing Heidegger's language of "enframing." For Heidegger, "enframe the future" is the directive that every denizen of our technological civilization must obey, one that we are in no position to refuse as long as technology asserts its "challenging claim" on us. "Modern technology as an ordering revealing is, then, no merely human doing,"[8] he concludes. "Only to the extent that man for his part is already challenged to exploit the energies of nature can this ordering revealing happen."[9] But how did technology come to claim us in this way? And are there other ways of interpreting ourselves and our place in the world that release us from the imperious technological stance toward nature to which we have become addicted?

SOFT WAX, HARD SCIENCE, AND REDEEMING LOVE

This event of "enframing" that reveals the natural world as "standing reserve" predates the emergence of modern machine technology in the same way that the blueprint for the new element Tony synthesizes in *Iron Man 2*, hidden in the design of the 1974 Stark Expo, precedes the actual synthesis of the element. The blueprint for our modern technological civilization was drawn up in the seventeenth century and its draftsmen were two of history's greatest philosophers, Francis Bacon and René Descartes. Bacon's most famous adage—"Knowledge is power"—was his pithy way of saying that the goal of scientific study should not be the edifying contemplation of nature's forms, as earlier natural philosophers had taught, but achieving practical control over nature. We must tear away nature's veil of modesty and uncover her hidden workings in order to make her work for *us*, rendering the natural world "the slave of mankind."[10] If Bacon's great achievement was to inspire future generations with a new vision of what might be possible for human beings, it fell to Descartes to describe the effective means for realizing that vision. In addition to pioneering the mathematics that made modern physics possible—it is no accident that every classroom and corridor of Tony's alma mater MIT is infused with a Cartesian zeal for graphs and equations—Descartes also taught modern science to interpret the natural world *not* as a heterogenous collection of beings, each with its own distinct nature and purpose, but rather as homogeneous matter-in-motion, obeying the same mathematical laws everywhere and thus masterable once we discover those laws.

In a memorable passage from his *Meditations on First Philosophy*, Descartes compares the material world to soft wax that possesses no essential qualities other than its infinite malleability. Just as a piece of wax should not be identified with such mutable qualities as its size, shape, color, or smell that change when we hold it close to fire—as Icarus discovered to his doom—so too, Descartes implies, we should think of the material world as a substance "capable of innumerable changes . . . even though I am incapable of running through these innumerable changes using my imagination."[11] And if the material world really is like mutable soft wax, then a full understanding of its properties and workings should allow us to reconfigure its matter and forces to suit our whims, even to the point of manufacturing entirely novel objects and processes that have no model or precedent in nature, such as the new element Tony synthesizes to power his Iron Man suits. Heidegger's standing reserve is the direct descendent of Descartes's soft wax, an apt metaphor for an assault on the world that "pursues and entraps nature as a calculable coherence of forces."[12] In *essence*, then, the technological paradigm is already present at the outset of modern science as envisioned in the program laid out by Bacon and Descartes. Both philosophers interpreted the natural world in a way that denuded it of any meaning other than as a store of resources and energies to be harnessed. Once we have come to fully understand its workings, we will have the potential to enrich and empower ourselves even beyond the wealth and power the Wakandans extract from the stores of vibranium deposited by the meteor that crashed there millennia ago.

In his *Discourse on Method*, Descartes was especially candid about the technological potential of this new science, describing its ultimate goal as making us "masters and possessors of nature"—an implicit challenge to the Supreme Being who was regarded by most of Descartes's contemporaries as the sole possessor of the title to the natural world, a realm in which we only sojourn as grateful pilgrims. Any doubt that Descartes really intended to displace God's traditional sovereignty is dispelled when he explained that our mastery of nature is "desirable not only for the invention of an infinity of devices that would enable us to enjoy without pain the fruits of the earth and all the goods one finds in it, but also principally for the maintenance of health . . . [so that we might rid ourselves] even perhaps also of the enfeeblement brought on by old age."[13] His language seems to have been deliberately chosen to recall two of the three curses laid upon Adam and Eve for their hubris: a life of painful toil and then physical decline culminating in death (Genesis 3:17–19).[14] Descartes's ambition might thus be characterized as an attempt to reconquer by technological means the Garden from which human beings were expelled as punishment for their prideful overreach.[15] One of the greatest intellectual founders of our technological civilization not only shared the same hubristic aspirations that we earlier associated with Tony Stark, but was bold enough to declare its defiant implications in shockingly stark terms.

Four centuries after Descartes, we are all too acutely aware of the countless ways this promise of a reconstituted Eden has not panned out. In addition to the ecological crisis that Pope Francis addresses, which has taught us that nature may not be quite as pliable as soft wax, after all, we are menaced by weapons of mass destruction and the ever-looming possibility of a renewed arms race between hostile nations. We are reminded of these dangers every time Tony's technology gets away from him, sometimes taken by others or, in the case of Ultron, leaving by its own accord. But, for Heidegger, the greatest danger of technology is *spiritual* in nature: its threat to the human essence. In particular, he worries that we will become so captive to this "enframed" way of interpreting the world that it will crowd out every other way of understanding ourselves and nature. When that happens, Heidegger believes we have come "to the brink of a precipitous fall."[16] Habituated to view everything as "standing reserve" from which energy can be extracted and reconfigured for our use, the inhabitant of modern technological civilization is moving steadily to "the point where he himself will have to be taken as standing reserve."[17] At this point, not only will the meaning of the world have been reduced to mere fodder for human exploitation, but we will have lost a sense of where our true humanity lies, namely, as the beings who allow things to "reveal" themselves in inexhaustible ways—not just as wax to be reshaped by the human will but as, among other things, epiphanies of the divine that elicit reverence and wonder. Consider the Asgardians' view of nature, their knowledge of how to work with the heterogeneous beings and forces of their world to let the sacred dimension of existence shine through them. Perhaps that way of "revealing" is what allowed them to evolve into god-like beings. On the other hand, a world dominated by "enframing" is one from which, as Heidegger puts it, "the gods have fled."[18] Having conquered the natural world, human nature becomes the final frontier to be re-engineered, mastered, and modified. We witness a particularly dire form of this phenomenon with the nano-powered Extremis formula, which effectively treats the entire human body and its physiology, including its DNA, as a kind of standing reserve—in the words of Aldrich Killian, as mere "bioelectrical potential" to be redesigned or "upgraded"—with consequences that are literally explosive.

Though Heidegger's account of our plight is bleak, he still holds out the hope that we might somehow wean ourselves of our infatuation with technology "to enter into a more original revealing and hence to experience the call of a more primal truth."[19] George Parkin Grant, a twentieth-century Christian philosopher profoundly influenced by Heidegger, offers some specifics about the sort of truth the "modern paradigm," as he calls it, has obscured. Within the modern technological paradigm embraced by scientific engineers like Tony Stark, the way to know and thus obtain power over a being is to treat it as a mere "object," "summoning" it before us and "putting it to the question, so that it gives its reason for being the way it is as an object."[20] But to know a being as an object to be mastered, Grant argues, is incompatible with knowing it as *loveable*. Of course, one might protest that there is a sense in which we "love" those things we appropriate for use. Tony presumably loves his fleet of sports cars, his Iron Man suits, and the vast wealth at his disposal. What he really delights in, however, is not the existence of such things *per se*, but the pleasure and other benefits he derives from them. What Grant means by "love" is more than just desiring an object as a means to augment one's power or even as something to be pleasantly consumed, like the single-malt scotch Tony enjoys so much. To consume something or to turn it into an extension of oneself is in fact nearly the opposite of what Grant means by "love." "Love is consent to the fact that there is genuine otherness,"[21] he tells us, adding that otherness is loveable precisely "because it is beautiful"[22] and that to premodern thinkers—we might call them pre-technological thinkers—"beauty was known as an image of goodness itself."[23] A world seen as beautiful and intrinsically lovable is not a world we can ruthlessly mine for its resources.

We might recall Heidegger's contention that the meaning of the world emerges not through detached rational scrutiny, but through our active and affective engagement with the beings around us. For Grant, those beings show themselves as good, as things to be cherished rather than subdued, to those who are open to their beauty. He directs us to an experience of the world as an epiphany of meaning very different from the "modern paradigm" with its imperative to order everything as a standing reserve. Dimming the beauty of the world with its drive to mastery, the technological paradigm ultimately occludes, in Grant's words, "the affirmation—so incredible to everyone at one time or another—that the cause of being is beneficence."[24] That affirmation is at the heart of our religious traditions but it is also present, if only tacitly, in every genuine experience of beauty. Consequently, technology's grip on us can never be total so long as we remain open to the beauty of the world, which, Grant reminds us, "manifests itself most intensely for us in the beauty of other people."[25] We see in *Iron Man 3* how Tony's entrapment within the technological paradigm—and, in particular, his obsession with building an army of suits controlled by Jarvis—imperils his relationship with Pepper, whom he has every reason to cherish. But we also see how that relationship offers him an escape from the technological paradigm that would otherwise consume him. If the Soul Stone grants power to those willing to destroy what they love most, it is love that ultimately saves us from the soul-destroying appetite for power.

"I THINK I'D JUST CUT THE WIRE"

Within the broad theological worldview shared by the major Abrahamic traditions—Judaism, Christianity, and Islam—the ongoing "civil war" that began with the fall of Adam and Eve involves not only the violence that humans inflict on each other—beginning with Cain against Abel (Genesis 4:1–16)—but also enmity between humans and the rest of the world: "cursed is the ground because of you; in toil you shall eat of it all the days of your life; thorns and thistles it shall bring forth for you" (Genesis 3:17–18). As noted earlier, Bacon and Descartes attempted to describe how human powers could be expanded to allow us to overcome this divine curse, though the implementation of their program has led to the ever-increasing disruption of our relationship with the rest of nature. And, while humanity has been largely successful in wresting not merely sustenance from the soil, but also building upon that soil cities that rival Jericho and skyscrapers—like Stark Tower—that put the Tower of Babel to shame, such accomplishments have betrayed what Pope Francis interprets as God's primordial command to exercise responsible stewardship over the goods provided for our use. As he notes, in language that recalls Heidegger's critique of modern civilization's aggressive stance toward nature,

> Men and women have constantly intervened in nature, but for a long time this meant being in tune with and respecting the possibilities offered by the things themselves. It was a matter of receiving what nature itself allowed, as if from its own hand. Now, by contrast, we are the ones to lay our hands on things, attempting to extract everything possible from them while frequently ignoring or forgetting the reality in front of us. Human beings and material objects no longer extend a friendly hand to one another; the relationship has become confrontational.[26]

Again, the issue at hand is not the development and use of technology *per se*. Given his concern with the limits of nonrenewable energy sources that we are rapidly using up, Francis would likely applaud Tony's creation of the Arc reactor that powers Stark Tower and could potentially provide renewable energy for the entire world. Rather, it is that we have fallen into a "technocratic" mindset in which, instead of believing that nothing is impossible with God (Luke 1:37), we imagine that nothing is impossible *for us* if we have a sufficiently well-designed Iron Man suit. Francis warns, however, that

> Our freedom fades when it is handed over to the blind forces of the unconscious, of immediate needs, of self-interest, and of violence. In this sense, we stand naked and exposed in the face of our ever-increasing power, lacking the wherewithal to control it. We have certain superficial mechanisms, but we cannot claim to have a sound ethics, a culture and spirituality genuinely capable of setting limits and teaching clear-minded self-restraint.[27]

Pope Francis is diagnosing the same problem Tony recognizes does when he admits that he had "become part of a system that is comfortable with zero accountability":

> We have to accept that technological products are not neutral, for they create a framework which ends up conditioning lifestyles and shaping social possibilities along the lines dictated by the interests of certain powerful groups.[28]

The temptation on the part of those with power to use technology to advance their own end of maintaining and increasing their power echoes the primordial temptation of Adam and Eve to become "like God." Just like the serpent's whisper, "Technology tends to absorb everything into its ironclad logic."[29] Yet, Francis affirms his hope that humanity can break itself out of this dominant technocratic paradigm: "We have the freedom needed to limit and direct technology; we can put it at the service of another type of progress, one which is healthier, more human, more social, more integral."[30]

As discussed above, the disharmony between humanity and the rest of the natural world is also exhibited in our own relationship to our natural *bodies*, which we seek to technologize through biomedical and cybernetic means:

> It is enough to recognize that our body itself establishes us in a direct relationship with the environment and with other living beings. The acceptance of our bodies as God's gift is vital for welcoming and accepting the entire world as a gift from the Father and our common home, whereas thinking that we enjoy absolute power over our own bodies turns, often subtly, into thinking that we enjoy absolute power over creation. Learning to accept our body, to care for it and to respect its fullest meaning, is an essential element of any genuine human ecology.[31]

Tony's damaged body is dependent on technology just for him to survive. However, when he powers his Iron Man suit with the mini-arc reactor that keeps the shrapnel from entering his heart, he fuses himself with the suit so totally that he proclaims that he and it are *one*, which is why he cannot simply turn it over to the U.S. government. Of course, this fusion is not literal, since he can step out of the suit, and others—first Brody and later Pepper and Bruce—are able to use various versions of the suit themselves. In a *phenomenological* sense, though, Tony certainly experiences himself as more his *authentic* self when he is in the suit, saving the world. As discussed earlier, Tony's obsession with expressing himself through an increasing multitude of types of Iron Man suits disrupts his relationship with Pepper and, for Tony not to lose his identity to "Iron Man," he must destroy all of the suits he has created at the end of *Iron Man 3*. Yet, he cannot help building a nanotech version of the suit to wear in case his worst nightmare comes true and Thanos shows up.

PROOF THAT TONY STARK HAS A HEART

Thanos's ultimate defeat requires the cooperation of all of the Avengers and their allies, who all use various tools to assist them, including Thor's hammer,

Cap's shield, and Wanda's psychic powers. All of their efforts would have been in vain, though, if not for two self-sacrifices—Black Widow's and Tony's—motivated by love. Both willingly give their lives to save the half of the universe's population that had been snapped out of existence five years prior, thereby demonstrating a heroic sense of duty to others reaching far beyond their intimate circles of friends and family. But they also both do so out of their love for particular persons—in Natasha's case, for her most trusted friend Hawkeye; in Tony's, for his family and Peter Parker, whose death in *Infinity War* hit him the hardest. Tony's love for particular others, in whom he glimpses the beauty through which the goodness of the world shines, grants him the freedom to serve a purpose that, as Francis describes, is "more human" than the merciless logic of the technological paradigm. That paradigm can tell us how to transform and command nature's energies, but it cannot tell us why any of the existing beings of nature are worth saving. That is something truly known and articulated in deed only by self-sacrificial love, first modeled for Tony by Yinsen, who died with the expectation of being reunited with his slain family. Tony Stark may have lived his life wed to the technological paradigm, but the events surrounding the birth of his Iron Man, as well as the circumstances of his death, testify to how we might transcend it.

NOTES

1. In Martin Heidegger, *The Question Concerning Technology and Other Essays*, translated and with an introduction by William Lovitt (New York: Garfield Publishing, Inc., 1977), 3–35.
2. Francis, *Laudato Si'* [*LS*]: http://www.vatican.va/content/francesco/en/encyclicals/documents/papa-francesco_20150524_enciclica-laudato-si.html.
3. See Jacques Ellul, *The Technological Society* (New York: Vintage Books, 1964).
4. Francis, *LS*, nos. 67–68.
5. Heidegger, *Question*, 4.
6. Ibid.
7. Heidegger elaborates this understanding of what it means to be human at length in his magnum opus *Being and Time*, translated by Joan Stambaugh, revised edition (New York: SUNY Press, 2010).
8. Ibid., 19.
9. Ibid., 18.
10. Among Bacon's major writings on this subject is his *Novum Organum*, translated and edited by Peter Urbach and John Gibson (Peru, IL: Open Court, 1994).
11. René Descartes, *Meditations on First Philosophy*, translated by Donald A. Cress (Indianapolis: Hackett Publishing Company, 1991), 22.
12. Heidegger, *Question*, 21.

13. René Descartes, *Discourse on Method*, translated by Donald A. Cress, 3rd edition (Indianapolis: Hackett Publishing Company, 1991), 35.

14. Descartes does not allude to the other curse, which was directed solely at the woman. Perhaps the promise of finding ways to alleviate the pain of childbirth was not considered a strong selling point to include in a prospectus to be circulated almost exclusively among men.

15. The impious rhetoric of this section of the *Discourse on Method* contrasts sharply with Descartes's reputation for religious orthodoxy, which he diligently courted in works such as the *Meditations*.

16. Heidegger, *Question*, 27.

17. Ibid.

18. Ibid., 117.

19. Ibid., 28.

20. George Grant, *Technology and Justice* (Concord, ON: House of Anansi Press, 1986), 21.

21. Ibid., 38.

22. Ibid., 39.

23. Ibid., 41.

24. Ibid., 42.

25. Ibid., 51.

26. Francis, *LS*, no. 106.

27. Francis, *LS*, no. 105.

28. Francis, *LS*, no. 107.

29. Francis, *LS*, no. 108.

30. Francis, *LS*, no. 112.

31. Francis, *LS*, no. 155.

REFERENCES

Bacon, Francis. *Novum Organum*. Translated and edited by Peter Urbach and John Gibson. Peru, IL: Open Court, 1994.

Descartes, René. *Meditations on First Philosophy*. Translated by Donald A. Cress. Indianapolis: Hackett Publishing Company, 1991.

Ellul, Jacques. *The Technological Society*. New York: Vintage Books, 1964.

Francis. *Laudato Si'*. Accessed on March 15, 2021. http://www.vatican.va/content/francesco/en/encyclicals/documents/papa-francesco_20150524_enciclica-laudato-si.html.

Grant, George. *Technology and Justice*. Concord, ON: House of Anansi Press, 1986.

Heidegger, Martin. *Being and Time*. Translated by Joan Stambaugh. New York: SUNY Press, 2010.

———. *The Question Concerning Technology and Other Essays*. Translated and with an introduction by William Lovitt. New York: Garfield Publishing, Inc., 1977.

Chapter 2

Mimesis, Conflict, and Sacrificial Crisis in Black Panther

Matthew Brake

In the movie *Black Panther*, Eric Killmonger, the son of N'Jobu, a prince of Wakanda who dies by the hand of his brother King T'Chaka, seeks to expose the truth about his father's death and usurp the throne of Wakanda in order to gain access to its vibranium weapons and distribute them to oppressed peoples of color around the world. He wins a duel with T'Challa, the Black Panther and king of Wakanda, and believing him to be dead, takes the throne, donning a variation of the Black Panther suit. However, T'Challa does not die and returns to face Killmonger. The two Black Panthers fight, with the forces of Wakanda split between them. In the end, Killmonger dies but not without inspiring T'Challa to end Wakanda's isolation and take steps toward making the world a better place.

In many ways, the story of *Black Panther* mirrors the thought of the twentieth-century philosophical anthropologist and literary critic René Girard. Girard is probably best known for his mimetic theory—the idea that humans are imitative creatures. Not only do humans imitate each other's behaviors, but humans learn what to desire by watching other humans. This mimetic desire often brings us into conflict with others, eventually culminating in an act of violence, and the original object of the conflict ceases to matter. One act of violence, however, demands a reciprocal act of violence. For Girard, violence is like a contagion, sparking a cycle of revenge that will not end until one of the parties is able to strike the final blow. When violence breaks out, the very social order breaks down.

In order to curb violence, human beings developed a mechanism to channel our violent impulses elsewhere—religious sacrifice. This victim of sacrifice or "scapegoat" becomes the foundation on which an entire mythology and "noble lie" is built that constructs and maintains social order. In *Black Panther*, one can think of Ulysses Klaue, against whom all of Wakanda directs its rage, and more importantly, T'Chaka's brother N'Jobu, whose secret death remains hidden and allows the isolationist social order of Wakanda to continue. Unfortunately, Killmonger's arrival reveals the truth of this death and the role it played in continuing Wakanda's isolationist social structure, and as Girard postulates, once the myth inaugurated by the scapegoat is unraveled and the truth revealed, the social order created by sacrifice breaks down, inaugurating what Girard calls the "sacrificial crisis."

One of the telltale signs of a sacrificial crisis is the presence of twins. Girard notes how in world literature, twins are always an omen of social disaster. He postulates that this is due to the acknowledgment of the mimetic nature of violence (can there be any greater imitation than literal twins?), such that the arrival of twins foretells the breakdown of the social order and the spread of the contagion of violence. Once violence is unleashed, it takes on a life of its own, and both parties lose the moral high ground. Killmonger and T'Challa embody this quite literally in their final battle, and it is not a coincidence that many moviegoers felt a great deal of sympathy for Killmonger's perspective. The distinctions of right and wrong between the two men became blurred.

Finally, the sacrificial crisis can only end with the death of a new scapegoat, which becomes the foundation for a new social order. In this case, the death of Killmonger inaugurates a new era of world intervention for Wakanda. From Killmonger's death, a new myth arises that takes Wakanda into its Marvel Cinematic Universe (MCU) future. Girard notes that while the victim of sacrifice is the victim of violence in life, he is venerated in death.

This chapter will analyze the film *Black Panther* through the lens of Girard's mimetic theory, including his views on scapegoating and the sacrificial crisis. I will evaluate the sacrificial crisis instigated by Killmonger's arrival in Wakanda, the role of vengeance in escalating the crisis in Wakanda, and the means by which the crisis is brought to an end through Killmonger's death.

MYTHS, SACRIFICES, AND SCAPEGOATS

Black Panther is a film of myths and scapegoats. The story begins with an ancient myth about the birth of Wakanda and the discovery of a meteorite containing the fictional substance vibranium, one of the most durable metals in the MCU. Viewers learn that five African tribes warred over the fabled substance until the first Black Panther gained his powers by eating a heart-shaped herb affected by the vibranium in the meteorite. He was able to unite four out of five tribes, all except the Jabari tribe, and Wakanda isolated itself from the rest of the world.

Here at the very beginning, a Girardian reading of this "text" reveals all of the basic elements of Girard's mimetic theory. Wakanda's story begins with a type of sacrificial crisis, a war of all against all, instigated by a mimetic conflict over the vibranium. It is possible to see the Jabari as a type of scapegoat whose seclusion from the rest of the tribes does line up with the peace of Wakanda. Scapegoats and sacrifices are always necessary to found not only a religion but the social order itself, as well as the myth that glosses over the messy details and violence against an innocent victim. Reading Wakanda's founding myth through a mimetic lens, Girard himself would argue that such a mythological tale of origins covers over a much messier reality, one where all parties involved avoid appearing as the "purely" good side (which is the way the tale is told, the four tribes of Wakanda are obviously meant to be read as "good," while the Jabari are meant to be "bad").[1] In Girard's estimate, the use of violence in mimetic conflicts forecloses the possibility of either side being separated into "good" and "bad" sides. While M'Baku of the Jabari tribe is initially portrayed as a villain (in the comics, an archnemesis of Black Panther problematically named Man-Ape), the end of the movie shows that M'Baku is not truly villainous and "bad," nor are the tribes aligned with T'Challa truly noble and "good." Violence and mimetic conflict produce an ambiguity to human action, an ambiguity covered over by lies and myths.[2] These lies are further reinforced by the perpetuation of a given culture's rituals, particularly the ritual of sacrificing a scapegoat. Myth is a type of "cover-up" for the real truth about the sacrifices that maintain a society's social order.

Ulysses Klau also might be thought of as a type of scapegoat. True, he is an arms dealer who breaks the laws of Wakanda by stealing its natural resource of vibranium, but the blame placed on Klau covers over a more ambiguous truth—a member of the royal family of Wakanda, King T'Chaka's brother N'Jobu, was working with Klau to steal vibranium in order to provide Wakandan weapons to people of color throughout the world to free them from the oppressive systems they live under. In order for scapegoats to work, there must be a unanimity surrounding the choice of the scapegoat, of all against one. If there is a remaining "divide" within society, the scapegoat won't be effective and mimetic violence in society will continue.[3] A scapegoat must stand alone in order to avoid the fear of reprisals, which would allow the mimetic conflict to continue.[4] It is easier to maintain social order by blaming a lone villain than it is to address the complicated moral and political motivations of N'Jobu, motivations which a number of his Wakandan comrades sympathize with. Again, at the center of the conflict is the object of desire itself—vibranium.

N'Jobu himself is another scapegoat, albeit an ineffective one, as I will unpack in a moment. When T'Chaka confronts his brother in 1992, he is forced to kill him. T'Chaka and his friend Zuri then perpetuate a lie that his brother disappeared, a lie that allowed Wakanda to continue its status quo policy of isolation from the rest of the world. The death of his brother, and the lie covering it up, act as Girard's scapegoat and obscuring myth. There is, however, a problem with N'Jobu's status as a scapegoat. Girard makes clear that the scapegoat must be a solitary figure. There can't be anyone on its side who will then retaliate with vengeance.[5] But that is exactly what happens. Erik Stevens, aka Killmonger, aka N'Jadaka, son of N'Jobu, remembers what happened and returns to Wakanda.

VENGEANCE, VIOLENCE, AND MIMETIC DESIRE

Girard describes human violence with words such as "contagion" and "contamination."[6] He writes, "The slightest outbreak of violence can bring about a catastrophic escalation. Though we may tend to lose sight of this fact in our own daily lives, we are intellectually aware of its validity, and are often reminded that there is something infectious about the spectacle of violence."[7] This can make vengeance itself "an intolerable menace . . . because the only satisfactory revenge for spilt blood is spilling the blood of the killer."[8] Girard explains, "Vengeance professes to be an act of reprisal, and every reprisal calls for another reprisal. The crime to which the act of vengeance addresses itself is almost never an unprecedented offense; in almost every case it has been committed in revenge for some prior crime."[9] As such, Girard states, "Vengeance, then, is an interminable, infinitely repetitive process" that threatens "the whole social body," for "[t]here is the risk that the act of vengeance will initiate a chain reaction whose consequences will quickly prove fatal to any society of modest size. The multiplication of reprisals instantaneously puts the very existence of a society in jeopardy."[10] In *Black Panther*, we see the very escalation of violence that Girard warns us about.

The story of *Black Panther* is driven by nothing if not vengeance. T'Challa is driven to avenge his father in *Captain America: Civil War*, leading to a sacrificial crisis of sorts for the Avengers. Now, in *Black Panther*, the theme of vengeance comes to the forefront again. T'Challa seeks vengeance for the entire nation of Wakanda by pursuing Ulysses Klaue in South Korea, driven in part by his friend W'Kabi, whose parents had been killed by Klaue. Killmonger arrives in Wakanda to avenge his dead father. In a way, Killmonger's father was seeking to avenge the oppression of people of color around the world by distributing Wakanda's weapons, a plan later picked up by Killmonger. In such conflicts, no matter who is right or wrong, vengeance and violence taints all those who are involved.[11]

It is worth noting here that I feel the same way about Killmonger and his cause as many other moviegoers. A brief internet search will bring up a number of articles with titles like "Why Killmonger is the Greatest Villain

Ever"[12] and "All Hail King Killmonger, the Best Superhero Villain Since Heath Ledger."[13] As Dani Di Placido writes in *Forbes*:

> And the uncomfortable truth about Killmonger is, his anger is entirely justified. In a strange way, he's much more relatable to the audience than T'Challa will ever be. He's American, born into poverty, and has struggled throughout his life to achieve a fraction of what T'Challa inherited. He's an extremely sympathetic villain, and if it wasn't for the whole "race war" thing, we'd be happily rooting for him. But of course, he offers a terrible solution to the dilemma facing T'Challa, forcing the ousted king to reject both isolationism and bloody uprising, and conceive a third option.[14]

I will address the viability of that "third option" toward the end of the chapter. For now, I am content to address Killmonger's reception among audiences and the issue of revolutionary violence. Killmonger is viewed as a sympathetic villain, as Placido points out in his article. It is hard not to watch *Black Panther* and think that Killmonger may have a point—people of color around the world have been oppressed, historically and presently. If one has the resources to help and doesn't, isn't that an issue of justice? While I'm not sure it's fair to pejoratively describe Killmonger's position as that of a "race war," there is certainly an aversion in the West to revolutionary violence, particularly by people of color, as Malcolm X highlighted in "The Ballot and the Bullet."

However, Girard would caution against the use of revolutionary violence because "conflicts arising over an original act of injustice . . . develop a mimetic momentum."[15] As Girard writes, "mimetic violence grows behind the backs of those involved."[16] A person may think they are using violence for a noble end, but according to Girard, violence ends up using *them*.[17] It's not that Girard doesn't recognize the presence of injustice in the world. He acknowledges that modern global terrorism is "a response to the oppression of the Third World as a whole."[18] In this statement, Girard merely wishes to highlight the reality of mimetic violence in the world's geopolitics,[19] and he cautions against violent responses to injustice because of the mimetic escalation that follows.[20] He writes, "One cannot exert violence without submitting to it."[21] It is worth noting at this point how Girard's writings could lead to an anti-revolutionary reading, one that disenfranchises or minimizes communities of color and could be said to be argued from a place of privilege. This is where it is helpful to refer to Martin Luther King and his seeming mimetic understanding of violence that is in some ways very much in line with Girard's own views of the contagious nature of violence:

> Violence as a way of achieving racial justice is both impractical and immoral. It is impractical because it is a descending spiral ending in destruction for all. The old law of an eye for an eye leaves everybody blind. It is immoral because

it seeks to humiliate the opponent rather than win his understanding; it seeks to annihilate rather than to convert. Violence is immoral because it thrives on hatred rather than love. It destroys community and makes brotherhood impossible. It leaves society in monologue rather than dialogue. Violence ends by defeating itself. It creates bitterness in the survivors and brutality in the destroyers.[22]

It isn't that King (or even Girard) did not recognize the legitimate cries for justice inherent in some acts of violence, but like Girard, he recognized that violence carries its own momentum beyond the intentions of its agents. However, in regard to privilege, whatever criticisms can be leveled at Killmonger, T'Challa is not above reproach by any means.

Perhaps this is what makes *Black Panther* such a compelling movie because as true as this is for Killmonger, it is also true for T'Challa, with the late, great Chadwick Boseman saying as much:

> At the start of *Black Panther*, T'Challa is no hero. This isn't exactly a secret - the alt-right has been snickering at the resemblance between T'Challa and Donald Trump's ideologies for months. Even Chadwick Boseman said of his character, "I am the enemy.... It's the enemy I've always known. It's power. It's having privilege." Indeed, before Killmonger came along and smacked some sense into him, T'Challa is more than happy to keep Wakanda's doors firmly closed. This is the way it's always been after all, and nobody wants to be the guy who ends centuries of tradition for an untested idea—you might mess things up.[23]

Violence is a collective effort, and participation in it means that everyone involved loses moral high ground.[24] As Girard asserts, the mimetic nature of violence ensures that "[n]obody ... incarnates the true oppressor or the true oppressed," for "the roles of dominating and dominated are constantly reversed."[25] There are no true "good guys" and "bad guys" where violence and mimetic desire is concerned.[26] This further cements *Black Panther* as a movie that highlights the mimetic nature of human life and conflict, and according to Girard's standards, by doing it, it makes it a well-written "text."[27]

For Girard, violence and vengeance is not driven simply by a desire for justice or reprisal, but it ultimately has its inception in mimetic rivalry and desire, for "violence is always mingled with desire."[28] As Girard makes clear in one of his earliest works, humanity believes "the lie of spontaneous desire" and the "illusion of autonomy."[29] Humans believe that their desires arise spontaneously, but humans are essentially mimetic creatures. They not only learn behavior but they learn what to desire from others.[30] Girard writes:

> The rival desires the same object as the subject, and to assert the primacy of the rival can only lead to one conclusion. Rivalry does not arise because of the fortuitous convergence of two desires on a single object; rather, *the subject*

desires the object because the rival desires it. In desiring an object the rival alerts the subject to the desirability of the object. The rival, then, serves as a model for the subject, not only in regard to such secondary matters as style and opinions but also, and more essentially, in regard to desires.[31]

This is the foundation for violence, for "[t]wo desires converging on the same object are bound to clash. Thus, mimesis coupled with desire leads automatically to conflict."[32]

The conflict in Wakanda is driven by mimetic desire. When Killmonger confronts T'Challa and his council, he makes it clear that he does not simply want vengeance or justice: "I want the throne." There is something Killmonger wants that someone else possesses. But as Girard makes clear, desire for an object is not actually about the object in question. He writes, "Imitative desire is always a desire to be Another."[33] In many ways, we can see how Killmonger, the abandoned royal youth, the kid from Oakland who came from nothing and fought his way into a position of power, wants to become T'Challa, the son of the king who killed his father and the man who was raised with all of the privileges that Killmonger was deprived of. Girard states that "metaphysical desire is never aimed at an accessible object."[34] Instead, "he desires *being*, something he himself lacks and which some other person seems to possess. The subject thus looks to that other person to inform him of what he should desire in order to acquire that being."[35]

While humans receive their desires from others or "models," what they actually desire is the "being" of the other. Scott Cowdell writes:

> So, what Girard came to call acquisitive mimesis is revealed to be at best partial. Desire is fixed most truly on its model, and the real focus of acquisition is the being of that model—that is why acquiring an object typically fails to satisfy because this or that object is only ever a proxy for the being of the model, which remains elusive.[36]

Kingship as an ancient institution very much awakens this desire for the being of the other. Girard notes, "The king's subjects may feel ill at ease in his presence, awed by his sheer superabundance of power."[37] In T'Challa's case, this is particularly true given that he is literally endowed with superpowers from the heart-shaped herb. Killmonger desires to literally consume T'Challa's being, a thing he is able to accomplish by defeating him in ritual combat and partaking of the heart-shaped herb. In a way, this relates to Girard's insights about cannibalism whereby "[m]imetic desire, once frustrated, seeks at once to destroy and to absorb the violence incarnated with the model-obstacle."[38] Killmonger literally consumes or absorbs that which gives T'Challa his "being," for as Girard states, "We know that all victims of metaphysical desire seek to appropriate their mediator's being by imitating him."[39] Killmonger seeks to do this, seemingly killing T'Challa in ritual combat, and in the throes of metaphysical desire, also orders the burning of all the heart-shaped herb plants. Those who saw the movie, however, know that not only did T'Challa survive, but his love interest Nakia saved one of the heart-shaped herbs. This sets up a rematch between T'Challa and Killmonger and ultimately creates a sacrificial crisis for the nation of Wakanda.

SACRIFICIAL CRISIS, TWINS, AND A NEW MYTH

Mimetic desire and the violent rivalry it leads to, particularly when one's myth is unveiled and no longer efficacious, leads to a sacrificial crisis. Part of what distinguishes a sacrificial crisis is a lack of differentiation or distinctions. Girard writes:

> The sacrificial crisis can be defined . . . as a crisis of distinctions—that is, a crisis affecting the cultural order. This cultural order is nothing more than a regulated system of distinctions in which the differences among individuals are used to establish their "identity" and their mutual relationships.[40]

Violence drives the loss of these distinctions "and the demise of justice."[41] Whatever the original dispute, "the two rivals become more and more concerned with defeating the opponent for the sake of it," and the original dispute becomes "an excuse for the escalation of the dispute. Thus, the rivals become more and more undifferentiated, identical: doubles."[42] Through their violence, the two sides become identical.[43] In this conflict, "a crisis of undifferentiation . . . erupts when the roles of subject and model are reduced to that of rivals," and "[t]his crisis not only escalates between the contenders, but it becomes contagious with bystanders."[44] The entire community gets pulled into the conflict between mimetic rivals.

Girard sees this reality as the reason for "the phobia of resemblance" in many cultures.[45] He notes, "In some primitive societies twins inspire a particular terror."[46] Here, Girard sees the inspiration for the many stories about enemy brothers, from Cain and Abel to Romulus and Remus.[47] He further comments that "[t]he proliferation of enemy brothers in Greek myth and in dramatic adaptations of myth implies the continual presence of a sacrificial crisis . . . . In fact, the theme itself is a form of violence."[48] These brothers or twins "mask and reveal the universal antagonism of doubles at the height of a crisis. One of the brothers must die in order for the doubles to disappear . . . in order to provide for the reappearance of difference and the subsequent founding of the city."[49] To put this another way, "the combat of *doubles* results in the expulsion of one of the pair, and this is identified directly with the return to peace and order."[50] With the death of a new surrogate victim, a new myth, and thus a new community, is born.[51]

Black Panther itself ends with a sacrificial crisis. As Killmonger prepares to send out Wakandan weapons to communities across the world, T'Challa returns. As T'Challa suits up as the Black Panther, viewers are treated to the cite of Killmonger suiting up in his own gold-laced version of the Black Panther suit, and in doing so, the two of them take on the role of mimetic twins, signaling the culmination of mimetic violence and the peak of the sacrificial crisis. This conflict, however, isn't limited to the "enemy brothers," but overflows into the entirety of Wakanda. The community itself divides between those loyal to Killmonger and those loyal to T'Challa, with W'Kabi and his tribe supporting the former, and the Dora Milaje supporting T'Challa, with M'Baku and the Jabari tribe also joining T'Challa's side. This war of all against all leads to the division of even the closest of relationships, not only between T'Challa and his friend W'Kabi, but even between W'Kabi and his spouse Okoye. In the sacrificial crisis, Girard notes that the breakdown of social order and justice means the breakdown of the most essential relationships in society.[52]

Girard indicates that in order for the sacrificial crisis to end, "[o]ne of the brothers must die" to allow for the restoration of peace and the founding of a new social order.[53] In this way, Killmonger becomes a type of scapegoat for the future of Wakanda. While Killmonger is largely responsible for the breakdown of Wakanda's previous isolationist social order, he inspires T'Challa to establish Wakanda as an actor on the international stage. This is in keeping with Girard's contention that while the scapegoat is blamed in life for the problems plaguing a community, once the scapegoat meets its end, he or she is often divinized and becomes the basis of a new myth.[54]

In speaking of "a new myth," I am referring to T'Challa's "third way" or restructuring of Wakanda's international engagement. At the end of the movie, T'Challa tells Shuri that he has bought a number of buildings in Oakland, including the very building where Killmonger grew up and where his father T'Chaka killed N'Jobu. He plans on making them the beginning of an initiative to start a number of educational centers around the world to reach out to communities of color. With this ending, we can briefly discuss one of the most glaring criticisms of the movie. Christopher Lebron writes:

> [T]he bad guy is the black American who has rightly identified white supremacy as the reigning threat to black well-being; the bad guy is the one who thinks Wakanda is being selfish in its secret liberation; the bad guy is the one who will no longer stand for patience and moderation—he thinks liberation is many, many decades overdue.[55]

What is T'Challa's solution? Lebron writes, "he gestures at all the buildings he has bought and promises to bring to the distressed youths the preferred solution of mega-rich neoliberals: educational programming."[56] David O'Bryant writes elsewhere:

> If this formula sounds familiar, it's because these are exactly the contours of the neoliberal project pursued by the United States and rich-world nations since the end of the Cold War (arguably, since its start). While the film pays lip service to the CIA and U.S. special operations forces' history of destabilizing nations and toppling their leadership through the deftly tokenized white character CIA officer Everett K. Ross, T'Challa's personal agenda is perfectly in line with that pursued by those very power structures for decades. Of course, it's by no means surprising that a major Hollywood movie studio wouldn't offer up anything more politically challenging than a film that centers neoliberal development economic aid based on non-renewable resource extraction and exploitation as a positive model for Black empowerment, rather than a narrative that centers the agency of African diasporatic communities to resist white supremacy on the international stage independent of wealth.[57]

As Di Placido pointed out earlier, in the struggle between isolationism and revolution, T'Challa's strategy is to adopt "a global interventionist project to develop communities around the world in its image by applying its tightly controlled wealth to education projects."[58] As Simon Critchley points out though, this, too, is a myth or "fiction," in that all such political systems and ideologies are fictions,[59] which, as far as someone like Girard is concerned, are built upon scapegoats and misconceptions.[60] Even though our "good guy" is the hero, a deeper analysis of his chosen strategy reveals flaws, demonstrating Girard's point that even our heroes can't claim a monopoly on goodness. And the potential exists for a new sacrificial crisis to arise.

CONCLUSION

Black Panther presents audiences with a visual mimetic "text." If great art and literature is that which reveals the mimetic nature of humanity, as Girard contends, then *Black Panther* can be considered a great movie.[61] In it, viewers see the workings of mythology, the system of scapegoating and sacrifice that founds those myths, and the sacrificial crises which they cover up. Though the MCU is not without its faults, and while it certainly does not lack its critics, a Girardian analysis of *Black Panther* gives us greater insight into the human condition, our violence, and the structures that our violence establishes.

NOTES

1. René Girard, *Violence and the Sacred*, translated by Patrick Gregory (Baltimore: The Johns Hopkins University Press, 1977), 78.

2. Ibid.
3. Ibid., 100–101.
4. Ibid., 13.
5. Ibid.
6. Ibid., 28.
7. Ibid., 30.
8. Ibid., 14.
9. Ibid.
10. Ibid., 14–15.
11. Ibid., 150. I do realize my own positionality in this discussion as a white cis-gender male may undercut this observation. I recognize that it is easy to condemn violence "from below" when one is endowed with privilege "from above." Nevertheless, I believe that the contagious nature of violence cannot be overstated.
12. Wyatt Donigan, "Why Killmonger is the Greatest Villian Ever," *Medium*, https://medium.com/@wyattdonigan/why-killmonger-was-quite-possibly-the-greatest-villain-ever-on-screen-2a1288413065, accessed 01/16/20.
13. Frazier Tharpe, "All Hail King Killmonger, the Best Superhero Villain Since Heath Ledger," *Complex*, https://www.complex.com/pop-culture/2018/02/black-panther-killmonger-michael-b-jordan-best-superhero-villain-since-dark-knight, accessed 01/16/20.
14. Dani Di Placido, "Why Killmonger was such a Compelling Villain in *Black Panther*," *Forbes*, https://www.forbes.com/sites/danidiplacido/2018/03/05/why-killmonger-was-such-a-compelling-villain-in-black-panther/#6dd0397424aa, accessed 01/16/20.
15. Roberto Farneti, *Mimetic Politics: Dyadic Patterns in Global Politics* (East Lansing, MI: Michigan State University Press, 2015), 85.
16. René Girard, *Battling to the End: Conversations with Benoît Chantre*, translated by Mary Baker (East Lansing, MI: Michigan State University Press, 2010), 183.
17. Girard, *Violence and the Sacred*, 261.
18. Girard, *Battling to the End*, 211.
19. Ibid., 213.
20. René Girard, *The One by Whom Scandal Comes*, translated by M. B. DeBevoise (East Lansing, MI: Michigan State University Press, 2014), 19–20.
21. Girard, *Violence and the Sacred*, 245.
22. Martin Luther King, Jr., "Stride Toward Freedom," in *A Testament of Hope: The Essential Writings and Speeches of Martin Luther King, Jr.*, edited by James Melvin Washington (New York: HarperOne, 1986), 482.
23. Di Plicado, "Why Killmonger was such a Compelling Villain," 2020.
24. Girard, *Violence and the Sacred*, 150, 204.
25. Ibid., 150, 153.
26. Ibid., 150.
27. René Girard, *Deceit, Desire, and the Novel: Self and Other in Literary Structure*, translated by Yvonne Freccero (Baltimore: The Johns Hopkins University Press, 1965), 3.

28. Girard, *Violence and the Sacred*, 145.
29. Girard, *Deceit, Desire, and the Novel*, 16.
30. Girard, *Violence and the Sacred*, 145–146.
31. Ibid., 145.
32. Ibid., 146.
33. Girard, *Deceit, Desire, and the Novel*, 83.
34. Ibid., 209.
35. Girard, *Violence and the Sacred*, 146.
36. Scott Cowdell, *René Girard and the Nonviolent God* (Notre Dame, IN: University of Notre Dame Press, 2018), 10.
37. Girard, *Violence and the Sacred*, 269.
38. Ibid., 277.
39. Girard, *Deceit, Desire, and the Novel*, 185.
40. Girard, *Violence and the Sacred*, 49.
41. Ibid., 51.
42. René Girard, *Evolution and Conversion: Dialogues on the Origins of Culture*, edited by P. Antonello and J. C. de Castro Rocha (London: Continuum, 2008), 57.
43. Girard, *Battling to the End*, 14.
44. Girard, *Evolution and Conversion*, 57.
45. Girard, *Violence and the Sacred*, 59.
46. Ibid., 57.
47. Ibid., 61.
48. Ibid.
49. René Girard, *Things Hidden since the Foundation of the World*, translated by Stephen Bann and Michael Metteer (Stanford, CA: Stanford University Press, 1987), 39.
50. Ibid., 142.
51. Girard, *Violence and the Sacred*, 79.
52. Girard, *Violence and the Sacred*, 51. While Girard highlights the breakdown of the relationship between father and son, one can imagine that the breakdown between spouses carries similar stakes outside of a patriarchal culture.
53. Girard, *Things Hidden*, 39, 142.
54. Girard, *Violence and the Sacred*, 85–87.
55. Christopher Lebron, "*Black Panther* is Not the Movie We Deserve," *Boston Review*, https://bostonreview.net/race/christopher-lebron-black-panther, accessed 01/24/20.
56. Ibid.
57. David O'Bryant, "Beyond Wakanda: Diaspora, Neoliberalism, and the Mythic Kingdom," *Medium*, https://medium.com/@davidobryant/beyond-wakanda-diaspora-neoliberalism-and-the-mythic-kingdom-65f4b12cf14c, accessed 01/24/20.
58. Ibid.
59. Simon Critchley, *The Faith of the Faithless: Experiments in Political Theology* (New York: Verso, 2014), 84–85.
60. Girard, *Battling to the End*, 22–23.
61. Girard, *Deceit, Desire, and the Novel*, 3.

REFERENCES

Cowdell, Scott. *René Girard and the Nonviolent God*. Notre Dame, IN: University of Notre Dame Press, 2018.

Critchley, Simon. *The Faith of the Faithless: Experiments in Political Theology*. New York: Verso, 2014.

Di Placido, Dani. "Why Killmonger was such a Compelling Villain in *Black Panther*." *Forbes*. https://www.forbes.com/sites/danidiplacido/2018/03/05/why-killmonger-was-such-a-compelling-villain-in-black-panther/#6dd0397424aa. Accessed 01/16/20.

Donigan, Wyatt. "Why Killmonger is the Greatest Villian Ever." *Medium*. https://medium.com/@wyattdonigan/why-killmonger-was-quite-possibly-the-greatest-villain-ever-on-screen-2a1288413065. Accessed 01/16/20.

Farneti, Roberto. *Mimetic Politics: Dyadic Patterns in Global Politics*. East Lansing, MI: Michigan State University Press, 2015.

Girard, René. *Battling to the End: Conversations with Benoît Chantre*, translated by Mary Baker. East Lansing, MI: Michigan State University Press, 2010.

———. *Deceit, Desire, and the Novel: Self and Other in Literary Structure*, translated by Yvonne Freccero. Baltimore: The Johns Hopkins University Press, 1965.

———. *Evolution and Conversion: Dialogues on the Origins of Culture*, edited by P. Antonello and J. C. de Castro Rocha. London: Continuum, 2008.

———. *The One by Whom Scandal Comes*, translated by M. B. DeBevoise. East Lansing, MI: Michigan State University Press, 2014.

———. *Things Hidden since the Foundation of the World*, translated by Stephen Bann and Michael Metteer. Stanford, CA: Stanford University Press, 1987.

———. *Violence and the Sacred*, translated by Patrick Gregory. Baltimore: The Johns Hopkins University Press, 1977.

King, Jr., Martin Luther. "Stride Toward Freedom." In *A Testament of Hope: The Essential Writings and Speeches of Martin Luther King, Jr.*, edited by James Melvin Washington. New York: HarperOne, 1986.

Lebron, Christopher. "*Black Panther* is Not the Movie We Deserve." *Boston Review*. https://bostonreview.net/race/christopher-lebron-black-panther. Accessed 01/24/20.

O'Bryant, David. "Beyond Wakanda: Diaspora, Neoliberalism, and the Mythic Kingdom." *Medium*. https://medium.com/@davidobryant/beyond-wakanda-diaspora-neoliberalism-and-the-mythic-kingdom-65f4b12cf14c. Accessed 01/24/20.

Tharpe, Frazier. "All Hail King Killmonger, the Best Superhero Villain Since Heath Ledger." *Complex*. https://www.complex.com/pop-culture/2018/02/black-panther-killmonger-michael-b-jordan-best-superhero-villain-since-dark-knight. Accessed, 01/16/20.

Chapter 3

Bulletproof Love

Luke Cage, *Race, and Religion*

Ken Derry, Daniel White Hodge, Laurel Zweissler, Stanley Talbert, Matthew J Cressler, and Jon Ivan Gill

Luke Cage is, to my own admission, a somewhat lesser-known character in the public pantheon of the Marvel Universe.[1] Not, that does not make him any less important or valuable—in fact, I know I would have enjoyed seeing more of him used in Avengers in the fight against Thanos. I mean, was he one of the vanished? How did the community react to that? I will also confess that until Netflix announced their series on Cage, I was not aware of his role within the Marvel Cinematic Universe (MCU). Thus, what would a book on the MCU be without talking about the value of Luke Cage? Yes, exactly!

I cannot go forward without acknowledging that this whole chapter is a revised version of one that was published with several other authors attached to it. The great minds of Ken Derry, Laurel Zwissler, Stanley Talbert, Matthew J. Cressler, and Jon Ivan Gill contributed to the shaping of this multi-authored journal article. The genesis of this piece came from a presentation we all did at the American Academy of Religion's (AAR) annual conference where each of us took a specific section of the Luke Cage series on Netflix. Annual conferences of large academic societies are typically, by their very nature, slow to respond to current events. The logistics in putting together such meetings are incredibly complex, the result being that the planning of sessions begins up to a year before the actual meeting itself. To its credit, the AAR has been sensitive to this issue and endeavored to open up ways in which scholars can offer analyses of more recent phenomena. At the November 2016 meeting of the AAR in San Antonio, Texas, for example, several sessions were offered in response to the results of the U.S. election that had taken place just slightly more than a week before.

With this sense of timeliness in mind, members of the AAR's Religion, Film, and Visual Culture (RFVC) group were able to get a last-minute roundtable discussion on the first season of the superhero series *Luke Cage* (Netflix, US 2016), released in October 2016.² Not only is Luke the first Black superhero to be featured in his own comic book *and* his own television show, but the Netflix portrayal of him in a hoodie, being shot at by police (figure 3.1), was clearly meant to resonate instantly with critically important, and deeply troubling, of-the-moment occurrences. He is, in the words of *Rolling Stone*'s Rob Sheffield, "the first Black Lives Matter superhero."³

The diversity of our roundtable panel fits well with one of our broad critical aims, which was to demonstrate that there are many ways to think about religion and popular culture. One starting point would be to ask where and when we see what might be commonly understood as "religious tradition(s)" explicitly on display. Regarding superhero narratives, this question invites us to analyze ostensibly religious images and tropes in various media incarnations including comics, film, and television. Such analysis could include, for instance, identifying characters modeled on religious archetypes, such as Jewish messianic figures, Buddhist arhats, or Anishinaabe tricksters. It could also include allusions to religious texts, such as the Qur'an, the Bhagavad Gita, or the Bible.

Another direction would be to think about superhero narratives themselves *as* "religious" in some way. Following theorists such as Jonathan Z. Smith, Talal Asad, and Tomoko Masuzawa, if we regard "religion" as a conceptual tool that scholars use to categorize and thereby better understand particular dimensions of human experience, we can begin to recognize the ways in

Figure 3.1 Film Still, "DWYCK," *Luke Cage* (2016), S01/E09, 19:10.

which superhero narratives (and the worlds they create) may serve some of the same functions typically reserved for "the religious."[4] This hermeneutic can illuminate aspects of such narratives that might otherwise go unnoticed.

This chapter, therefore, takes a variety of approaches to understanding religion in relation to *Luke Cage* (2016). Doing so highlights the polysemic nature of popular culture in general, and superhero stories in particular cross-sectioned with racial tropes. Like religious traditions themselves, the show is complex and contradictory: it is both progressive and reactionary; emphasizes community and valorizes an individual; critiques and endorses Christianity; subverts and promotes violence. Depending on the questions you ask, *Luke Cage* (2016) has many, many different answers.

"SENSATIONAL ORIGIN ISSUE!"

The character of Luke Cage was created in 1972 by two white men, Archie Goodwin and John Romita Sr., in the spirit of the Blaxpoitation films of the time. He first appeared in *Luke Cage, Hero For Hire* #1, written by Goodwin and Roy Thomas, and drawn by George Tuska. Born Carl Lucas, Luke is framed by his old friend Willis Stryker, ending up in Seagate Prison. He is tormented by a sadistic white guard, Albert Rackham, and volunteers for an experiment run by Dr. Noah Burstein in exchange for early release. Rackham sabotages the experiment in an effort to kill Carl, causing an explosion. But as is the way in comics things go bizarrely awry—Rackham is killed instead and Carl emerges from the wreckage with super strength and invulnerability, breaking out of prison and changing his name to Luke Cage. Cautious about whom he can trust he makes few close friends; an early one is Claire Temple, who helps Luke when he's hurt and who dates him for a while.

All of these details are repeated in the 13-episode Netflix series, which unlike the original comics was made by Black artists, including creator and showrunner Cheo Hodari Coker. Despite some of the big picture similarities to Luke's original incarnation, these artists made many changes to his character, bringing him into the twenty-first century and out of white stereotypes. He is much quieter, more thoughtful, and reserved; instead of shouting bombastically and punching supervillains, he reads books and eschews violence. Pointedly unlike his comic book self, the Netflix Luke refuses to be paid for helping people, preferring to earn his living as a janitor in Pop's barbershop. Changes were also made to his childhood: no longer raised in Harlem by a police detective father, Luke is now from Georgia and the son of a philandering preacher. In the television show, therefore, he is an outsider in Harlem, working to help people he has only recently come to know and love. Claire too undergoes important shifts as her character is translated from the comics: she is now a Hispanic nurse, instead of a Black doctor.

The reasons why Harlem needs Luke's help are laid out in two main story arcs: the first seven episodes of the series focus on local gangster Cornell "Cottonmouth" Stokes and his cousin Mariah Dillard, a corrupt local councilwoman. Together they unsuccessfully attempt to recover first from the betrayal of an underling during a weapons deal with a rival gang, and then from the crippling damage that Luke inflicts on Cornell's organization. As Luke's vigilante activities against Harlem's criminal world gather steam he finds himself the focus of a police investigation, led by Detective Misty Knight.

The second arc of the series begins when Mariah kills Cornell in a rage over his accusation that she "wanted" the sexual abuse she suffered as a young girl. At this point, the mysterious "Diamondback"—Cornell's powerful unseen supplier—emerges from the shadows. He reveals himself to be Willis Stryker, who is not only Luke's childhood friend and betrayer but also, it turns out, his half-brother. During the final six episodes, Mariah gradually steps into her dead cousin's crime boss's shoes, while Diamondback repeatedly tries to kill Luke for the unforgivable sin of being the publically "accepted" son, rather than the one whose origin was a shameful secret. He shoots Luke twice with "Judas bullets" derived from alien technology that actually pierce his skin, before donning a super-suit for a climactic hand-to-hand street battle. Luke wins the fight and ends the series by giving himself up to the police as an escaped convict.

"DISHWASHER LAZARUS"

Our consideration of religion and *Luke Cage* (2016) begins with this question: What kind of a hero is Luke? The second time that we see him use his powers is to protect a young boy when one of Cornell's henchmen, Tone, shoots up Pop's barbershop (E02; figure 3.2).[5] When the shooting is done, Luke does not charge out of the shop to punish the gunman; he instead stays to help the injured and check on Pop, who tragically has been killed. Much of *Luke Cage* (2016) focuses on the lead character's transformation from escaped convict to hero, as he is pushed and inspired by circumstances and people (particularly Pop and Claire Temple) to emerge from hiding and use his powers to help others. But even as this emergence takes place, Luke continues to help by shielding victims to *prevent* harm, as much as (if not more than) he hits villains to inflict it: he stands in front of the injured corrupt police detective, Rafael Scarfe, when Cornell's men try to run him over (E06); he protects Misty from being shot during the hostage crisis at Harlem's

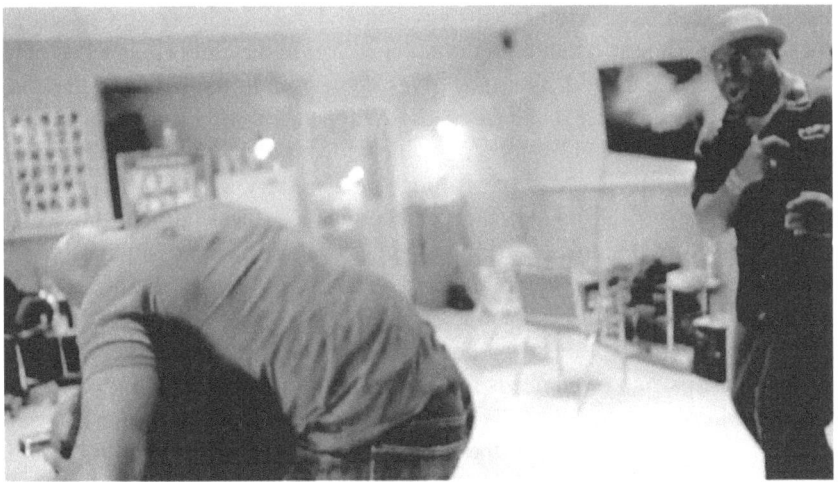

Figure 3.2   Film Still, "Code of the Streets," *Luke Cage* (2016), S01/E02, 42:31.

Paradise (E10-11); and he covers a police officer with his body when that man's partner starts firing at Luke (figure 3.2).

There are other ways in which Luke submits to violence of different types, rather than leading with his fists. When his landlords are being threatened, he first asks the four men to stop being disrespectful, and then stands still while one of them hits Luke in the face and shatters his own hand (E01).[6] After Cornell threatens to expose Luke as a fugitive he decides to leave Harlem, before Claire convinces him to stay and fight back (E07). He tells the two officers who stop him that he just wants to walk and mind his own business (E09). Despite his innocence, he does not resist being taken back to prison at the end of the series (E13). Even during his final showdown with Diamondback, he simply decides to stop trading blows: "I'm not doing this any more. . . . You want me dead? Then kill me" (E13).[7]

This is unusual behavior for a superhero. We are used to seeing these characters—despite their ostensive commitment to peace—embracing violence with much more enthusiasm than Luke does. As Robert Jewett and John Shelton Lawrence have argued in several works,[8] superheroes most often embody a troubling perspective—derived originally from certain biblical responses to crisis—that they have termed "zealous nationalism."[9] This perspective is one rooted in moral dualism, as a lone savior driven by a commitment to justice is faced with corrupt and/or ineffective laws, and so becomes a vigilante in order to save the community by destroying the evildoers who threaten it.[10] There are some elements of this perspective in *Luke Cage* (2016), especially regarding problems with the police and Luke's justification for using violence to make Harlem safer.[11] But Luke never directly or even inadvertently kills anyone; and even after seeing Cornell let out of jail (E07) he still hands Diamondback over to the authorities when their fight is done (E13)—and, again, he gives *himself* up to the police in the end.

In many ways, in fact, *Luke Cage* (2016) appears to represent the opposing worldview—also biblically rooted—which Jewett and Lawrence refer to as "prophetic realism." Instead of wishing for a solitary hero who ignores the law to save everyone from evil, this perspective recognizes human complexity and valorizes communities working together to improve their situation using due process. This focus on community is evident throughout the series, from the importance of Pop's barbershop as a refuge and meeting place, to the fact that Luke has no mask or "superhero" identity: he is always Luke Cage and he openly helps, and often needs the help of, the people around him.[12] He also tries to *understand* the people who are hurting Harlem, and the series itself slowly peels off the masks of the villains—Cornell Stokes, Mariah Dillard, Willis Stryker—to show us the painful histories that have shaped their current identities and actions.[13]

One other feature of Luke's character stands out as unique in a way that is connected to prophetic realism: his role as a Christ figure. While a great many superheroes also symbolize Jesus, they do so while waving the flag of zealous nationalism. There are by no means any universally agreed-upon parameters for identifying cinematic Christ figures, but Lloyd Baugh's influential *Imaging the Divine* (1997) offers a useful starting point.[14] And while he does not even mention superheroes, almost all of his criteria are in fact part of standard superhero tropes: they are saviors with mysterious origins; they perform miracles; they suffer and bleed; they have devoted followers or helpers; and they are committed to justice, which often leads to conflicts with authorities. In addition, many heroes are often scapegoated, and it has become increasingly common for them to die and resurrect, sometimes literally. In the film, the Christ-like nature of these (literal or figurative) deaths is often indicated by showing the hero in a crucifixion pose.[15]

Luke meets all of these Christ-figure criteria. Initially, no one knows who he is or where he is from. He has miraculous strength and seems impervious to harm, although he suffers and bleeds when hit by the Judas bullets. He is helped by several people, including Pop, Claire, Misty, and (in a great cameo) Method Man. His sense of justice is what compels him to finally step out of the shadows to protect the community.[16] He struggles against several authorities including the police, Mariah, and Cornell. He is falsely accused of killing both Cornell and a police officer. He is not prone to crucifixion poses, although he possibly appears in one after he has been shot by Diamondback and is helped by Claire and Dr. Burstein, his arms across their shoulders. More directly, after his eulogy for Pop he is shown walking with a neon crucifix over his shoulder and a street lamp halo; during the opening, a crucifix is projected onto Luke's back; and at the very end of the series, as Luke is being driven out of New York by the police, he passes by a brightly lit "Jesus Saves" cross. Finally, we see Luke "resurrected" at least twice: after Dr. Burstein's Seagate prison experiment explodes, giving Luke his powers and leading everyone to think he is dead (E04);[17] and when he appears to actually die for a moment while being treated for the Judas wounds, brought back to life when Claire throws a live electrical hot plate into the acid bath that contains him (E10).

Luke Cage (2016) contains several other possible Christ-figure elements not mentioned by Baugh but included in Anton Kozlovic's extensive list.[18] He is poor, and his submission to the police at the end is a "willing sacrifice."[19] He has a dual nature, "one fantastic and the other mundane,"[20] beautifully captured by the name that Cornell gives Luke: "Dishwasher Lazarus" (E05). He is betrayed by a Judas figure,[21] his old friend Willis Stryker. As for Pop, in both his encouragement of Luke and his death he is analogous to John the Baptist, someone who "identifies and/or points the way to the Christ figure, and fades away."[22] It is even possible to see Luke's hoodies as a gesture toward the "popular image of Jesus in his iconic white robes."[23] And of course the show several times goes out of its way to tell us directly that Luke is a Christ figure. When he confronts Cornell after surviving another attack he is advised to consider his next actions carefully: "[It]

Figure 3.3 Left: *Black Jesus* Painting. Right: Film Still, "Moment of Truth," *Luke Cage* (2016), S01/E01, 52:46.

costs to be a savior. Ask Jesus" (E05). And when Shades tells Cornell about the Judas bullet he points out, "If you wanted to kill Jesus, that's the bullet you'd use" (E05).[24]

As many critics have noted, simply labeling a character as a "Christ-figure" is not in itself all that meaningful, as it begs the question: "So what?"[25] One possible answer for most superhero narratives is that being presented as a messiah supports the perspective of zealous nationalism. This perspective depends heavily on claiming the moral authority to decide who is good and who is evil; aligning your hero with Christ conceivably can do a good deal of work toward this end.[26] *Luke Cage* (2016), however, explicitly tells us that Luke will be a very different kind of savior when he recites Luke 4:18 and renames himself after the gospel writer: "The spirit of the Lord is on me, because I have been anointed to preach good news to the poor. He sent me to proclaim freedom for the prisoners, and recovery of sight for the blind. To release the oppressed" (E04). Luke will be, that is, a savior more interested in helping people in need than in defeating evil. This is a much more down-to-earth mission, a more human mission, than we see most in most superhero stories.

In this regard, while Luke is clearly special in many ways, the show also works to humanize him. This is evident in his fear of being recognized and sent back to jail, and his determination to earn a living with honest work, whether sweeping hair or washing dishes. There is also the simple but important fact that he can in fact be physically hurt: he is shot by Diamondback, he bleeds, and he almost dies. When Cornell facetiously comments that people act as if Luke "can walk on water," Shades asks in all seriousness, "Can he?" (E07). This question, along with Mariah's suggestions for trying to kill Luke—drowning, burning, poisoning (E06)—points to the vulnerabilities that he shares with the rest of humanity. This shared connection is movingly underscored when men in the community wear hoodies with holes in them, risking their own safety to make it harder for the police to find and capture Luke (E12).[27] As he becomes us, in other words, we become him: ordinary/special, criminal/hero, human/divine: Dishwasher Lazarus.

"WHO'S GONNA TAKE THE WEIGHT? HIP HOP'S NARRATIVE IN CAGE"

The use of Hip Hop culture throughout *Luke Cage* (2016) is pervasive. From the soundtrack to the location of Luke's community, Hip Hop culture is prevalent and provides a foundational grounding for the series and for the character of Luke. His connection to the community, the father figure in Pop, the oversized picture of Biggie Smalls in Cornell's office, and the underground aura gives *Luke Cage* (2016) a strong connection to a culture much larger than just its music.

Hip Hop, as it has been asserted by scholars,[28] is much more complex than just music videos, lyrics, and "bling." It is a culture by which those who have been disinherited can find identity, space, place, and being.[29] Moreover, Hip Hop is a contextual manufacturing of those oppressed and cast aside into DJing, rhythms, MCing, dance, language, street entrepreneurialism, street fashion, knowledge, and spirituality.[30] Thus, *Luke Cage* (2016) and the themes within the first Black comic book hero, present a reassertion of Black narrative and theology. *Luke Cage* (2016) is a secular articulation of the spiritual of the profane reimagined within a Hip Hop context and ethos. To that, Luke takes on three of Hip Hop's theological concepts:[31]

1. A theology of social action
2. God of the profane
3. A theology of community

Jon Michael Spencer's theomusicology provides a framework to better comprehend Luke's connection to Hip Hop, its culture, and its theology. Theomusicology[32] is defined as "a musicological method for theologizing about the sacred, the secular, and the profane, principally incorporating thought and method borrowed from anthropology, sociology, psychology, and philosophy."[33] It is, as Cheryl Kirk-Duggan and Marlon Hall state, "Music as spiritual practice ... [to] hear the challenges and evils in the church and the world as the music reveals."[34] Theomusicology is distinguished from other methods and disciplines such as ethnomusicology:[35]

> Its analysis stands on the presupposition that the religious symbols, myths, and canon of the culture being studied are the theomusicologist's authoritative/normative sources. For instance, while the Western music therapist would interpret the healing of the biblical patriarch Saul under the assuagement of David's lyre as a psychophysiological phenomena, the theomusicologist would *first* take into account the religious belief of the culture for whom the event had meaning. The theomusicological method is therefore one that allows for scientific analysis, but primarily within the limits of what is normative in the ethics, religion, or mythology of the community of believers being studied.[36]

The theomusicologist[37] is thus concerned with multi-level data within the context of the people they study, and subsequently analyzes the material within the proper time, culture, and context in which it was created—something that LUKE CAGE (2016) provides a particularly good space for, and precisely what is needed when examining Hip Hop culture within the series.

A hero suitable for the post-civil rights[38] context in which Hip Hop finds itself. Luke's use of violence, often as a last resort as when protecting his landlords, is a just use of that force when seen through the Hip Hop lens of rules of engagement. In other words, force should be used only when necessary and to protect those whom you love.[39] In one sense, Luke focuses primarily on his own community to do the work of a hero—much unlike other superheroes who take on a more meta-savior role to "save the world" or humankind from some far-off evil. In Luke's sense, this far-off evil is present in the local and using the advice from Pop, can create a space for heroic measures. Luke's use of his power is communal, yet, he is still cisgendered and attracted to women; as is the case with his sexual encounters with Misty. For those in traditional religious contexts, this could pose a problematic scenario, yet, for a post-civil rights hero, this is part of the context and lifestyle.[40]

When interpreting a character like Luke in terms of religion and Hip Hop, we might consider three guiding categories:

1. The Sacred: not only those elements within a society that are set apart and forbidden for ritual, but those elements within the given society and culture that are aspiring toward both a pious stance, and search for deity.
2. The Secular: those items designated by a given society and culture as having little to no connection with a form of deity.
3. The Profane: those areas in a society labeled or given the designation of being outside the given morals, codes, ethics, and values established as "good" and/or "right" by the society and culture being studied.

With these understandings in mind, we can see Luke as a sacred, secular, and profane hero. An example of this trinary perspective is when he speaks at Pop's funeral (E05; figure 3.4). Luke is in a conventionally sacred space, a church, in front of a sign that connotes transcendence. But while he is the son of a minister he himself is not ordained; he is as secular as his suit, and a key part of the message he delivers in this moment is very much about *this* world, about the community of Harlem. The profane is all that Luke embodies of the streets and his invoking of violence for good, his secular jacket covering the profane bullet holes in his shirt. The angle of this shot also suggests that Luke commands respect and those who follow must listen; the subtext could mean he possesses something of deity himself, rooted in the sacred, secular, and profane.

Figure 3.4 Film Still, "Just to Get a Rep," *Luke Cage* (2016), S01/E05, 44:46.

The notion of a secular, sacred, and profane hero is not a foreign concept for those within the Hip Hop community. Heroes come in all forms, shapes, genders, and sizes. Take Biggie, for example, a hero that embodied an apotheosis approach to God and faith, yet, was in all manner still "secular" and "profane." For the Hip Hop community, the good outweighs the bad and Biggie is representative of an ongoing debate as to the connection of God to the pimps, thugs, baby-mammas, and "niggas." Biggie provided that sacred, secular, profane connection to God and re-articulated it back in his music, poetry, and work with his community. Someone like Luke is that conduit as well, a person that is able to utilize their context and begin to create a "better way" while not using conventional methods.

The Hip Hop community regularly experiences violence, death, nihilism, and war-like conditions. One might argue that this is at the center of most of the social critique Hip Hop has toward dominant societal structures and systems. Equality, justice, fairness, impartiality in the law, and a social voice is where many Hip Hoppers—especially the underground community in which Luke finds himself—push toward and give a lot of their energy. Thus, Luke, a reluctant hero at first, and not originally from Harlem, roots himself into his space and place and rises to give that voice back to the community. This arc fits well with a messianic narrative or a Hip Hop Jesuz that The Outlawz or even Kendrick Lamar describes. Luke is someone not too perfect, not too saintly, not too connected to divinity, a hero that the post-civil rights Hip

Hopper can connect with and to. Luke is the answer to the question posed by the title of the Gang Starr track (and episode 3), "Who's Gonna Take the Weight?" This is something worthy of notice and, especially using the image of a strong Black man in Luke, something that is much more complex than just all good or all evil.

"THAT'S THE LAST TIME YOU WILL EVER CALL ME A BITCH"

Constructions of masculinity and femininity inevitably implicate each other. In approaching any discussion of gender and sexuality, intersectional theory, formulated by Kimberlé Williams Crenshaw[41] and further championed by Patricia Hill Collins,[42] is crucial. It becomes even more crucial when considering gender in a series like *Luke Cage* (2016), which actively wrestles with race and class stereotypes, often using Christian tropes to do so. The characters struggle within a context that bell hooks has named "imperialist white-supremacist capitalist patriarchy."[43] That is, the show is not just about race, not just about gender, but about these identity markers as interconnected ways of distributing power within our social context, in combination with religion, sexuality, material dis/advantage, and so on. Character responses to their histories of violence flow down gendered lines. This section highlights three themes: absent parents, that is, a lack of constructive gender models; sex; and the relationship of gender to power.

From the beginning of the series, the issue of absent parents surfaces. As Pop is explaining why it is important to create a safe space for the young men of the neighborhood, Luke says, "Everyone has a gun, no one has a father" (E01). The link between a lack of positive male role models and community violence is made explicit. Pop's approach to the boys of the neighborhood also reflects what Patricia Hill Collins has called, "other-mothering,"[44] the practice, common in stressed communities, of "taking in strays," taking responsibility for under-parented or neglected children and integrating them into non-biological kin networks. This practice is something we see not only with Pop but also with Mama Mabel and then Mariah (E07).

Here begins a gendered split between the constructed parenting provided by Pop and by Mama Mabel. Pop gives emotional support and mentoring, consciously creating a sanctuary space free from violence. Mabel, on the other hand, brings abandoned children, Cornell and Mariah, into her world of hustle and violence. Mariah further takes on the role of "other mother" to Cornell. Though she tries to provide a different kind of care to him than Mabel provided to them, in the end, she cannot help but reproduce the violence of her past, bringing death rather than life. This parallels the role she is trying to play for her neighborhood: her dream is to uplift, but in the end she cannot help but consume.

Mariah's collapse into devouring mother connects to the series' meditations on sexual violence. Even in episode 1, Luke assists a coworker, Candace, who is uncomfortable serving the VIP room alone, for fear of harassment or assault. The show acknowledges sexual violence as one of the multifaceted forms of violence it addresses, one that swirls around with and refracts other forms of violence, including structural. When Misty is speaking with a counselor after her attack on Claire (E08), he suggests that she needs to acknowledge her adolescent guilt over the murder of her cousin, who was abducted and raped (E09). In juxtaposing the exploitation and destruction of this body—young, Black, female, characteristics interpreted by her assailants and by the police as evidence of its disposability[45]—Misty's narrative offers a contrast to Luke's body as invulnerable. However, this contrast also highlights ways that, while vulnerability to physical and structural violence is shared across disadvantaged communities of color, it affects men and women in different ways.

There is also the tragedy and complexity of Mariah's childhood sexual abuse, for which Cornell ultimately pays. Her crazed reaction to Cornell's accusation that she "wanted it" is multivalent (E07). On the one hand, her powerful denial of the accusation offers a clear demonstration of how inaccurate and self-serving the cultural commonplace of blaming victims is. On the other, her actions afterward also reinforce the stereotype that abused women are crazy and dangerous.[46] Further, her character arc does not challenge the trope, fodder for exploitation films galore, that requires that women be raped before they are socially sanctioned or morally excused for mobilizing their own power as physical violence. Finally, there is also the last scene with Shades, who has just fallen in love with Mariah as a result of her violence, when she echoes her words to Cornell, "I did not want this" and Shades replies, "I think you did." What do we do with the juxtapositions that such an assault narrative provides in the context of rape culture?

Any discussion of sexuality in *Luke Cage* (2016) must also consider the forms of sexuality that are visible and those that are invisible. It is not difficult to take a queer reading to the relationship between Luke and Cornell.[47] They are both as smooth as protagonists from 1970s soul cinema, showing each other up, engaging in repartee parallel to that between Luke and the major female characters, and vying for the soul of their fictional Harlem. Through the male-desiring gaze, they can be read as competing suitors, the tragically Luciferian Cornell and the reluctantly messianic Luke, but also, therefore, as completing each other.

The homoeroticism between the two must remain subtext, however. This message is reinforced by the continued rhetorical use of the term "bitch" as an insult for men, angrily ascribed, for example, not only by Cornell (E01) but also Misty (E07) and Turk (E12). The word's repression specifically of women is symbolically subverted by the clear inclusion in the series of powerful women, is made light of when Claire successfully recovers her bag from a mugger, and is explicitly challenged when Mariah tells Shades, "That's the last time you will ever call me a bitch" (E08). Yet, the word's specifically homophobic power is never challenged, whether subtly or directly, as it would be by the visible presence of openly LGBTQ characters.

The foreclosure of latent desire between Cornell and Luke comes not only as Cornell is removed, but with the simultaneous arrival of Diamondback, with his Old Testament rules and punishments. An erotically charged story of rival Brothers is overwritten with a literal one of rival brothers, explicitly presented in the show as a Cain and Abel story. However, behind this story of hate and fratricide is also an Isaac and Ishmael story, sons of the same man by different women. As Delores Williams has deftly demonstrated, peering behind the androcentric and patriarchal narrative actually gets us to a story of two women, mothers to sons from the same man, that is, to the shadows of Hagar and Sarah.[48] In Williams' analysis, Hagar's story is the story of African American women's historical experience. Her appearance here only as a back-story in the conflict between two powerful men is consistent with the historical androcentrism of Christianity, shared by the Black Church, that Womanist theologians such as Williams deconstruct. Predictably then, the shadow mothers also set up some "yo mama" insults (E13).

Finally, a consideration of gender and sexuality in the series would be incomplete without a meta-view about the place of the show in its broader social context. The series features numerous, significant roles for people of color and more specifically women of color. In a media landscape in which roles for actors of color are often both deliberately and unconsciously limited,[49] *Luke Cage* (2016) provides an important exception. It is resplendent with beautiful women of color, of various ages, whose characters represent different avenues of agency, empowerment and choice, even if the writing does not always do them justice.[50] It is also refreshing that sexuality is represented as a normal part of adult life; the series skips the cheap will-they/won't they plot points; Misty and Claire don't have to compete over a man, but instead, come to admire each other through cooperation in the trenches. Further, while the series attends to sexual violence, as discussed above, it is significant that the sexual encounters actually depicted on-screen are consensual, in great contrast to many competing series, though consistent with JESSICA JONES (Netflix, US 2015), which introduced Luke's character.

"I'M NOT A MONSTER"

In the tenth episode of *Luke Cage* (2016), Luke reenters the acidic waters of baptism from whence his salvation comes (E10). Luke undergoes his initial baptism as a scientific experiment at Seagate Prison (E04; figure 3.5). He dies as Carl Lucas and becomes a new creature. When Claire confronts Dr. Burstein for transforming Luke Cage, he responds, "I . . . I'm not a monster (E10)." Burstein's response offers a crucial point of departure for evaluating the theological significance of LUKE CAGE (2016). Indeed Dr. Burstein and his creation confront us with an interesting paradox. Who is the monster?

Luke Cage (2016) opens us up to a particular moment in the United States and abroad when militarism, racism, and economic exploitation have crippled Black and Brown lives. The show invites theological reflection and interrogation because of its themes of freedom, art, and humanity. Black Theology and Womanist Theology offer unique vantage points for engaging Luke Cage methodologically. Because both theologies are grounded in the reality of Black lives, these theological frameworks are relevant in regard to Luke and the Harlem community. For James Cone, the parent of Black Liberation Theology, Black experience, Black history, Black culture, revelation, scripture, and tradition encompass the sources for Black Theology.[51] Concern for the community and liberation in light of Jesus' gospel guides the theological norm or hermeneutical principle in Black Theology. Womanist theology concerns itself primarily with the liberation of Black women and the family, establishing a positive quality of life for women and the family, and forming political alliances with other marginal groups struggling to be free of the oppression imposed by white-controlled American institutions.[52]

In understanding the concept of a monster, James Baldwin is useful. In the documentary *Take This Hammer* (Richard Moore, US 1963), Baldwin says, "I'm not describing you when I talk about you. I'm describing me. . . . We invented the nigger. I didn't invent it. White people invented it." Baldwin articulates that the creation of the monster (nigger) emerged from white supremacist fears imposed on Blacks. In *Democracy Matters*, Cornel West describes niggerization as the act of American terrorism on Black people, treating them as niggers for over 350 years, making them "feel unsafe, unprotected, subject to random violence, and hated."[53] Like the Tuskegee syphilis experiments in the late twentieth century, Dr. Burstein takes Luke's Black body without any concern for his humanity. Burstein objectifies Luke into a thing that can benefit U.S. imperialism and militarism.

For centuries, the white gaze has invented slaves, Sambos, welfare queens, Jezebels, Hulks, and even animals out of Black bodies. These catastrophic misnomers are made possible by what Emilie Townes calls "the fantastic hegemonic imagination." Townes says, "The fantastic hegemonic imagination

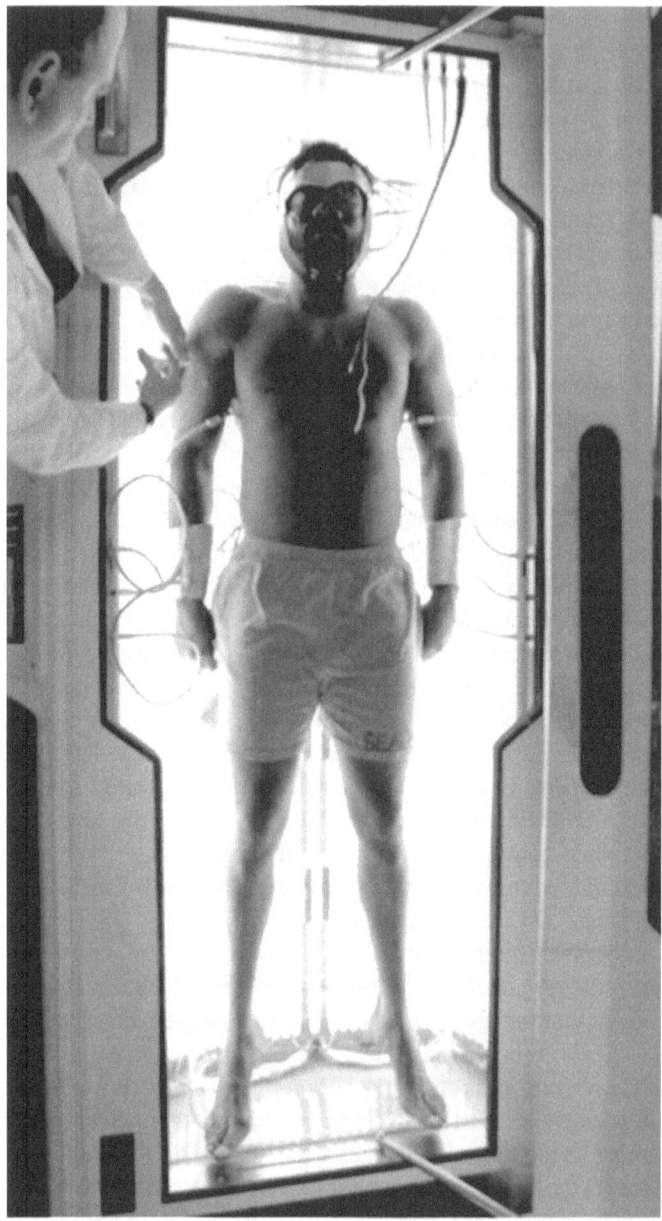

Figure 3.5 Baptism/Rebirth. Film Still, "Step in the Arena," *Luke Cage* (2016), S01/E04, 39:34.

traffics in peoples' lives that are caricatured or pillaged so that the imagination that creates the fantastic can control the world in its image."[54] In this way, we may understand Luke Cage's impenetrable Black body as a result of white supremacist fantastic hegemonic imagination. The creation of Luke Cage emerges from the imagination of Dr. Burstein and not Luke himself. Luke's impenetrable body raises questions about how the United States sees itself concerning Black bodies. Does the United States understand itself to be impenetrable like Luke because of its military power? Does fear within the psyche of the white gaze perpetuate police brutality, harsh punishment, and the disproportionate imprisonment of Black bodies in the prison-industrial complex due to false conceptions of the Black body? Who is the monster?

In *Future of Ethics*, Willis Jenkins articulates the ways in which the earth is connected to women's bodies. In particular, Jenkins evokes Womanist voices to demonstrate how the earth's vulnerability relates to the vulnerability of women. The penetrable bodies of women in *Luke Cage* (2016)—Candace, Mariah, Misty's cousin—contrast with Luke's normally impenetrable male body. When Luke too is pierced, his insides ravaged by the Judas bullets, this gender distinction breaks down somewhat. Jenkins also helps us to go beyond the binary of female/male, as well as that of human/non-human, considering *all* those who are susceptible to harm. In this regard we remember that the United States continues to assert its imperial self not only through patriarchy and racism, not only through war and colonialism, but also through fracking, polluting, razing, and drilling.

What is Luke's response to his tragic condition and paradoxical self? He answers the niggerization imposed on his body like Emmett Till's mother who responded to the murder of her 14-year-old son by saying, "I don't have a minute to hate. I'll pursue justice for the rest of my life."[55] Out of love, Baldwin tells his nephew that he does not have to confine himself to the definitions of the white world. With these two formulations, we may understand Luke Cage pursuing love and justice as a response to the various cages in which he exists. When Luke chooses his name, he quotes a central text in Black Theology—Luke 4:18 (E04). In reference to Luke 4:18, Cone says, "Jesus' work is essentially one of liberation."[56] Like the Jesus of Black Liberation Theology, Luke Cage is anointed to bring liberty to the oppressed. As Jesus enters the human condition of those who experience systemic violence, Luke steps into the experience of those who are economically exploited, those who encounter police brutality, and those who encounter gang violence.

When two police officers stop Luke, many viewers may have had people in mind, such as Sandra Bland, Tamir Rice, Renisha McBride, Trayvon Martin, Mike Brown, and many others. Police inquiries have resulted in the deaths of too many Black and Brown people in the United States. However, the scene presents liberative tones when the bullets bounce off of Luke (E07). This scene is very similar to Kendrick Lamar's music video *Alright* (Colin Tilley, US 2015), where Kendrick's body levitates against the gravity of state-sanctioned violence. Even in the face of the monstrosity of police brutality, Luke shields one police officer from the bullets of the other. He demonstrates a central claim in the thought of Baldwin and Black Theology—the liberation of the oppressed is tied to the liberation of the oppressor.

"NO ONE CAN CAGE A MAN IF HE TRULY WANTS TO BE FREE"

In his brief yet influential introduction to the subject Eddie S. Glaude Jr. argues that if "African American religion" is to have any analytical purchase, it must mean more than simply the religious life of people who happen to be Black. He insists, instead, that we understand it as a religious formation that "emerges in the encounter between faith, in all its complexity, and white supremacy."[57] African American religion responds to the political and social context of the United States in three ways. It represents a "sign of difference," insofar as it "explicitly rejects, as best as possible, the idolatry of white supremacy." African American religion operates as a "practice of freedom," wherein the "black religious imagination is used in the service of opening up spaces closed down by white supremacy." And it "insists on its *open-ended orientation*," meaning "African American religion offers resources for African Americans to imagine themselves beyond the constraints of now."[58]

We have already seen the ways in which Luke Cage, our "dishwasher Lazarus," stands as a *sign of difference* with regard to the traditional superhero story. If we take the archetypal comic-book superhero who doles out violence in his (or occasionally her) quest to redeem the masses as an embodiment of the white savior—the figure who takes up the white wo/man's burden to save those who cannot save themselves—then we can read Luke Cage's reluctance to do harm and commitment to protecting the vulnerable as a rejection of one logic of white supremacy.

To this sign of difference, we can add that the show opens up spaces closed down by white supremacy by reclaiming the image of the Black man in a hoodie which figures so prominently in the racist fantasies of the collective American subconscious in recent memory. Cheo Hodari Coker, the show's creator, brought to life a bulletproof Black man who shields other Black and Brown bodies from harm at a time when, for viewers of color, their bodies are as vulnerable as they have ever been. Nothing is more indicative of the show's birth in the Black Lives Matter moment than Coker's choice to dress Luke Cage in an array of hoodies. Here, Coker directly intervenes in the demonization and criminalization of Black bodies. Responding to the grim reality that a hoodie could, in the eyes of a vigilante like George Zimmerman, condemn Trayvon Martin to death, Coker reclaims the hoodie and opens an imaginative space wherein "heroes could wear hoodies, too."[59]

In many respects, *Luke Cage* (2016) can also be understood as a *practice of freedom*. This is, after all, the meaning behind the titular character's name. Freedom is a central theme of the show, which is oriented around the wrongful conviction of a man who has escaped from prison. "No one can *cage* a man if he truly wants to be free," Luke states as he explains his adopted surname (E04). He demonstrates this ideal repeatedly as he escapes an impressive array of both figurative and literal confinements, including Seagate Prison, his father's low expectations, his own fears and anxieties, and the rubble that he's buried under when Cornell shoots him with a missile (E03–04; figure 3.6). As

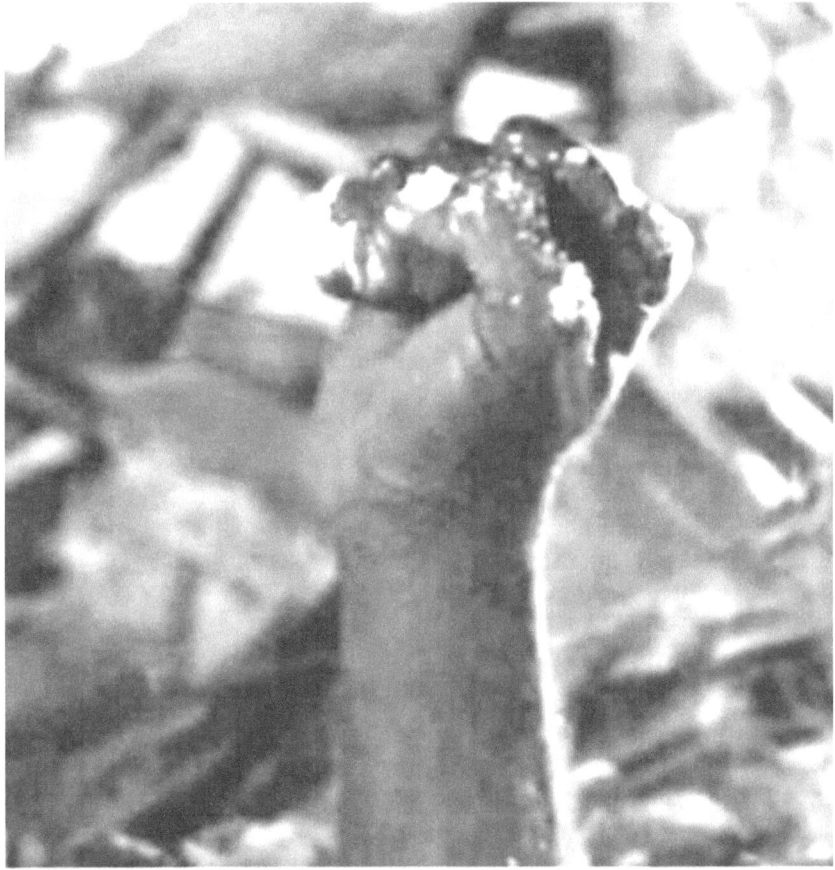

Figure 3.6 Luke's Fist Breaks Free of the Rubble and Symbolizes Solidarity with Black Liberation Movements. Film Still, "Step in the Arena," *Luke Cage* (2016), S01/E04, 44:10.

for "Luke," he takes his first name from the gospel where Jesus proclaims he has come to "preach good news to the poor . . . freedom for the prisoners, and recovery of sight for the blind" (E04, Luke 4:18).

Nowhere does the show exemplify the features of African American religion more poignantly than in its *open-ended orientation*. *Luke Cage* (2016) achieves something that has long remained a defining feature of African American religion: the creation of an imaginative space in and through which Black people can conjure worlds beyond the violence and degradation of daily life in a racist society. David Walker prophesied that God would wipe white supremacy off the face of the earth in wrath. The Exodus story of slaves set free by plagues and the parting of seas served as the mythic model for the liberation of the enslaved in the South, and later, for a second Exodus out of Jim Crow in the Great Migrations. Martin Luther King insisted that African Americans "as a people will get to the Promised Land" even if he also admitted, on the eve of his assassination no less, that he might "not get there with you."[60] And *Luke Cage* (2016) brings a world into being where a Black man in a hoodie is impervious to the bullets of police officers and gangsters alike, where that hoodied hero unites his beloved community (Harlem) against the death dealers set out to destroy them from without and within.

Coker characterizes this open-ended orientation as a sort of wish fulfillment, noting "superheroes to a certain extent are always wish fulfillment."[61] Another way to think about the show, though, would be as an example of what Robin D. G. Kelley calls "freedom dreams." Reflecting on the significance of the imagination in the Black radical tradition, Kelley quips, "call me utopian, but I inherited my mother's belief that the map to a new world is in the imagination, in what we see in our third eyes rather than in the desolation that surrounds us."[62] When we view *Luke Cage* (2016) through the lens of African American religion, we begin to see the ways in which Black superhero narratives can function *as* religion, especially in the present moment when one must insist that Black lives matter in the face of a society that too often insists otherwise.

"ALWAYS FORWARD, FORWARD ALWAYS"

The content of *Luke Cage* (2016) demonstrates what one could call an "ultimate concern" in the Tillichian sense. It looks through the unconditional aspects of the existential situation of the context within which it is situated and subtly and overtly voices the situation through summarizing its multiplicity into themes/questions/problems that can be addressed.[63] In other words, we enter into the dynamic social, political, economic, racial, and other dilemmas of the New York City where the story is set without an explanation of those problems as problems, but with a Heideggerian "thrownness" right in the middle of the "action" from which the concerns that need to be addressed emanate.[64]

Luke Cage's role in this context is one of synthesis: he embodies the ultimate concern as displayed in the whole of the fucked up situation manifested in the struggle that ensues between Cornell and the drug kingpin Colon (E01), the political maneuvering of Mariah as a disguise for her own balancing act between the legal and the illegal for personal benefit (E01), and the campaign of extortion of local businesses executed by both Cornell and Mariah (E03). In the embodiment and synthesis of this multiplicity, Luke Cage becomes a God in the Whiteheadian sense. He does not create an answer ex nihilo, but takes the jagged bricks of his context and theopoetically makes a house of liberation in which Harlem residents "relocate" and experience a transformation of their understanding of themselves, their worth, and their potential for greatness, even in the midst of the multifaceted oppression plaguing them.[65] In the words of Jerome Stone, this might be thought of as "minimalist transcendence," a humanistic response/intervention that replaces the need for a divine response, or at least the affirmation that transcendence described in this way is more logically defensible due to an empirical experience and location of such transformation.[66] Luke represents the "creative transformation" that John Cobb describes as "the call forward,"[67] a notion echoed by Pop's sacred mantra/dying words: "always forward" (E02).

One of the most interesting themes of *Luke Cage* (2016) that goes largely unstated is that of the "world within a world." The Harlem as presented has autonomous existence in the way that Indigenous communities in North America have a sort of sovereignty: it is dependent on the world from which it comes in a peripheral way, yet operates on its own rules. It has its presidents and its pawns, its members with social capital and those without. This is Whiteheadian interconnectivity. The parent world's racism, poverty, classism, sexism, and other deities of white supremacy that converge in the "event" of Harlem, all play a role in how Harlem functions.[68] But the blatant existence of this parent world and its diseases are rarely made explicitly evident, except occasionally. One key example is Cornell's identification of what in his exegesis is the curse/blessing of the underestimation of Afro-diasporic individuals in the parent world of the United States in his statement, "It's easy to underestimate a nigga. You never see them coming" (E01). Another is the recurring appeal to literary works written by people of Afro-diasporic descent born in the United States as a source/instance of reclamation of identity such as Langston Hughes and Walter Mosley (E01). The liberation strategy here is processual, emphasizing in glimpses how the humanistic wise use of the thematic background of a context (even the background that is virtually inaccessible) can set a brighter future for even the darkest situation.[69]

Another theme of the series is "Switzerland," or Pop's Barber Shop. In this rhizomic meeting place, the hierarchical tensions of key influential people in the Harlem World become nonfactors, as all who enter this shrine of the barbershop lose the stance of competitors and become colleagues. This is not the cancellation of difference, but the acceptance of the contrast of multiplicity so that difference is not solved but courageously engaged within this beautiful mess, this chaosmos, many times uncomfortably (E02). The role of space is important in *Luke Cage* (2016) as a process liberation philosophy, for Switzerland is a freeze frame of the moment of decision. In Switzerland, there are no decisions but only possibility. In Switzerland, entities are presented with choices that could lead to their progressive liberation if they enact them outside of the Harlem World. Pop's Barber Shop is a prime liberating thematic instance of the secular transcendence Whitehead alludes to and Stone clearly spells out.[70]

The pinnacle of this liberating process/secular transcendence unearthed by Luke Cage is the notion of secular Gods that shows up in the background of the series, sometimes literally. There are allusions to the transcendent Gods of classical Christian theism, such as the funeral service for Pop (E05) and the biblical recitations of Luke's nemesis Diamondback (E08). But these are either figureheads which symbolize empty religiosity or use it subversively, even perversely. These Gods, in other words, are dead.[71] The "true religion"

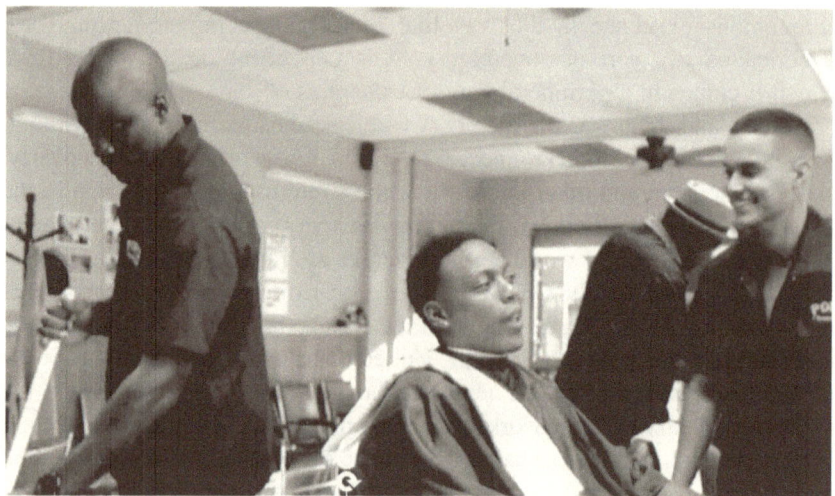

Figure 3.7 Conflicting Theologies: Shameek Swaggers, Luke Sweeps. Film Still, "Moment of Truth," *Luke Cage* (2016), S01/E01, 2:57.

of the Harlem World of *Luke Cage* (2016) lies elsewhere. You don't get much more religious than having a picture of the Notorious B.I.G. on your wall as the focal point of honor. The MCs are some of the Gods of Harlem, along with the drug lords. These are the people who many of the residents of the city—like Shameek, done in by hubris and Cornells' fists—aspire to be. They set the tone of the town. So does Luke Cage. While the drug lords take the position of disconnected coercion to influence Harlem, Luke presents a different way of life that is interconnected persuasion. In the poetry of his Godhood, he takes the vileness of the world and creatively transforms it to a beautiful mess that influences the dwellers of Harlem to follow his modest whispers of liberation, whispers infused with a contagious renewed sense of hope and power.[72]

"DO WHAT YOU CAN, KID"

So where does all this get us? What is the point of this shared rumination on *Luke Cage* (2016), which is, in the end, just a Netflix series based on some comic books? Why should scholars of religion care? Why should anyone care?

Circling back to J. Z. Smith, he has theorized religion as a way of envisioning how the world should be, in contrast to how it is, and acting out ways to reconcile that gap.[73] Creating a show, watching its episodes, participating in its fan culture, even ragging on it through criticism can be analyzed as part of this practice. After all, disappointment only makes sense in comparison to a better what-could-be. In a sense this idea speaks to the tension within the concept of the superhero itself: it is an imperfect response to the problems of the world in which we live, the envisioning of a solution that is not only impossible but also itself problematic. In the words of Method Man as he concludes his ode to Luke, "Bulletproof Love": "People say we don't need another hero, but now we got one" (E12).

Our first roundtable discussion at the AAR and this ensuing chapter analyze, and ultimately contribute to, the meta-process of a culture reflecting on itself through its own products. I am excited about working in collaboration to allow for a richer sense of context than any of our individual approaches to *Luke Cage* (2016) could provide on its own. Rather than a single scholarly take, this chapter is intended to provide a kaleidoscope of different perspectives, each lens allowing us to see new pieces and shifting our vision of the whole.

The sections share what can be read in Smith's formulation as a dialectic of hope and disappointment. In its conscious engagements, the show has the potential to offer subversive alternatives to the expected messages of mainstream entertainment. Luke is a more thoughtful, more human, Christ figure than usually found within superhero narratives, yet the genre's default to purifying violence ultimately proves impossible to completely escape. The series introduces

Figure 3.8 Misty Tries to See the Whole Picture. Film Still, "Manifest," *Luke Cage* (2016), S01/E07, 10:45.

not one, but several compelling characters who are women of color, but also at times disempowers them in conventional and therefore perplexing ways. The image of a righteous Black man in a hoodie, immune to bullets, is a messianic dream in this moment in which "Black Lives Matter" is a supposedly controversial statement. Yet, the image can also be twisted into White-supremacist sadism. The Harlem of the show represents an autonomous alterity, but does so by appropriating a real, thriving African American community into a fictional vision largely of deprivation. There are so many ways that the show is invigorating, entertaining, and inspiring and so many ways that it inevitably falls short. Discussing together is part of the way we reconcile the gap.

Tracing religious elements within the show, putting the series in relationship to cultural phenomena with which it is in dialogue, and considering its trajectories of influence demonstrate that *Luke Cage* (2016) wrestles with some of the major issues of our cultural moment—racism, violence, sexuality, and power—issues with which, as scholars of religion, we must also engage. In the end, there is no single answer or meaning. The show is multivalent, as are the best scholarly conversations.

NOTES

1. This chapter was originally published in the *Journal for Religion, Film, and Media* (2017). It is revised for this book and used with permission.

2. The authors would like to thank one of the members of the Religion, Film, and Visual Culture group, Dr. Syed Adnan Hussain (of St. Mary's University in Halifax),

for the initial inspiration to propose this session. The panel featured six scholars from several groups within the AAR in addition to RFVC: Anthropology of Religion; Black Theology; Critical Approaches to Hip-Hop and Religion; and Religion and Popular Culture. Many of the participants had never encountered one another before, and so the roundtable became an opportunity to cross disciplinary lines, bring together a diverse range of voices and perspectives, and meet some seriously excellent people.

3. Sheffield 2016.

4. Smith 1982; see also Asad 1993; Masuzawa 2005.

5. All references to *Luke Cage* are to the first season of the series, which as of this writing is the only season that has aired.

6. This is in fact the first time that we see Luke's powers in action.

7. As it turns out Luke is employing a rope-a-dope strategy, letting Diamondback wear his suit out beating on him before being dispatched by our hero with three quick hits. Still, the fact is that Luke wins by submitting to violence.

8. See, e.g., Jewett and Lawrence 1977, 2002, 2003, 2010.

9. For a concise account of both zealous nationalism and prophetic realism (which is discussed below), and the biblical origins of each perspective, see Jewett and Lawrence 2003, 44–54.

10. Examples of American cinematic superheroes who embody zealous nationalism include the protagonists *Batman* (Tim Burton, US 1989), *Spider-Man* (Sam Raimi, US 2002), *Superman Returns* (Bryan Singer, US 2006), *Iron Man* (Jon Favreau, US 2008), *The Dark Knight Rises* (Christopher Nolan, GB/US 2012), and *Man of Steel* (Zack Snyder, GB/US 2013).

11. One of the most zealous moments in the series comes after Pop's funeral (E05), when Misty upbraids Luke for antagonizing Cornell and says that she will get him "the right way," using due process, and that "the system will win." Luke is having none of it: "Forget the system. Arrests lead to indictments, and indictments lead to pleas. There's always a bigger fish. A bigger angle. A slap on the wrist. And boom. Right back in business. I ain't going for that." This conversation is an example of the wonderfully complex, shifting dynamics of LUKE CAGE (2016), given that Luke as noted below does end up trusting the "system" in several respects, while Misty moves further into vigilante territory: she attacks Claire during an official interrogation (E08) and circumvents police protocol when trying to protect a key witness against Mariah, which leads to the witness' death and Mariah's freedom (E13).

12. In his eulogy for Pop, Luke admits that he used to be "selfish" in his responses to violence, and that Pop taught him a critical lesson: "If we try to protect only ourselves, without looking out for those people closest to us, then we lose" (E05). He concludes the eulogy by affirming, "I don't believe in Harlem. I believe in the people who make Harlem what it is." This faith is returned at several points in the series, notably when many of Harlem's people put on hoodies with holes in them to help Luke evade the police, and when they all start chanting "Luke! Luke! Luke!" during his final fight with Diamondback (E13).

13. Pop too worked to understand the value and humanity of all people, regardless of their past. As Luke notes in his eulogy, "Pop saw the shine in everyone that walked

into his barbershop. . . . He made them feel better about the world, and themselves. We have to strive on a daily basis to do the same for each other" (E05).

The most striking way in which *Luke Cage* (2016) fails to do this very thing involves Willis Stryker, who is portrayed as cartoonishly evil. The attempt to understand his horrifying behavior is weak and unsatisfying; simply having a thoughtless and hypocritical father hardly accounts for Stryker's murderous rampages. And the parental indifference he experienced in no way comes close to the horrors suffered by Cornell and Mariah, who are shown to us as infinitely more complex, conflicted, and interesting adults than Stryker.

That said, to its credit the series remarkably does not end with the standard climactic/apocalyptic superhero battle between mimetic enemies. It certainly appears to be going in this direction, especially when the penultimate episode ends with Diamondback in a super-suit confronting his half-brother Luke. But this fight is actually quite brief and ends very near the start the final episode, leaving a great deal of time for people to simply have *conversations* about what is next for themselves, for others, and for the community.

14. The criteria for identifying Christ figures listed in this paragraph come specifically from chapter six of Baugh's text ("Essential Dimensions and Typical Guises of the Christ-figure"). There are of course any number of criteria not mentioned by Baugh that could be used instead; see, e.g., Kozlovic 2004. Also, as noted below, many objections have been raised regarding the ways in which Christ figures are generally identified and interpreted.

15. The one criterion mentioned by Baugh that appears least often in superhero films is prayer, although this is not unheard of (e.g., Superman's very Gethsemane-esque visit to a church in *Man of Steel* [2013]). In keeping with this pattern, prayer is arguably the one Christ-figure requirement from Baugh's list that Luke does not clearly fulfill—although he does give a eulogy for Pop in a church (E05).

16. Referring to his role as the savior of Harlem, Angelica Jade Bastién (2016) says that she has come to think of Luke as "Hood Jesus."

17. This moment also represents the death of Carl Lucas as an identity. As Luke angrily tells Dr. Burstein after his post-Judas resurrection, "I'm Luke. Carl died at Seagate" (E10).

18. Kozlovic 2004.

19. Kozlovic 2004, ¶61, ¶51.

20. Kozlovic 2004, ¶33.

21. Kozlovic 2004, ¶40.

22. Kozlovic 2004, ¶43.

23. Kozlovic 2004, ¶63. The hoodie appears to evoke the image of Jesus specifically as *shepherd*, as taking care of others and Black; which fits Luke's reference to Luke 4:18 (discussed below). In fact, the first time he wears a hoodie in the series is also the first time he uses his powers, when he protects his landlords from Cornell's men (E01). When the fight is done Mrs. Lin says that she wants to pay Luke to help them, and he replies: "I'm not for hire. But you have my word ma'am: I've got you." And then he pops his hood on (figure 3.4).

24. See Campbell 2016 for a theological discussion of the ways in which Luke functions as a Christ figure in contrast to Matt Murdock from *Daredevil* (Netflix,

US 2015, 2016). Campbell argues that each hero represents very different aspects of the Christian messiah's salvivic role, with Matt as the suffering Jesus and Luke the risen Christ. He contrasts the fact that Matt's "body is broken time and time again for the sake of those he seeks to save" with the understanding that Luke is "indestructible": "Freed from death and physical pain, after his resurrection, Luke Cage is able to tackle oppression in Harlem fearlessly. Mostly." While Campbell makes many good points, his use of "mostly" here is, I would argue, an understatement. Unlike Daredevil, who is in fact called "the man without fear," Luke is filled with a great deal of anxiety—and (arguably) fear—about taking on oppression. And while he is certainly much less susceptible to physical harm than Matt Murdock, *Luke Cage* (2016) makes the point in several ways noted below that Luke is far from indestructible.

25. See, e.g., Deacy 2006; Derry 2012, 189–191; Jasper 1997; Lyden 2003, 24; Plate 2003, 158, 160 n. 12.

26. It is thus not surprising that most superhero films end with a huge, enormously destructive fight. The protagonist essentially becomes the savior figure of Revelation, triumphing in an apocalyptic battle against evil.

27. A television news report on this community action highlights the iconic/religious significance of Luke's hoodie by referring to him as "The 'Hole-y' Hero" (E12).

28. Dyson 2001; Hodge 2009, 2010; Johnson 2013; Miller and Pinn 2015; Miller, Pinn, and Bun 2015.

29. Forman 2002, 173–211.

30. Hodge 2010, 42–43.

31. Hodge 2010, 73–187.

32. While the central premise of this framework focuses on music, I have expanded its use to also explore cultural phenomena within Black and city contexts along with adding symbolic imagery and cultural mores—all of which are a part of *Luke Cage* (2016).

33. Spencer 1991, 3.

34. Kirk-Duggan and Hall 2011, 77.

35. There is no universal or singular definition of ethnomusicology, as William Darity states; several words come to mind for ethnomusicology such as sound, music, performance, context, and culture. For some, it is the study of music in culture, or, more broadly, the study in context (Darity 2008, 20–22).

36. Spencer 1991, 3–4.

37. Theomusicology broadens the discussion of religion within Hip Hop contexts and asks the question "What is the Hip Hop community saying in the context in which the music, the art, the album, and the artist were created?"

38. This is the generation of young adults born during the post-soul era/ context (1980-2001), raised on a transmediated diet, disconnected from previous generations both locally and ideologically, and currently have non-binary issues to contend with in a post-9/11 society living in Western society. This generation does not have the binary issues to contend with that the Civil Rights generation did (e.g., more Blacks in leadership or the right to vote). While those issues are still present, they manifest

themselves in a matrix of problems, which involve police brutality, sexuality, sexual orientation, socioeconomics, transgender, class, and race.

39. Hodge 2017, 116–148.

40. I would note that there is still a strong patriarchal feel within *Luke Cage* (2016), and that this continues to be one of Hip Hop's major flaws. Gender and sexuality tend to favor men and heteronormative standards, leaving little to no room for LGBTQ and other variances to that norm.

41. Crenshaw 1989 and 2012.

42. Collins 1990, 2013, and 2014.

43. hooks 2004, 29.

44. Collins 1995.

45. See Crenshaw 1991, especially 1266–1271.

46. Merry 2008; Levy 2009.

47. On queer theory and the academic study of religion, see Wilcox 2012.

48. Williams 1993.

49. I am thinking here of critiques of "white washing" characters as other media forms are adapted to film, of the marketing concern that more than one significant character of color will pigeon-hole a show (e.g., as dramatized in "Indians on TV," *Master of None* [Netflix, US 2015], S01/E04, and of the lack of recognition for actors of color who do manage, in spite of systemic racism, to land important roles (#OscarsSoWhite).

50. Bastién 2016.

51. Cone 2010 [1970], 24–35.

52. Williams 1994, 53.

53. West 2004, 20.

54. Townes 2006, 21.

55. West 2004, 21.

56. Cone 1997 [1969], 35.

57. Glaude 2014, 6.

58. Glaude 2014, 11–12.

59. Kim/Shifflet, 2016.

60. King 1991 [1968], 286.

61. Kim/Shifflet, 2016.

62. Kelley 2002, 2–3.

63. Tillich 1951, 10–11.

64. Heidegger 1996 [1927], 127.

65. Whitehead 1978 [1929], 346.

66. Stone 1992, 109–110.

67. Coleman 2008, 87.

68. Massumi 2009, 5–6.

69. Whitehead 1967 [1933], 256–257.

70. Stone 1992, 109–110.

71. Nietzsche 2007 [1882], 71–72.

72. Walker 2004, 59–60, 62, 69–71.

73. Smith 1987.

REFERENCES

Asad, Talal. 1993. "The Construction of Religion as an Anthropological Category," in: *Genealogies of Religion: Discipline and Reasons of Power in Christianity and Islam*. Baltimore: Johns Hopkins University Press, 27–54.

Bastién, Angelica Jade. 2016. "LUKE CAGE Recap." Family First, Vulture, 10 October. http://www.vulture.com/2016/10/marvels-luke-cage-recap-season-1-episode-7.html [accessed 2 January 2017].

Baugh, Lloyd. 1997. *Imaging the Divine. Jesus and Christ-Figures in Film*. Kansas City: Sheed and Ward.

Campbell, Nathan. 2016. "How Luke Cage and Daredevil are (Good) Images and Imitators of Jesus (and Why the Original is Still Better)." St. Eutychus, 10 October. http://st-eutychus.com/2016/how-luke-cage-and-daredevil-are-good-images-and-imitators-of-jesus-and-why-the-original-is-still-better [accessed 12 November 2016].

Coleman, Monica A. 2008. *Making a Way Out of No Way. A Womanist Theology*. Minneapolis: Fortress Press.

Collins, Patricia Hill. 1990. *Black Feminist Thought. Knowledge, Consciousness, and the Politics of Empowerment*. New York: Routledge.

Collins, Patricia Hill. 1995. "Black Women and Motherhood," in: Held, Virgina (ed.), *Justice and Care: Essential Readings in Feminist Ethics*. Boulder: Westview, 117–138.

Collins, Patricia Hill. 2013. *On Intellectual Activism*. Philadelphia: Temple University Press.

Collins, Patricia Hill. 2014. "Intersectionality's Definitional Dilemma." *Annual Review of Sociology* 41: 1–20.

Cone, James. 1997 [1969]. *Black Theology and Black Power*. Maryknoll: Orbis, 3rd ed.

Cone, James. 2010 [1970]. *A Black Theology of Liberation*. Maryknoll: Orbis, 3rd ed.

Crenshaw, Kimberlé Williams. 1989. "Demarginalizing the Intersection of Race and Sex: A Black Feminist Critique of Antidiscrimination Doctrine, Feminist Theory and Antiracist Politics." *University of Chicago Legal Forum* 140: 139–167.

Crenshaw, Kimberlé Williams. 1991. "Mapping the Margins: Intersectionality, Identity Politics and Violence against Women of Color." *Stanford Law Review* 43: 1241–1299.

Crenshaw, Kimberlé Williams. 2012. "From Private Violence to Mass Incarcerations: Thinking Intersectionally about Women, Violence and State Control." *UCLA Law Review* 59: 1418–1473.

Darity, William A., Jr. 2008. "Ethnomusicology," in: Darity, William A., Jr. (ed.), *International Encyclopedia of the Social Sciences*, vol. 3. Detroit: Macmillan Reference USA, 19–20.

Deacy, Christopher. 2006. "Reflections on the Uncritical Appropriation of Cinematic Christ-Figures: Holy Other or Wholly Inadequate?" *Journal of Religion and Popular Culture* 13: 1. http://dx.doi.org/10.3138/jrpc.13.1.001.

Derry, Ken. 2012. "Believing is Seeing. Teaching Religion and Violence in Film," in: Pennington, Brian (ed.), *Teaching Religion and Violence*. New York: Oxford University Press, 185–217.
Dyson, Michael Eric. 2001. *Holler If You Hear Me. Searching for Tupac Shakur*. New York: Basic Civitas.
Forman, Murray. 2002. *The 'Hood Comes First. Race, Space, and Place in Rap and Hip-Hop*. Middletown: Wesleyan University Press.
Glaude, Eddie S., Jr. 2014. *African American Religion: A Very Short Introduction*. Oxford: Oxford University Press.
Heidegger, Martin. 1996 [1927]. *Being and Time*. Translated by Joan Stambaugh. Albany: State University of New York Press.
Hodge, Daniel White. 2009. *Heaven Has a Ghetto. The Missiological Gospel & Theology of Tupac Amaru Shakur*. Saarbrucken: VDM Verlag Dr. Müller.
Hodge, Daniel White. 2010. *The Soul of Hip Hop. Rims, Timbs and a Cultural Theology*. Downers Grove: Inner Varsity Press.
Hodge, Daniel White. 2017. *Hip Hop's Hostile Gospel. A Post-Soul Theological Exploration*. Boston: Brill.
hooks, bell. 2003. *The Will to Change. Men, Masculinity and Love*. New York: Atria.
Jasper, David. 1997. "On Systematizing the Unsystematic. A Response," in: Marsh, Clive/Ortiz, Gaye (eds.), *Explorations in Theology and Film: Movies and Meaning*. Oxford: Blackwell, 235–244.
Jenkins, Willis. 2013. *Future of Ethics. Sustainability, Social Justice, and Religious Creativity*. Baltimore: Georgetown University Press.
Jewett, Robert/Lawrence, John Shelton. 1977. *The American Monomyth*. Garden City: Anchor Press.
Jewett, Robert/Lawrence, John Shelton. 2002. *The Myth of the American Superhero*. Grand Rapids: Eerdmans.
Jewett, Robert/Lawrence, John Shelton. 2003. *Captain America and the Crusade Against Evil: The Dilemma of Zealous Nationalism*. Grand Rapids: Eerdmans.
Jewett, Robert/Lawrence, John Shelton. 2010. "Heroes and Superheroes," in: Lyden, John (ed.), *The Routledge Companion to Religion and Film*. London/New York: Routledge, 384–402.
Johnson, Andre E., ed. 2013. *Urban God Talk: Constructing a Hip Hop Spirituality*. Lanham: Lexington Books.
Kelley, Robin D. G. 2001. *Freedom Dreams: The Black Radical Imagination*. Boston: Beacon Press.
Kim, James/Shifflet, Jonathan. 2016. "Why 'Luke Cage' Creator made his Superhero Costume a Hoodie." The Frame, 15 September. http://www.scpr.org/programs/the-frame/2016/09/15/52135/why-luke-cage-creator-made-his-superhero-costume-a [accessed 26 January 2017].
King, Martin Luther, Jr. 1991 [1968]. "I See the Promised Land (3 April, 1968)," in: Washington, James M. (ed.), *A Testament of Hope: The Writings and Speeches of Martin Luther King, Jr.* New York: HarperCollins, 279–286.
Kirk-Duggan, Cheryl/Hall, Marlon. 2011. *Wake Up! Hip Hop Christianity and the Black Church*. Nashville: Abingdon.

Kozlovic, Anton Karl. 2004. "The Structural Characteristics of the Cinematic Christ-figure." *Journal of Religion and Popular Culture* 8: 1. http://dx.doi.org/10.3138/jrpc.8.1.005.

Levy, Barrie. 2008. *Women and Violence*. Berkeley: Seal.

Lyden, John C. 2003. *Film as Religion. Myths, Morals and Rituals*. New York: New York University Press.

Massumi, Brian. 2009. *Semblance and Event: Activist Philosophy and the Occurrent Arts*. Cambridge: MIT Press.

Masuzawa, Tomoko. 2005. *The Invention of World Religions: Or, How European Universalism was Preserved in the Language of Pluralism*. Chicago/London: The University of Chicago Press.

Merry, Sally Engle. 2009. *Gender Violence. A Cultural Perspective*. Malden: Wiley-Blackwell.

Miller, Monica R./Pinn, Anthony B., eds. 2015. *The Hip Hop and Religion Reader*. New York: Routledge.

Miller, Monica R./Pinn, Anthony B./Bunn, B., eds. 2015. *Religion in Hip Hop. Mapping the New Terrain in the U.S.* New York: Bloomsbury.

Nietzsche, Friedrich. 2007 [1882]. "The Gay Science," translated by Peter Fritzsche, in: Fritzsche, Peter (ed.), *Nietzsche and the Death of God: Selected Writings*. Boston: Bedford/St. Martin's, 68–78.

Plate, S. Brent. 2003. "The Re-creation of the World: Filming Faith." *Dialog* 42: 155–160.

Sheffield, Rob. 2016. "Luke Cage: Meet the First Black Lives Matter Superhero." Rolling Stone. 5 October. http://www.rollingstone.com/tv/news/luke-cage-meet-the-first-black-lives-matter-superhero-w443198 [accessed 16 March 2017].

Smith, Jonathan Z. 1982. *Imagining Religion: From Babylon to Jonestown*. Chicago: The University of Chicago Press.

Smith, Jonathan Z. 1987. *To Take Place: Toward a Theory in Ritual*. Chicago: University of Chicago Press.

Spencer, Jon Michael. 1991. *Theological Music. An Introduction to Theomusicology*. New York: Greenwood.

Stone, Jerome. 1992. *The Minimalist Vision of Transcendence: A Naturalist Philosophy of Religion*. Albany: State University of New York Press.

Tillich, Paul. 1951. *Systematic Theology Vol. 1*. Chicago: University of Chicago Press.

Townes, Emilie. 2006. *Womanist Ethics and the Cultural Production of Evil*. New York: Palgrave Macmillan.

Walker, Theodore. 2004. *Mothership Connections: A Black Atlantic Synthesis of Neoclassical Metaphysics and Black Theology*. Albany: State University of New York Press.

West, Cornel. 2004. *Democracy Matters*. New York: Penguin.

Whitehead, Alfred North. 1967 [1933]. *Adventures of Ideas*. New York: The Free Press.

Whitehead, Alfred North. 1978 [1929]. *Process and Reality*. New York: The Free Press, corrected ed.

Wilcox, Melissa. 2012. "Queer Theory and the Study of Religion," in: Boisvert, Donald/Johnson, Jay Emerson (eds.), *Queer Religion, Vol. 2: LGBT Movements and Queering Religion*. Westport: Praeger, 227–251.
Williams, Delores. 1993. *Sisters in the Wilderness: The Challenge of Womanist God-Talk*. Maryknoll: Orbis.
Williams, Delores. 1994. "The Color of Feminism: Or Speaking the Black Woman's Tongue," in: Daly, Lois K. (ed.), *Feminist Theological Ethics: A Reader*. Louisville: Westminster John Knox.

FILMOGRAPHY

Alright (Colin Tilley, US 2015).
Batman (Tim Burton, US 1989).
Daredevil (Netflix, US 2015, 2016).
The Dark Knight Rises (Christopher Nolan, GB/US 2012).
Iron Man (Jon Favreau, US 2008).
Jessica Jones (Netflix, US 2015).
Jesus of Nazareth (FRANCO ZEFFIRELLI, GB/IT 1977).
Luke Cage (Netflix, US 2016).
Man of Steel (Zack Snyder, GB/US 2013).
Master of None (Netflix, US 2015).
Spider-Man (Sam Raimi, US 2002).
Superman Returns (Bryan Singer, US 2006).
Take This Hammer (Richard Moore, US 1963).

Part II

POWER, WORTH, AND SOCIETY

Chapter 4

Old Gods in New Films

History, Culture, and Religion in Black Panther, Doctor Strange, *and* Thor: Ragnarok

Rhiannon Grant and Jo Henderson-Merrygold

In this chapter, we compare the content, context, and especially the religious and cultural aspects of three Marvel films: *Doctor Strange* (2016), *Thor: Ragnarok* (2017), and *Black Panther* (2018). We argue that each of these films reveals something about the way that religion is currently understood in the Western, Anglophone, and mainly American society within which the films were made, precisely because each of them involves an interaction with another more or less fictional and non-Western society. Because religion is bound up with culture and especially with the transfer of power in each narrative, the ways in which Eastern religion (in *Doctor Strange*), African religion (in *Black Panther*), and alien religion (in *Thor: Ragnarok*) are imagined by the filmmakers tells us a good deal about how power and religion are assumed to relate universally. We briefly consider each film individually, before introducing some key themes in the religious content of the films. We then move into a substantial discussion of the ways in which religion is portrayed, both appropriatively and appreciatively, and show how the films ultimately support a white Protestant Christian hegemony.

INTRODUCING THE FILMS

The films central to this discussion are taken from the third phase of the Marvel Cinematic Universe (MCU, 2016–2019), the concluding arc of The Infinity Saga (2008–2019). Each was launched into an established canon and the basic formula for such films is well established. Yet, each of the films featured here—*Doctor Strange* (2016), *Thor: Ragnarok* (2017), and *Black Panther* (2018)—has something noteworthy to say about the way religion is understood in and through the MCU. In his interrogation of *Black Panther*, Ken Derry allies Christianity with colonialism, persuasively arguing that the enduring model of superhero films, especially those in the MCU, draws heavily on biblical apocalypses and hegemonic, white colonialism. Indeed, he describes the oeuvre of such films as based in a messianic model, typified by a singular act leading to the hero (almost) singlehandedly overcoming a biblical-level apocalypse—all while ensuring that the idyllic society that the hero enables to take root affirms rather than undermines established political hegemony.[1] Derry also notes that in this body of work there is a predominance of everyday Joes who are transformed and ascend to legendary status following a singular—miraculous—event. These three films differ from that model in that the central heroes combine their messianic duties with a status established by tradition and lineage. The ascension model central to these films is bolstered through religious imagery that highlights the narrative centrality of lineage in each character's story.

Doctor Strange introduces us to an antisocial, misogynistic, egotistical but nevertheless gifted, white, American surgeon (Stephen Strange: Benedict Cumberbatch) who experiences profound, life-altering damage to his hands early in the film. He treks off in search of a miraculous cure only to be found under the tutelage of The Ancient One (Tilda Swinton) in Kamar-Taj, a remote village possibly in Tibet.[2] The Ancient One is Sorcerer Supreme of a religious order whose East Asian location and saffron-colored robes connote an orientalist representation of Buddhism despite Swinton's whiteness and the character's apparent Celtic heritage.[3] After initial frustration, Strange soon finds himself excelling in the "mystic arts" of which he will become an eventual master and successor to The Ancient One as the Sorcerer Supreme. Faced with a threat to the order who have provided him with these gifts, Strange chooses to embrace his life as hero and eventually saves the day, overtaking those who have trained far longer and with more familiarity with this religious tradition.

Black Panther is widely celebrated as the first Marvel film to feature a lead and director who are black as well as a predominantly black cast. Engaging with wider moves in American science fiction toward Afrofuturism, the film is largely set in the fictional isolationist nation of Wakanda.[4] T'Challa (Chadwick Boseman) is the eldest son of the recently deceased king T'Chaka (*Captain America: Civil War*, 2016), whose inherited status as both king and Black Panther is both threatened and established throughout the film. Erik Killmonger (Michael B. Jordan), the film's antagonist, is T'Challa's U.S.-born cousin whose birth was kept from the family in Wakanda. Throughout the film, the ideologies of religion, nationhood, tradition, and identity are juxtaposed.⁵ At its conclusion, T'Challa finds himself the undisputed king and Black Panther following the death of Killmonger, for which he is culpable. The tradition into which he has been raised continues through him, albeit with a shift toward a less isolationist national model. The film has attracted significant critical engagement as a marked contrast with the white messianic Americo-centric hero figures and has been praised for its blurring of the hero/villain dichotomy and foregrounding of postcolonial and Afrocentric perspectives.⁶

The final film, launched between the two just introduced, is the only one to feature a non-human protagonist and is a sequel rather than the originating film.⁷ *Thor: Ragnarok* (2017) follows 2011's *Thor* and 2013's *Thor: The Dark World* but marks a departure from the "hero faces down threat in order to save the day and get the girl" model that typified the earlier films. In *Ragnarok*, Asgardian prince and god of thunder Thor (Chris Hemsworth) is trying to adapt to single life and embarks on a journey of self-discovery that coincides with the death of his father Odin and the introduction of a hitherto unknown villainous elder sibling, Hela, God of War (Cate Blanchett). Simultaneously the viewer encounters the extent to which Asgardians, through Odin, have erased the problematic "old ways" of Hela's era, replacing the divine imagery with that of Thor. Meanwhile, Thor himself is marooned and enslaved on an apparently inescapable planet. The resultant voyage of self-discovery is one for both Asgard and the prince who understood himself to be heir apparent. Unlike the earlier films, *Ragnarok* concludes with the destruction of the planet and an articulated understanding that "Asgard is a people not a place." Thor is marked by the physical costs of his journey and the battles symbolized by the loss of his right eye. Through the directorship of Taika Waititi, the film thus presents a noteworthy engagement with postcolonialism. These challenges render Thor a remarkably different character through this film than in his previous (and subsequent) incarnations.⁸

Each of these films presents heroes in marked contrast with those figures identified by Derry (2018) as lone messianic figures created through singular acts, as they each embody MCU versions of the divine right of kings. For that kingship to be exercised, there must be some exploration of how that *divine* right is understood within that story world. While Derry notes the biblical and messianic model that endures through Iron Man (2008, 2010, 2013), Hulk (2008),⁹ Captain America (2011, 2013, 2016), and Spider-Man (2017, 2019), there remain questions about how religion is portrayed beyond the white, anglo-saxon, Christian environments that inform the American religious context central to these messianic figures.¹⁰ Can the divine kings, whose stories appear distant, be free from the influences of Eurocentric Christian colonization—whether in an isolated African nation (Wakanda), the Himalayan mountains (Kamar-Taj), or the planets Asgard and Sakaar (where

Thor is enslaved)—or do they end up reproducing similar Christianized ideologies to those so dominant in the rest of the MCU?

RELIGIOUS THEMES

What is the significance of religion in these three Marvel films? At first glance, it might seem that, especially in *Black Panther* and *Doctor Strange*, religious ideas appear only as decoration around plots that are based mainly on magic—or at least a form of technology which, in the way of these things in superhero movies and as Arthur C. Clarke predicted,[11] has long since become indistinguishable from magic.[12] Mentioning the names of deities or a religious concept does not make a film about religion, and similarly, a throwaway line ("There's only one god, ma'm, and he doesn't look like that" (*Avengers* 2012)) is not enough to establish (or reject) religion as a theme in a film. Even using characters from a mythology, as in *Thor*, substantially re-written from ancient sources, only starts to scratch the surface. However, in this chapter, we argue that these three films do engage with religion, both on a superficial and a much deeper level, and that understanding the role of religion in storytelling, especially in the modern American comic-book context, is vital to an accurate analysis of these films.

Most English speakers know a religion when they see one—it is most commonly used to refer to the "world religions," a list usually starting with Christianity, Judaism, Islam, Hinduism, and Buddhism—but the term is difficult to define.[13] Many of the problematic aspects of the category of "religion" stem from the way in which Protestant Christianity is usually taken as the baseline or prototype of a religion, and other traditions and faiths are compared to that model. Buddhism is considered to be a religion despite a widespread denial in a supernatural deity, because it is similar enough to Protestant Christianity in social function and practice. Hinduism was constructed as a "religion" by the British and other Europeans colonizing India, who chose to treat a diverse collection of traditions as a single religion based mainly on geography. Traditions in which individuals might both lack belief and participate more or less fully in religious life and rituals, such as atheist Jews or lapsed Catholics, also present puzzles for this Protestant Christian model of religion in which belief is primary. In this relatively narrow model, the sporadic invocation of the goddess Bast by characters in *Black Panther* is a sign of religion, but there is little else to indicate its presence in the film. In a more expanded model, based on the multiple ways in which the word "religion" can be used in ordinary modern English, belief, practice, family, history, and culture all figure as important aspects of religion. In that light, other aspects of the film—encounters with ancestors, debates over the ownership of historic and culturally significant artifacts, moral duties to family, a nation, and the world, and so on—all become relevant to a discussion of religion. Furthermore, it will be hard to make useful generalizations about religion as a whole, and much more useful to think in terms of the study of religions, plural.

Any scholar operates within some communities and outside others. Their family of origin, friendship networks, academic community, languages, and wider society all affect the work they are able to do, from the practical (funding sources) to the theoretical (available concepts). As belonging to a faith community is an important part of many people's, the study of religions is inevitably affected by the faith position of the researchers involved. This is sometimes discussed in terms of a distinction between work done on one's own religious community, by an insider, or work done on a religion to which one does not belong, as an outsider. It can also be framed in terms of work done from an emic perspective, looking at how faith works from the inside, or an etic perspective, which examines faith from the outside view. The extent to which it might be possible for someone to come from outside a community but research the emic perspective, or operate in an edge space between the two approaches, is a matter for debate.[14]

The positioning of the characters and filmmakers is therefore of importance in exploring religion in these films. Strange moves from outside the tradition of the Ancient One, through a series of initiations, to taking on a significant role in the organization (from "Have you seen *that* in a gift shop?" through being abandoned in the Himalayas to becoming the guardian of New York). In creating a fictional Afrofuturist society, the makers of *Black Panther* aim to set up a nation and a tradition, including religion, in which some of their characters are insiders but everyone else is necessarily an outsider.

Finally, as with any question about society or groups of people, issues of power, privilege, and relative status are always present in questions about religions. Religious practices and imagery can be stolen or reused in offensive and damaging ways, just like other aspects of culture (such as music and language). The power and other social relationships between originator and user are the determining factors here, with some appropriations "punching up" and being generally regarded as ethically acceptable and other appropriations taking money, status, and power away from the originators of the cultural material and thus judged to be unacceptable.

RELIGION, POWER, AND THE DIVINE RIGHT OF KINGS

How is power passed from one generation to the next? In the films under analysis in this chapter, there is a movement in each from the beginning to the end of the film, with power resting in new hands. In *Doctor Strange*, the power passes from the Ancient One to Strange, some to other characters who are trained by the Ancient One and/or dispute her rightful ownership. In *Black Panther*, kingship passes from T'Chaka to T'Challa—and to Killmonger and back to T'Challa—and with the kingship goes the magical power of the Black Panther as well as the scientific and technological power of Wakanda. In *Thor: Ragnarok*, kingship passes from Odin to Thor, but this progression is challenged by Hela and Loki, and circumstances. These narratives provide an opportunity to examine the rules which underlie the transfer of power in the societies involved. All three are fictional societies unique to the Marvel universe, although all have connections with real-world societies. In this section, we will argue that each is actually based on very standard European historical ideas about the role of a king and the process of power transfer. Three key underlying ideas are primogeniture, the divine right of kings, and might makes right.

In *Black Panther* and *Thor: Ragnarok*, it is assumed by the narrative and most characters involved that kingship would naturally pass from the dead man to his eldest son. There are opportunities to challenge this progression, a formal ritual in *Black Panther* and an ad hoc violent challenge in *Thor: Ragnarok*, but that it would normally and rightly be so is established by the behavior of the characters and the endings which are reached. This might seem so obvious that it hardly needs saying. After all, is that not how European monarchies do work? Why would it be otherwise? There are two reasons to think that it might be otherwise. First, even in the European tradition within which this model is indeed standard, other competing or variant models also exist. Women can have the right to inherit if they are the eldest living child, as they now do in the British monarchy. Kingship systems can rest on election (as at some times in Poland) or selection from a group of aristocrats—many kings in history have attained power by a route more like Strange's, proving themselves in battle, than like T'Challa's inheritance. Secondly, why would a film produced by filmmakers in a nation which prides itself on being a strong democracy and exporting democracy to other countries want to promote any kind of kingship system? That American films include stories about kings at all, and not elected officials—especially when they set out to imagine an idyllic society, like Wakanda—perhaps tells us something about the heritage of these stories, in European-based fantasy. (And, in the case of Wakanda, about what Americans imagine when they picture a peaceful, technologically advanced, but culturally African society.) Could filmmakers tell the same story about a democratic society? The plot might remain largely the same. If T'Chaka's assassination meant that T'Challa had to fight an election, he could still want Nakia to come home and help and have a dramatic encounter with a political opponent. It probably wouldn't make less sense if they held presidential hustings topless in a waterfall.

What would change would be the cultural assumptions which come with this. Inheriting the kingship, rather than being elected, is a vital part of the religious background because T'Challa needs to have the otherworldly encounter with his father, figured as a literal ancestor, to gain plot-relevant information. To have that scene in a film where T'Challa was elected and not born to the role of the king would require a broader understanding of what it is to have ancestors. In a world where adoption is never quite complete (we all have to know that Loki is adopted, he is only sometimes regarded as truly Odin and Frigga's son, and Thor is happy to use it as the punchline of jokes) for T'Challa to inherit in a metaphorical sense would not be narratively acceptable.

APPROPRIATION, APPRECIATION, OR ANNIHILATION?

How does that power translate into a religious context for our superheroes and their story worlds? With the kingship model so successfully, but subtly, embedded in these non-messianic superheroes we now consider how power is consolidated through the religious imaginary of the films. Just as the lineage route for each hero follows models in evidence throughout Europe's Christian and colonial history, the use of religion in each film appears in a similar way. As the religions that feature in these films are overtly non-Christian it is important to consider whether they are presented appreciatively or appropriatively. Ultimately the question will be whether the pantheon of the MCU makes space for multiple divinities and multiple religions or, will end with the threat of religious annihilation

The complex relationships between viewer and hero, and between hero and religious context, comes to the fore. The films present the heroes as tour guides for our encounters with these unfamiliar religious landscapes, enabling viewers to assimilate our familiarity with white, American Protestant Christian norms to intentionally different locations. We are presumed to require translators or characters with etic perspectives through which we can append our preexisting understandings of religion. It is particularly valuable to consider how familiar assumptions about gender, class, and race are used in these apparently unfamiliar religious contexts. In each case, it is important to begin with the recognition that the tour comes with a royal guide—the hero—who epitomes privilege and an insider status no matter how different *his* context may ostensibly, or originally, be.

Strange is the tour guide for Kamar-Taj and the world of the mystic arts. Like him, the viewer is assumed to be fluent in the American context (read: white, Protestant, Christian, financially stable).[15] The world of the Ancient One needs translating but teases us with the prospect of confronting assumptions, although ultimately it consolidates rather than undermines those presuppositions. Strange is enticed into perceiving an elderly Asian man, dressed in dark robes, as the Ancient One, before being introduced to a younger white, European/Celtic, woman. While the magical, mythical strangeness of the mystic arts is visible, a Hollywood and appropriative approach toward Buddhism is clearly signaled. Swinton's Ancient One relies on familiar tropes in her presentation of an orientalized Buddhist character: bald head, saffron robes, skilled in martial arts, and surrounded by an entourage of largely nameless Asian men. This has long been a stock part of the portrayal of the appropriation of Tibet and Buddhism, especially in Marvel Comic's Iron Fist as well as *Doctor Strange*.[16] Daniel Martin suggests there is a pattern of "a consistent fetishization of Oriental society that expressed both Asiaphilia and Asiaphobia—in contrast to American values—raising issues of ethnicity, morality, and social identity."[17] Add to that list, gender, as the Ancient One's casting was a gender swap in addition to the race and (arguably) class switches.

In the comic, the Ancient One is more visually akin to the man lampooned in the film than the European, upper-class woman. While there are countless problems in the fetishized portrayal of Buddhism and Tibetan identities in *Doctor Strange*, class, gender, and race switching does not resolve those issues.[18] Instead, it invites scrutiny of those very features. There is something quite WASPy about both Strange and the Ancient One in *Doctor Strange* that connotes both Protestant Christianity and Buddhism. The adoption of a model of Buddhism that has roots in Asian heritage but becomes consolidated into something notably different in particularly a British context is core to the idea of Protestant Buddhism.[19] Such a European influence on the Buddhism of *Doctor Strange* is particularly evident in the casting of white British actors Swinton and Cumberbatch in addition to Dane Mads Mikkelsen as Kaecillius, the film's antagonist who are juxtaposed with Karl Mordo and Wong. These roles are played by British actors of color, Chiwetel Ejiofor and Benedict Wong, but there are marked differences in the portrayal. Mordo and Wong are seen as fundamentalist and traditionalist respectively, while Kaecillius, the Ancient One and Strange repeatedly question, challenge and, at times, appropriate the secrets of the order for their own ends. Kaecillius's aims are nefarious, the Ancient Ones are morally ambiguous even as she entices Strange (alone) to disregard the strictures of tradition, and Strange's are applauded. It is the discontinuity with the inherited teachings that vexes Mordo—and places him on the journey to future villainy.[20] Here, race and ethnicity are used to signify whether a perspective on religion is emic or etic, and to align it with that of the assumed viewer: White, anglo-saxon, anglophile, European/American. We, the viewer, are treated as if we are Strange in this etic exploration of the mystic arts and Kamar-Taj; he is our interpreter and his assumptions become ours. When it becomes clear he is fully committing to the new life and religion, as indicated by a life-and-death battle, the film fast forwards us ensuring that we remain on the outside of Strange's religious encounter. At the film's end, Strange has returned to New York—his previous home—no longer a medic but Sorcerer Supreme and head of the New York sanctum. His physical disability which led him to Kamar-Taj is no longer evident and his personal style has changed. He has adopted robes and a goatee, which is slightly reminiscent of the orientalist fu Manchu moustaches. Thus, the viewer leaves Strange: on the one hand to return to the familiar religious landscape but knowing we have seen—and ultimately rejected—the alternative put in front of us; on the other hand, we are presented with the epitome of hegemonic whiteness, religiosity, class, and gender safely established as the new king of the mystic arts.

The new Sorcerer Supreme, in a mid-credit scene, passes the baton for religious education to Asgard's heir apparent. Strange encounters Thor and directs him toward the missing figure Odin, God-King of Asgard, by way of a teaser trailer for *Thor: Ragnarok*. Having served as a reliable guide, he hands over to someone with a more established relationship with both his religious heritage and the viewing audience. In his first film, Thor finds himself the alien on earth, trying to understand our strange ways. In the second, human love interest Jane Foster, acts as an interpreter while she is on Asgard. Together Thor and Jane have parsed some of the strangeness of the Asgardian pantheon and their mutual fluency becomes ours. It also helps that there is an inferred familiarity in the mystical world of a planet loosely based on a northern European mythscape—it is not as dangerous, alien, unfamiliar or inaccessible as either Kamar-Taj or Wakanda. Even the rainbow bridge of the Bifrost offers an accessible entrance or exit. Yet this familiarity is transformed effectively in *Thor: Ragnarok* so that these locations of safety and security are upended as much for us as for Thor. Nevertheless, we still find ourselves accompanied by interpreters when needed: Strange handed over the reins to Thor, particularly for the time he (re)visits earth, before we are joined by Bruce Banner/Hulk when the landscape becomes less familiar.

After being exiled to Norway by Loki, Odin is met by his sons shortly before his death. His dying words advise these reluctant siblings that there is a third, older child who has been imprisoned for the safety of Asgard and her incarceration is tied to Odin's life. Hela greets her brothers on their father's death and almost immediately smashes Mjolnir, Thor's hammer. Mjolnir symbolizes Thor's power and fecundity and, until this point, the MCU canon has held that the only person who can wield it is someone as righteous as Thor. Thus, Hela overpowers her brother and his virtues, and sets in motion a crisis of identity. As they try to escape Hela, Thor falls through the Bifrost and lands in the hostile waste planet of Sakaar. Here he is missing his status, recognition of his identity, and the reassurance of his hammer. He is scavenged and sold by someone we later discover to be Valkyrie, another Asgardian who left following the massacre of her military troop and is hiding from her identity. Thor is humiliated by his loss of status and identity, which becomes symbolized in the cutting of his luxuriant locks, recalling the biblical story of Samson (Judges 16). Without hair or hammer, Thor is symbolically powerless and ends up facing the unnamed champion of the gladiatorial ring. This champion turns out to be Hulk who has repressed Bruce Banner. So, the film constructs a motley crew, comprised of a man forcibly reduced from status and identity and two counterparts who do not wish to recall who they were. Yet, in asserting his authority over Hulk and Valkyrie, Thor dominance as king and god forces them to facilitate his return to Asgard (somewhere Valkyrie has said she will never return, while Banner just wants to return to earth).

It is in this interaction that Thor's power becomes clear, although it is on Asgard that a more nuanced account of religion and religious culture appears. While Thor is stranded on Sakaar, Hela returns to Asgard. Angered by her excision from the Asgardian pantheon and accompanying stories she recounts the stories of the violent colonization of the nine realms by her and her father Odin. She queries how these proud endeavors have given way to supposedly friendly—perhaps asinine—stories of benevolence. As she rips through a pastoral stucco depicting Thor, Frigga, and Odin in happy times, she cries out that her history should be known. Such wealth does not come without violence, she reminds viewers, in a statement about Christian colonization as much as its fictional counterpart in the nine realms. Hela stands accompanied by a hapless Asgardian who has aligned himself to her but there is no other character to provide the translation: none is needed and the meaning successfully crosses the fourth wall without any further interpretation. Steve Rose notes that "even the jokey *Thor: Ragnarok* smuggled in a message about wealthy civilizations erasing their history of colonial violence and exploitation" (2020).[21] It is the link between the religious imagery and the violence of the colonialism of wealthy civilizations that comes through so effectively in this film. Hela takes issues with the metanarratives and divine stories that give shape to both the religious and broader socio-cultural landscape. When combined with Thor's own journey of self-discovery, it is a powerful account of the problems that arise when religion is combined with totalizing political discourses.

Once Thor's return to Asgard is discovered by Hela, she directs her violence toward her younger brother and usurper. She takes his eye, marking him with the same injury their father bore, but this leads Thor to find within himself a hitherto unknown strength. He erupts with lightning as his remaining eye glistens with its flashing lights and bringing to viewers—both the Asgardians around him and the film's viewers—a renewed sense of the power of their god and anticipated savior. In any of the messianic films discussed above, no doubt Thor's lightning would have smited his sister into oblivion. Here there is no such fortitude. Thor realizes that none of his assembled team can defeat this enemy and save his world; on this occasion, his divine intervention will not prevent his world's end. Rather he compels Loki to unleash Surtur, destroyer of worlds, to take down Asgard and, with it, Hela.

This markedly different departure visually depicts the annihilation of cherished religious truths—including quite literally the old gods of the story. Odin and Hela's deaths, along with that of the planet Asgard, are presented clearly to the viewer. Added to that are the deaths of the perceived religious truths of Asgardian creation narratives and the authority of the pantheon. The most powerful of all, though, is the annihilation of the belief in an innocent, unrevised, and nonviolent model of colonization. Despite these deaths, Thor still remains a divine king and one whose hero status and authority remain undiminished. At the film's end, Thor's entourage includes his brother Loki, loyal companion and all-seeing guardian of the Bifrost Heimdall, and fellow gladiatorial 'prisoners with jobs' Korg and Miek alongside Valkyrie and Hulk whose desires have already been set aside for their king. As the ship, carrying what remains of the Asgardian population, departs with the combusting planet behind them the easy links to earth—the destination of the ship—such as the Bifrost and instant travel are gone. Gone too are the simplistic imaginaries of religion that require a translator to make them palatable and easily open to appropriation.[22]

Black Panther presents a different religious imaginary to its forebears, despite the perpetuation of the Eurocentric, Christianized, divine right of kingship model. There is a juxtaposition between the enduring legacies of the MCU franchise, with its white, anglophone Christian foundations, and the intentional shifts expedited by Waititi's *Thor: Ragnarok* and Ryan Coogler's *Black Panther*. How possible is it for an appreciative model of religion without a risk of annihilation or appropriation? The Afrofuturist landscape makes space for an imagination free from the colonizing effects of European Christianity; Islam also does not appear to have crossed the border. Freedom from the influence of the slave trade and with it the links to European Christianity are to be praised according to Ebony Elizabeth Thomas.[23] In an analysis of the Harry Potter book and film franchises, Thomas argues that there is subtle and regularly overlooked evidence that the isolated magical world must have been affected by the legacy of the Western Passage like its muggle counterpart. Black magical characters follow the conventions of white, British naming patterns, with Thomas citing Dean Thomas and

Angelina Johnson as examples (cf. Padma and Parvati Patel). She argues there is significant value to creatively imagining black communities free from the influence of colonialism. *Black Panther* seeks to offer such a perspective but that may be more of a challenge than it initially seems, especially when unintentionally adopting models of leadership so enmeshed in the political and religious heritage of Europe's Christian authorities. Despite this, there is a plurality within the religious landscape that does reach beyond its fictional borders.

Hidden in plain sight under the guise of another of the miscellany of easily forgotten deprived African countries, Wakanda hides its wealth, security, and technological developments. As the opening scene with Nakia's spy mission highlights, there are covert links with neighboring countries. It is here that the initial introduction to religion emerges: Nakia is hidden among a number of veiled women in an apparent convoy of refuges. Presented as nameless, voiceless Islamic women, Nakia stands alone when adopts and then promptly drops these signifiers of religiosity. This differentiation, in combination with the reliance on Wakanda's advanced status—notably shown through technology—creates a problematic dialogue with Islam as it does not feature noticeably elsewhere in the film. As such, any presentation of religious or cultural beliefs *within* Wakanda is held as distinct from those beyond its borders.

Within the Wakandan religious framework, spiritual links to the ancestors, especially through the lineage of the kings, a clear and narratively significant part of the story.[24] T'Challa needs the wisdom and strength of his ancestors in re-establishing his claim on the throne. In addition to those ancestral beliefs there comes an interesting challenge in creating and understanding the religious landscape. Given that Wakanda has, apparently, escaped the waves of colonizing proselytism associated with both Christianity and Islam that continue to have such a marked effect on the continent more widely, there is a challenge to create a religious imaginary recognizable to the intended American audience. The link between the Egyptian feline god Bast and Black Panther is made clear; she is the ancestor who grants power to the Black Panther and each generation continues in her legacy. She is a recognizable figure thanks to the popularity of Egyptian mythology and fellow members of her pantheon appear in the comic canon.[25] Her rival, and the divinity followed by the outlawed Jabari tribe, led by M'Baku, is a different story. The White Gorilla Tribe are described as following Hanuman, one of the Hindu pantheon. Here, then we encounter the challenge faced in the Afrofuturist landscape, made for a predominantly American audience: How to create a religious imaginary that resonates with the viewer and connotes recognizable religiosity while also emphasizing difference? It is a particularly pertinent challenge for the filmmakers as they reimagine

M'Baku, intentionally distancing this iteration from the comic character who shares both his name and the racist title of Man-Ape assigned to him in his role as a villain. Reconceived as the antagonistic (rather than villainous) leader of a rival tribe M'Baku's status as peer to T'Challa but acolyte of an alternative God found within the Wakandan pantheon initially looks promising but there remain questions as to the validity of such syncretism. The tension between appreciation and appropriation is evident here: the move to adopt (appropriate?) Hanuman provoked controversy in India. The cry "Glory to Hanuman" was bleeped by the Indian Board of Classification to avoid offense; however, this enraged some viewers who found pride in the inclusion of the god complicating the inclusion of this as an inappropriate and appropriative term.[26]

The adoption of Hanuman by the filmmakers to accompany Bast in the Wakandan religious imaginary is fascinating but provokes more questions than it answers. Why they opted for an Indian divinity when "there are several ape deities among African-centered religious traditions" is particularly pertinent.[27] How and why these figures made their journeys from their homes in India and Egypt to Wakanda remains unanswered. The approach to the adoption of Gods, especially beyond those signaled by the comics, appears as something akin to Neil Gaiman's approach to divinities in *American Gods*. Gaiman imagines countless gods who travel with their adherents through the migrant routes—forced and chosen—to find themselves needing a home in the United States.[28] Despite the success of the journeys made by Bast and Hanuman—and perhaps their devotees— the Wakandan borders have remained closed to the influences of Islam and Christianity. Their absence is all the more notable, especially when combined with the perpetuation of a European, Christian divine kingship model discussed. Given the value added to the film by close attention to detail in the creation of the Afrofuturist context, this portrayal of religion seems a little clumsy. Added to this is Torin Dru Alexander's recognition that despite the aim "to acknowledge the deep historical connections between the Africans and the peoples of the Indian subcontinent," the appropriation of Hanuman is an artistic misstep in the film.[29] This sense of clumsiness endures through the portrayal of Killmonger's understanding of the religious landscape of Wakanda. Darius Hills argues that Killmonger represents the "'Western, Americanized and hierarchical embodiment' of his upbringing that translates into a desire to 'invade and destroy the sacred spaces of 'others'."[30] His sense of anger and abandonment seems to reach from Wakanda into the divine realm, as is symbolized by his destruction of the divinely magical flowers that imbue power on the Black Panther. His interest in religion, particularly Wakandan rites and rituals, is functional and allows him to both secure and destroy his legacy in a single act. With Killmonger's apparent ambivalence, combined with his adoption of colonial approaches to its destruction, the picture of religion in *Black Panther* becomes necessarily complicated. Ultimately it cannot serve as an appreciation of a celebration of Afrofuturist religion when it still relies on colonialist tropes of appreciation and annihilation of the practices of the other. Nevertheless, it is still a marked development in the understanding of religion within the MCU.

CONCLUSION

At the end of *Black Panther* diversity of religion has appeared in its most appreciative form to date in the MCU. However, as the adoption of Hanuman highlights it is not free from the trappings of religious appropriation or syncretism. This is a problem long associated with Marvel comics and in the *Black Panther* stories in particular.[31] Despite an overt desire to imagine a model of African culture free from the effects of European, Christian colonialism, the perpetuation of the kingship model demonstrates the difficulty in annihilating its influence. So embedded in both the cultural imagination and the anticipated perception of the imagined audience is the legacy of Euro-Christian colonial influences that they endure even in this new landscape. The impossibility of this challenge is also evident in the conclusion of *Thor: Ragnarok* as the diminished but nevertheless, the regal king holds command of his newly displaced people. Yet, these films show that there is value in facilitating an emic engagement with religion, even where it may initially appear unfamiliar to the audience. We as viewers have moved from a solely etic engagement with religion—even though always working from an assumed fluency with white, anglophone Christian (predominantly Protestant) religiosity—to an appreciation of the emic insights. The lack of validity of *Doctor Strange*'s appropriative approach to unfamiliar, especially Asian, religion is called out through Waititi's envisioning of Thor. In *Ragnarok*, the supposed benign superiority of white, hegemonic, European models of colonizing religion is shown to be inherently violent and problematic. Only following the destruction of the myth of innocent exportation of religion—in this case by Hela—can an alternative imagination come to the fore. *Black Panther* offers a glimpse of the potential of a more mutually appreciative religious imaginary. But even in this new filmscape, the specter of those hegemonic, white, Christian models of religion remains inescapable. The old gods of Bast and Hanuman may find themselves created anew but, for now at least, the most omnipresent and inescapable god of the MCU remains that of the God of hegemonic white, Protestant Christianity.

NOTES

1. Ken Derry, "The Semi-Anti-Apocalypse of Black Panther," *Journal of Religion & Film.* 22, no. 1 (2018), Article 42: 1–2.

2. Joel Gruber, "The Dharma of Doctor Strange: The Shifting Representation of Tibet and Tibetan Buddhism within a Comic Book Serial," *Implicit Religion.* 18, no. 3 (2015): 347–371.

3. In the film only, the comics portray the Ancient One as of unspecified East Asian—perhaps Tibetan—heritage. This led to justifiable complaints that *Doctor Strange* whitewashed the role even while Swinton's performance was praised for the balance and nuance it bought to the film. See Alan Evans, "Doctor Strange 'Whitewashing' Row Resurfaces with New Criticism of Swinton Casting," *The Guardian.* Nov. 4, 2016. Available from: https://www.theguardian.com/film/2016/nov/04/doctor-strange-tilda-swinton-whitewashing-row. Accessed Jan. 16, 2020. cf. Peter Bradshaw, "The 20 Best Marvel Films—Ranked!" *The Guardian.* Nov. 15, 2018. Available from: https://www.theguardian.com/film/2018/nov/15/the-20-best-marvel-films-ranked. Accessed Jan. 16, 2020.

4. Afrofuturism is understood to be African-American in origin; African writers, such as Nnedi Okorafor, use the term Africanfuturism. For the wider movement, see Lisa Yaszek, "Afrofuturism, Science Fiction, and the History of the Future," *Socialism and Democracy.* 20, no. 3 (2006): 41–60.

5. Torin Dru A. Alexander, "Africana Religion, *Black Panther*, and the Marvel Cinematic Universe (MCU)," *Africology: The Journal of Pan African Studies.* 11, no. 9 (2018): 64–67; Giana M. Eckhardt, "Black Panther: Thrills, Postcolonial Discourse, and Blacktopia," *Markets, Globalization & Development Review.* 3, no. 2 (2018); Lleuella Morris, "To the Ancestral Plane: African Spiritism in Ryan Coogler's *Black Panther* (Marvel Studios, 2018) and the Desensitization to Spiritualism in Hollywood," *Africology: The Journal of Pan African Studies.* 11, no. 9 (2018): 73–76; Laurel Zwissler, "Black Panther as Spirit Trap," *Journal of Religion & Film.* 22, no. 1 (2018). Article 41.

6. Jon Ivan Gill, "Ancestors Change Constantly: Subversive Religious Colonial Deconstruction in the Religion of Black Panther," *Journal of Religion & Film.* 22, no. 2 (2019); Darrius Hills, "Killmonger's Quandary: Notes on Religious Meaning, Freedom, and Identity in *Black Panther*," *Journal of Africana Religions.* 8, no. 1 (2020): 62–83.

7. While Doctor Strange and Black Panther are originating films, neither were anticipated to be the sole feature for their eponymous heroes. Prior to the death of Chadwick Boseman (*Black Panther*) in August 2020 sequels for all three films had been scheduled within the fourth phase of MCU. Before the COVID-19 pandemic delayed production, these sequels had been scheduled for release in 2021 and 2022 see Aaron Couch, "Marvel Confirms Kit Harington for 'Eternals,' Sets 'Black Panther II' Date," *The Hollywood Reporter.* Aug. 24, 2019. Available from: https://www.hollywoodreporter.com/heat-vision/black-panther-2-release-date-kit-haringtons-role-eternals-confirmed-1233149. Accessed Jan. 22, 2020.

8. Siddhant Adlakha, "'Thor: Ragnarok': Marvel From a Postcolonial Perspective," *The Village Voice.* Nov. 10, 2017. Available from: https://www.villagevoice.com

/2017/11/10/thor-ragnarok-marvel-from-a-postcolonial-perspective/. Accessed Sept. 25, 2019.

The continuations of the storyline in *Avengers: Infinity War* (2018) and *Avengers: Endgame* (2019) present somewhat problematic accounts of Thor, as they lose the careful and considered engagement with colonialism central to Waititi's *Ragnarok*. By returning an eye (albeit an apparent prosthetic) to Thor in *Infinity War* the physical marker of external transformation tied to genocidal violence is erased. Thor's response to both the destruction of his planet and the subsequent genocide of the majority of the refugees en route to earth (*Infinity War*) becomes individualized and becomes the subject of (fatphobic) mockery in *Endgame*. Here, we treat *Ragnarok* as no more or less a stand-alone film than either *Black Panther* or *Doctor Strange*, treating the characters as portrayed in their self-titled films rather than across the canon more broadly.

9. Hulk (Edward Norton) in *The Incredible Hulk* (2009) did not become an enduring part of the MCU. Rather he was replaced by a second iteration of the Hulk played by Mark Ruffalo (since 2012) who has not featured in any stand-alone films.

10. Derry, "Semi-Anti-Apocalypse of Black Panther."

Ant-Man (2015, 2018) does not adequately follow either the divine right of kings model nor the singular messiah. The Guardians of the Galaxy films (2014, 2017), the final components of the franchise, showcase a team model rather than offering a single individual a headline slot.

11. Arthur C. Clarke, *Profiles of the Future* (New York: Harper & Row, 1973).

12. Indeed, CIA Agent Ross remarks that it must be magic rather than Wakandan technological prowess that has saved his life. For further discussion of this dialogue and its value in confronting colonization, see Giana M. Eckhardt, "Black Panther: Thrills, Postcolonial Discourse, and Blacktopia," *Markets, Globalization & Development Review*. 3, no. 2 (2018). Article 6: 5–6.

13. For a review of options previously proposed, see Victoria S. Harrison, "The Pragmatics of Defining Religion in a Multi-cultural World," *International Journal for the Philosophy of Religion*. 59 (2006): 133–152.

14. Fiona Beals; Joanna Kidman; Hine Funaki, "Insider and Outsider Research: Negotiating Self at the Edge of the Emic/Etic Divide," *Qualitative Inquiry*. April (2019): 1–9; Rhiannon Grant, "Breaking Sixteen Walls: Deadpool as Philosopher and Sociologist," in *Deadpool and Philosophy*, eds. Nicolas Michaud and Jacob May (Chicago: Open Court, 2017).

15. Although Strange does mention at one point being short of money, this is specifically for further healthcare—an experience which is common in the USA but not necessarily shared internationally.

16. Gruber, "Dharma of Doctor Strange"; Daniel Martin, "The Americanization of the Hong Kong Kung Fu Hero: Orientalism and Social Glass in Marvel Comics' *Iron Fist*," *The Journal of Popular Culture*. 51, no. 6 (2018): 1521–1538; Eve Mullen, "Orientalist Commercializations: Tibetan Buddhism in American Popular Culture," *Journal of Religion and Film*. 2, no. 2 (2016). Article 5.

17. Martin, "Americanization of the Hong Kong Kung Fu Hero," 1522.

18. Evans, "Dr Strange 'Whitewashing' Row."

19. Philip A. Mellor, "Protestant Buddhism? The Cultural Translation of Buddhism in England," *Religion.* 21, no. 1 (1991): 73–92.

20. See also Netflix's *Iron Fist.* Sacha Dhawan, a northern British-Indian actor, takes on the role of Davos/Steel Serpent. Introduced in Season One and a Big Bad for Season Two, Davos is unhappy with Danny Rand/Iron Fist. Like Strange, Rand finds himself marooned in the Himalayas (this time, K'un Lun) and becomes heir apparent ahead of more established, emic members of the order such as Davos (or Mordo). Like Strange, Rand is played by a white British actor, Finn Jones, also adopting an American accent.

21. Steve Rose, "Taika Waititi: 'You Don't Want to be Directing Kids with a Swastika on Your Arm'," *The Guardian.* Dec. 26, 2019. Available from: https://www.theguardian.com/film/2019/dec/26/taika-waititi-flight-of-the-conchords-thor-ragnarok-jojo-rabbit-nazi-dictator. Accessed Dec. 26, 2019.

22. Despite the model of religion presented in Ragnarok, much of the critical engagement presented in Waititi's envisioning of Asgard and religion is undermined by the *Avengers: Infinity War* and *Endgame* films. However, as Waititi returns to direct a fourth film, with a working title *Thor: Love and Thunder* (anticipated release 2022) these themes remain unresolved.

23. Ebony Elizabeth Thomas, *The Dark Fantastic: Race and the Imagination from Harry Potter to the Hunger Games* (New York: NYU Press, 2019).

24. Morris, "To the Ancestral Plane."

25. Alexander, "Africana Religion, *Black Panther*," 65.

26. The Indian Express, "Black Panther Fans in India Angry Over Beeping Out the Hanuman Reference," *The Indian Express.* Apr. 12, 2018. Available from: https://indianexpress.com/article/trending/trending-in-india/black-panther-fans-in-india-angry-over-beeping-out-hanuman-reference-twitter-reactions-5073987/. Accessed Jan. 23, 2020.

27. Alexander, "African Religion, *Black Panther*," 66.

28. Neil Gaiman, *American Gods* (London: Headline, 2001).

29. Alexander, "African Religion, *Black Panther*," 66.

30. Hill, "Killmonger's Quandary," 71.

31. Alexander, "African Religion, *Black Panther*."

REFERENCES

Adlakha, Siddhant. "'Thor: Ragnarok': Marvel From a Postcolonial Perspective." *The Village Voice.* Nov. 10, 2017. Available from: https://www.villagevoice.com/2017/11/10/thor-ragnarok-marvel-from-a-postcolonial-perspective/. Accessed Sept. 25, 2019.

Alexander, Torin Dru. "Africana Religion, *Black Panther*, and the Marvel Cinematic Universe (MCU)." *Africology: The Journal of Pan African Studies.* 11, no. 9 (2018): 64–67.

Beals, Fiona; Kidman, Joanna; Funaki, Hine. "Insider and Outsider Research: Negotiating Self at the Edge of the Emic/Etic Divide." *Qualitative Inquiry.* April (2019): 1–9.

Bradshaw, Peter. "The 20 Best Marvel Films—Ranked!" *The Guardian*. Nov. 15, 2018. Available from: https://www.theguardian.com/film/2018/nov/15/the-20-best-marvel-films-ranked. Accessed Jan. 16, 2020.

Clarke, Arthur C. *Profiles of the Future*. New York: Harper & Row, 1973.

Couch, Aaron. "Marvel Confirms Kit Harington for 'Eternals,' Sets 'Black Panther II' Date." *The Hollywood Reporter*. Aug. 24, 2019. Available from: https://www.hollywoodreporter.com/heat-vision/black-panther-2-release-date-kit-haringtons-role-eternals-confirmed-1233149. Accessed Jan. 22, 2020.

Derry, Ken. "The Semi-Anti-Apocalypse of Black Panther." *Journal of Religion & Film*. 22, no. 1 (2018), pp. 1–8, Article 42.

Eckhardt, Giana M. "Black Panther: Thrills, Postcolonial Discourse, and Blacktopia." *Markets, Globalization & Development Review*. 3, no. 2 (2018), pp. 1–7, Article 6.

Evans, Alan. "Doctor Strange 'Whitewashing' Row Resurfaces with New Criticism of Swinton Casting." *The Guardian*. Nov. 4, 2016. Available from: https://www.theguardian.com/film/2016/nov/04/doctor-strange-tilda-swinton-whitewashing-row. Accessed Jan. 16, 2020.

Gaiman, Neil. *American Gods*. London: Headline, 2001.

Gill, Jon Ivan. "Ancestors Change Constantly: Subversive Religious Colonial Deconstruction in the Religion of Black Panther." *Journal of Religion & Film*. 22, no. 2 (2019), pp. 1–11, Article 38.

Grant, Rhiannon. "Breaking Sixteen Walls: Deadpool as Philosopher and Sociologist" in *Deadpool and Philosophy*. Edited by Nicolas Michaud and Jacob May. Chicago: Open Court, 2017.

Gruber, Joel. "The Dharma of Doctor Strange: The Shifting Representation of Tibet and Tibetan Buddhism within a Comic Book Serial." *Implicit Religion*. 18, no. 3 (2015): 347–371.

Harrison, Victoria S. "The Pragmatics of Defining Religion in a Multi-cultural World." *International Journal for the Philosophy of Religion*. 59 (2006): 133–152.

Hills, Darrius. "Killmonger's Quandary: Notes on Religious Meaning, Freedom, and Identity in *Black Panther*." *Journal of Africana Religions*. 8, no. 1 (2020): 62–83.

The Indian Express. "Black Panther Fans in India Angry Over Beeping Out the Hanuman Reference." *The Indian Express*. Apr. 12, 2018. Available from: https://indianexpress.com/article/trending/trending-in-india/black-panther-fans-in-india-angry-over-beeping-out-hanuman-reference-twitter-reactions-5073987/. Accessed Jan. 23, 2020.

Martin, Daniel. "The Americanization of the Hong Kong Kung Fu Hero: Orientalism and Social Glass in Marvel Comics' *Iron Fist*." *The Journal of Popular Culture*. 51, no. 6 (2018): 1521–1538.

Mellor, Philip A. "Protestant Buddhism? The Cultural Translation of Buddhism in England." *Religion*. 21, no. 1 (1991): 73–92.

Morris, Lleuella. "To the Ancestral Plane: African Spiritism in Ryan Coogler's *Black Panther* (Marvel Studios, 2018) and the Desensitization to Spiritualism in Hollywood." *Africology: The Journal of Pan African Studies*. 11, no. 9 (2018): 73–76.

Mullen, Eve. "Orientalist Commercializations: Tibetan Buddhism in American Popular Culture." *Journal of Religion and Film.* 2, no. 2 (2016). Article 5.

Rose, Steve. "Taika Waititi: 'You Don't Want to be Directing Kids with a Swastika on Your Arm'." *The Guardian.* Dec. 26, 2019. Available from: https://www.theguardian.com/film/2019/dec/26/taika-waititi-flight-of-the-conchords-thor-ragnarok-jojo-rabbit-nazi-dictator. Accessed Dec. 26, 2019.

Thomas, Ebony Elizabeth. *The Dark Fantastic: Race and the Imagination from Harry Potter to the Hunger Games.* New York: NYU Press, 2019.

Yaszek, Lisa. "Afrofuturism, Science Fiction, and the History of the Future." *Socialism and Democracy.* 20, no. 3 (2006): 41–60.

Zwissler, Laurel. "Black Panther as Spirit Trap." *Journal of Religion & Film.* 22, no. 1 (2018). Article 41.

Chapter 5

The Worthiness of Thor

Adam Barkman and Bennet Soenen

What do we mean when we call someone worthy? More specifically, what does it mean that Thor is worthy to wield Mjolnir? We often refer to figures from religion and mythology as "worthy," but these characters are very different from one another. Is the worthiness of the mythological Hercules the same as the worthiness of Christ? This chapter will discuss various theories about the worthiness of Thor. There are three main theories that we will discuss and evaluate: worthiness as charity to others, as a warrior's spirit, and as the approval of Odin. Before delving into these three theories, we will have a general discussion about what worthiness is and its background in the films that Thor appeared in, although this background will appear throughout the chapter after our initial incursion. Finally, we will discuss the most important comic book storylines relating to the theme of worthiness and the implications they hold for the future of Thor and the Marvel Cinematic Universe (MCU).

This question of worthiness is the theme and driving force of the first *Thor* film. In this film, Thor makes a plethora of rash, selfish decisions, consistently putting his desires and needs in front of the desires of others. This culminates in him attacking the Frost Giants in vengeance for a minor act.[1] This attack by Thor reignites a war between the Asgardians and Frost Giants. After this brash and selfish act, Thor's father, Odin, declares him unworthy and strips him of his powers and hammer, sending him to earth to live as a human. Throughout the course of the rest of the film, Thor learns multiple lessons and eventually regains the worthiness to wield his hammer.

Take note of what Odin says when he casts Thor's hammer into Midgard (the Asgardian name for the realm of Earth). Odin says, "Whosoever holds this hammer, if he be worthy, shall possess the power of Thor."[2] This implies that anyone can be worthy of Thor's hammer and power if he has the right power or character. This is seen a few times in the comics when noble characters such as Beta Ray Bill[3] and Captain America are able to lift Thor's hammer.[4] In the films, we have both Vision and Captain America lifting Thor's hammer. This all goes to show that anyone, not just Thor, can lift his hammer and gain the powers of Thor if they are worthy. The question is not specifically about what makes Thor, the son of Odin, worthy, but what it takes for a person as such to wield Mjolnir.

The first theory that we will cover is the idea of worthiness as self-sacrificial charity to others. In the beginning of the first Thor movie, Odin is about to pass the crown to Thor. During the crowning ceremony, Odin has Thor make a few oaths, the most important of which is, "Do you swear to cast aside all selfish ambition and to pledge yourself only to the good of the realm?" This oath implies that to be king of Asgard, you must not think of yourself and your desires, but only of the good of others, more specifically your subjects and the realm that you rule. When Thor attacked the Frost Giants, he showed that he is unable to fulfill this oath to put his own ambitions behind himself and think of the good of the realm. He is unable to become the king. Odin calls Thor "a vain, greedy, cruel boy."[5] All of this points to the idea that Thor is declared unworthy because he is self-centered.

We have further confirmation of this idea later in the movie. Thor's worthiness returns at the moment when he dies for the good of others. In the third act, Thor has come to the conclusion that the people of earth are worth dying for and that he must take responsibility for what he has done. Referring to Loki wreaking havoc on Earth, Thor says, "Brother, however I have wronged you, whatever I have done that has led you to do this, I am truly sorry. But these people are innocent, taking their lives will gain you nothing. So take mine, and end this."[6] He comes to the realization that these weak, often helpless creatures are worth just as much as he is and that it is his actions that have brought this danger to them. Loki unleashes a blast from his machine, and nearly kills Thor. The only thing that saves Thor is the return of his powers. His worthiness returns because he is not only willing to sacrifice his own life for the safety of others but has actively done so.

Before going further into the worthiness of Thor, let us consider a similar story of near death to powerful resurrection. When we compare the Christ narrative to Thor's there are obvious differences (the primary one being the perfection of Christ in comparison to the obvious imperfection of Thor), but there are also important similarities. In reference to the incarnation (becoming man) of Christ, C. S. Lewis notes, "The story of the Incarnation is the story of a descent and resurrection. When I say 'resurrection' here, I am not referring simply to the first few hours, or the first few weeks of the resurrection. I am talking of this whole, huge pattern of descent, down, down, and then up again."[7] Think of how this relates to Thor. Thor not only came to

Earth, learned his lesson, and then went back to being a god, but instead had to live as a man. Much of the second act of the first Thor film is about him realizing his own weakness in his new, human form (think of the many times he gets hit by a car or loses fights with mere humans, all while screaming that they are no match for the mighty Thor). This is not only to punish Thor for his unworthiness and selfishness but also in order to show Thor the worth of humans and the dignity of those that Thor considers "lower" than himself. In a similar way, Christ had to actually become a man if he was to be the payment for their shortcomings (Anselm: man sinned, so man must pay for sin), and Thor had to be a man to realize the worth of man.

These are two very different reasons for taking on a human form, but the similarities in reasons are interesting. For Jesus, it was important not only that he was a man but also that he lived the life of a man. There would have been something incomplete about Christ's sacrifice if he had not lived the life of man. Jesus needed to feel the temptations to sin, to feel the grief of loss, and the joy of human friendship in order to actually be human. The incarnation was more than just the creator degrading himself to the level of the creation, it was God truly becoming the creation and living a life as the creation. Think of how Thor's "incarnation" compares to this. In order to understand, to truly understand, those that were less powerful than him, his powers needed to be removed. It instilled in Thor compassion and willingness to sacrifice himself for them. Christ needed to be incarnate in order to be a proper sacrifice for the failings of mankind, and Thor needed to be incarnate in order to be a willing sacrifice and defender of mankind.

Back at the beginning of the movie when Odin was giving a speech on kingship, he said, "Today I entrust you with the greatest honor in all the Nine Realms. The sacred throne of Asgard. I have sacrificed much to achieve peace. So, too, must a new generation sacrifice to maintain that peace. Responsibility, duty, honor. These are not merely virtues to which we must aspire, they are essential to every soldier and to every King."[8] Before Thor became incarnate as a human, he did little in the way of sacrificing anything for his people. He would fight for the glory and thrill of battle instead of for his people. His mighty acts made him popular with the people but did not make him fit to rule them. His life as a human and willingness to sacrifice himself for the good of those that he once perceived as less than him made him truly worthy, not only of the hammer but to become king.

This idea of incarnation is even more poignant in the comics. Stripping Thor of his powers, Odin says, "Though thou art supreme in thy power and thy pride . . . thou must know weakness . . . thou must feel pain! But, such lesson can ne'er be learned by Thunder God! Thus thou shalt leave the Golden Realm . . . and shed thy godly trappings!"[9] Thor then asks his father where he is being sent, and Odin answers, "Tis known as earth . . . where fragile mortals dwell! And there shalt thou reside . . . and there shalt thou learn that none can be truly strong unless they be truly humble!"[10] Thus, Thor was turned into a surgeon with an injured leg. He was not only a human, but one with a disability.[11] Despite his injury, Thor became a kind and loving human. He helped the sick and eased the suffering of others. After Thor regained his worthiness and powers, Odin said, "Thou didst treat the sick and the afflicted! Thou didst walk amongst the weak . . . and give them strength!"[12]

We already outlined how the films show a similarity between Thor's life as a human and Christ's, but the comics show an even more poignant similarity between Christ's life and Thor's. Thor is placed into a med school as a student and eventually becomes a surgeon. He chooses to live his human life helping the sick and ill. He learns patience, mercy, and, most important to Odin, humility. Thor was not even a healthy human, but one with a bad leg. He required a cane to get anywhere and was not a great warrior by any measure.

In the first *Avengers* movie, we can see Loki trying to tempt Thor away from this newfound understanding of the human race. Loki is trying to split the Avengers by playing on their various weaknesses, and targets Thor's pride, the pride that was the main issue in the first *Thor* film. He goads the Avengers into infighting and specifically goads Thor into viewing the others as less than him because of it. Loki is trying to have Thor turn his back on his newfound understanding of those less powerful than himself. Succumbing to this temptation for a moment, Thor says, "You people are so petty, and tiny."

The Bible itself refers to Christ as "worthy" of certain things because of his sacrifice on the cross. In a similar way that Thor is worthy to hold Mjolnir, there is a kind of worthiness that is attributed to Christ. Revelations 5:2–5 says,

> And I saw a mighty angel proclaiming in a loud voice, "Who is worthy to break the seals and open the scroll?" But no one in heaven or on earth or under the earth could open the scroll or even look inside it. I wept and wept because no one was found who was worthy to open the scroll or look inside. Then one of the elders said to me, "Do not weep! See, the Lion of the tribe of Judah, the Root of David, has triumphed. He is able to open the scroll and its seven seals."

It is generally agreed upon that the scroll that this passage is referring to is the harbinger of the end times, Christ being the only one worthy to bring that about. It also seems to imply that Christ is worthy to do this because he has triumphed in his sacrificial death and resurrection. Christ obviously had the attributes to be worthy, but until the act of sacrifice, there was something missing. In a similar way, it seems likely that Thor gained the attributes needed to be worthy again somewhere near the end of the second act of the movie, but did not actually become worthy until these attributes culminated in his act of sacrifice during the third act.

This self-sacrificial charity was obviously what triggered the returning of Thor's worthiness in the first movie, but what about Thor's worthiness prior to the first movie? He most definitely did not seem to be any Christ-like paragon of virtue—a great warrior, but also something of a self-absorbed narcissist. This leads us to the second theory for the basis of Thor's worthiness, the warrior's spirit. In this section, we will be comparing Thor with the likes of Hercules and Samson.

The basis of this theory is the idea that Thor's worthiness hinges on his abilities as a warrior. In the film, Dr. Erik Selvig at first doubts that Thor is who he says he is. He refers to Thor as part of the child stories he was told when he was young. Later in the film, he actually pulls out a children's book about Norse mythology. The page it opens to is about Mjolnir and reads,

> Mjolnir, or 'that which smashes,' is the hammer carried by Thor, the god of thunder. Odin, king of the Norse people, ordered the dwarves to create Mjolnir. The blacksmiths used the core of a star as a mold. In the process the star exploded and almost took Earth with it. Although powerful, the hammer also holds several magic spells from Odin, who killed the frost giants with it. Much later, Mjolnir was bestowed to Thor, after proving himself worthy through many challenges. The history of Mjolnir is the history of Thor.[13]

Although this may seem like an odd piece of evidence, most of what it says is in line with the in-universe explanation of the origins and history of Thor's hammer in *Thor: Ragnarok* and *Avengers: Infinity War*. We have little reason to doubt that is anything but an accurate in-universe explanation of the Mjolnir's history. The part that is specifically of interest to us is where it says, "Mjolnir was bestowed to Thor, after proving himself worthy through many challenges."[14]

This idea of challenges unto worthiness can be seen in multiple religions and mythologies, the most obvious connections being the labors of Hercules and the challenges that Samson faced. In the Greek mythos, Hercules had to complete various challenges in order to redeem himself from the murder of his wife and child, an act he did under the influence of the constantly jealous wife of Zeus, Hera.[15] The labors that Hercules undertook include the slaying of the Nemean Lion,[16] the slaying of the Hydra,[17] and the subduing of Cerberus.[18] The main tool that Hercules has in these tasks is his immense strength, but he also displays a surprising amount of ingenuity. His burning of the heads of the Hydra so that they could not grow back, for example. This theme is not only found in the ancient Mediterranean but all over the ancient world.

In the biblical stories, Samson was the strongest man to ever exist. Samson's story is perhaps more similar to Thor's story in that he loses his powers due to his own hubris and regains them in a redemption narrative. Prior to this redemption, Samson does not take his duty toward God seriously. Instead, he lived life for himself, disregarding the rules and guidelines that God had set in place for him. He does many amazing feats, proving himself a mighty warrior and that God's favor was with him through various acts of strength and courage, much the same as Hercules did. Much like Thor was brought low in finding out he was unworthy to lift his hammer, in Judges 16:1–21, Samson is brought to his lowest point. Not only does his strength leave him, but verse 20 says that the Lord himself had left him. In the finishing narrative in verses 25–31, Samson again relies on God and defeats his enemies, killing himself in the process. Important to the theory of the warrior's spirit is that Samson, despite acting directly against many aspects of his vow to God, he maintained his power for a long time. He defended the Israelites against their enemies through multiple acts of strength and valor, such as his killing of a thousand Philistines with the jawbone of a donkey in Judges 15 or killing a lion in Judges 14. It seems that despite his moral failings, his defending of the people of God was the basis for the worthiness of the powers bestowed upon him. According to the in-movie children's book, Thor underwent similar challenges to Hercules and Samson. He fought multiple battles and countless foes and was then deemed worthy of wielding his now-signature hammer.

Now, there is one thing that the in-movie children's book says that is not quite true. In fact, this untruth is repeated in other films of the MCU as well. It says that "Although powerful, the hammer also holds several magic spells from Odin, who killed the frost giants with it." It says that Odin used Mjolnir to kill the Frost Giants. This was commonly believed throughout Asgard but is untrue. Hela, not Odin, used Mjolnir to defeat the Frost Giants. This is seen in *Thor: Ragnarok* in a mural depicting Hela wielding Mjolnir with Odin next to her and the armies of Asgard behind them. However, until the events of *Thor: Ragnarok,* this mural was completely hidden. It was covered and forgotten. Explaining this past event to Skurge, Hela says, "We were unstoppable. I was his weapon in the conquests that built Asgard's empire. One by one, the realms became ours. But then, simply because my ambition outgrew his, he banished me, caged me, locked me away like an animal."[19] This is to say that Odin changed, and thus the requirements for worthiness changed with him.

This brings us to the third theory of worthiness, that of Odin's approval. Thor is worthy because Odin declares him worthy. This is very similar to the moral theory called divine command theory. Unrestricted divine command theory is the idea that there is an unrestricted relationship between the rulings of God and morality.[20] In this theory, there are three categorizations of actions. Philosopher Mark Timmons explains these three categories as such,

An action A is *obligatory* if and only if (and because) God commands that we A.
An action A is *wrong* if and only if (and because) God commands that we not A.
An action A is *optional* if and only if (and because) God neither commands that we A nor that we not A.[21]

This is to say that if we have God's commands on a subject, we can then see that subject as black and white. If he has commanded we do something, we must do it. If he has commanded that we do not do something, we must not do it. In this lies the basis of morality. If divine command theory is to be believed, right and wrong are determined by the most powerful entity.

This issue is brought up by Plato in his dialogue, *Euthyphro*. In this dialogue, Plato and Euthyphro are discussing whether or not an act is pious because the gods love it, or whether the gods love an act because it is pious.[22] Plato further clarifies the question by asking whether the holy is loved simply because it is loved, or whether it is loved because it is of the sort that is supposed to be loved.[23] In Marvel terms, we can ask if Thor is worthy because Odin decrees him worthy, or if Odin declares Thor worthy because Thor truly—or objectively—is worthy. There are four definitions that are given by the titular character of the *Euthyphro* and that are argued against by Plato through Socrates, but we will only go over the two that are most pertinent to us. First, the idea that what is holy is that which is loved by the gods.[24] Plato takes issue with this by pointing out that there is often disagreement between the gods.[25] This means that what may be pious, holy, or good to one god may be impious, unholy, or evil to another.

This leads Plato into his second definition, which that what is pious is that which has the universal love of the gods and that which is impious is that which has the universal hate of the gods.[26] This is where Plato starts leading the dialogue toward the question of whether the good conforms to the will of the gods or whether the gods conform to the good. While this difference may seem arbitrary to some, Plato uses the example of carrying something or being carried by something to explain his point.[27] The difference is as stark as the difference between someone carrying a box and a box carrying a person.

For our purposes, the question becomes whether Odin conforms to the good, or whether what is considered to be good conforms to the will of Odin. Does Odin declare Thor worthy because Thor has truly become worthy through a self-sacrificial change in character, or because Odin has deemed Thor worthy once again? As much as we might want to believe that Odin is a morally perfect being who not only orders the good, but actually is good, this is not the case. Just take the wars that Odin and Hela waged. Warning Thor of Hela, Odin says, "Her violent appetites grew beyond my control. I couldn't stop her, so I imprisoned her. Locked her away. She draws her strength from Asgard . . . and once she gets there, her powers will be limitless."[28] Odin paints himself as a victim here, but, unsurprisingly, Hela has a different way of viewing these events. She says, "Look at these lies. Goblets and garden parties? Peace treaties?"[29] and later, "Odin, proud to have it, ashamed of how he got it."[30] For much of Odin's rule, it seems as though he was a warmonger. He waged countless wars before finally realizing the error in his ways. The fact that he realized he was wrong and changed his ways implies that there is a moral authority or essence that is higher than himself. Despite being one of the most powerful beings in the Marvel universe, and the most powerful god in the Asgardian pantheon, there is something that binds even his conscience.

This is a similar conclusion to what Plato was trying to lead Euthyphro into, but with a less charitable view of the gods. For Plato, the gods would never say or do anything that was wrong or immoral. Any record of them doing wrong, records that were common among the Greek poets of Plato and Socrates' day, were either errors or outright lies. The gods of Plato were thought to be perfectly in line with his form of the good. They were perfect beings. In the Marvel universe, the gods are more like the myths and poems that Plato thought were lies. The gods of Marvel are, at times, brutal, lying, and self-absorbed. At other times, they are imminently wise and thoughtful peacemakers. If Plato was to hear of Zeus waging brutal wars for completely selfish reasons, he would immediately reject the notion as a falsification by the poets.

In describing a perfect state's stance on allowing for the poetic stories of the gods to be taught to Children, Plato writes,

> No, we shall never mention the battles of the giants, or let them be embroidered on garments; and we shall be silent about the innumerable other quarrels of gods and heroes with their friends and relatives. If they would only believe us we would tell them that quarrelling is unholy, and that never up to this time has there been any, quarrel between citizens; this is what old men and old women should begin by telling children... for a young person cannot judge what is allegorical and what is literal; anything that he receives into his mind at that age is likely to become indelible and unalterable.[31]

Plato is saying that the events described by Homer are not true, but even if they were true, they should not be taught to children because of their poor moral quality. His main reasoning behind this ban is so that the youth are not corrupted, but a secondary reason is that these stories about the gods are simply untrue. He noted that there may be allegorical value to them, but due to the difficulty in discerning the literal from the allegorical, they should be left aside.

Speaking again of her and Odin's exploits, Hela says, "Odin and I drowned entire civilizations in blood and tears. Where do you think all this gold came from? And then one day he decided to become a benevolent king." We can just imagine Plato dealing with this kind of story. Even if it were real, there is no way he would want it taught as history. Plato would want it hidden, as Odin did. We can actually see what Plato was talking about in the first Thor film. Thor always wished to grow up and fight the Frost Giants as his father once did. Given how seemingly bloodthirsty Odin was in his youth, the advice that he gave to Thor at the beginning of the movie is incredibly interesting. Responding to a young Thor saying that he wishes to slay monsters as his father once did, Odin says, "A wise king does not seek out war, but he is always ready for it."[32] This shows maturity and goodness in Odin that was hard-earned from age and experience. The issue is that it does not show any sort of Platonic conformity to the good. If Odin is thought to be in line with the unchangeable, Platonic good, then how is it that he was matured and changed with time?

There is one last question that we must ponder. Since Odin died during the events of *Thor: Ragnarok*, what now happens to the enchantment that was laid upon Mjolnir? There is precedent in the comics for the enchantment existing apart from the existence of Odin or even growing beyond Odin's power to control. In Jane Foster's run as Thor, Odin completely loses control of the enchantment. Before going into that, however, we need to discuss Thor losing his worthiness.

Thor losing his worthiness was a long time coming. It started with his massive battle against Gorr the God Butcher that began in *Thor: God of Thunder* issue 2 and lasted until *Thor: God of Thunder* issue 11. Gorr had been traveling the cosmos, finding and slaughtering any and every god that he found. Upon discovering this, Thor confronted and battled Gorr, eventually being victorious alongside a younger version of himself and an older, All-Father, version of himself. Although the story is suspenseful and the artwork breathtaking, what really sets this series apart are the deep themes that run through it. Gorr initially sets out on his bloody mission because the gods never answered him when he most needed them.[33] As a child, Gorr watched his mother get torn apart and eaten by monsters right beside the altar where they had just sacrificed their last bit of food to their gods.[34] The gods did nothing. As a young man, Gorr watched helplessly as a natural disaster took his wife and unborn child.[35] The gods did nothing. A few years later, Gorr and his sick child are dying of thirst in the desert. His son expired, and again the gods did nothing.[36] This final death breaks Gorr. He rejects the idea of the gods altogether. Referring to his unanswered prayers he says, "The gods don't hear your prayers because there are no gods. There never were. No gods in the sky. No gods who made us. No gods watching over us. No gods who give a damn. There's only us."[37] For this heresy, the rest of his tribe attempted to stone him, but they settle on simply exiling him.[38]

Gorr is now an atheist. The problem of evil was too much for him. How can gods exist in this horrible world that has been so cruel to Gorr? His atheism is not long lived. Walking alone in exile, he comes across two gods fighting. The one kills the other but is badly wounded in the process. The injured god asks Gorr for help. Gorr is in disbelief. These gods had never answered his pleas for help. In a rage, Gorr takes the weapon of the fallen God and murders him.[39] Armed with the cosmic weapon he obtained from the god, Gorr begins a killing spree that will take place across dozens of realms, hundreds of planets, and over thousands of years. Thus begins the tale of the God Butcher. This spree was only ended when three Thors, each from a different era of the main Marvel universe's timeline, came together to fight him.

What does this have to do with Thor's worthiness? In the seventh issue of the *Original Sin* storyline, Nick Fury whispers something to Thor, causing Thor to become immediately unworthy to wield Mjolnir.[40] It is later revealed that all that Fury said was that Gorr was right.[41] Gorr was correct in his evaluation of the gods of the Marvel universe. Thor goes on to explain, saying, "Gods are vain and vengeful creatures. Always have been. The mortals who've worshipped us for centuries would all be better off without us. We gods do not deserve love. No matter how much we fight to fool ourselves. We are *all* unworthy."[42] First and foremost, Thor is not just referring to Mjolnir in his evaluation of the gods as unworthy. They are unworthy of worship and love from the mortals who so revered them. Second, Thor is not declaring the gods unworthy because of their ontological status as gods. He is declaring them unworthy because of the ethical framework that developed from their ontological status. Their being gods is not what makes them unworthy, but the pride and selfishness that develops from their being nearly ageless and nearly omnipotent is what makes them unworthy.

This is best demonstrated by the way that Odin acts upon finding out that Thor has become worthy, and even more so when he finds himself unworthy. Attempting and failing to lift the hammer, Odin says, "Move, you blasted hunk of Uru! Odin commands thee! I am the way and the wrath and the wonder! I am him who speaks while galaxies obey!"[43] There is no real reason given as to why Odin can no longer control the enchantment, but upon Odin being unable to lift the hammer, Freyja says, "It would appear the enchantment has grown beyond even the enchanter. Perhaps that is for the best."[44] This scene shows both the arrogance and wisdom of the gods. Odin is shown to be belligerent and self-involved. He shoves aside his broken-hearted son and goes to the hammer, becoming irrationally angry when he cannot lift it. This is the attitude that Gorr, and eventually Thor, came to so despise. On the other hand, we see a tenderness and care in Thor's stepmother, Freyja. She is first and foremost concerned about the well-being of Thor, not the dishonor of being counted unworthy by Mjolnir. The attitude that Odin displays in the comics is comparable to the attitude that Thor had at the beginning of the first *Thor* film.

Eventually, the hammer is picked up by Jane Foster, a storyline that will likely be included in the fourth Thor film, *Thor: Love and Thunder*. In the comics, Jane Foster had been dealing with breast cancer for years when she eventually picked up the hammer.[45] Picking up the hammer transformed her into the mighty Thor, allowing her to completely change her appearance and gain all the powers of Thor.[46] The issue was that every time that she transformed from Jane Foster into Thor and back again, her cancer would revert to a worse state. Eventually, she could no longer transform without her cancer running its full course and dying. With the fate of her friends and Asgard at stake, she makes this sacrifice. She transforms into Thor, defeats the threat to Asgard, and then expires.[47]

This act of sacrifice is how the gods should act. Mjolnir, now out of Odin's control, looks for a self-sacrificial charity—a willingness to put others in front of yourself, even if the cost is your life. Jane Foster is worthy because of her willingness to sacrifice herself, much the same reason that Thor's worthiness returned in the first *Thor* film. This truly seems to be what Mjolnir is looking for in the films as well. The three characters that have wielded Mjolnir (Thor, Vision, and Captain America) all put the needs and safety of others far in front of their own wants and needs. Thor we have already discussed, but Vision was willing to die so that the mind stone would not fall into the hands of Thanos[48] and Captain America sacrificed himself by piloting his plane into the frozen waters.[49]

In this chapter, we have gone over and discussed various frameworks for the worthiness of Thor in comparison to religious and philosophical systems of worthiness and morality. The first was that Thor was considered worthy because of an attitude of charity and self-sacrifice. The second was that Thor was considered worthy through the completion of a set of challenges, similar to those faced by the Greek Hercules or the biblical Samson. The third was that Thor was worthy simply because Odin declared him worthy. All of these frameworks had aspects of truth in them but the third ends up best fitting the evidence available to us. Finally, we discussed the implications of Odin having died in the MCU on the enchantment placed on Mjolnir. Through careful consideration of the comic books where similar events have transpired, we settled on self-sacrificial charity as a lasting and final framework for the consideration of worthiness.

NOTES

1. *Thor*, directed by Kenneth Branagh (Marvel Studios, 2011), DVD.
2. Ibid.
3. Walter Simonson, *The Mighty Thor*, Issue #337 (New York, NY: Marvel Comics Group Inc., 1966), 20.
4. Tom Defalco, *The Mighty Thor*, #390 (Marvel Entertainment Group Inc., 1966 and Marvel Characters Inc., 2013), 15.
5. *Thor*.
6. Ibid.
7. C. S. Lewis, *God in the Dock: Essays on Theology and Ethics*, ed. Walter Hooper (Grand Rapids, MI: William B Eerdmans Publishing Company, 1970), 82.
8. *Thor*.
9. Stan Lee, Jack Kirby, and Vince Colletta, *The Mighty Thor*, Issue #159 (New York, NY: Marvel Comics Group, 1968), 18.
10. Ibid.
11. Ibid., 19.
12. Ibid.
13. *Thor*.
14. Ibid.
15. Thalia Papadopoulou, *Heracles and Euripidean Tragedy* (New York: Cambridge University Press, 2005), 58.
16. Michael R. Huber, *Mythematics: Solving the Twelve Labors of Hercules* (Princeton, NJ: Princeton University Press, 2009), 1.1.
17. Ibid., 2.2.
18. Ibid., 12.2.
19. *Thor: Ragnarok*, directed by Taiki Watiti (Marvel Studios, 2017), Digital.
20. Mark Timmons, *Moral Theory: An Introduction* (Lanham, MD: Rowman and Littlefield, 2012), 23.
21. Ibid., 24.
22. Plato, *Euthyphro*, trans. Reginald E. Allen (New Haven, CT: Yale University Press, 1984), 50.
23. Ibid., 51.
24. Ibid., 46.
25. Ibid., 47.
26. Ibid., 49.
27. Ibid., 50.
28. *Thor: Ragnarok*.
29. Ibid.
30. Ibid.
31. Plato, *The Republic of Plato*, trans. Benjamin Jowett, July 26, 2017 [EBook #55201], 153.
32. *Thor*.
33. Jason Aaron and Tom Palmer, *Thor: God of Thunder*, Issue #6 (New York, NY: Marvel Characters Inc., 2013).

34. Ibid., 2.
35. Ibid., 4.
36. Ibid., 6.
37. Ibid., 7.
38. Ibid., 8–9.
39. Ibid., 13–14.
40. Jason Aaron, Mike Deodato, and Frank Martin, *Original Sin*, Issue 7 (New York, NY: Marvel Characters Inc., 2014), 14.
41. Jason Aaron, Olivier Coipel, Kim Jacinto, Pascal Alixe, Mat Lopes, and Jay David Ramos, *The Unworthy Thor*, Issue 5 (New York, NY: Marvel Characters Inc., 2017), 14.
42. Ibid.
43. Jason Aaron, Russell Dauterman, and Matthew Wilson, *Thor*, Issue #1 (New York, NY: Marvel Characters Inc., 2014), 10.
44. Ibid.
45. Ibid., 21–22.
46. Ibid., 22.
47. Jason Aaron, Russell Dauterman, and Matthew Wilson, *The Mighty Thor*, Issue #705 (New York, NY: Marvel Characters Inc., 2017), 17–19.
48. *Avengers: Infinity War*, directed by Anthony Russo and Joe Russo (Marvel Studios, 2018), Digital.
49. *Captain America: The First Avenger*, directed by Joe Johnston (Marvel Studios, 2011), DVD.

REFERENCES

Aaron, Jason, Mike Deodato, and Frank Martin. *Original Sin*, Issue #7. New York, NY: Marvel Characters Inc., 2014.
Aaron, Jason, Olivier Coipel, Kim Jacinto, Pascal Alixe, Mat Lopes, and Jay David Ramos. *The Unworthy Thor*, Issue #5. New York, NY: Marvel Characters Inc., 2017.
Aaron, Jason, Russell Dauterman, and Matthew Wilson. *Thor*, Issue #1. New York, NY: Marvel Characters Inc., 2014.
Aaron, Jason and Tom Palmer. *Thor: God of Thunder*, Issue #6. New York, NY: Marvel Characters Inc., 2013.
Avengers. Directed by Joss Whedon. Marvel Studios, 2012. Digital.
Avengers: Age of Ultron. Directed by Joss Whedon. Marvel Studios, 2015. Digital.
Avengers: Infinity War. Directed by Anthony Russo and Joe Russo. Marvel Studios, 2018. Digital.
Captain America: The First Avenger. Directed by Joe Johnston. Marvel Studios, 2011. DVD.
Defalco, Tom. *The Mighty Thor*, Issue #390. Marvel Entertainment Group Inc., 1966 and Marvel Characters Inc., 2013.

Huber, Michael R. *Mythematics : Solving the Twelve Labors of Hercules*. Princeton, NJ: Princeton University Press, 2009.

Lee, Stan, Jack Kirby, and Vince Colletta. *The Mighty Thor*, Issue #159. New York, NY: Marvel Comics Group, 1968.

Lewis, C. S. *God in the Dock: Essays on Theology and Ethics*. Edited by Walter Hooper. Grand Rapids, MI: William B Eerdmans Publishing Company, 1970.

Papadopoulou, Thalia. *Heracles and Euripidean Tragedy*. Cambridge Classical Studies. New York: Cambridge University Press, 2005.

Plato. *Euthyphro*. Translated by Reginald E. Allen. New Haven, CT: Yale University Press, 1984.

Simonson, Walter. *The Mighty Thor*, Issue #337. New York, NY: Marvel Comics Group Inc., 1966.

Thor. Directed by Kenneth Branagh. Marvel Studios, 2011. DVD.

Thor: Ragnarok. Directed by Taiki Watiti. Marvel Studios, 2017. Digital.

Timmons, Mark. *Moral Theory: An Introduction*. Lanham, MD: Rowman and Littlefield, 2012.

Chapter 6

"Who Are You?"
René Girard, W. E. B. Du Bois, and Black Panther

Ryan Smock

April 2016 was buzz month at my former school, an all-minority high school located smack in the middle of the projects. *Captain America: Civil War* had just released, meaning the adolescent-fueled fervor among our blerds could barely be contained. To this point, there had been a dearth of minority superheroes worthy of being called role models: Blade wasn't exactly nice or family friendly, Hancock didn't paint a good character portrait, and Steel was cringeworthy to say the least. For the first time in their 18-year history, my students would get to see (as one of them put it) a triple-A superhero "who looked like them." The Monday after release, toward the end of the day, two of them ran up to me in a fluster. "Mr. Smock," said one, "tell me, who do you think was the absolute BEST superhero in *Civil War*?" They both froze with bated breath, as though I were King Minos handing down some eternal sentence. "If I'm going to be completely honest," I said, "I'd have to say Black Panther." One looked at the other, his face coldly sober but his eyes shining with joy. "See, I told You! Get out my face, boy!" I reprimanded him for his rudeness, but inside I smiled at his enthusiasm. I can only wonder how much these boys squeed about the *Black Panther* movie itself, since I took a position across the country and lost contact with them before it came out. But if they were anything like I remember, and if they were anything like me, then the very moment King T'Chaka stepped out of the shadows and into his traitorous brother N'Jobu's apartment . . . it was on.

Little did I know, however, that it would be on in more ways than one. After watching T'Challa brave the dangers of ascending the throne, strive to step out from his father's long shadow, and struggle to find a sense of self among strictures of duty and social tension, I was awed to see him subtly address the central questions posed by Christian thinker René Girard: "How do we overcome and turn away from the 'satanic' mechanisms of blame, victimization, and scapegoating? Is there a sense of self which isn't enthralled by imitative desire, conflict, and violence?"

Black Panther is unique within the Marvel Cinematic Universe because, unlike any other film, its hero rises above immense social and political adversity to realize W. E. B. Du Bois's charge to "be himself, and not another."[1] By the end of the film, T'Challa emerges as a humanitarian and a teacher as opposed to a mere warrior. (No offense, Thor fans.) His lesson? How to answer the simple question which plagues us all: "who are you?"

GIRARD ON THE ROOT OF ALL CONFLICT

From the very opening of *Black Panther*, we are immersed in the terrible consequences of a long-standing rivalry. King T'Chaka has come to confront his brother Prince N'Jobu about stolen vibranium—a rare and extremely valuable mineral that is the foundation for much of the Marvel universe's advanced technology. They both want to use the material for their own ends, and so each perceives the other as an enemy thwarting their desires. Although the opening scene fades out just after T'Chaka orders N'Jobu to come home and report his crime, we know how that meeting really ends. N'Jobu moves to shoot the person who ratted him out, only to find panther claws suddenly driven into his chest. N'Jobu dies on the spot, and a small child is left to deal with the fallout on his own. But surely, some argue, there could have been another resolution. The Black Panther character has superhuman speed and reflexes, after all, so he would have been able to knock away the gun and subdue his brother rather than spill his blood. How then did it get to such a point, that the choice was made to kill? One answer can perhaps be found in the work of French literary critic and philosopher René Girard.

In *Deceit, Desire, and the Novel* Girard lays out his concept of "triangular" or "mimetic" desire—that is, the idea that we copy our desires from others. Suppose a boy (Boy 1) enters a room full of toys and walks around, trying to decide which one to play with. He picks up a stuffed giraffe to see how it feels, what it does, and whether it makes any sounds. At this moment, imagine that another boy (Boy 2) enters the room also wanting to play. Unlike the first boy, this second one immediately seems to know which toy he wants: the giraffe. But when he goes to grab it, Boy 1 suddenly recoils and shouts "mine!" even though mere seconds ago he could not have cared less. What accounts for this change, Girard suggests, is that desire was first modeled and then imitated between the two.

Let us assume that Boy 2 is our acting *subject*. We would ordinarily want to depict his desire by drawing a straight line between him and the giraffe, known as the *object*.

Boy 2—Giraffe

Boy 2 sees the giraffe, then desires the giraffe. But such an approach fails to consider that, even though every other toy in the room is available, he fixates on the giraffe for some reason. This is because when Boy 2 enters the room and sees Boy 1 holding the toy, Boy 1 unwittingly becomes the *mediator* or *model* of desire. The very moment Boy 2 sees the giraffe being held, certain ideas occur to him which may or may not even be true: that the other knows which toy is best, perhaps, or that there is some reason the other is holding that particular toy. These are called *tutelary beliefs*, and their truth value is not as important for Girard as their effect on the subject.[2] So long as Boy 2 merely believes Boy 1 has a reason for holding the toy giraffe, that giraffe becomes desirable. This desire becomes imitated or "mimetic" when Boy 2 reaches for the toy. Boy 1 sees the other's desire and copies it, now believing the giraffe is desirable. When Boy 2 goes to grab the giraffe, however, there is a sudden shift in the relationship: each instantaneously becomes perceived as a rival standing in the way of the other's acquisition of the object. What we now have is a triangular relationship between the three.

Boy 2—Giraffe
\ /
\ /
Boy 1

We can replace the characters in this triangle with those from *Black Panther*, casting N'Jobu as the subject, T'Chaka as the mediator, and vibranium as the desired object. That vibranium is much rarer and more useful than the toy giraffe only augments its desirability, and only heightens the passion felt toward each other and the object itself.[3]

In his analysis of Max Scheler, Girard suggests a distinction between our ideas of *hatred, jealousy,* and *envy*.[4] Hate, he states, develops when someone models desire and then prevents us from fulfilling it. Jealousy, then, is what we feel when seeing our rival possess the desired object and contend for it. By hoarding the vibranium under the pretense of keeping it safe, T'Chaka prevents N'Jobu from utilizing it to free oppressed minorities around the world. But by stealing the mineral in response and enabling others (like Klaue) to do so as well, N'Jobu threatens T'Chaka's ability to keep it secret and safe.

That each actively deprives the other of the object only cements their mutual perception of the other as an antagonist. Furthermore, that each has now expressed a desire to defeat or otherwise remove the other now elicits an escalating reciprocal response:

> What was for him in the beginning only a whim is now transformed into a violent passion. We all know that every desire redoubles when it is seen to be shared. Two identical but opposite triangles are thus superimposed on each other. Desire circulates between the two rivals more and more quickly, and with every cycle it increases in intensity like the electric current in a battery which is being charged.[5]

There are two opposing triangles, according to Girard, because N'Jobu and T'Chaka each see themselves as the desiring subject and interpret the other as the model/rival. Conflict is born and begins to cycle between the two, growing stronger with each interaction, until it explodes into aggressive violence. So even though the brothers' living room confrontation is only the beginning of the film for us, for them it marks the culmination of a long, bitter, and vicious altercation.

Envy, unlike jealousy, "occurs only when our efforts to acquire [the object] fail and we are left with a feeling of impotence."[6] The shocking horror spreading across N'Jobu's face when Zuri reveals his true identity, and the bleak defeat which registers as T'Chaka recaptures the stolen canister, leaves little doubt concerning N'Jobu's final feelings in this scene. He has tried to usurp his rival, but utterly failed. Powerless to strike down the king due to his current role as the Black Panther, N'Jobu instead lashes out at a proxy—a person he believes can assault without consequence. There is only one way to end the conflict for good, however, and T'Chaka is the one to make the fateful move.

MODELING ACTION VERSUS MODELING IDEAL

To this point, our analysis has confined itself to *internal mediation*, where the desire for a limited is mediated by someone within our social sphere, and people inevitably become drawn into the vortex of rivalrous conflict. Girard, however, maintains there is a more positive form of mimesis to be found in *external mediation*.[7] This happens when a role model outside our social sphere—like a teacher, a statesperson, or a religious leader—mediates desire away from objects and toward ideals. The ultimate role model for Girard is Jesus Christ as portrayed by the gospels; for he alone reveals the mimetic mechanism and offers an alternative model which protects us from rivalries rather than involves us in them.[8] Christ is unique because he invites us not to imitate his actions, as other models do, but rather his desire "to resemble

God the Father as much as possible."[9] What does it mean, though, to resemble God? One example Girard gives is to practice "detached generosity," to be kind and freely give of oneself without favoritism or prejudice.[10] Since internal mediation directs us to think in materialistic or acquisitive terms, Christ counters this by modeling compassion and care for everyone he meets. Just as God "makes the sun rise on the evil and the good," Jesus heals, preaches to, and otherwise supports any who ask of him; not just those in his favor.[11] By freely showing kindness toward everyone and sharing what we have, mimetic rivalry and violence can be stymied before they ever develop.

But even Jesus is not without competition. Girard writes, "Satan likewise presents himself as a model for our desires, and he is certainly easier to imitate than Christ, for he counsels us to abandon ourselves to all our inclinations in defiance of morality and its prohibitions."[12] It is important to note here that, for Girard, Satan is not a literal being but rather a presence represented by the overall cycle of internally mediated desire and violence. The "invitation," then, is Satan's seducing us to think the prohibition against desiring what our neighbors have (the tenth commandment) is just "the resentment of grumpy men eager to prevent young men from having a good time."[13] Having accepted this view, we might feel free to pursue all our desires without constraint. But this is a false sense of liberation: by dropping our prohibitions and indulging ourselves, we really become enthralled to copying others' desires and reciprocating hateful acts when they get in our way.

A significant aspect of *Black Panther*'s narrative is that T'Challa exclusively takes T'Chaka as his role model. In an early scene, after prevailing over the Jabari challenge and consuming the heart-shaped herb, T'Challa finds himself wandering across a velvety plain to meet the spirit of his deceased father. Midway through their conversation T'Challa says to him, "I want to be a good king, baba, just like you." While his intention may be entirely noble, the issue is that T'Challa focuses more on the *action* of being king than the *ideal* of being king. Imitating his father's desire to hoard the vibranium and keep it safe, he rebuts Nakia's claim that Wakanda should be helping those in need and instead dedicates his energy to hunting down the man who had stolen from Wakanda thirty years prior. "Not capturing him," T'Challa says, "is perhaps my father's greatest regret." Use of the present tense here indicates that T'Challa has become subsumed within his father's identity: his pursuit of Klaue is nothing but reciprocal violence masquerading as justice. "Wakanda does not need a warrior right now," a councilwoman admonishes, "we need a king!" Already enslaved within satanic mechanisms, however, T'Challa is oblivious to Nakia's and her prompts toward a Christ-like bearing.

The real evil of Satan, however, lies in his role of "the accuser."[14] When two people are seen fighting over something, others tend to notice and begin desiring it as well. This leads to what Girard calls "scandal," a situation in which every member of a community desires the same thing yet works to prevent anyone from achieving their desire. The community becomes divided in a "war of all against all," otherwise known as a *mimetic crisis*.[15] When this happens, the community must express its collective violence, and yet cannot attack itself without serious repercussions. The community therefore heaps its anger and frustration and hostility upon a single, innocent victim—a *scapegoat*—and then blames it as being the one responsible for their problems. For Girard, Satan is "the violent contagion" which convinces them of the scapegoat's guilt, and which drives the community to expel the victim through sacrifice or exile.

Toward the end of the film, after the true details of T'Chaka's rivalry have been revealed by N'Jadaka, the son of N'Jobu, there is a moment where T'Challa stands before the tribal elders and demands an explanation from his father.

"Why," he pleads, teary-eyed. "Why didn't you bring the boy home? Why, baba?"

"He . . . He was the truth I chose to omit."

"You were wrong to abandon him."

"I chose my people. I chose Wakanda. Our future depended."

Although T'Challa angrily cuts him off, the implication has already been made: N'Jadaka was the scapegoat, the innocent victim T'Chaka sacrificed to preserve Wakanda's safety and unity. The admission finally reveals the false model T'Challa had set for himself, lifting once and for all the shadow which had loomed overhead since his coronation, but at a steep cost. By this point the return of Prince N'Jadaka has ignited a war of all against all, dividing and pitting Wakanda's most loyal citizens against each other and threatening to repeat the satanic cycle of violence, blame, and victimization. Unless, of course, T'Challa can do something about it.

KILLMONGER'S MIMETIC ORIGIN

It is here that we must pause and appreciate the complex, multifaceted nature of the so-called villain, for T'Challa is not the only son dedicated to fulfilling his father's desires. N'Jadaka, also known as "Erik" or "Killmonger," clearly expresses his desire to realize N'Jobu's vision when accosting the Wakandan leadership: "Y'all sittin' up here comfortable. Must feel good. It's about two billion people all over the world that looks like us. But their lives are a lot harder. Wakanda has the tools to liberate 'em all. [What tools?] Vibranium. Your weapons." What is interesting about N'Jadaka is that he considers himself part of a global community while T'Challa adamantly clings to his

Wakandan ethnicity. It is this quality which led many viewers and critics to consider Erik as both a product of and a commentary on African American history.[16] Indeed, his own association with the African slave trade reveals a mimetic quality to his character which must need be explored. After all, if Girard's understanding of mimesis need not be limited to physical objects or social prestige, then it can also help us better understand how personal identity is formed.

Vickie Mays, quoting Erikson, Berger, and Luckmann, maintains that "human identity must be examined . . . in terms of the individual's relationship within the social and historical development of society," further noting that "no human thought is immune from the ideologizing influences of its social context."[17] The notion of someone "fitting in" with society is predicated on living up to other people's standards and fulfilling their expectations. We take our measure from socially sanctioned ideas of the "good," the "honorable," and the "just," internalizing the collectively modeled abstract desires. When Mays writes that black identity "develops in a culture which teaches that all their behaviors, beliefs, and characteristics are inferior, maladjusted, and inadequate,"[18] she unknowingly references Girard's idea of mediation—only the mediation is directed at a kind of cultural transmission rather than a tangible desire.

Girard does allow for all sorts of transmissions through the mimetic process, stating that "it is not only desire that one borrows from those whom one takes as models; it is a mass of behaviors, attitudes . . . prejudices, preferences, etc."[19] These prejudices and attitudes all too readily fuel passion and conflict; for if we scratch through the surface of "racial ideals," what we find modeled is a type of manipulative selfishness, a desire for the self to be victorious over the other, which leads straight toward mimetic violence. But one cannot contend with society (from where Mays argues African American stereotypes derive) as one would a rival in the sense detailed by internal mediation. While one can physically overcome a rival and take an object—like the toy giraffe or the vibranium—one cannot physically extract ideas from another's mind. To contend with society, we must change the thoughts themselves, which means externally mediating a different ideal much like Christ did. The catch, and we have ample evidence of this, is that the person who stands against a unified society usually only succeeds in encouraging them to cast that person as a scapegoat and reaffirm their own ideas.[20] The person and the idea stood for both become vilified.

The perpetually negative mediation—the negative behaviors, attitudes, preferences, and prejudices which society continually transmits—causes African Americans to experience what W. E. B. Du Bois calls a "double-consciousness"; a "sense of always looking at one's self through the eyes of others, of measuring one's soul by the tape of a world that looks on in amused contempt and pity."[21] Historically, this disorientation began with the very group N'Jadaka associates himself: the African slaves. Mays suggests they modeled—or as Girard would say, imitated—"whites' stereotypes about blacks" as a defensive coping strategy.[22] By internalizing and acting out these stereotypes, slaves often experienced less violent treatment and were rewarded with comfort, favors, positions of authority, and even education.[23] The same fruits, incidentally, which N'Jadaka enjoyed by conforming to dominant cultural standards at MIT, in the military, and in the CIA.

By the time abolitionism took hold, however, and all through desegregation and the equal rights movements, such imitation had already become an internalized part of black culture and caused the development of a "dual identity." While their "real self" featured natural pride arising from self-awareness and personal achievement, their "pseudo-self" was plagued with depersonalization, anxiety, fear, and feelings of inadequacy.[24] Du Bois acknowledges this in his own reflections, stating that "One ever feels his two-ness—an American, a Negro; two souls, two thoughts, two unreconciled strivings; two warring ideals in one dark body, whose dogged strength alone keeps it from being torn asunder."[25] It is here that we can see N'Jadaka at his most sympathetic. Born to the American culture which champions personal industry and success, he is racially bound by that selfsame culture's mediation of social degradation, objectification, and subservience. At the same time, he is a legitimate prince of the wealthiest and most powerful nation on the planet (Wakanda); he is nevertheless forced to live among poverty and death, all the while watching his cousin grow up being valued and groomed to achieve greatness. It should come as no surprise that Erik has three names: two names for each of his "pseudo-selves" which are products of culture, and one name for the "real self," which emerges from his persistent inner conflict. But which, then, is the real name and which are false? Unfortunately, his speech to T'Challa just before their ritual combat provides irrefutable confirmation: "I've lived my whole life waiting for this moment. I trained, I lied, I killed just to get here. I killed in America, Afghanistan, Iraq. I took life from my own brothers and sisters right here on this continent. And all this death, just so I could kill you." Forged in the satanic flames of hatred and resentment, in part from the mediation of negative cultural values and in part from the rivalry with T'Challa, he truly is the Killmonger seeking violent retribution.

CALL TO RESPONSIBILITY

One thing Girard admittedly waffles on is whether there is such a thing as *authentic* desire, or a desire according to oneself. Sometimes he professes that all desires are mediated in some way, and other times it seems he wants to hold out hope for a true sense of autonomy. From the very beginning of his first book, though, Girard insists that Don Quixote "surrenders" his "fundamental prerogative."[26] These three words together seem to presume personal agency as the foundation for being an individual. One pitfall of trying to assert our individualism, however, is that we become just as obsessed with what others are doing as those Girard calls *vaniteux*, vain people who rely upon others to determine their desires for them.

How, then, do we find an authentic sense of self which is not in thrall to the mimetic process? Ironically, according to Luca di Blasi, the first step toward retaking our autonomy is to "give up a promethean egotism" and realize that we are inseparable from mimetic desire. The more we attach to the idea of an "I" in control of everything, after all, the more we adopt a "me-victorious" mindset which forms the basic snare of mimetic conflict. "The acceptance of being part of mimetic desire," writes di Blasi, "permits us to overcome an illusory autonomy and replace it with a real autonomy."[27] For Girard, it would ideally be Christ who wakes us up to the mimetic process and then offers a new model, but anyone who is outside the mimetic triangle could serve a similar function. The idea is that once we are aware of the various models of desire available to us, we then autonomously choose which of them to follow.

T'Challa faces this exact problem throughout the film, as we have seen. Wanting to be a "good king," he wraps his sense of self inside his father's identity. Yet, writes Du Bois, for one "to attain his place in the world, he must be himself, and not another."[28] T'Challa is fortunate in that that he has not one but two surrogates for Christ which help him ultimately see through the mimetic matrix in which he has been entangled. The first is his girlfriend Nakia, who at the beginning of the film encourages T'Challa to lead Wakanda in providing humanitarian aid. Maintaining that Wakanda is strong enough to protect itself and help others, she insists it is their responsibility to help people in need. Then, when T'Challa mournfully reflects upon the truth about N'Jobu's death and N'Jadaka's exile, she tries to console him: "You can't let your father's mistakes define who you are. You get to decide what kind of king you are going to be."

At the time she relays this sage advice, T'Challa is primed, for he has already experienced a significant moral split from his father's code. Earlier in the narrative, Agent Ross (T'Challa's second surrogate) had jumped in front of a bullet to protect Nakia from Killmonger's assault, suffering a life-threatening spinal injury. Okoye, the head of his kingsguard, had demanded they leave Ross behind. He was a foreign agent, after all, and would be required to report back to the United States anything he saw. But deferring to Okoye's advice, strongly reminiscent of T'Chaka's desire to protect Wakanda and keep its technology secret, would entail letting Ross die. This is something T'Challa's conscience would not allow him do.

Daniel Fleming, referencing the Catholic document *Gaudiam et Spes (Hope and Joy)*, holds that the conscience is our primordial call to goodness; that it is the law written by God which we are naturally bound to follow.[29] This law, he continues, has three parts: the call to do good and avoid evil, the search for moral truth, and the commitment to act in a particular way. The deepest experience of conscience, Fleming argues, invoking the philosophy of Emmanuel Levinas, involves the "call to responsibility," which is brought to mind in any encounter with the Other. As a sort of analogy for how the call to responsibility appears, he refers to the image of a pebble caught in one's shoe. Human consciousness is understood to be fundamentally concerned with itself, with its own maintenance. This is called the *conatus essendi*, which is Latin for "being tried." There is also, however, a sort of "scruple" which for Levinas is a primary part of human nature. It is a program of sorts which questions the conatus essendi to differentiate between good and evil, or right and wrong. An encounter with the Other interrupts the conatus essendi, "causing the scruple to be moved" so that it cannot be ignored. This is the pebble in the shoe, or the call to responsibility.

The conatus is then confronted with a choice "between self-interest and otherwise than being."[30] The motion toward otherwise than being is where the conatus "exceeds itself as involvement in the good" and becomes "good will" or "unselfishness." The fact that the conatus seems pre-intentioned toward goodness—toward otherwise than being—reveals a natural goodness in human beings: "we are created as our brother's keeper before we ourselves could have any idea, longing or intention to want to be such a keeper."[31] One implication here is that the conscience, understood as the call to responsibility, operates specifically counter to the selfishness of internal mediation. Paying close attention to our conscience when we encounter another, then, may well be another way to find the "authentic sense of self" we seek.

To build on this idea Fleming quotes Tallon's understanding of responsibility:

> [It is] not something first understood in concepts or reached as a conclusion in judgements, nor is it freely chosen or decided on after deliberation. Rather, one is affected by meaning, one is commanded by proximity, held hostage by an experience, not after representation but before it, in presence, presentation, vulnerability, embodiment, in affectivity as its own kind of intentionality, its own access to meaning.[32]

When Nakia first asks T'Challa to set aside his father's directive and instead help those in need, her request is easy to dismiss because those vulnerable others appear distant and vague. The immediacy and urgency of Ross's condition, however, interrupts T'Challa's mimetic process and forces a confrontation between two possible models: that of T'Chaka, and that of Nakia and Ross. The call to do good rather than evil compels T'Challa to save Agent Ross's life in spite of his "duty" to keep Wakanda secret. "I cannot just let him die," he tells Okoye, "knowing we can save him." Furthermore, with respect to Girard, it enables him at long last to choose his own object of desire: brotherhood. By the end of the film, T'Challa is newly motivated by conscience to "right the wrongs" committed by his ancestors and his father. Renouncing the mimetic violence, he once espoused, T'Challa tries to save Killmonger rather than condemn him. Moreover, through his commitment to open up Wakanda and provide humanitarian aid to other struggling people, T'Challa finally answers the question which had begun to plague him upon first ascending the throne: "Who are you?"

He is one who has stepped out of the shadow of his father, and who has broken free of the cycle of violence.

He is himself.

NOTES

1. W. E. B. Du Bois, *The Souls of Black Folk (Dover Thrift Editions)* (Dover Publications: Kindle Edition), 4.
2. Paisley Livingston, "What is Mimetic Desire?" *Philosophical Psychology*, Vol. 7, No. 3 (1994), 291–305. By using the term "tutelary belief," Livingston refers to any beliefs which inform the subject's choice of a model. While Livingston presumes these beliefs about the model exist beforehand, I contend they can and do arise spontaneously.
3. René Girard, *I See Satan Fall Like Lightning* (Maryknoll: Orbis Books, 2001), 10.
4. René Girard, *Deceit, Desire, and the Novel: Self and Other in Literary Structure* (Baltimore: Johns Hopkins Press, 1965), 12–13.
5. Girard, *I See Satan*, 14.
6. Girard, *Deceit*, 12–13.
7. René Girard, *Evolution and Conversion: Dialogues on the Origins of Culture* (New York: Continuum International Publishing), 76; Girard, *I See Satan*, 14.
8. Girard, *I See Satan*, 13–14.
9. Ibid.
10. Ibid.
11. Ibid.
12. Ibid., 32.
13. Ibid., 12.
14. Ibid., 35.
15. Ibid., 24.
16. Doreen St. Felix, "On Killmonger, the American Villain of *Black Panther*," *The New Yorker*. February 20, 2018.

17. Vickie M. Mays, "Identity Development of Black Americans: The Role of History and the Importance of Ethnicity," *American Journal of Psychology*. Vol. XL, No. 4 (October 1986).
18. Mays, "Identity Development of Black Americans," 582.
19. Girard, *I See Satan*, 15.
20. Ibid., 25.
21. Du Bois, *The Souls of Black Folk*, 3.
22. Mays, "Identity Development of Black Americans," 585–586.
23. Ibid.
24. Mays, "Identity Development of Black Americans," 581.
25. Du Bois, *The Souls of Black Folk*, 3.
26. Girard, *Deceit*, 1.
27. Luca Di Blasi, "Within and Beyond Mimetic Desire," *Mimesis, Desire, and the Novel: René Girard and Literary Criticism* (Michigan: Michigan State University Press, 2015), 50.
28. Du Bois, *The Souls of Black Folk*, 5.
29. Daniel Fleming, "Primordial Awareness: Levinas, Conscience, and the Unavoidable Call to Responsibility," *Heythrop Journal*, Vol. LVI (2015), 604–618.
30. Ibid., 608.
31. Ibid.
32. Ibid.

REFERENCES

Di Blasi, Luca. "Within and Beyond Mimetic Desire." In *Mimesis, Desire, and the Novel: René Girard and Literary Criticism*. Michigan: Michigan State University Press, 2015.

Du Bois, W. E. B. *The Souls of Black Folk (Dover Thrift Editions)*. Dover Publications, Incorporated; Unabridged edition (July 14, 2016).

Fleming, Daniel. "Primordial Awareness: Levinas, Conscience, and the Unavoidable Call to Responsibility." *Heythrop Journal*. Vol. LVI (2015), 604–618.

Girard, René. *Deceit, Desire, and the Novel: Self and Other in Literary Structure*. Baltimore: Johns Hopkins Press, 1965.

———. *Evolution and Conversion: Dialogues on the Origins of Culture*. New York: Continuum International Publishing. Bloomsbury Academic; Reprint edition (February 23, 2017).

———. *I See Satan Fall Like Lightning*. Maryknoll: Orbis Books, 2001.

Livingston, Paisley. "What is Mimetic Desire?" *Philosophical Psychology*. Vol. 7, No. 3 (1994), 291–305.

Mays, Vickie M. "Identity Development of Black Americans: The Role of History and the Importance of Ethnicity." *American Journal of Psychology*. Vol. XL, No. 4 (October 1986), 582–593.

St. Felix, Doreen. "On Killmonger, the American Villain of Black Panther." *The New Yorker*. February 20, 2018.

Chapter 7

The Failure of a God

Thor, the Snap, and Post-Holocaust Political Theology

Andrew T. Vink

In the face of tragedy, a weighty question is often asked in the midst of grief, anger, and sorrow: Why didn't God prevent this? It is a genuine reaction and an understandable one. If God is Almighty, then why are lives lost or damaged in acts of senseless violence. To some, such acts of violence are considered failures of an omnipotent, omniscient, and benevolent God to act.

This concept of tragedy brings to mind two events that parallel these seeds of reflection: the Snap, which ends *Avengers: Infinity War* and establishes the context for *Avengers: Endgame*, and the Holocaust, the mass murder of millions of Jews, LGBTQ+ persons, and others during the reign of the Third Reich in Germany. The Snap comes to mind as it is the climatic failure of the Avengers to prevent Thanos from erasing half of all living creatures from the universe. The Holocaust, on the other hand, is an event that required a reconsideration of how theology—the study of God—can respond to such horror. To put it concisely, how do we make sense of an apparent failure of (a) God in light of an atrocity?

While the parallel of these events could apply to the entire Avengers roster, a particularly interesting point of focus is Thor's journey. As the resident god on the team, Thor's power puts him on a higher level than the rest of the Avengers fighting in Wakanda. Thor's final attack on Thanos could have changed the outcome of the Battle of Wakanda, even potentially preventing the Snap if he had "gone for the head." The atrocity of the Snap was within Thor's power to stop, and yet he failed. This failure requires the viewer (and in many cases, die-hard Avengers fans) to reconsider who Thor is and what his godhood really means.

In this essay, I will frame Thor's situation in light of one of the most significant atrocities in the twentieth century: the Holocaust. This framing will occur by looking at the insights of German political theologians Johann Baptist Metz (1928–2019), Jürgen Moltmann (1926–present), and Dorothee Sölle (1929–2003). Writing in Germany in the 1960s and 1970s, these figures confront the problem of believing in an all-powerful God in light of the atrocity of genocide. Each thinker provides ideas that can serve as analogs to how to interpret Thor's status and self-perception after the five-year time jump in *Endgame*. Metz argues that Christianity must reinterpret itself from the foundational level in light of its complicity with the Third Reich. Moltmann directly deals with the question of how a merciful God can stand impassibly while God's people, and God's son Jesus, suffer. Sölle follows a parallel line of reflection, arguing God suffers with God's people. By examining these theologians, the understanding of Thor as a passible god suffering with those he protects provides a new context for understanding his journey through the two most recent Avengers films.

"JUST SO WE ARE ALL IN AGREEMENT": SETTING TERMS AND RELATIONS

Before beginning the argument in earnest, there is a significant difficulty that must be addressed: an outright comparison between Thor and the Judeo-Christian God is unfair, given Thor never claims to be omnipotent or omniscient. While this contradiction appears to be a non-starter, it can be broken down into three smaller challenges which can be overcome by making careful distinctions.

The first of these challenges of making this kind of argument with the MCU iteration of Thor is that the audience is never given a full explanation of the limits of his powers. It is clear that Thor is neither omnipotent nor omniscient, but the audience is never given a clear definition of how powerful Thor actually is. The second challenge is linked to this first, namely distinguishing between Thor's power as displayed in the films as only part of his potential and Thor's power as his potential fully actualized. Finally, the third challenge is, assuming that Thor is neither omnipotent nor omniscient, how could have Thor even hoped to stop Thanos with the fully assembled Infinity Gauntlet, which gives the bearer the power to reshape the entirety of reality. In other words, how could a hero with finite power defeat an omnipotent villain?

The first challenge can be overcome by an emphasis on the point that we do not actually need to know the absolute definition of Thor's power set, but rather a relative definition. When we reach the Battle of Wakanda in *Infinity War*, Thor has gone through major changes since his first theatrical appearance in 2011's *Thor*. Using this first theatrical appearance as a baseline, Thor's power set does not show any kind of development until *Thor: Ragnarok*, where he loses Mjolnir at the hands of Hela and is forced to learn to control his thunder-based powers without the aid of a focus. His powers are upgraded once again with the addition of Stormbreaker, which gives him additional powers, such as being able to summon the Bifrost. As Eitri says when Thor, Rocket, and Groot visit Nidavellir, Stormbreaker is "a king's weapon," and it shows Thor's powers have been elevated to meet his station as King of Asgard.[1] This allows us to make a definitive statement that when Thor makes his appearance at the Battle of Wakanda, he is the strongest that the audience has ever seen him.

An answer to the second challenge can be found in answer to the first, particularly dealing with Thor's arc in *Ragnarok*. In the final act of the film, Thor, after losing an eye and finding himself on the edge of defeat at the hands of Hela, has a vision where a conversation with Odin allows him to unlock his potential and have full control over his godly powers. Since he does not seem to lose control of these powers at all during *Infinity War*, we can say that his powers at the Battle of Wakanda are at his full potential with nothing held back by mental blocks or the like.

Finally, the question of Thor's ability to genuinely deal with the threat of Thanos's omnipotence is the most significant, as this assumption is the lynchpin for the rest of the essay. Fortunately, the answer is rather simple. In the climatic final attack, Thor is able to use Stormbreaker to deflect an assault from the complete Infinity Gauntlet, even cutting through the Gauntlet's power to hit Thanos squarely in the chest. This means that when armed with Stormbreaker, Thor is on a similar level as Thanos in terms of power, meaning that Thor had a genuine chance of preventing the Snap.

Yet, Thor failed to stop Thanos multiple times. He failed to prevent the slaughter of the Asgardians, including Heimdall and Loki, in the opening scene of *Infinity War*. He failed to prevent the Snap, missing a fatal blow by less than a foot. Finally, he, along with the other Avengers, were unable to reverse the Snap when confronting a wounded Thanos at The Garden before *Endgame*'s five-year time jump. When we see Thor next in *Endgame*, he is a broken god. Thor is clearly dealing with severe post-traumatic stress, hiding away from his responsibilities not only as a founding member of the Avengers but also as King of New Asgard, leaving Valkyrie to lead in his absence.[2] He no longer has the heroic confidence and focus he had before the jump. What, then, is one supposed to do with a God who has failed?

METZ, MOLTMANN, SÖLLE: OMNIPOTENCE IN THE FACE OF ATROCITY

Now that we have clearly established the problematic of Thor's situation, we can now look to the resources of the political theologians of post-Holocaust Germany. As the first generation of theologians to be formed in a world after the devastation of World War II and the atrocities committed by the Third Reich, Metz, Moltmann, and Sölle saw it as their responsibility to address the point that theology as a discipline cannot continue to act as though such atrocities never happened. By looking at the work of these three theologians, we will gain valuable insights that will help us think through Thor's failure to prevent the Snap.

Johann Baptist Metz: Finding God in Dangerous Memories

The first theologian we will discuss is Metz, the Roman Catholic theologian who was a student of Karl Rahner. After reflecting on his own traumatic experience as a teenager forced into the German army at the end of World War II, Metz understood that theology must take a different path than what has come before.[3] The culture of contemporary Christianity, writes Metz, is an amnesiac culture; it prefers to relegate painful truths to matters of history and focus on the joyful over the sorrowful.[4] This form of Christianity, called bourgeois religion, is one that ignores the radical message of the Gospel in favor of platitudes and easy answers. It seeks to forget the dangerous memory of Christ on the cross as it would be too damning of the bourgeoise attitudes of avoidance and complicity in atrocity.[5] It is this form of Christianity that allowed many Christians to turn a blind eye to the Third Reich's discriminatory practices and allowing Jews, LGBTQ+persons, and other dissidents to be herded off to camps to be killed. Metz, critiquing this influence on theology as a discipline, writes:

> Whenever Christianity victoriously conceals its own messianic weakness, its sensorium for dangers and downfalls diminishes to an ever greater degree. Theology loses its own awareness for historical disruptions and catastrophes. Has not our Christian faith in the salvation achieved for us by Christ been covertly reified to a kind of optimism about meaning, an optimism which is no longer really capable of perceiving radical disruptions and catastrophes within meaning? Does there not exist something like a typically Christian incapacity for dismay in the face of disasters? And does this not apply with particular intensity to the average Christian (and theological) attitude toward Auschwitz?[6]

This forceful question requires us to recognize Christians as constitutive of the universal Church have a responsibility to face these horrendous evils and recognize the sorrow and suffering the world must endure.

How, then, is the universal Church to do this? Metz's answer lies in the dangerous memory of the crucified Christ. The crucifixion, carried out as a political punishment by the Roman government against someone who sought to disrupt the established order in both Roman and Jewish society, is a dangerous memory. Even if Jesus's disruption was a call for love and justice for the poor and marginalized in society, it was enough for those comfortable with the arrangements of Roman rule to see him executed. According to Metz, this memory of Jesus, which is central to the Church's mission, cannot be one of content at the comfort of one's situation with a sunny optimism.[7] Instead, it must be a memory of hopelessness and despair, requiring a disruption that liberates one from one's complacency. The dangerous memory makes one vulnerable, forcing us to look at those who suffer.[8] This stands in opposition to nationalist sentiments, which use memories to focus on past sufferings for the sake of self-assertion.[9] For Metz, a contemporary dangerous memory that permeates his German context is that of Auschwitz, that which no prior evil can truly capture by way of analogy. It is a horror not only of senseless deaths but also of widespread ignorance of events.[10] The memory of Auschwitz is meant to remind us that atrocities happen without warning and without even knowing about it; our social structures and even the best of intentions are not enough to stand guard against horrendous evils. The only hope lies in following Christ's example of solidarity with the victims and an active remembrance of their pain.

It is this concept of the dangerous memory that becomes important for evaluating Thor's status as a failed God. Thor's failures are dangerous memories, reminding the population of the MCU, the audience, and Thor himself that the God of Thunder is not truly omnipotent: that some catastrophes are beyond even Thor's power to contain. When Professor Hulk and Rocket force Thor to confront this dangerous memory, it reveals Thor's burden that is buried deep under the distractions of pizza, beer, and video games: the suffering caused by his failure.

Jürgen Moltmann: Rejecting an Impassible God

A second theologian who addresses the question of God in the face of the Holocaust is the Reformed theologian Jürgen Moltmann. Moltmann, sharing Metz's context as a German theologian after World War II, saw it was impossible to think about God in the same way after Auschwitz. God cannot be understood, writes Moltmann, as anything if not the companion in suffering of the victims of the Holocaust.[11]

Moltmann's concern for a God's relationship to suffering comes from one of the divine attributes of classical theism. Classical theism makes use of the ancient Greek philosophical traditions to make inferences to make assertions about God's nature that are distinct from what one would find in scripture. St. Thomas Aquinas, for example, dedicates the first 26 questions of the *Summa Theologiae* to making deductions about the divine attributes of a monotheistic God. The attribute Moltmann takes issue with is a corollary of divine immutability (God does not change): divine impassibility (God does not suffer). Also known as the divine apathy, the attribute of divine impassibility claims that God is swayed by emotion or pain; God is constant and untroubled by elements that can lead a person to potentially err. The reason this becomes significant is the chain reaction this has not only on understanding the nature of the monotheistic God's attributes, but also the impact it has on the believer. The argument can be formulated in the following way: if one assumes God can suffer, then one must conclude God can change, shifting between states of suffering and not suffering. If God can change, then by the classical definition of perfection as something unchanging, God is not perfect. If God is not perfect, then one cannot have perfect hope in God. This is the central point of the significance of divine impassibility: a God who is can suffer and engages in passions in a way that human beings do cannot be relied upon perfectly for the salvation of the human race.

Moltmann's critique of this point comes from several different points. One of these points is Moltmann's assertion that if God is loving, then God must suffer. Moltmann breaks the argument down into a series of direct propositions with some commentary.[12] For the sake of brevity, we will focus on the direct line of argumentation to understand what precisely Moltmann is arguing. First, Moltmann defines love as the self-communication of the good, and next claims every self-communication presupposes the capacity for self-differentiation.[13] Moltmann's next claims that in God's decision to communicate Godself,[14] God reveals God's own being, making God vulnerable to humanity just as any person makes themselves vulnerable to another person when they choose to love. In this decision, God also chooses to limit Godself, opting to set aside divine omnipotence in favor of omnipresent compassion and love as a part of creation.[15] This leads Moltmann to the conclusion that God's creative love necessarily entails suffering. He writes: "Creative love is ultimately suffering love because it is only through suffering that it acts creatively and redemptively for the freedom of the beloved. Freedom can only be made possible by suffering love. The suffering of God with the world, the suffering of God from the world, and the suffering of God for the world are the highest forms of his creative love, which desires free fellowship with the world and free response in the world."[16] In short, in choosing to create something that is not Godself and communicate with the creation, God makes Godself vulnerable to suffering. God's suffering, however, does not imply God loves any less or in a changeable way. This suffering is simply a necessary part of loving God's creation in an omnipresent way.

The second point Moltmann makes is how the vision of an apathetic God contradicts scripture, particularly the Old Testament. Relying on the work of Jewish theologian Abraham Heschel, Moltmann points out that images of the Lord as experiencing passion as an example of the Lord's freedom.[17] Since God can choose to be free of passion and suffering, God limits Godself through fidelity to the covenant made with the people of Israel. God enters into the suffering of the people of Israel through their persecution, freely engaging with a divine "self-humiliation" as an expression of love.[18] This stands in opposition to the Greek-influenced theology of divine *apatheia*, where God does not limit God's power for the sake an emotional connection grounded in love. Instead, God pours Godself out as a libation not only in the form of these self-humiliations with the people of Israel but also in sending God's son to be incarnate in the form of a first-century Palestinian Jew known as Jesus of Nazareth.

The most significant of these points is the suffering Christ experiences during his crucifixion. Moltmann considers the idea of Jesus the crucified, God incarnate hanging on the cross, has serious implications on the idea of God that classical theology has not properly considered. With the crucified Christ as the starting point for Christian theology, the philosophical conception of God mentioned above once again becomes problematic. If, Moltmann says, one holds the theological presupposition of one's God as the immutable, apathetic deity brought through philosophical reasoning, then Christ's death on the cross must be devoid of divinity.[19] The Christian conception of God must instead overcome this philosophical concept and recognize its radicality of the Christ event. Moltmann writes: "In the cross of his Son, God took upon himself not only death, so that man might be able to die comforted with the certainty that even death could not separate him from God, but still more, in order to make the crucified Christ the ground of his new creation, in which death itself is swallowed up in the victory of life and there will be 'no sorrow, no crying, and no more tears'."[20] This conception of God once again implies compassion for God's creations in a way that the God of divine apathy cannot have. God must, therefore, transcend such categories.

This transcendence takes place in the dual natures of Christ. In his analysis of the Christological doctrines of the Council of Nicea, Moltmann asserts the importance of simile in understanding the Nicean doctrine that God cannot change. While this statement is correct, says Moltmann, the definition of change cannot be taken absolutely.[21] God cannot change in the way human beings and other creatures can change. If I decide that I want a hot coffee but change my mind as I walk up to barista and order a cold brew, it is because I am finite, having changing needs and desires. God does not fit into this category and therefore cannot change in this way. If God were to change, it would be in a way totally alien to finite creatures. By this logic, God's suffering must be different than human suffering, making God therefore able to love. Since God loves God's Son, an inherent trinitarian relation, God must be able to suffer in relation to the death of Jesus on the Cross. If the crucifixion, says Moltmann, is to be understood as a divine event, then the trinitarian doctrine must be contained within the crucifixion, meaning that the suffering of the Godhead over the loss of the Son is a significant piece of trinitarian life.[22]

After this prolonged discussion of Moltmann, how can our findings apply to our discussion of Thor? There are three main ways that Moltmann's thoughts translate well to our understanding of Thor after the Snap. The first of these is the idea of a passionate God. Thor, while neither omnipotent or omniscient, is clearly passionate. He revels with his fellow Asgardians and the Avengers, feels anger at injustice and slight, and experiences grief. The second way is that of the relationship between love and suffering. It is clear that Thor loves throughout the films. He loves the people of Asgard who he has agreed to lead at the end of *Ragnarok*, his fellow Avengers, and even Jane Foster, if the *Endgame* briefing scene is to be believed. This love opens him to suffering, and when he comes to recognize that loss, he indeed suffers the grief already mentioned. The final way Moltmann's thought applies to Thor is that this suffering is intrinsic to his identity as a god. From his earliest appearances, Thor makes it clear that both Asgard and Midgard are under his protection. Thor's adamant defense of both realms makes him who he is; he identifies as a protector of the realms and their people. When he fails to protect both of these realms from Thanos's deadly encounters, it breaks him in a way that becomes central to who he is, just as the crucifixion becomes central to trinitarian doctrine. These ideas about Thor lead to the next idea that is the next logical step from Moltmann's thought: a God who suffers with the rest of humanity.

Dorothee Sölle: A God That Suffers with Us

The final theologian that enters into our conversation is Sölle, a Lutheran theologian who, distinct from Metz and Moltmann, brings a feminist perspective to her political theology. Sölle's theology provides three ideas that assist in our reflections on Thor: God's compassion as understood through the lens of the feminine metaphor for God, God's connection to humanity through grief, and the idea of God suffering alongside God's people.

In developing a feminist political theology of God's suffering, Sölle first shifts the primary analogy of God as Father to God as Mother. With this shift in metaphor, Sölle shows God not as the proud, stoic, masculine ideal, but as the embodiment of feminine virtues. She writes: "This God is our mother, who weeps over the things that we do to each other and our sisters and brothers, the animals and plants. God comforts us like a mother: God cannot make the pain go away by magic (although that occasionally happens too!) but she holds us in her lap until we stand up again with renewed strength."[23] This image of God as nurturing and compassionate, genuinely caring about the pain of God's creatures, provides a level of comfort that is foreign to the masculine ideal perpetuated by the traditional images of God.

Following Sölle's image in the preceding quote, there are a few other ideas that can be explored. The first of these is how the traditional, masculine image of God is often depicted as distant, an unappealing quality for those who are suffering. The closeness of the comforting, feminine God makes up for this statuesque quality. Second, a comforting God also implies a God involved with the world, actively attentive to the needs of God's people. Sölle claims that a God without pain is cannot truly be with God's people, meaning a God without pain cannot be the god Christians claim to worship.

Sölle goes on to develop the idea of the closeness of God by emphasizing God's connection to humanity through godly grief, which she develops from the New Testament, specifically from 2 Corinthians 7. While Sölle only cites verse 10 of the epistle, verses 8–9 provide further context:

> For even if I made you sorry with my letter, I do not regret it (though I did regret it, for I see that I grieved you with that letter, though only briefly). Now I rejoice, not because you were grieved, but because your grief led to repentance; for you felt a godly grief, so you were not harmed in any way by us. For godly grief produces a repentance that leads to salvation and brings no regret, but world grief produces death.[24]

Sölle's interpretation of St. Paul on this point is interesting because she focuses on how to link God's experience of feelings, particularly grief and pain, and how human beings experience those feelings.[25] Sölle is, like Moltmann above, emphasizing the analogical nature of the language about God, seeing that God responds to grief and pain in ways that are transformative and salvific as opposed to the worldly responses that lead to death. Given humanity's finite nature, it follows that human beings are limited in the way we respond to grief and pain, leading ultimately to death because we are not only finite but fallen. God, on the other hand is infinite and not sinful, allowing God to transform grief and pain into salvific growth that can be overcome. This is all to say that while God's response to these feelings is radically different than that of finite human beings, there is still a closeness of God to human beings in the fact that God also experiences pain and grief, showing God is not distant to human concerns.

Sölle's most significant point on the question of suffering is the affirmation that God suffers from human beings and does not leave us to suffer alone. Sölle explores two different ways that this is true: the mystical affirmation and the Bitter Christ. The mystical affirmation that God suffers with us serves as a presupposition to be able to learn from one's suffering.[26] According to Sölle, this affirmation is an affirmation of life and the undying hope that life provides. This undying hope allows for the one who experiences suffering to possess a love that "is more invulnerable and serene than in any other life situation."[27] This love grants a strength that allows one to endure that suffering and to grow from it.

The second aspect of Sölle's discussion on suffering is the bitter Christ or the idea that Christian discipleship entails suffering of one kind or another. The idea of the bitter Christ serves as a contrast to the honey-sweet Christ, which leads the believer to think that Christian discipleship allows one to be free of suffering, and to consider the suffering of the world to be insignificant and barely worthy of notice.[28] The honey-sweet Christ, of course, is a false prophet, leading believers away not only from the suffering inherent in discipleship but also from the suffering, marginalized groups that Christ ministers to in the Gospels. In recognizing that Christ suffers alongside humanity as it suffers from injustice and atrocities, God's closeness is revealed and, quite literally, incarnate.

The final question we must ask of Sölle and her work is how does this very Christocentric understanding of suffering and God's compassion aid us in our reflection on Thor. One way that Sölle's contribution adds to the conversation surrounding Thor is her emphasis on a God that weeps for us, which Thor clearly does. He is moved by not only his own pain, but also the pain of his friends. Thor's frustration at the beginning of *Endgame* could be read as simply stewing in his own failure, but it also reflects the idea that he let his friends, living and dead, down.

Another aspect of Sölle's thought that plays a role is in placing Thor's grief in a particular context: he experiences what St. Paul and Sölle would call a worldly grief, and it shows in Thor's choice to become a recluse and live a life of pizza, beer, and video games. Thor's grief is self-destructive, as it causes him to ignore his responsibilities as king. His grief is not able to transform until his conversation with his mother, comforting and consoling, reminds him that he is still worthy.

Finally, Sölle's discussion in *Suffering* provides a hermeneutic lens for analyzing Thor's conversation with his mother in 2012. It is her love, a divine love from a female god, that allows Thor to handle his grief and suffering in a way that strengthens him and prepares him to be the god the Avengers need him to be the final battle at the Avengers complex.

RETHINKING THOR (AND THE AVENGERS) AS A PASSABLE GOD

After thinking through the work of Metz, Moltmann, and Sölle, we can make the assertion that Thor is a passible god, suffering alongside his people, whether it be Asgardian or Midgardian, while facing the dangerous memory of Thanos's snap and the dust in the wind. Thor's divinity is not lessened by his pain, but perhaps it provides a comforting closeness to see a god-hero in a similar grief-ridden suffering like the rest of us. This is a quality not only of Thor but of the entire surviving Avengers roster. Captain America, Black Widow, Hawkeye/Ronin, Hulk, Iron Man, and the others all deal with grief in different, but very human, ways.

But what does this mean for the failure of Thor, and the rest of Avengers, to save half of all life from Thanos's random slaughter? As shown by all three political theologians discussed above, we cannot reflect on God, or heroes in this context, with offering consideration of what one must say to the victims that have not been saved. Heroes cannot only be judged by their failures, but these failures cannot be totally ignored either. If nothing else, we must recognize the virtue in the solidarity that the Avengers show, some in admittedly better ways than others. Perhaps this is why *Endgame* worked as well as it did: the Avengers, showing solidarity with and compassion toward those who were suffering, risked everything yet again to bring back everyone Snapped out of existence. Their passibility, in light of their failures, allows them to be redemptive heroes as well.

NOTES

1. One may be tempted to say Thor's title is now All-Father, similar to Thor's rise to the status of All-Father in Jason Aaron's *War of the Realms* #6. However, in the MCU, we are never given a clear indication that Thor has been granted the power set one would expect as All-Father other than his ability to summon the Bifrost. Therefore, to maintain continuity with the MCU exclusively, I will not refer to Thor as All-Father.

2. One aspect of Thor's post-Snap trauma that needs to be addressed is the way his weight gain was played for comedic effect. While this is intimately linked to his trauma, and the Russo brothers' failure to take the issue seriously is worthy of serious consideration, it actually distracts from the argument of this piece, so it will be left for a potential future project.

3. Johann Baptist Metz, "In Place of a Foreword: On the Biographical Itinerary of My Theology," in *A Passion for God: The Mystical-Political Dimension of Christianity*, trans. J. Matthew Ashley, New York: Paulist Press, 1998, 1–2.

4. Johann Baptist Metz, "The Church after Auschwitz," in *A Passion for God: The Mystical-Political Dimension of Christianity*, trans. J. Matthew Ashley, New York: Paulist Press, 1998, 125–6.

5. For Metz's detailed reflection on the category of bourgeois religion, see Johann Baptist Metz, *Faith in History and Society: Toward a Practical Fundamental Theology*, trans. J. Matthew Ashley, New York: Herder & Herder, 2007, 43–59.

6. Johann Baptist Metz, "Christians and Jews after Auschwitz: Being a Meditation Also on the End of Bourgeois Religion," in *Love's Strategy: The Political Theology of Johann Baptist Metz*, ed. John K. Downey, Harrisburg, PA: Trinity Press International, 1999, 45–6.

7. Johann Baptist Metz, "The Dangerous Memory of the Freedom of Jesus Christ: The Presence of the Church in Society," in *Love's Strategy: The Political Theology of Johann Baptist Metz*, ed. John K. Downey, Harrisburg, PA: Trinity Press International, 1999, 94.

8. Ekkehard Schuster and Reinhold Boschert-Kimming, *Hope Against Hope: Johann Baptist Metz and Elie Wiesel Speak Out on the Holocaust*, trans. J. Matthew Ashley, New York: Paulist Press, 1999, 34.

9. Schuster and Boschert-Kimming, *Hope Against Hope*, 34–5.

10. Schuster and Boschert-Kimming, *Hope Against Hope*, 14. Metz discusses here how the general population was unaware of what the Nazi regime was doing, mainly through the lens of a conversation with his mother. This is a significant moment for his thinking, but the details distract from the main direction of the argument.

11. Jürgen Moltmann, "The Question of Theodicy and the Pain of God," in *History and the Triune God: Contributions to Trinitarian Theology*, trans. John Bowden, New York: Crossroads, 1992, 27.

12. Jürgen Moltmann, *The Trinity and the Kingdom*, trans. Margaret Kohl, Minneapolis: Fortress Press, 1993, 57–60.

13. Moltmann, *The Trinity and the Kingdom*, 57.

14. While the three authors I am in dialogue with use the masculine pronoun for God, as was standard convention, I am actively choosing to avoid a gendered pronoun for God out of the recognition that the Christian God transcends gender and should not limited based on patriarchal biases in traditional language.

15. Moltmann, *The Trinity and the Kingdom*, 58–9.

16. Moltmann, *The Trinity and the Kingdom*, 60.

17. Moltmann, *The Trinity and the Kingdom*, 25.

18. Moltmann, *The Trinity and the Kingdom*, 27.

19. Jürgen Moltmann, *The Crucified God*, Minneapolis: Fortress Press, 2015, 312.

20. Moltmann, *The Crucified God*, 315–16.

21. Moltmann, *The Crucified God*, 336.

22. Moltmann, *The Crucified God*, 363.

23. Dorothee Sölle, "God's Pain and Our Pain," in *The Future of Liberation Theology: Essays in Honor of Gustavo Gutiérrez*, ed. Marc H. Ellis and Otto Maduro, Maryknoll, NY: Orbis Books, 1989, 326.

24. 2 Cor 7: 8-10, NSRV.
25. Sölle, "God's Pain and Our Pain," 327–8.
26. Dorothee Sölle, *Suffering*, trans. Everett Kalin, Minneapolis: Fortress Press, 1975, 127.
27. Sölle, *Suffering*, 127.
28. Sölle, *Suffering*, 129.

REFERENCES

Metz, Johann Baptist. *Faith, History, and Society: Toward a Practical Fundamental Theology*. Translated by J. Matthew Ashley. New York: Herder & Herder, 2007.

———. *Love's Strategy: The Political Theology of Johann Baptist Metz*. Edited by John K. Downey. Harrisburg, PA: Trinity Press International, 1999.

———. *A Passion for God: The Mystical-Political Dimension of Christianity*. Translated by J. Matthew Ashley. New York: Paulist Press, 1998.

Moltmann, Jürgen. *The Crucified God*. Minneapolis, MN: Fortress Press, 2015.

———. *History and the Triune God: Contributions to Trinitarian Theology*. Translated by John Bowden. New York: Crossroads, 1992.

———. *The Trinity and the Kingdom*. Translated by Margaret Kohl. Minneapolis, MN: Fortress Press, 1993.

Schuster, Ekkehard, and Reinhold Boschert-Kimming. *Hope Against Hope: Johann Baptist Metz and Elie Wiesel Speak Out on the Holocaust*. Translated by J. Matthew Ashley. New York: Paulist Press, 1999.

Sölle, Dorothee. "God's Pain and Our Pain." In *The Future of Liberation Theology: Essays in Honor of Gustavo Gutiérrez*. Edited by Marc H. Ellis and Otto Maduro, 326–33. Maryknoll, NY: Orbis Books, 1989.

———. *Suffering*. Translated by Everett Kalin. Minneapolis: Fortress Press, 1975.

Chapter 8

Mysterio as Antichrist in *Spider-Man Far From Home*

George Tsakiridis

Spider-Man: Far From Home presents a satisfying end to the arc of the Marvel Universe. Tony Stark has died, and we are able to put our focus on Spider-Man as the hero of the day. Despite the vestiges of The Avengers and their influence on the film, this film is a coming-of-age story for Peter Parker as he fully embraces the role of Spider-Man. It takes a great villain to show that greatness, and this film does not disappoint. *Spider-Man: Far From Home* exemplifies this arc by giving us Peter's toughest adversary to date, Quentin Beck, aka Mysterio. Being that Mysterio had not yet appeared in Spidey movies since the 2002 reboot, this was a welcome introduction and one that raises the stakes to a global level. It is with this framework that we see a clear parallel between Mysterio and the Antichrist in the Christian scriptures. In this chapter, I present this development in three ways. First, I look at the Antichrist of the Christian Bible and its theology. Second, I connect this to the relationship between Mysterio and Peter Parker (as well as the world) in *Spider-Man: Far From Home*. Finally, I present the full coming of age of Peter Parker in a post-Avengers world that might be viewed as Spider-Man's "millennial" age. In the same way that Christ's triumph over evil is both accomplished and yet to come, we see the fulfillment of Spider-Man's promise come to fruition in his defeat of Mysterio, the cosmic level Antichrist, which supersedes the triumph over Vulture that we find in *Spider-Man Homecoming*.

THE ANTICHRIST IN CHRISTIAN SCRIPTURE

Although the average person will jump to the book of Revelation when they hear the term "antichrist," we find this concept in many places in the

New Testament, both in the Gospels and the Epistles. For purposes of this study, and to give some diversity of genre, first we will look at references in Johannine epistles, then the Gospels, and finish with the book of Revelation and early Christianity. As a disclaimer, because of the nature of this piece, I am only briefly touching on a complex grouping of scripture and tradition.[1]

Starting with the Johannine epistles, in the book of 1 John 2:18–25, we see many references to antichrist(s).

> [18] Children, it is the last hour! As you have heard that antichrist is coming, so now many antichrists have come. From this we know that it is the last hour.[19] They went out from us, but they did not belong to us; for if they had belonged to us, they would have remained with us. But by going out they made it plain that none of them belongs to us.[20] But you have been anointed by the Holy One, and all of you have knowledge.[21] I write to you, not because you do not know the truth, but because you know it, and you know that no lie comes from the truth.[22] Who is the liar but the one who denies that Jesus is the Christ? This is the antichrist, the one who denies the Father and the Son.[23] No one who denies the Son has the Father; everyone who confesses the Son has the Father also.[24] Let what you heard from the beginning abide in you. If what you heard from the beginning abides in you, then you will abide in the Son and in the Father.[25] And this is what he has promised us, eternal life.[2]

Here, we see the development of one of the major themes of the epistle, comparing truth with lie, light with darkness. There is an emphasis on Jesus as the Christ, and anyone who denies this as the antichrist. The concept of antichrist is not limited to a single figure as many assume in referencing the book of Revelation and modern tradition. Antichrist is a term set for those who are in opposition to Christ. Notice the theological development in this passage. Those who are against Christ "went out from us." The antichrists come from within the Christian movement, though they never belonged to it. Those who are in Christ know the truth, and they know that lies do not come from truth. The emphasis is on the true confession of Christ and opposition to any lie that has no part of this truth in Christ. The main idea here is that deception does not come from truth. Those who purport to be Christians, yet aim to deceive, are not of Christ, but are antichrists. Not only is there an emphasis on what an antichrist looks like, but an even stronger one on what one "anointed by the Holy One" looks like. If one knows the truth, he can discern a lie. If one knows Christ, he will see through the deception of the antichrist.

Further, the author of 1 John is drawing on a number of possible Jewish motifs in using the term "antichrist." In his commentary on the Johannine epistles, Raymond Brown mentions four: "The Sea Monster," "The Satan or Angelic Adversary," "The Human Ruler Embodying Evil," and "The False

Prophet." He states that "the most comprehensive combination" of these images is found in Revelation.[3] The author of 1 John insists that it is the last hour because of the antichrists that have already appeared, indicating that the end is near. This passage connects the antichrist to the final apocalypse, linking it to other New Testament texts such as Matthew 24 and Revelation 13.

We also see mention of the term antichrist in 2 John 7. It states, "Many deceivers have gone out into the world, those who do not confess that Jesus Christ has come in the flesh; any such person is the deceiver and the antichrist!"[4] This is particularly interesting as there seems to be some allusion to a Gnostic view of Christ—one in which Christ was not of flesh. Implicitly this tells us that anyone who deceives others in regard to Christ is an antichrist. The emphasis is not necessarily on the apocalyptic end but on the act of deception itself. Deception, however, in regard to Christ might be seen as an apocalyptic act because of the cosmic nature of the person of Christ and His salvation. The deception that is connected to the ultimate truth of Jesus Christ is itself apocalyptic evil because it undermines the future hope of eternity for those that follow Christ. The commentator I. Howard Marshall mentions that this verse is a fulfillment of the prophecy that Jesus made in Mark 13:5–6, 22, that many will come in His name to deceive.[5] There are obviously differences of opinion as to the interpretation, but this general approach to the antichrist is consistent with the passages in view.

Moving forward to the Gospels, we see a continued apocalyptic theme of the antichrist(s). This is clear in Matthew 24 and Mark 13. In Matthew 24, Jesus is presenting the many deceivers who will appear in the end times. In verses 23–24, he states, "Then if anyone says to you, 'Look! Here is the Messiah'! or 'There he is'!—do not believe it. For false messiahs and false prophets will appear and produce great signs and omens, to lead astray, if possible, even the elect."[6] Here, the setting is the end of days, the judgment, and there is a warning against false messiahs or antichrists. In verse 15, Jesus has already linked back to the prophet Daniel's words, both looking forward to a final apocalyptic day. The Matthew text follows Mark's lead in presenting this warning, adding some material from Q.[7] These passages focus on the coming judgment and the deception that will take place in that time. Notice the emphasis on the deception in verse 24, stating that even the elect would be deceived if that were possible. Jesus is presenting this as a great deception, one that would fool anyone whom it would be possible to fool.

The book of Revelation puts a cap on the discussion of the term antichrist, presenting this final enemy for Christ to overcome. When most people describe the Antichrist they are thinking of these texts. In this apocalyptic text, the Antichrist is a deceiver to the nations, who is leading many astray. In chapter 13 of Revelation, we see this beast, who is like a leopard, with bear's feet, and the mouth of a lion. This beast impresses his followers by overcoming a mortal wound in verse 3: "One of its heads seemed to have received a death-blow, but its moral wound had been healed. In amazement the whole earth followed the beast."[8] This antichrist is allowed to destroy the righteous and to rule over the nations in verses seven and eight: "it was allowed to make war on the saints and to conquer them. It was given authority over every tribe and people and language and nation, and all the inhabitants of the earth will worship it" except for those found in the "book of life of the Lamb."[9] Further on in verse 11–14, we see a second beast that speaks for the first. Specifically in verses 13–14, this beast "performs great signs . . . and by the signs that it is allowed to perform on behalf of the beast, it deceives the inhabitants of the earth, telling them to make an image for the beast that had been wounded by the sword and yet lived."[10] The chapter finishes with the well-known mark of the beast whose number is 666.

Looking at this passage, we see the Antichrist ruling over the nations, deceiving them in opposition to the true Christ of the Christian scriptures. We see that the beast gets his authority from Satan, paralleling the authority of the Lamb (Christ) who is given that authority by God the Father.[11] The main emphasis in the passage is on the deception of the nations through an antichrist. The imagery is drawing on the Roman Empire, as the powers of this world are those opposed to the true Christ. Revelation sets up this final showdown with the beast as an ultimate deception before Christ comes to save the world from evil for the last time. It is set in an apocalyptic genre, maximizing the tension and power of evil as the greater the evil, the greater the good needed to overcome it.

To further the discussion, we see references to antichrist in the Early Church. As early as the *Didache* we see mention of the antichrist, who will "come as the Son of God, doing miracles."[12] The Early Church was rife with descriptions of the Antichrist, which makes perfect sense considering much of the early writings are a systematization of biblical scripture in the context of the challenges they were facing. Irenaeus, Tertullian, and Cyprian of Carthage all discussed the Antichrist in the first three centuries, with differing opinions and emphases.[13] Specifically, in the cases of Tertullian and Cyprian, they saw the Roman Empire of their day connected to the Antichrist and end times, though in very different ways.[14] Beginning early on, and continuing to the present, theologians and clergy have looked for the Antichrist among their contemporaries for centuries. The twentieth and twenty-first centuries have been no different with emphasis on the pretribulational/premillennial rapture and the popularity of the fictional book series starting with *Left Behind* and Tim LaHaye.[15] That said, what does this have to do with *Spider-Man: Far From Home*?

MYSTERIO AS ANTICHRIST

Okay true believers, I mean, readers, you have been patient. It is time to look at the world of Spider-Man. In the most recent installment, *Spider-Man: Far From Home*, Mysterio embodies the Antichrist in an attempt to fill the void of leadership left behind by Tony Stark and The Avengers. In this film, we see the culmination of evil in this same void. Spider-Man is left to be the messiah of the world in the absence of the Avengers. He is reluctant to take on this mantle, given his age and insecurity, but also his humility and his character. Peter Parker is trying to make it in the world of high school and hormones while being asked to take on leadership and heroism of a cosmic nature. It is in the midst of this struggle and the void of leadership that the Antichrist arises: Quentin Beck, aka, Mysterio.

Mysterio is first revealed to us through the confirmation of a rumor. Early in the movie, we find Nick Fury and Maria Hill investigating an unusual storm in Ixtenco, Mexico, coming face-to-face with Mysterio and the earth monster. This sets the deception for Spider-Man indirectly, through Nick Fury. Peter Parker's first true encounter with Mysterio happens about twenty minutes into the film, with the water monster attacking Venice. Peter is able to help Mysterio defeat this monster. It is not until much later that the audience is made aware of the deception. If you are viewing the film, you will get to almost fifty-four minutes in before there is a strong hint of deception, bringing the viewer along for the ride.[16]

That said, the four elemental monsters (air, earth, water, and fire) are illusions with a narrative laid over them—that Quentin Beck is from another dimension and trying to save earth. He was not able to save his own world, but now is set up to make the ultimate sacrifice for our world. He carries out this illusion using projectors to create the image, and drones to create actual damage.[17] It is an intricate and grandiose plan to deceive both Spider-Man and the nations. We see parallels in the film and the biblical narrative. An antichrist (Mysterio) rises up to deceive the nations, and presents an illusion so real as even to deceive "the elect," in this case our hero. There are three major parallels between Mysterio and antichrist. First, the deception is on a massive scale. The intention is to deceive the nations. Second, the ultimate battle is over truth. Third, the "Antichrist" appears as good. It is through this misrepresentation that the deception takes place. This is because the ultimate intention of the deception is the undermining of the hero in our story—Spider-Man, the proxy for Tony Stark.

First, one of the strongest themes we see in this film is the cosmic/global nature of the deception. Mysterio himself repeats this theme multiple times in the movie. At the 72-minute mark, Mysterio states, "We need maximum damage . . . more casualties, more coverage . . . I mean if I'm going to be the next Iron Man, I need to save the world from an Avengers level threat. But when its new savior descends, all those casualties will be forgotten."[18] He re-emphasizes the importance of the substantiality of the threat as the final battle settles on London. Maria Hill says, "it's a hundred times bigger than the previous ones." A few minutes later Mysterio states, "Now, that is an Avengers-level threat."[19] It is only by creating a threat on such a grandiose scale that Mysterio can gain the full trust of the nations in the same way the biblical Antichrist is set up as an apocalyptic figure to deceive the world.

In the aftermath of the Avengers films, where cosmic battles are the norm, Spider-Man is also brought into a cosmic level battle in his engagement with Mysterio. This point is especially notable because of the movement through Europe. Despite Spider-Man's continual reminder in this movie and *Spider-Man: Homecoming*[20] that he is just a "friendly neighborhood Spider-Man," he is fighting on a broader stage, one in which the very nature of truth is at stake.

This brings us to the great deception, the second major parallel, which is the battle over truth. Because of the cosmic nature of the battle, the very essence of truth is in the balance. During the first battle scene where Spider-Man is fighting Mysterio's illusions, the latter states, "I created Mysterio to give the world someone to believe in. I control the truth. Mysterio is the truth."[21] His illusion is focused on worldwide delusion, bringing everyone into his truth. This is in direct opposition to Jesus Christ's statement in John 14:6: "I am the way, and the truth, and the life. No one comes to the father except through me."[22] Mysterio is claiming to be the ultimate arbiter of truth, raising his deception to a definitive level.

In this vein, the battle is not just over limited power, it is over the nature of absolute truth. The ultimate triumph over evil is accomplished through the truth. As it states in John 8:32, "you will know the truth, and the truth will make you free."[23] Spider-Man defeats Mysterio by seeing through the illusion. He sees Mysterio's mirage for what it is, which allows him to deal with the reality of the evil. This plays out in the final battle scene with the drones, and then ultimately in the Tower Bridge interior where he prevents Mysterio from killing him because he now sees through the illusion. The truth allows him to avoid his own destruction. He uses his spider-sense to see the lie: "Your lies are over, Beck."[24] At this point, Spider-Man has his mask off, also revealing his true nature.[25] Soon after, Beck utters one of the critical lines of the movie: "People, they need to believe. And nowadays . . . they'll believe anything."[26]

In this process, Mysterio goes so far as to delude himself. In the 99th minute of the film, he calls for the illusion to be killed and when warned about this he says, "They'll see what I want them to see!"[27] Quentin Beck's lust for power and absolute control of the message leads to even his own delusion. If truth is up for grabs, even those who try to manipulate truth may be manipulated by their own deception. As viewers, we never find out what Mysterio had planned for an explanation, but it is clear that his message of control and his declaration of truth reach beyond the rational. If Mysterio is indeed the truth, then anything he utters is a declaration of truth. His deception continues, even beyond death, as the scene after the initial credits reveal a fake news story with J. Jonah Jameson. In this story, he presents a doctored clip that makes Spider-Man look like the villain, and reveals his secret identity to the world.[28]

This theme is further emphasized by other characters, with MJ being an important narrator for the nature of truth. When Brad is trying to out Peter's supposed backroom tryst with the woman at the rest stop, he states, "Is no one else here interested in the truth?" MJ retorts, "The very concept of objective truth is fading out of the world," quoting George Orwell, as Brad notes. A bit later, when she is trapped in the London Tower vault with Happy, Flash, Ned, and Betty and they all share confessions, she utters, "I'm obsessed with telling the truth even if it hurts other people's feelings."[29] Perhaps, it is the virtuous nature of Peter Parker/Spider-Man that attracts him to MJ as a truth-teller. In the later scene on Tower Bridge where they declare their feelings for one another, he seems to reveal that MJ's quirky, direct nature is attractive. She is a constant source of blunt truth, both for the viewer and for Peter.

Third, the deception aims at creating the image of goodness for Quentin Beck/Mysterio. This is due to his ultimate goal of usurping the power that was given to Peter Parker/Spider-Man, who is now the representative of Tony Stark on earth. Without pressing the metaphor too far, we do see at least some parallels between Tony Stark as God the Father and Peter Parker as Jesus Christ. If we were really pressing the issue, we might even look to E.D.I.T.H. as a representation of the Holy Spirit. I realize this parallel is flawed due to the imperfect nature of our heroes (and of metaphor itself), but there is imagery to be found here that might bear further exploration.

In viewing the treatment of truth in *Spider-Man: Far From Home*, we see the juxtaposition of truth and deception in the same way the biblical text presents it to us. Anyone who deceives is called antichrist. Mysterio is the chief deceiver, making him the ultimate antichrist of our cosmic struggle. Just as the Antichrist usurps power from Christ, Mysterio's aim is at usurping the power that Peter Parker has been given by Tony Stark through E.D.I.T.H. He is aiming to fill the void that Tony has left, the void that is meant to be filled by Peter. This is exemplified around the midpoint of the film when Mysterio gives a speech to his support team, following the great deception he has just pulled on Peter Parker in the bar. He states:

> Tony Stark is gone. There is a window of opportunity and someone will step up. But these days, you can be the smartest guy in the room, the most qualified, and no one cares. Unless you're flying around with a cape or shooting lasers

from your hands, no one will even listen. Well, I've got a cape and lasers. With our technology and with E.D.I.T.H., Mysterio will be the greatest hero on earth! And everyone will listen. Not to a boosy man-child. Not to a hormonal teenager. To me and to my very wealthy crew. To us. To Mysterio! To Peter Parker. Poor kid. Let's get to work.[30]

Mysterio's whole play utilizes the leadership vacuum left by Tony Stark. Mysterio is a manufactured Christ, an antichrist, and one for which the public is ready.

I would also be remiss if I were not to mention the royal purple cape of Mysterio, which echoes the triumphal inauguration of his perceived royalty. It is true that the original Mysterio of Spider-Man lore also had a purple cape, but the writers of *Spider-Man: Far From Home* did a masterful job of alluding to the cape ever so slightly as to indicate its importance. In the lead up to the final scene, Mysterio mentions the cape, which Janice is steam cleaning to get wrinkles out because he might meet the queen in a few hours. This continues later around the 99th–100th minute when she asks him if he still needs the cape when he kills the illusion. He replies affirmatively. The fact of the matter is that Quentin Beck sees himself as royalty and buys into his own illusion of power.

In sum, we see in the narrative of the film that Quentin Beck, aka Mysterio, is clearly the figure of the Antichrist for the present Marvel age. He is the great deceiver, attempting to fill the shoes of the true messiah, Spider-Man. The battle hinges on what is truth, and ultimately the truth that wins out over this great deception. Spider-Man is the rightful owner of E.D.I.T.H., the savior, that will save the day.

SPIDER-MAN/PETER PARKER AS THE FULFILLMENT OF THE PROMISE

In his defeat of Mysterio, by seeing through the deception to the truth, Spider-Man has reached his true fulfillment as a superhero. He is no longer just "your friendly neighborhood Spider-Man," but as the film's title alludes to, he is now far from home and has conquered evil on a global level. As a fan of the traditional character, part of this is unappealing, because I believe the true nature of Spider-Man is to be the hero of New York; that is where he belongs. But, as the Marvel Universe of the film shows us, he has taken a role far beyond this. Even in *Spider-Man: Homecoming* he does some of his most heroic work in Washington D.C. It is almost a paradox to see the ultimate promise fulfilled in Peter Parker because it is his humility that has prevented him from taking on this mantle. We first see this in *Homecoming*, as he declines to join the Avengers, and then in *Far from Home*, where he passes Tony Stark's mantle on to a great deceiver before realizing it is his responsibility to hold. This is in direct opposition to Iron Man/Tony Stark, who is the antithesis of humility.

Humility is a primary virtue in the Christian tradition and is key to the incarnation of Christ, as well as ascetic development. We see this initially in the Christian scriptures. The exemplification of this theology is found in Philippians 2:6–8, speaking of Jesus Christ, "who, though he was in the form of God, did not regard equality with God as something to be exploited, but emptied himself, taking the form of a slave, being born in human likeness. And being found in human form, he humbled himself and became obedient to the point of death—even death on a cross."[31] As with the true Christ of Christianity, the messiah of *Spider-Man: Far From Home*, shows humility. Unlike Jesus Christ, however, he initially avoids taking up the mantle of Tony Stark. He passed on The Avengers in *Homecoming*, and he does it again here, till the point at which he can no longer deny his birthright. It is after he realizes he has also been deceived by Mysterio that he works to make it right. His virtue shines in his attempt to save his friends and to become the caretaker of the power of The Avengers in the "person" of E.D.I.T.H.

Humility is also notable in the Desert Fathers and the ascetic tradition of Christianity. It is a continued theme in the *Apothegmata*. John the Dwarf states in verse 22, "'Humility and the fear of God are above all virtues'." Speaking of a spiritual old man and drawing on Luke 14:11, he also states in verse 38, "The more he wished to flee from the glory, the more he was glorified. In this was accomplished that which is written: 'He who humbles himself will be exalted'."[32] John of the Thebaid also states the monk must first gain humility, and Macarius the Great recalls the story of a devil who could not defeat him; he did all that Macarius did, but did not have the power of humility.[33] I could go on, but if one studies the Christian tradition (as well as other religious traditions), one sees that humility is one of the chief virtues. It is from this foundation Peter Parker emerges.

There are many hints of Peter's humility and unease with being the hero/messiah of our story. Early on in the film, Nick Fury mentions to him, "Uneasy lies the head that wears the crown," as he hands him the glasses.[34] Even the error he commits in giving E.D.I.T.H. to Quentin Beck is founded on a misguided approach to humility. Peter's sympathetic nature is used against him as he is roped into Beck's narrative about his wife dying on another world. In fact, in the first ten minutes of the film we see Peter's unease with being a cosmic hero when he is confronted by reporters about taking over for Tony Stark. The pressure is building. Mysterio later plays on the insecurity of Peter in his illusion, attempting to find out who he told about Mysterio's deception.

Contrast this with the fulfillment of Peter's promise as the messiah as he overcomes the deception of Mysterio, first giving E.D.I.T.H. to him in error, and then giving up his friends in a misguided attempt to save them. After connecting with Happy, he rains down from the clouds in the 97th minute, mirroring a Christ-like triumphal entry to earth. This time, he is equipped with knowledge of the deception, and affirming to himself that it is not real. Knowledge is now added to his humility and this knowledge allows him to fight the drones. It reaches its ultimate fulfillment in the final battle with Mysterio inside Tower Bridge. At this point, he faces Beck's illusions once again, but this time he puts trust in his spider sense. I think it is helpful to view this as trusting the unseen truth versus the seen lie. It is reminiscent of 1 Samuel 16. In this passage, the Lord is speaking to Samuel as Samuel is looking for the next king of Israel to replace Saul. The person in question is David, in contrast to his brother Eliab. 1 Samuel 16:7 states, "'Do not look on his appearance or on the height of his stature, because I have rejected him; for the Lord does not see as mortals see; they look on the outward appearance, but the Lord looks on the heart'."[35] This is a continued theme of Christian (and Jewish) scripture. The inner human is what matters, not the outer appearance. Just like Mysterio's grandiose illusions and his formidable stature, they are a deception. They cover the rot and impurity of the inner self that Quentin Beck is. He is an illusion of heroism. On the other hand, Peter, as Spider-Man, is small in stature, and humble in heart, and his inner self is pure. When Peter trusts his spider-sense (or as the movie playfully calls it, his Peter-tingle), he sees the truth by trusting the power that is within him. He sees through Mysterio's ultimate lie, saving the world, as well as his own life. Even in the aftermath of Beck's defeat, he asks E.D.I.T.H. if it is real. He is now no longer naïve to the lie. He is the "Christ" of the story, while Mysterio is the Antichrist. Even in the humorous epilogue scene, the voiceover talks about him facing a lot of deception, but that he is tired of the lies. The film then cuts to Happy and May. Even in humor, the emphasis on truth is clear.

CONCLUSION

In sum, *Spider-Man: Far From Home* presents a great metaphor for the Christian tradition's narrative of Jesus Christ and the overcoming of the Antichrist. Deception presents itself as heroism and lies as truth. The Christian scriptures continually warn us to be vigilant against those who deceive, and this film does the same.[36] Both present an apocalyptic level threat that the messiah of the story must overcome. Although the stakes are clearly higher in the Christian apocalypse, *Spider-Man: Far From Home* mirrors the message found in traditional Christianity. We can draw some important truths. First, one must know the truth and be aware of the deception, especially darkness that looks like light. Second, the outward appearance is often deceiving. If one knows the truth, they will not be fooled by the lie. They will look beyond the surface. Third, good will triumph over evil in a final sense. Though many are deceived, the true Christ will overcome this apocalyptic deception.

Spider-Man is an enjoyable character, and Tom Holland's recent incarnation of him on screen is both entertaining and true to the spirit of the character. That said, we can learn through the virtuous character of Spider-Man. His innocence and joy are virtues that have become less prominent in hero genres of the twenty-first century. Spider-Man can point us to the greater good and help humanity reexamine their own virtue and faith, whether they subscribe to Christian belief or not. Although Mysterio is the Antichrist of *Spider-Man: Far From Home*, the savior in the story points us to a virtuous life and the Christian message that good will triumph over evil, not just in the "neighborhood" but also in a cosmic sense.

NOTES

1. We should also be aware of other relevant passages, such as 2 Thessalonians 2:1–12 that could be used in this discussion, but hey, you're here to read about Mysterio, so we don't want spend too much time on exegesis.

2. *The Holy Bible: New Revised Standard Version* (New York: Oxford University Press, 1989).

3. Raymond E. Brown, *The Epistles of John*, The Anchor Yale Bible (New Haven, CT: Yale University Press, 1982), 333–335.

4. *The Holy Bible*, NRSV.

5. I. Howard Marshall, *The Epistles of John*, The New International Commentary on the New Testament (Grand Rapids, MI: William B. Eerdmans Publishing Company, 1978), 69.

6. *The Holy Bible*, NRSV.

7. M. Eugene Boring, "The Gospel of Matthew: Introduction, Commentary, and Reflections," in *The New Interpreter's Bible: Volume VIII* (Nashville: Abingdon Press, 1995), 441.

8. *The Holy Bible*, NRSV.

9. *The Holy Bible*, NRSV.

10. *The Holy Bible*, NRSV.

11. Craig R. Koester, *Revelation*, The Anchor Yale Bible (New Haven, CT: Yale University Press, 2014), 570.

12. Koester, *Revelation*, 534.

13. Koester, *Revelation*, 534–5.

14. Koester, *Revelation*, 535. Tertullian saw a unified Rome holding off the Antichrist, whereas Cyprian saw the Decian and Valerian persecutions as a premonition of the Antichrist to come.

15. Tim LaHaye and Jerry B. Jenkins, *Left Behind: A Novel of Earth's Last Days* (Carol Stream, IL: Tyndale House Publishers, 1995).

16. As I am assuming those reading this chapter have seen the film, I will present the narrative from that point of view. In other words, there are going to be "spoilers."

17. I might even argue that the drones appear like an apocalyptic plague of locusts.

18. *Spider-Man: Far From Home*, Directed by Jon Watts (Culver City, CA: Columbia Pictures, 2019).

19. *Spider-Man: Far From Home*, 2019.

20. *Spider-Man: Homecoming*, Directed by Jon Watts (Culver City, CA: Columbia Pictures, 2017).

21. *Spider-Man: Far From Home*, 2019.

22. *The Holy Bible*, NRSV.

23. *The Holy Bible*, NRSV.

24. *Spider-Man: Far From Home*, 2019.

25. I believe a study of the Peter Parker/Spider-Man identity divide would be interesting in viewing both *Spider-Man: Far From Home* and *Spider-Man: Homecoming*. He is more forthcoming with his secret identity than in other incarnations of the character, and a closer study of when he has his mask on or off and what is going on in those scenes might be enlightening.

26. *Spider-Man: Far From Home*, 2019.

27. *Spider-Man: Far From Home*, 2019.

28. I must take this opportunity to say that the use of the Go-Go's *Vacation*, while being one of my favorite songs, is a perfect match for this film.

29. *Spider-Man: Far From Home*, 2019.

30. *Spider-Man: Far From Home*, 2019.

31. *The Holy Bible*, NRSV.

32. *The Sayings of the Desert Fathers: The Alphabetical Collection.* Trans. by Benedicta Ward. Cistercian Studies 59 (Kalamazoo, MI: Cistercian Publications, 1975), 90, 93.

33. *The Sayings of the Desert Fathers*, 106, 129–130.

34. *Spider-Man: Far From Home*, 2019.

35. *The Holy Bible*, NRSV.

36. In the 55th minute of the film, Nick Fury even warns about staying vigilant, as this is not the last threat they will face. The context is the aftermath of Quentin Beck's defeat of the fire monster—the height of his deception.

REFERENCES

Boring, M. Eugene. "The Gospel of Matthew: Introduction, Commentary, and Reflections." In *The New Interpreter's Bible: Volume VIII*. Nashville: Abingdon Press, 1995.

Brown, Raymond E. *The Epistles of John*. The Anchor Yale Bible. New Haven, CT: Yale University Press, 1982.

The Holy Bible, New Revised Standard Version. New York: Oxford University Press, 1989.

Koester, Craig R. *Revelation.* The Anchor Yale Bible. New Haven, CT: Yale University Press, 2014.

LaHaye, Tim, and Jerry B. Jenkins. *Left Behind: A Novel of Earth's Last Days.* Carol Stream, IL: Tyndale House Publishers, 1995.

Marshall, I. Howard. *The Epistles of John.* The New International Commentary on the New Testament. Grand Rapids, MI: William B. Eerdmans Publishing Company, 1978.

The Sayings of the Desert Fathers: The Alphabetical Collection. Trans. by Benedicta Ward. Cistercian Studies 59. Kalamazoo, MI: Cistercian Publications, 1975.

Spider-Man: Far From Home. Directed by Jon Watts. Culver City, CA: Columbia Pictures, 2019.

Spider-Man: Homecoming. Directed by Jon Watts. Culver City, CA: Columbia Pictures, 2017.

Part III

DECONSTRUCTING NORMS, IMAGINING THE NEW

Chapter 9

Science and the Marvel Cinematic Universe

Deconstructing the Boundary between Science, Technology, and Religion

Lisa Stenmark

Many of us involved in the task of exploring the relationship between religion and science (the "Science and Religion Discourse," or SRD) have argued that there is a need to reexamine our assumptions about the relationship between religion and science, in order to develop a framework for discourse that is more prophetic, meaning more able to challenge structures of injustice and envision a way forward that is more just and more inclusive. One of the main stumbling blocks to developing this prophetic vision is our inability to think beyond the categories themselves so that we implicitly reinforce the underlying beliefs and practices encompassed by "religion" and "science," including, in particular, colonial ideologies. I say stumbling block, but a more apt metaphor is a thicket, because "colonial ideology" does not describe one or two ideas but a myriad of intertwined and entangled beliefs and practices that together encompass the worldview we designate as "modernity." At the heart of these narratives is a view of reality, and our ideas about that reality, as both singular and universal, meaning that there is one true reality and one Truth about that reality, a truth that is necessarily universal and applies to everyone, everywhere. This framework leads to the idea of universal religion (there is One God, and so there is one Truth about that God that is true for everyone, everywhere), universal science (there is one reality, and one truth about that reality which is true for everyone everywhere) and universal history (there is one stream of time, one history, which involves all people everywhere). This singular/universal view of reality/truth is connected to a number of other strands of colonial ideology, including narratives of progress, scientific triumphalism, and center-periphery thinking—in which some ideas and practices are designated as primitive, backward, or "non-modern" in order to define other ideas as rational, scientific or "modern." Until we can disentangle these ideas, we will never be able to transform our practices. But this is a herculean task, because the innumerable strands of colonial ideology are intertwined, and they all support and reinforce one another, so while the individual ideas may be small and seemingly insignificant, and even easy to identify, each strand is held in place by the others, so that no matter how determined we might be, when we pull and tug it is impossible to remove.

I have argued that science fiction can be a valuable tool for exposing these underlying ideologies and for rethinking our understanding of "religion" and "science" and the relationship between them. As a genre, science fiction has long been "deployed as a means to think about . . . contemporary social, cultural, political, and technological transformations" and to reveal and comment on "the delusions we all share."[1] Science fiction is particularly important for those of us involved in the religion and science discourse not only because it is closely connected to the emergence of scientific rationalities, but because of its connection to colonial ideologies as well.[2] While the superhero genre is not necessarily science fiction, the Marvel Cinematic Universe (MCU), because of its emphasis on science and technology and its commitment to a scientific framework can clearly be classified as science fiction, which makes it a useful resource for those interested in exploring the relationship between science, technology, and religion.

In this paper, I begin by examining the basic framework for understanding science and technology in the MCU, focusing on Phase One, and especially *Iron Man* and *Captain America*.[3] Phase One establishes science and technology as positive forces, a utopian view in which (Western) science and technology are seen as the keys to a good global future. Utopian visions are connected to dystopian warnings, however, which means that the MCU can provide resources for a prophetic critique of the dangers of overconfidence in science and technology and warnings about their misuse. There are limits to this critique, however, largely because the MCU does not question the centrality of Western science and technology or challenge the basic narratives of progress, and so it does not address the underlying ideologies behind a particular view of science, making it insufficient for a fundamental rethinking of our understanding of science and technology. This more fundamental challenge can be found in a variety of tropes that lie outside what might be called "mainstream" science fiction, and in the broader category of speculative fiction, which includes afro- and indigenous futurism, postcolonial and third world science fiction, and other genres.[4] These various genres and subgenres include a variety of tropes and narratives that can help reveal and disentangle the colonial ideology embedded in our construction of science, and thus of religion. In the third part of this paper, I will look at three that are part of the MCU: Magic, (Thor, Dr. Strange), which problematizes center/periphery thinking in the relationship between religion and science; Afrofuturism (Black Panther) which challenges the modern/colonial narratives of progress about science and technology; and the multiverse, which challenges the view of singular truth/reality. While each of these has the potential to "queer" our understanding of religion and science, revealing what is hidden and obscured by colonial ideologies, none of these fulfill their potential within the MCU, largely because they are subsumed into a framework that remains committed to a Western scientific framework that is singular, universal, and progressive. My point is not that there is something wrong with the MCU, quite the opposite, I am not only a fan, I think that the MCU and other forms of science fiction have a lot to offer as we attempt to rethink our way of approaching the relationship between religion and science, but they fail because they address one aspect but miss another. The thicket of coloniality is dense and complex, and addressing it will be both difficult and require narratives that are messy.

SCIENCE AND TECHNOLOGY AND UTOPIA

The attitude of the MCU toward science and technology is fundamentally positive, with science and technology seen as keys to a better life. This is a utopian view, but one which reflects more contemporary sensibilities than the story told by Sir Thomas More. Through his play on words, More's *Utopia* described a good place (*eutopia*) that is no place (*outopia*), a thought experiment that allowed More and his contemporaries to critique the flaws of their society by *imagining* a place that existed apart from and in contrast to that society. The utopian vision of the MCU reflects a more modern sensibility where utopia is projected into the future, and is therefore more properly described as *euchronia:* the good future. Influenced by Enlightenment optimism, utopia became a historical possibility, a view that was further transformed by a progressive view of history, theories of global evolution, and attitudes toward Western science and technology. The good future was a global future, a historical goal that was increasingly dominated by both science and technology. Technology—ships, time machines, and space ships—did not just allow one to travel to the good place, they became tools for creating a utopian future, which was itself defined in terms of scientific advancements and technological mastery of the natural and material world.

Although utopia and science fiction are distinct genres, in contemporary literature they have become closely linked and both reflect important elements of colonial ideologies.[5] This connection is temporal—More's utopia was modeled on the travel literature of the times which described the "discovery" of other people and other ways of life, and science fiction also develops as a distinct literary genre in tandem with colonialism growing confidence in Western science and technology—but also ideological, reflecting important components of colonial ideology, including a history as progress along a single, universal timeline along which all human societies develop (with some being further along than others), progress as the ability of humans to control and intervene in natural processes, largely through technology and science, and other narratives important for justifying and maintaining European colonialism. Europeans' perception of their own material superiority, "particularly as manifested in scientific thought and technological innovation," was a key component of the civilizing-mission ideology that justified Europe's global hegemony and the way European power was exercised.[6] This sense of superiority was not new, of course, but prior to the nineteenth century it was Christian faith, not mastery of the natural world, that was seen as the source of European distinctiveness and superiority. By the end of the nineteenth century, Europeans had come to believe that it was their ability to understand and control nature by means of science and technology that proved that Europeans were culturally superior.[7] Science developed *only* in Europe because it was *only* in Europe that science and reason had triumphed "over the forces of superstition and ignorance"; while other cultures remained "unable to extract their scientific and technological concerns" from superstition and religion, lacking the "political climate for self-critical thought."[8] The ability to control the natural environment marked the line between savagery and civilization, and the evangelizing impulse was now directed toward "civilizing" indigenous peoples and improving the conditions of their lives. The religious impulse was not gone, but the White Man's Burden was no longer the command to evangelize the heathen, but the command to save the savages, and "Fill full the mouth of Famine, And bid the sickness cease" on a global scale.

MCU PHASE ONE: UTOPIAN VISIONS AND DYSTOPIAN WARNINGS

Phase one of the MCU provides an excellent example of a utopian view of science and technology, with Iron Man and Captain America, Hulk and The Avengers, each demonstrating an overwhelming faith in technology and science. Scientific and technological prowess are celebrated and glorified, connected to power (especially military power) and a sense of "advancement," reflecting a utopian belief in the ability of science to create a better future. Captain America is a super-soldier, a perfect man created by science: 6'2" tall, muscular, with super strength, speed, agility, reflexes, and, of course, blue eyes with bits of green.[9] When confronted by a reporter about dealing in weapons of death, Stark echoes Kipling's admonition to Fill full the mouth of Famine, and bid the sickness cease: "do you plan to report on the millions we've saved by advancing medical technology or kept from starvation without intelli-crops."[10] In the MCU, technology and science are tools that secure peace and freedom and the repeated message is that science and technology will save us, protect us and lead to a better world. Captain America, Iron Man, and the rest of the Avengers are tasked with securing peace and protecting the world, and later the universe and the multiverse. And in true White Man's Burden fashion, the world is rarely grateful, and the Avengers must face "the blame of those ye better."

The catch, of course, is that global peace and prosperity is defined and achieved on Western terms—the science and technology that will save us is Western, as are the scientists who are our saviors. In this first phase at least, all of the superheroes are Western, almost all are men (the exception is Black Widow—but she is a weapon—an object of science, a tool, and not herself a scientist),[11] and none of the scientists are women, except for Jane Foster. Even when women exist, they are peripheral: Captain America's love interest ceases to exist after the origin story; Jane Foster, Thor's love interest, the sole female scientist, disappears after her original appearance, and virtually all of her action occurs off screen (and is described by male characters); Hawkeye's wife, Laura Barton, sits in a farmhouse in the middle of nowhere with their kids, waiting in limbo for him to return (it's not clear what she does out there, although it's possible that she is an artist since there are art supplies laying around).

The connection between advanced science and technology and the West is especially pronounced in *Iron Man*, where the technological achievements of Stark Industries and the West are contrasted with those of the Afghani rebels who attempt to steal his tech (presumably unable to come up with it on their own). When Stark is demonstrating his new weapons system–Jericho—he tells the military brass that these weapons are so advanced that after seeing them in action, "the bad guys won't even want to come out of their caves." And they do, of course, live in caves, in "primitive" conditions, heating themselves, and even smelting metal, with open fires. These Middle Eastern savages beg, bribe, and steal technology that they do not understand. The leader of the rebels, anxious to get his hands on Western tech, observes that at one point the bow and arrow were the pinnacles of technology, and this allowed Ghengis Khan to rule a great empire. The suggestion is that the Afghani's have not advanced much past that stage, so they must rely on Stark (Western) weapons. As Obadiah Stane tells Raza Hamidmi Al-Wazar, Afghani leader, "Technology has always been your Achilles heel in this part of the world."

Even casual readers of contemporary science fiction will by now have taken at least some issue with my emphasis on the utopian elements of modern SF, since so much of contemporary SF is dystopian. But, dystopia is closely related to utopia, incorporating the logic of utopia and euchronia. Both utopia and dystopia project the present into the future, they just predict that things will turn out badly. Dystopias begin with a utopian ideal that somehow becomes distorted. Furthermore, while dystopias seem pessimistic, they actually share utopian optimism; dystopias issue a warning because of a belief that people can and want to change.[12] In this way, dystopias are a kind of prophetic literature, warning against continuing along our current path: if we don't change something now, something bad will happen in the future (turn aside from sin or God will punish us). In *1984*, for example, George Orwell was concerned that Western intellectuals did not see Stalinism for what it was, Ray Bradbury wrote *Fahrenheit 451* because he was worried about the impact of censorship, and *Handmaid's Tale* resulted from Margaret Atwood's concerns about nuclear/environmental disaster and the rise of religious fundamentalism.

The MCU includes this critical, dystopian edge, warning of the dangers of idolatrous overconfidence in our ability to solve problems through technology and science alone. We are continually reminded that Steve Rogers and Tony Stark are Good Men, heroes, who are worthy of the great power that comes from being Captain America and Iron Man. And the narrative arcs of Iron Man, Captain America, the Avengers, and so on, also raise concerns about the dangers of militarism, hubris, and unintended consequences (e.g., *Avengers: Age of Ultron*). This critical edge is helpful for the SRD in further developing a prophetic voice, and we need to continue this engagement. But, none of this negates the essentially utopian view. The MCU warns about the dangers of science and technology, warnings that have been integral to SF from the beginning—the shift from utopia to dystopia was partially influenced by a growing concern about and suspicion of science and technology. Significantly, these criticism are not aimed at science and technology itself, they are warnings about what happens when technology gets into the hands of "bad guys." The problem is not science and technology per se, the problem is in those who *misuse* science and technology, those who are motivated by greed and militarism. The solution is to make sure that the utopic potential of science and technology are not distorted and used for evil ends. Obadiah Stane is a problem, as is Hydra; Iron Man and the technological resources of the Avengers (and S.H.I.E.L.D.) is the solution. The idea that science and scientists are good, while bad science and bad scientists are an aberration is summed up by Maya in *Iron Man III*, who explains, "we all begin wide-eyed. Pure science. And then the ego steps in, the obsession. And you look up, and you're a long way from shore. We all start that way. Idealistic."

Captain America, Iron Man, and the Avengers might warn against the dangers of greed, militarism, or a lust for power, but ultimately science and technology are salvific; they are the solution to our problems and protection against threats, not problems or threats in and of themselves. This view of science and technology is inadequate because while it criticizes science and technology, it leaves the thicket of colonial ideology intact, and it cannot help us address the more fundamental problems with science and technology or challenge the structure of the relationship between religion and science and the categories of "religion" and "science" themselves. There is, however, the potential for a more fundamental critique of science and technology within the MCU, and I turn to this in the next part.

PHASES TWO AND THREE: MAGIC, WAKANDA, AND THE MULTIVERSE

While science fiction includes a number of elements that can help develop a prophetic critique of science and warn of the dangers of scientific triumphalism, we need a more fundamental challenge, one that can untangle the colonial ideology inherent in the categories of religion and science. One wonders if these more fundamental critiques are even possible for SF, which is so closely tied to colonial expansion and scientific triumphalism. Can a genre whose dominant tropes include strange aliens, empty lands ripe for conquest, and techno-utopian dreams provide the tools for dismantling colonial ideology? Jessica Langer and others have argued that it can, not by running away from those tropes, but by parodying, hybridizing, and otherwise transforming them in order to explore "the ways in which scientific discourse, both in terms of technology and in terms of culture . . . has interacted with colonialism and the colonial production of colonized peoples."[13] This bending of the colonial narratives and tropes of SF typically occurs outside of what might be called mainstream SF, in a number of genres and subgenres that fall under the broad category of "speculative fiction," including afro- and indigenous futurism, postcolonial and third world science fiction, and other genres. A number of these useful narratives and tropes can be found within the MCU, and I will touch on three. The first is magic (*Thor, Dr. Strange*), which problematizes the relationship between religion and science, challenging the center/periphery model of science. The second is Afrofuturism (Black Panther), which challenges the modern/colonial narratives about science and technology, and attempts to describe a more inclusive future. The third is the multiverse, which challenges the idea of a singular reality and a singular framework for understanding by introducing the idea of multiple realities.

Magic is useful for exploring the territory between religion and science, and for challenging the center/periphery model of science and religion. Beginning in the early modern period, the concept of "magic" has been integral to the development of the Western concepts of both "religion" and "science," and for regulating the boundary between them. "Magic" proved incredibly useful for legitimating and elevating certain practices, largely because it is a fluid concept. Accusations of magic were used by the Catholic Church against pagans in order to establish Catholic worship and practice as the sole legitimate form of religious expression and to consolidate church authority. Protestants used the same accusations against Catholics to legitimate Protestant forms of worship and practice, defining religion as a "rational" system by rejecting irrational/magical beliefs such as the claim that physical objects could be endowed with supernatural qualities (i.e., the consecration of the host). As Western science developed in relation to Western religion, "magic" was used to establish scientific practices as distinct from religious ones, and to mark the boundary between what was properly religious (spiritual) and what was properly scientific (material), thereby establishing what was both legitimate and illegitimate religion and science. "Magic" describes a kind of deviance against which *appropriate* religious piety and scientific rationality are brought into relief. Magic is the "stigmatized mediator" between religion and science, reinforcing a separation which legitimates two distinct channels through which human needs are constructed and resolved: a rational scientific realm, which has broad control over the material world, and a spiritual or religious realm, which is increasingly marginalized in regard to any kind of material concerns. Challenges to this system are described as deviant, irrational, and primitive.[14]

During colonial expansion, "magic" was called into service to further define and legitimate Western religious and scientific practices over and against those of other peoples, not merely to clarify the boundaries of (Western) science and religion, but consolidate Western norms and practices as "modern" (meaning "not primitive") by excluding certain practices, behaviors and ideas as primitive, superstitious or "magical thinking," thus establishing Western superiority and justifying Western colonialism. A wide variety of practices were lumped together to serve as the foil for describing these superior practices—indigenous, African, Pagan, savage, "folk," "old wives tales," to name but a few. Different scholars defined the boundary differently, but this fluidity allowed scholars to define Western forms as more evolved and more advanced by defining other practices—however disparate—as primitive, and Western beliefs and practices as more advanced and thus superior, while simultaneously appropriating any successes as "really" an embryonic form of a superior practice. This was particularly important in defining science, and through this process, science and scientific rationality came to serve "as the definitive markers of precisely what it means to be modern. Science is, in large measure, who 'we' are."[15] To be modern is, quite simply, to reject magic in favor of an understanding that is more "rational" and scientific. Imposing a European worldview on other cultures is merely to speed their progress by replacing the ignorance and superstition of a magical worldview with a rational and scientific worldview.

Because "magic" represents what has been excluded to create an idea of "religion" or "science" as a distinct, natural category—magic is the "queer" of religion and science—it can be an important tool in revealing what has been excluded by Western concepts of science and religion, deconstructing the concepts themselves, and exposing the ways these categories reinforce colonial ideologies. Magic in its various forms has long played a role in SF to bend and challenge our perceptions of the world and what we should deem "rational." At first blush, magic in the MCU serves a similar function. When magic is first introduced, it is scientists who first encounter it: Drs Jane Foster and Erik Selvig in *Thor*, and Dr. Strange in *Dr. Strange*. In both cases, the concept of magic is rejected as irrational, superstition, or childish. Selvig, for example, dismisses Thor's claim that he is the God of Thunder, who wields the hammer Mjölnir and traveled from Asgard via the Bifrost (the rainbow bridge) as "delusional," and "the stories I grew up with as a child," offering a picture of Mjölnir in a children's book as proof. Dr. Strange's rejection of the idea of magic is similarly dismissive. Having traveled to Tibet to seek a cure for his ruined hands, Strange meets the Ancient One who explains that the body can put itself together in all sorts of ways. Strange thinks this procedure for cellular regeneration must involve "bleeding edge" technology, but when the Ancient One suggests a more mystical explanation, he rejects it "because I do not believe in fairy tales . . . . There is no such thing as spirit! We are made of matter and energy and nothing more." The primacy of this scientific materialist understanding for both men is shattered by their experiences; Selvig, when Thor's friends, and a demon appear and Thor's hammer is restored; Strange when the Ancient One forces his astral body out of his physical one. In both cases, science cannot encompass their experience, so they widen their worldview to accept a nonscientific framework.

Except that is not what happens. This encounter with magic *could* have decentered the scientific worldview, positing it as one worldview among others, an interpretation that is at least suggested by Thor's assertion that he comes from a place where magic and science exist together, or when the Ancient One shows Strange a series of "maps" of the body—Chakras (Strange rolls his eyes and scoffs), acupuncture and an MRI—explaining that, "Each of those maps was drawn up by someone who could see in part, but not the whole." But, the idea of parallel frameworks, to say nothing of parallel realities, is never fully realized and, instead, the boundaries of science are expanded in such a way as to redefine magic in terms of science. Jane, for example, responds to Selvig's rejection of Thor's claim that he traveled on the Rainbow Bridge from Asgard by suggesting that the Rainbow Bridge is the same thing as an Einstein-Rosen Bridge. He scoffs, and she reminds him that he had pushed her to consider every possibility. Selvig: "I'm talking about science, not magic!" Foster: "Well magic's just science that we don't understand yet; Arthur C. Clarke." Magic is not magic; it is a primitive form of science, an idea that enters into the MCU early on: when Johann Schmidt captures the Tesseract he says to the Tower Keeper "what others see as superstition, you and I know to be a science," and later when a Nazi sneers that he wants "to win this war through magic," Schmidt responds, "Science. But I understand your confusion, great power has always baffled primitive man." These claims reflect both a singular view of reality/truth and the narrative of progress which are so prominent in dismissals of magic as primitive forms of what has become perfected in Western thought and culture.

The existence of multiple frameworks of reality and interpretation is not really an option, in part because the creators of the MCU believed they needed to create a universe with a single set of rules, and brought in scientists to act as consultants to help "develop a coherent and consistent universe of science," one "that respects the scientific process and that uses enough of real science to make things plausible or build off them."[16] Although the concept of magic has the potential to challenge our understanding of science, and its relationship with religion, as well as the colonial ideologies that are intertwined with it, this potential is never fully realized in the MCU, largely because magic is subsumed into science—that is, instead of using the concept of magic to problematize the idea of science, the MCU just repeats the historical trick of moving the goalposts to claim magic as a *kind* of science. The reference to Arthur C. Clarke above is instructive, since the idea that "magic" is primitive science was intentionally used to create a single framework that could encompass both science and magic, with science as a more advanced form of magic. In this framework—with scientists defining the terms—magic becomes a primitive form of science, which is perfected in Modern (Western) society. The suggestion that multiple frameworks could coexist is never realized, not because of the existence of a superior scientific framework, but because of the need to reduce all of reality and experience to a single framework which, in this context, is necessarily scientific. You can *introduce* the idea of magic, but it must be understood as science, or it will be implausible.

Challenging the colonial framework must involve more than merely decentering scientific paradigms, it should involve simultaneously decentering science, challenging a linear progressive model of history, and challenging a singular worldview to create space for the coexistence of multiple frameworks of understanding. For this, I turn to Afrofuturism and Black Panther.

Afrofuturism is not a subgenre of science fiction, but a distinct literary genre that parallels and intersects science fiction.[17] Combining elements of science fiction, historical fiction, fantasy, and magic realism, it is speculative fiction that explores race and racism in a political and social critique that necessarily addresses science and technology, using the language of science fiction to show how black alienation is exacerbated, not relieved by, science and technology, and demonstrating the ways that a future described by the dominant culture simply reproduces the racism of the past. Combining many elements of speculative fiction, Afrofuturism moves "seamlessly back and forth through time and space, between cultural traditions and geographic time zones," reclaiming and reinterpreting the past in order to describe a more inclusive future. Africa ceases to be a relic of the past and becomes "a harbinger of a new and more promising" future.[18]

Black Panther is clearly an example of Afrofuturism. Wakanda represents a reimagined past, an Africa that was never colonized, which provides an opportunity to imagine what Africa might have been, and could be still. Wakanda is a technologically advanced society, which disrupts the Eurocentric narrative of progress in which technology is inextricably linked to Western civilization, and Wakandan technology is distinctly non-Western, combining elements of technology, magic, and religion. It is worth noting that this challenge to the narrative of progress is somewhat flawed since Wakandan technology is *not* a cultural production, it exists *only* because a meteor made of vibranium crashed in Wakanda millennia ago. Wakandan technology is (literally) alien to Africa, which strangely echoes the claim that the pyramids could not have been built by Africans, so (perhaps) they were built by an alien race. But, even to the extent that it does bend the narrative of progress, the Afrofuturism of the MCU does not realize its full potential. Unlike *magic* in the MCU, which decentered science without challenging the narrative of progress, Afrofuturism in the MCU critiques the narrative of progress, but does not decenter the primacy of a scientific and technological worldview: Wakanda is civilized *because* of its advanced technology (alien or not). And on the MCU, neither magic nor Afrofuturism addresses the problem of a singular view of reality/truth. To achieve a more fundamental critique, the MCU would have to more fully embrace the messiness of Afrofuturism, which does not merely explore the queer area between religion and science, or challenge the narratives of progress, it also resists attempts to present a fixed and static alternative to Western constructs.

Which brings us to the multiverse, a concept introduced in *Dr. Strange* (although it plays a part in *Guardians of the Galaxy* and *Ant-Man*). When Strange first meets the Ancient One, she tells him that our universe "is only one of an infinite number. Worlds without end. Some benevolent and life-giving. Others filled with malice and hunger. Dark places, where powers older than time lie . . . ravenous . . . and waiting." In the MCU so far, we have encountered several of these dimensions, including the Astral Dimension, where the physical and material are distinct, the Mirror Dimension, which is an "ever present but undetected" dimension that parallels the real world, and is used to train and surveil, and the Quantum Realm, a subatomic realm where all concepts of space and time become irrelevant. There are many additional universes and dimensions that have been introduced in the comics, and presumably more will be introduced in Phase Four of the MCU, starting with *Doctor Strange in the Multiverse of Madness* in 2021. While the idea of the multiverse would provide a more comprehensive untangling of the thicket of colonial ideology, I remain somewhat skeptical of whether this will be realized, largely because I suspect that the MCU will remain committed to a singular/universal framework, even in the context of the multiverse. And that framework will continue to involve center/periphery thinking that creates a hierarchy of frameworks, as when the Ancient One assures Dr. Strange that what happens in the Mirror Dimension does not impact the *real* world.[19]

Any critique of colonial ideology will need to more fully articulating fluid—queer and messy—alternatives to a static universal (unified) worldview, and here I am imagining something more like Nalo Hopkinson's tricksters or Nnedi Okorafor's organic fantasy. Hopkinson is a Jamaican-born Canadian, who lives in California; Okorafor is a Nigerian American. Both women write stories that allow us to simultaneously inhabit different realities without somehow resolving them into one another. In trying to explain what she means by organic fantasy, Okorafor describes a bus ride through Nigeria, listening to her uncle tell stories, reading Stephen King, staring out the window, listening to Guns N' Roses: "American, to Nigerian, to American, to Nigerian, to American, I'm flickering back and forth . . . Why wouldn't it be logical to illustrate myself literally changing shape when I write about this bus ride? My reaction certainly was just as physical as it was mental. And everything about that bus ride was fantastical and surreal. There was far more going on than what was on the surface."[20] This experience is at the heart of organic fantasy, which "blooms directly from the soil of the real . . . . To write myself as a shape-shifter in that van to the village most accurately shows just how jarring the cultural shifts were to me. It is the most truthful way of telling the truth. For me, fantasy is the most accurate way of describing reality."[21] Okorafor's writing is an example of the ways SF can challenge our categories: in her words, her novels do not blend science, religion, technology, and magic:

> I don't feel I NEED to merge them. I feel they are naturally merged. Especially in African culture. To be African is to merge technology and magic. . . . In my

experience as an African, the mystical and the mundane have always coexisted. It's expressed within the explanation of things, in ways of doing things, the reasons for doing things . . . I'm not doing anything in my fiction that doesn't exist already.[22]

This is the kind of thinking that will be necessary to really dismantle colonial ideology.

CONCLUSION

In many ways, the MCU and the SRD (and, perhaps, the Western Academy in general) find themselves in the same place, wanting to move past the old paradigms so that we can envision and realize a world that is more just, more inclusive, and provides space for human and planetary flourishing. But we keep getting tangled in the bramble of colonial ideologies. I'm not saying that there is no hope. After all, Okorafor has been the author of several Black Panther graphic novels,[23] and the MCU itself will be far more diverse moving forward, in terms of characters and directors, if not writers and producers. But, real transformation will need more than greater diversity and pluralism because, to paraphrase Walter Mignolo, pluralism without decoloniality is another form of colonial expansion. Envisioning real alternatives to the current worldview will involve the hard work of clearing out the thicket of colonial ideology that chokes out the promise of a different world. But that might be asking too much of Hollywood movies based on comic books. Hopefully, it is not too much to ask of academia.

NOTES

1. Veronica Hollinger and Joan Gordon, "Introduction: Edging into the Future," in *Edging Into the Future: Science Fiction and Contemporary Cultural Transformation*, Veronica Hollinger and Joan Gordon, eds. (Philadelphia, PA: University of Pennsylvania Press, 2002), 3. See also John Rieder, *Colonialism and the Emergence of Science Fiction* (Middleton, CT: Wesleyen University Press, 2008), 308.

2. See, Rieder, *Colonialism and the Emergence of Science Fiction.*

3. For the purposes of this paper, titles will refer somewhat loosely to both the characters and the various movies they might appear in. So "Iron Man" refers to the character Iron Man, as well as *Iron Man I, II, III.*

4. "Speculative fiction" is a somewhat fuzzy category. It was originally described as a subgenre of science fiction, and sometimes a distinct genre, which focused on possible futures or alternative realities related to science and technology. More recently, speculative fiction has come to describe an extremely broad category that includes all genres that do something other than describing "consensus reality."

In Robert Heinlein's words, it is fiction that occurs "in a place that never existed, on a world we know nothing of, or on an earth that might have been or might be." (Robert Heinlein, "On the Writing of Speculative Fiction," in *Of Worlds Beyond; The Science of Science Fiction Writing*, Lloyd Arthur Eshbach, ed. (Chicago: Advent Publishers, 1964)), 2. Speculative fiction includes science fiction, but also horror, post-apocalyptic fiction, weird fiction, superhero tales, alternate history, steampunk, slipstream, magic realism, and more. (See also Mark Oziewicz, "Speculative Fiction," *Oxford Research Encyclopedia of Literature* (Online Publication Date: Mar 2017). Web. DOI: 10.1093/acrefore/9780190201098.013.78).

5. Fatima Vieira, "The Concept of Utopia," in *The Cambridge Companion to Utopian Literature*, Gregory Claeys, ed. (Cambridge: Cambridge University Press, 2010), Oziewicz, "Speculative Fiction"; Rieder, *Colonialism and the Emergence of Science Fiction*.

6. Michael Adas, *Machines as the Measure of Men: Science, Technology, and Ideologies of Western Dominance* (New York: Cornell University Press, 1989), 3–4.

7. Adas, *Machines as the Measure of Men*, 7.

8. Sandra Harding, *Is Science Multi-Cultural? Postcolonialisms, Feminisms, and Epistemologies* (Bloomington: Indiana University Press, 1998), 204.

9. At least according to Helmut Zemo in *Avengers: Civil War*.

10. Instead of referring to quotes by movie and time, all quotes have been taken from Movie Quotes and More (https://www.moviequotesandmore.com), and verified by the author while watching the movie.

11. While this is similar to Captain America—in his creation he is an object of science and technology, and there are a bunch of men running around in lab coats referring to him as the "subject," and so on. But, Cap achieves agency through his strength, he becomes the leader, the decision-maker, and so on. This is not the case with the Black Widow (at least not in Phase One and Two).

12. Vieira, "The Concept of Utopia," 17.

13. Jessica Langer, *Postcolonialism and Science Fiction* (New York: Palgrave Macmillan, 2011), 8.

14. Randall Styers, *Making Magic: Religion, Magic, and Science in the Modern World* (New York: Oxford University Press, 2004), 169.

15. Styers, *Making Magic*, 122.

16. Adam Frank, quoted in Meeri Kim, "Science of the Marvel Cinematic Universe," http://scienceandentertainmentexchange.org/blog/science-of-the-marvel-cinematic-universe/ (the website of the Science and Entertainment Exchange, which connects scientists to the entertainment industry to ensure accurate science), Butch Chalkley, "Astrophysicist Adam Frank Talks Consulting On Doctor Strange," MCU Exchange (November 4, 2016), https://mcuexchange.com/astrophysicist-adam-frank-talks-consulting-on-doctor-strange-multiverses-and-mcu-magic/.

17. The term itself was first used by Mark Dery in his essay "Black to the Future: Interviews with Samuel R Delaney, Greg Tate and Tricia Rose," in *Flame Wars: The Discourse of Cyberculture* (Duke University Press, 1994). It worth noting that it is not just a literary genre, and science fiction provides "apt metaphors for black life and history" and inspiration for "technical and creative innovations" for artists like

Jean-Michel Basquiat, musicians like Sun Ra and Janelle Monáe, and others working in a variety of media.

18. Lisa Yaszak, "Afrofuturism, Science Fiction, and the History of the Future," *Socialism and Democracy*. 20, no. 3 (2006): 47.

19. For a more generous interpretation, see Whitney Bauman and Imran Khan, "Religion, Science and the Marvel Universe: Re-Imagining Human-Earth Relations," in this volume.

20. Nnedi Okorafor, "Organic Fantasies," *African Identities*. 7, no. 2 (May 2009): 277–278.

21. Okorafor, "Organic Fantasies," 278–279.

22. Qiana Whitted, "'To Be African Is to Merge Technology and Magic': An Interview with Nnedi Okorafor," in *Afrofuturism 2.0: The Rise of Astro-Blackness*, Reynaldo Anderson and Charles E. Jones, eds. (Lanham, MA: Lexington, 2016), 209.

23. *Black Panther: Long Live the King* # 1-6 (2017–2018) as well as *Shuri (2018-19)* which tells the story of T'Challa's sister who is a technological genius, *Wakanda Forever* (2018), which focuses on the Dora Milaje—the women warriors of Wakanda.

REFERENCES

Adas, Michael. *Machines as the Measure of Men: Science, Technology, and Ideologies of Western Dominance*. New York: Cornell University Press, 1989.

Chalkley, Butch. "Astrophysicist Adam Frank Talks Consulting On Doctor Strange." MCU Exchange. November 4, 2016. https://mcuexchange.com/astrophysicist-adam-frank-talks-consulting-on-doctor-strange-multiverses-and-mcu-magic/.

Csicsery-Ronay, Istevan, Jr. "Science Fiction and Empire." *Science Fiction Studies*. 30, no. 2 (2003): 231–245.

Dery, Mark. "Black to the Future: Interviews with Samuel R Delaney, Greg Tate and Tricia Rose." In *Flame Wars: The Discourse of Cyberculture*, Mark Dery, editor. Durham, NC: Duke University Press, 1994. 179–222.

Harding, Sandra. *Is Science Multi-Cultural? Postcolonialisms, Feminisms, and Epistemologies*. Bloomington: Indiana University Press, 1998.

Harrison, Peter. *The Territories of Religion and Science*. Chicago: University of Chicago Press, 2015.

Heinlein, Robert. "On the Writing of Speculative Fiction." In *Of Worlds Beyond; The Science of Science Fiction Writing*, Lloyd Arthur Eshbach, editor. Chicago: Advent Publishers, 1964.

Kim, Meeri. "Science of the Marvel Cinematic Universe." http://scienceandentertainmentexchange.org/blog/science-of-the-marvel-cinematic-universe/.

Langer, Jessica. *Postcolonialism and Science Fiction*. New York: Palgrave Macmillan, 2011.

Movie Quotes and More. Online at https://www.moviequotesandmore.com.

Okorafor, Nnedi. "Organic Fantasies." *African Identities*. 7, no. 2 (May 2009): 275–286.

Oziewicz, Mark. "Speculative Fiction." *Oxford Research Encyclopedia of Literature* (Online Publication Date: Mar 2017). Web. DOI: 10.1093/acrefore/9780190201098.013.78.

Rieder, John. *Colonialism and the Emergence of Science Fiction*. Middletown, CT: Wesleyen University Press, 2008.

Styers, Randall. *Making Magic: Religion, Magic, and Science in the Modern World*. New York: Oxford University Press, 2004.

Vieira, Fatima. "The Concept of Utopia." In *The Cambridge Companion to Utopian Literature*, Gregory Claeys editor. Cambridge: Cambridge University Press, 2010. 3–27.

Whitted, Qiana. "'To Be African Is to Merge Technology and Magic': An Interview with Nnedi Okorafor." In *Afrofuturism 2.0: The Rise of Astro-Blackness*, Reynaldo Anderson and Charles E. Jones, editors. Lanham, MD: Lexington, 2016. 207–213.

Yaszak, Lisa. "Afrofuturism, Science fiction, and the History of the Future." *Socialism and Democracy*. 20, no. 3 (2006): 41–60.

Chapter 10

Religion, Science, and the Marvel Universe

Reimagining Human–Earth Relations

Whitney Bauman and Imran Khan

> I think hard times are coming when we will be wanting the voices of writers who can see alternatives to how we live now and can see through our fear-stricken society and its obsessive technologies to other ways of being, and even imagine some real grounds for hope. We will need writers who can remember freedom. Poets, visionaries, the realists of a larger reality.
>
> —Ursula K. LeGuin[1]

Hard times are coming? Hard times are here. As the epigram by Urusla Le Guin suggests, we need creative thinkers to help us through these hard times. If we are to get through the current problems of globalization and climate change, without continuing to assume the human exceptionalism that is inherent in Modern and Postmodern thought, then we need to think differently. Indeed, these are not just hard times, but some would even call them "dark times."[2] Hannah Arendt had a thing or two to say about the hard and dark times Le Guin sees for our future because she also lived through them in the form of the horrors of WWII. Arendt also called for new ways of thinking and understanding ourselves narratively and historically. She argued both that we have to go "out walking," take a break from ourselves, and try to experience and understand the world from different perspectives, but also that we must go "pearl diving," and perhaps sift through the detritus of our own histories for gems that can be useful to us today.[3] Neither Le Guin nor Arendt argued that we should forget history altogether, but they did argue for new self-understandings based upon new narratives (with an emphasis on multiple narratives).

This brief chapter engages the speculative/science fiction of the Marvel Multiverse, in an effort to think anew our relationships with one another and with the rest of the natural worlds in which we live. While Lisa Stenmark's chapter in this volume warns against the re-narration of colonial mentalities, attitudes, and ideas in the Marvel Universe, which is definitely one, valid reading, this chapter takes another reading. Multiple interpretations of these worlds exist and we need them all. If we are going to get through these dark and hard times, without repeating neoliberal globalization as usual or some sort of return to dangerous localisms and nationalisms, both of which ignore our planetary contexts and the ways in which we are deeply related evolutionarily, ecologically, historically and culturally, then we need to think about the "undercommons" or "hidden voices" within dominant modern, Western traditions,[4] as well as the multiple worlds, histories, and voices outside of modern, Western traditions. This chapter, then, tries to draw out some of the alternative histories and voices of the Marvel Universe and some of the possible implications of them for a planetary future. While the Modern, Western mentality is based upon pure identities and boundaries, we explore the hybridity between humans, technology, animality, and divinity that the Marvel worlds play around with. While the modern Western mentality forces everything into a single tunnel of historical time, which is inherently a colonizing process,[5] perhaps we can think of the multiple times, spaces, and histories of the Marvel Multiverse. While the Modern, Western mentality argues that historical agency resides with the human being alone (and within the category of humans, white, upper class, elite males are considered to have the most agency historically), perhaps we can think about the multiple and distributed types of agencies and powers throughout the Marvel Multiverse.

It may sound, at first, ridiculous and irresponsible to turn to fantasy at a time when there seem to be so many problems facing the planetary community. But, we argue, along with Le Guin, Donna Haraway, and others that there is an urgent need for this type of speculative thinking: and, not just human thinking, but thinking with the rest of the planetary community. As Haraway notes,

> The systemic stories of the linked metabolisms, articulations, or coproductions (pick your metaphor) of economies and ecologies, of histories and human and nonhuman critters, must be relentlessly opportunistic and contingent. They must also be relentlessly relational, sympoietic, and consequential.[6]

We must, then, think with the rest of the planetary community in ways that pay deep attention to the differences and textures of various embodiments. Furthermore, there will not be one world to rule them all, but multiple worldings all of which at any given moment in time make up the planetary community.[7] The way we think about the worlds in which we live and relate then is perhaps more about aesthetics and ethics than it is about metaphysics: how do our co-worldings affect different bodies differently for better and worse, and how can we co-create worlds that bring about more flourishing for the entire planetary community. We are not naive enough to think that there will be a final answer to this and in fact searching for a final answer is problematic to say the least. Rather, as long as the process of geo-evolution continues and as long as the universe keeps expanding there will always be new entities, new relations, and thus new horizons for our thinking. Much like the Guardians of the Galaxy, we are not necessarily saving the universe once and for all, but moving from project to project, from horizon to horizon, trying to carve out a meaningful process along the way. Most important to keep in focus is that this is a co-productive process, what Haraway calls sympoiesis rather than autopoiesis. She uses,

> sympoiesis for "collectively-producing systems that do not have self-defined spatial or temporal boundaries. Information and control are distributed among components. The systems are evolutionary and have the potential for surprising change." By contrast, autopoietic systems are "self-producing" autonomous units "with self defined spatial or temporal boundaries that tend to be centrally controlled, homeostatic, and predictable."[8]

One reason for this stress on sympoiesis is due to the hybrid nature of all entities and reality, so it is to a discussion of this hybridity that we now turn.

HYBRIDITY AND THE PROBLEM WITH DIVERSITY AND INTEGRATION

> Wakanda will no longer watch from the shadows. We can not. We must not. We will work to be an example of how we, as brothers and sisters on this earth, should treat each other. Now, more than ever, the illusions of division threaten our very existence. We all know the truth: more connects us than separates us. (T'Challa, Black Panther).

In order to think a bit about the hybrid nature of the Marvel Universe and its relevance to our own hybrid planetary community, we'd like to put forth three models based upon the old, Modern typologies of how Religion and Science might relate. This section explores how humans view themselves in the larger ecosystems of the planet, and as the opening quote suggests, differences are couched in an evolving world of connections that are ignored at their own peril. In the Marvel Universe, humans are forced to question their place in the pecking order given that mutants have challenged their place at the apex of the universe. Are mutants a devolutionary threat or are they a trans-/post-human threat? Or, are they no threat at all but a mutually emergent feature of the multiverse that can be worked with and evolved with other planetary entities. If we take the perspective of Professor X, mutants should fold into and integrate with the rest of the human society.

Let's call this the integration model. The civil rights of MLK Jr. or the centrist gay fight for marriage (vs. the queer abolition of marriage) and the second wave of feminism that sought to show women could live and thrive in a man's world are all examples of this integration model. This is the "expanding the circle of moral concern" model in which you extend moral concern from specific humans (Christians or Muslims) to all "men" (literally male historically) to women, to queer people, to people of color, to animals to the rest of the natural world. This is the "many made one" model of monotheism and inclusion; it has its problems as all "extensionist" ethics do, but also still redefines what the central "norm"/ideal "human" is. The problem from a postcolonial and/or decolonial perspective has to do with the center-periphery thinking and the idea of unity. The latter will be discussed further below, but the former is the process by which the center extends out to the periphery and attempts to incorporate all those entities by ranking them against a center.[9] The creation of such a center-periphery reality must either integrate, background, or eliminate differences. In other words, the attempt is to maintain a core, central, essential, or pure identity: and this comes at violent costs. Think here about the perpetuation of racisms and sexisms that maintain a racist and white political and economic structure at the heart of the United States. The political and economic inequality literally kills black and brown bodies: from the genocide of millions of native peoples that lies at the founding of the United States to the slavery and racism that killed and still kills black people. Something like "Black Lives Matter," and "Me Too" movements are derailing because they upset the center, the very heart, of power. It is not that the Marvel Universe doesn't present some of these same colonial ways of thinking, to which the integration and supersession models attest, but rather that if one looks at the whole of the Marvel multiverse, there are multiple centers and no single center into which all the stories and characters fit.

One example of the integration model in the Marvel Universe plays out in the Civil War storyline between Iron Man and Captain America. Iron Man, known for his rogue anti-establishment sentiment, suddenly acquiesces to a call from world leaders to submit the Avengers to governmental oversight. He feels adamantly that because the Avengers have acted without any accountability that they have inflicted undue harm. There is extreme pressure to fold the exceptional "otherness" of the Avenger's abilities into a working and established world order, in a way that works to maintain that order. However, Captain America, who would normally be the one to advocate for doing things the "right way," finds himself on the other side of the aisle because he understands that integration is fundamentally problematic. You have to make a square peg round in order to fit it into that hole. His view is that the Avengers and what they represent can't be folded into a model in which there is no space for their kind. Instead, for Captain America, the Avengers represent a new normal, which brings us to the next perspective we describe.

A second perspective is given to us by Magneto's view in which humans need to be separated and/or superseded or progressed past and fit into a new order developed by mutants. Let's call this the supersessionist, revolutionary model. Malcolm X and the Black Panthers (historically and in the speculative world of Marvel), lesbian separatists of the 70s (Amazonian narratives such as found in DC Comics, Wonder Woman; or perhaps even the new depiction of the lone powerful female, Captain Marvel), and the Act Up! queer movement that wants to completely overturn patriarchy and heteronormativity for a brand-new order, run by a brand-new power and identity, are all examples of this type of separatist, revolutionary model. In this perspective, humanity is one step along the way that needs to give way to the next phase of evolution. Christianity surpasses paganism and expands to incorporate the world in its own image. Science surpasses Christianity and all "religious" ways of knowing and seeks to enlighten the world in its own image. In these supersessionist models, the idea of the hybridity of humanity is ignored, and the tables are just turned to allow a new, essential identity into the center, which then measures all others. This is a "many made one" model: one must conform to the new reality (and it does too often seem to be singular), with new rules. This way of thinking is usually tied to progressive, utopic (no-place) visions that have no choice but to supersede whatever came before. This is a perspective of history that lies at the center of Marxism, Capitalism, Modernity, and Postmodernity alike. They all self-identify as progressive and "better than" what came before.

At least initially, this is the premise of Wakandan society as depicted in the comic Marvel Universe. The Wakandan kings, Black Panthers, chose to self-isolate themselves away from the society at large because they anticipated that they wouldn't be able to incorporate their technological superiority into the existing world order. So, they created a new world order hidden behind a veil. Their revolution wasn't to break what existed and create a new center for everyone but just for themselves within their own fiefdom. And, this is a necessary space to create voices that have been marginalized. One must find and define one's own voice, one's otherness and uniqueness apart from the dominant norms before one can reform and change the world toward different ways of becoming. Most other separatists/supersessionists in the Marvel Universe, like Magneto and Thanos, seek to create a new world order that does away with whatever the current world order is. Similarly, the Sovereigns in the Guardians of the Galaxy universe think of themselves as genetically, cognitively, and emotionally superior to all others. Their supersessionist and seperatist ideology evolves to thinking of themselves above all others: they are the carriers of the torch of progress that all others must conform to. However, the Wakandans carve out a third way and path, that seeks to change the world into something different from what was before, and something different from the unique Wakandan world that existed in separation from other worlds.

The Wakandans offer up, Black Panther, a third option in which many groups build a new society together that starts to classify both humans and mutants as part of new worlds moving forward. This is not a kind of return to order that Thanos thinks he can restore by killing off half the population of the universe. Nor is this an order that seeks to set up a brand-new monolithic order that displaces and destroys the old monolithic order. This is a hybrid, emergent, new world that holds open many possibilities for becoming.

In this scenario technology, humans, animals, and the rest of the natural world are all mixed up together in an ever-evolving pluriverse. Under this reimagining as Leguinn would have wanted, we start to take into account the needs of more than just humans but also the planet and other planetary entities as all central figures in the ongoing story of life. This third option, that we might call the synthesis model or the hybrid, monstrous model is the one we most want to stress in this chapter.[10] This is MLK Jr. and Malcolm, the reformer and the revolutionary together (though both of these civil rights figures obviously already had elements of both of these methods). This is the planetary vision of co-construction of new worlds with the full recognition that there is no single "one" that the many can be brought into, but the many can never be reduced to a single "one." This third option is a move beyond single stories, to multiple narratives and histories. Such multiperspectivalism does not place all agencies in one location but rather, the agency is diffuse and distributed (discussed in the final section). This type of multiperspectivalism is captured well by Donald Crosby. He writes,

> All the elemental particles, atoms, molecules, compounds, inorganic and organic entities and combinations of those entities, including human beings and their histories, cultures, and societies, and all of the actions, reactions, functions, qualities, and traits of these particular things and their relations are included. No two perspectives or systems of them are exactly alike.[11]

And this is where Chadwick Boseman's Black Panther lands. As a black person who has the superior technology and resources, he realizes that he must bring the riches of Wakanda to the world in order to create a new world. Not a totally separatist world, which within an interconnected planetary system is impossible, but it will not be a world that merely accommodates and re-attunes to the centers of power. His benevolent opening up of Wakanda is met with ridicule when in the final scenes of the Black Panther film, reporters scoff at what a poor African nation could share with the world. Little did they know. In fact, almost exclusively, this hybrid model that allows for interconnected multiplicity is employed by people of color and/or others from outside the established 'white male privilege' order. Because this new world will be a hybrid of many narratives, and it will generate multiple more narratives, time and history must also be thought of outside the singular.

BEYOND CHRONOLOGICAL SPACE-TIME: MULTIPLE TIMES AND MULTIPLE NARRATIVES

> Mutation: it is the key to our evolution. It has enabled us to evolve from a single-celled organism into the dominant species on the planet. This process is slow, and normally taking thousands and thousands of years. But every few hundred millennia, evolution leaps forward.
>
> —Professor Charles Xavier, *X-Men*

In order to think beyond purity and single narratives, such as the one professed by Professor Charles Xavier in the quote above, we may want to begin by questioning the underlying assumption of the unity of all things. We have questioned unity in terms of identity and humanity (above), and in this section we will question the unity of time and history. Instead of narrating the story of the universe and our earth in a single, chronological understanding of time and instead of narrating human history in the singular, perhaps we need to begin to think of a multiverse multiple times.[12] Such speculative thinking might allow us to move beyond an Anthropic understanding of the expansion of our universe and the evolution of our planet and open us to multiple trajectories and possibilities for becoming.

According to one speculative theory known as Rainbow Gravity, differently embodied entities are in time and space in different ways, and thus have different responses to gravity. As one article puts it: "The color of light is determined by its frequency, and because different frequencies correspond to different energies, light particles (photons) of different colors would travel on slightly different paths through spacetime, according to their energy."[13] There are not only multiverses beyond our own universe, but also multiverses within our universe. Might we be able to talk about the different stories and different times from the perspective of planets, trees, bees, galaxies, and different peoples around the world? Such an understanding breaks open not only the present and past from a single narrative but also the possibilities for future becoming. The Marvel world has been playing with time travel and the ideas of multiverses (in one way or another) since the 1970s. This is one primary source we might turn to, then, in order to think through these ideas a bit.

In this section, we will examine the idea of multiple and simultaneously existent times by looking at the Sorcerer Supremes and especially Dr. Strange. This drives home the idea of a multiperspectival reality. Second, we will look at the person of Quicksilver, who reveals that there is no common time but the time depends upon embodiment and context. Even within the same world or context, there exist worlds among worlds. As Walter Mignolo's work argues, "The Zapatistas taught many of us that to change the world as it is may be an impossible task, but to build a world in which many worlds would coexist is a possible task."[14] Antman and the Wasp also provide us with the sense of multiperspectival textures to any given context or world. Third, we will take the shifting of time in the Avengers movies as the context for understanding that time is radically open: the future is not a closed and single teleology, and though we might be able to shift future becomings in some ways, the consequences of our actions have ripple effects that cannot be imagined from the present. Part of doing this is to, again, drive home the idea that humans are not singular but hybrid (section 1), there is no single story of the Anthropos/Anthropocene (this section), and thus humans are only part of a much larger story, with many other agents, both known and unknown (final section).

Dr. Strange and the Multiverse (of Madness?)

Let me draw here, by way of analogy, what (re)attuning to our worlds in light of the multiverse might accomplish in terms of thinking and feeling. At the Rose Center for Earth and Space in the Hayden planetarium in New York City, there is a "Cosmic Pathway" walk based in large part on the current cosmological narrative such as found in Steven Hawking's, *A Brief History of Time*. This pathway also coincides with the more poetic version of the cosmos found in *The Universe Story* by Brian Swimme and Thomas Berry, which is a text important to many people who want to make religious and spiritual sense of what can seem like a cold dead universe. In this exhibit, you start at the top floor of the planetarium, and wind your way down the equivalent of several building stories on a spiraling walkway. As you walk, each step you take represents millions of years in the 13.7-billion-year-old universe. At the very end of the walkway is a human hair in a display box. The width of this hair (not the length) represents the time that humans have been around in the cosmos.

This perspective is mindblowing and challenges us to rethink and (re) attune to what it means to be human in the long, vast history of the cosmos. Just as Galileo and Copernicus had challenged anthropocentrism for the geocentric understanding of the universe, so now, the big bang cosmology does for us. However, as Mary Jane Rubenstein (among others) has pointed out, big-bang cosmology still holds tightly to the singular, unified, universe, and the "big bang" itself fits well aesthetically and intellectually with the idea of a God that creates, "out of nothing."[15] Such singularity, power, and purity is part of the problem of human exceptionalism that this chapter is trying to think beyond. Speculative thinking about the multiverse pushes our thinking even more, challenging the anthropomorphic God that creates a world for the Anthropos ex nihilo, and makes humans even less central to any single story, on the one hand. But, on the other hand, the multiverse also makes humans and every other possible entity equally important. As the entanglement of life on planet earth is impossible to transcend, so the entanglement with universes in the form of a multiverse. The loss of such transcendence, and objectivity and total abstraction and collapse into immanence can be frightening at first. The loss of unity and wholism as well. But as Latour notes, "Deprived of the help of transcendence, we at first believe we are going to suffocate for want of oxygen; then we notice that we are breathing more freely than before: transcendences abound."[16] This sense of loss that comes from the loss of a single narrative, and a single universe is also replaced by the excitement of multiplicity and hybridity. Difference makes us through and through; the multiverse constitutes our universe and the many worlds that exist within the planetary community co-constitute one another in an open process of becoming.

There is no better example of this multiplicity of time and history in the MCU than that of the Sorcerer Supreme, and not just Dr. Strange but also his predecessors. The Sorcerer Supreme is a practitioner of the mystical arts who has skills greater than all other practitioners and a greater portion of the ambient magical energy in the world. Within this world, they exist on several coexisting planes of existence: one mystical, one spiritual, one physical, and so on. When the Sorceress Supreme meets Steven Strange for the first time she propels his astral body from his physical form. And this radical moment not only shatters his worldview but also opens up the MCU to the existence of multiverses. It also challenges the traditional Western timeline in which humans think of the evolution of knowledge. As Dr. Strange comes to learn the mystical forces and energies of the mystical arts he realizes that they predate current human history. But also coexist on multiple planes. This challenges the idea that humans are at the center of the universe or are the central subjects of linear time. Not only are there different portals into different places, but there are connections between pasts, presents, and futures. Life does not come to us from the future, it bubbles up in the evolving interactions of pasts, presents, and futures. From the bubbling of time, one cannot hold onto a supersessionist theory of knowledge and life: that is, one cannot hold on to the "new is better than the old" or "religion supersedes magic which is superseded by science." Dr. Strange is a combination of science, religion, and magic, and all three have their place.

Quicksilver and the Contours of Our Worlds

Not only might there be different worlds with different laws and different possibilities for the future, but also any given moment is pregnant with many different worlds, times, and stories. Chronos time, anchored by the atomic clock and its GMT, tends to smooth over all textures and spaces. As Trish Ferguson notes, the construction and enforcing of a single time over the face of the planet was a colonial effort that then allowed for greater economic efficiency, including more efficient production and extraction of resources.[17] Further, chronos and time were also enforced through global temperance movements led mostly by factory owners who needed reliable labor. Drugs, alcohol, and mind-altering activities including meditation and religious experiences tend to take their own times, and draw us out of chronological time. So, in many ways, thinking about the planet and not just for humans means that we have to think about the multiple times taking place in the worlds in which we live. The slowing down of time many of us have experienced during the Covid crisis has also enabled many to see the different times of the planet. Social media is filled with stories of people noticing more stars and hearing more birdsong because of the decrease in human's fossil-fueled realities. The very climate of the planetary community is breathing a slight sigh of relief that the constant pressure of fossil-fueled chronos imposes upon its human and "more than human" systems.

There is no single time by which all lives and entities can be judged. There is, rather, the various life and times of humans, elephants, trees, rivers, mountains, and planets, just to name a few. Eduardo Viveiros de Castro, in his work among indigenous groups and building off of ideas of Nietzsche, and Delleuze and Guattari, describes this as "perspectivism." He writes that perspectivism is "the conception, common to many peoples of the continent, according to which the world is inhabited by different sorts of subjects or persons, human and non-humans, which apprehend reality from distinct points of view."[18] In other words, from the concept of "perspectivism," each species of the creature creates the world around themselves, they are at the center of their own world, they are the humans. And, I would add that all these overlapping worlds make up what we might call the planetary community.

Creating common grounds for a planetary community depends upon some recognition of the cacophony of time that makes up any given ground.

For example, Quicksilver lives on a time wavelength that is unique to him. The nanoseconds in between every moment for us is but a second or two for him. He uses his speed as a means to enter a new chronology. This allows him to exploit the moments in between. What if society could live at the pace of those moments in between. What would that do to our understanding of the world around us and the cosmos. This conversation is particularly relevant as the world is effectively shut down amidst a global pandemic. Many people in the modern Western world are taking a pause from our fossil-fueled time and noticing more of the "in between" places and moments. Indeed, the grounding of the entire household and working/schooling from home gives us a glimpse into the past and what the world must have been like a short few centuries ago for most people (and still some people today). Of course, for many others, those who have lost jobs, or are essential workers, and/or who must now do both jobs of educating and raising children and working outside the home, the sense of time has also been abnormal in a different way: there is not enough of it. These experiences of time in different ways highlight the experiential and malleable nature of time rather than its uniformity. It is this type of rubber time that can be stretched and that Quicksilver takes advantage of. Might we be able to take advantage of a different pace of life, perhaps a planetary pace instead of the fossil-fueled pace of progress?[19]

Time is also a queer concept in the cases of Antman and the Wasp where time shifts in scale with the actual physical size of the characters. Dr. Hank Pym uses his know-how to shrink himself down to a size that would allow him to jump into the quantum realm. Like Quicksilver living in the nanoseconds between the seconds we experience, Pym is venturing into the spaces between particles that are between the objects we experience in our daily lives. What happens to the human perspective if we could travel on a molecular level. As Pym discovers it shifts our understanding of chronological time, meaning that several years in the "real world" (the human world) could be a mere few hours in the quantum realm in between atoms. In the MCU this lays the basis for time travel. A fountain of youth or holy grail for nerds and scientists alike.

The Avengers and the Open Future

What types of times and narratives exist depend also on what types of futures exist. If there are many different histories and one telos, then all paths lead to the same mountain.[20] If this is the approach to multiplicity and plurality, then we still end up in oneness and unity. A monotheism still closes off the future of possibilities. Instead, what we might think about in terms of speculative possibilities for the future, are perhaps present moments pregnant with possibilities for multiple different futures. We might think of this as a "viable agnosticism" in regard to the past and the future.[21] From this perspective, we can only see, think, and feel our way (even through technologies) so far back into the past. What is before the big bang? What is the origin of humanity? What is before our own life? Likewise, we can only see, think, and feel our way so far into the future. We may be able to predict with some reliability the next few weeks, but after that (and sometimes even that) is a mystery. Furthermore, we can only "see" the microwave background radiation at the edges of our universe, but we have no idea what, if anything, is beyond that. Finally, we have no idea what will become of us after our own individual deaths. Rather than projecting everything in those unknown spaces (theism) or nothing (atheism), why not keep them open as spaces of emergent mystery. From these vibrant spaces, life continues to breathe, live, evolve, and emerge in multiple different ways.

In the Marvel Universe, there are many different examples of non-teleological futures, but in this chapter, we are going to focus on the multiple futures of the avengers. Each one of their isolated adventures leads to different stories in different worlds for possible futures. They move between them, connecting them, and make hybrid new narratives for the possibilities of future becoming. They are like the connections that Walter Mignolo talks about between worlds: not reducing worlds one to the other but serving as ecotones between worlds and shifting those worlds through that interaction into different trajectories that would otherwise not be possible. There is no final, single overall Telos or time toward which these characters are aiming. Rather, they are aimed at multiple, context-specific times and trajectories within those specific worlds. As Mignolo argues, "For a world composed of multiple worlds we need not have abstract universals and empty signifiers, but connectors that will link the Zapatistass' theoretical revolution and its ethical consequences with similar projects around the world emerging from the colonial difference (either as 'external' or 'internal' national forms of colonialism)."[22] We might argue that the avengers are not saviors, but rather trickster figures and pirates: helping to upend the dominant world for something new to emerge while connecting these different possibilities for the future.

Through these narratives, not only are humans decentered but their timelines become drops in the bucket of what the potential multiverse timeline could be. And this is further compounded by the idea of extraterrestrial species that may exist, which could be light years "ahead" of human technology and understanding. Finally, the different embodiments and abilities of the Avengers, the X-Men, and all marvel characters for that matter, point to the need for critical theory. We need critical theories (that focus on sex, gender, race, class, species, ableness, and other intersections) to help narrate the multiple times and multiple stories, experienced by different embodiments which linked together, make up the fabric of the multiverse.

The time heist that the Avengers venture to pull off in the final installment of the Infinity War storyline is a perfect embodiment of this idea. The team, led by Iron Man's intellect, unlocks the possibilities of the quantum realm and its use to travel back to specific moments in their collective history to undo Thanos' "snap" that eradicates half of all living things across the universe. The notion that the Avengers could slip into previous moments in time to recover the Infinity stones to undo the damage in their own timeline and then return those stones without creating parallel futures is fundamentally noble. However, as we know things don't necessarily work so easily when it comes to messing with time. As Robert Downey Jr.'s Iron Man so eloquently states, "when you mess with time, it tends to mess back." But the deeper understanding for us here is that in these parallel timelines, worlds and universes exist cohesively in both the MCU as well as in the world of the comics. There it is a given that these realities can coexist and ultimately there are more than just the Avengers, let alone humans, at the center. Captain Marvel is a perfect example of this idea. Although temporarily an Avenger she has a cosmic mission to be a protector on thousands of other planets within the universe. Each of which has its own chronology and sets of multiversal existences. For both Marvel and the Avengers, it is unacceptable to "save the universe" at the expense of half of the population of all living things in the universe. Captain Marvel goes even further in a critical, theoretical way in Endgame when she reminds the other Avengers on earth that they are protecting one planet and its inhabitants while she is doing the same for many worlds throughout the universe. Like much good critical theory, Marvel helps us to get out of our human centeredness.

3. DECENTERING HUMAN AGENCY / (THANOS, THE ETERNALS, AND THE KREE)

We expect rocks to play their part, which is to say, be totally passive. We're the top, they're the bottom and we expect them to stay that way. When they play at being the top, humans call it an earthquake and find it highly unpleasant. Or, consider a rock falling on one's car: there are road hazard signs showing how it happens, but we never read those signs as if the rocks somehow jump off the cliff and hurtle down toward us. We are hampered even from beginning to ascribe intention to rocks, the issue that lurks in the background of the notion of agency.[23]

One of the major implications of the ideas of identity hybridity (and embeddedness within the rest of the natural world) and multiple narratives, the multiverse, and/or the pluriverse is that humans can no longer be understood as the only agents and thus as the center of all value in the universe. This critique is not a new one and has roots in religious traditions that center upon nature, upon God or some sort of gods, and upon animisms or pantheisms. In Islam, for instance, God is precisely not the world and cannot be captured in human concepts or language: God is the iconoclast to our human hubris. However, the dominant, Christian *cum* modern Western narrative that has made "religion" and "science" into separate entities, has also in both religious and scientific traditions seen humans as somehow above the rest of the natural world, as the only agents in the world. Carolyn Merchant critiques this from the scientific side in the *Death of Nature*.[24] In that book, she began her now career-long effort to decenter humans in the universe or to "provincialize the human,"[25] and to restore value and agency to the rest of the natural world that (for her and other historians of science) was eliminated in the process that we now call "the Scientific Revolution." In religious studies, the effort to restore agency and value to the rest of the natural world and see humans as citizens of the planet (or at least as not having dominion over the planet) begins largely with the article by historian of science Lynn White, in which he argues that the problem of "human exceptionalism"[26] can be laid at the foot of monotheism, and particularly the biblical narrative of Genesis that gives humans "dominion" over the earth.[27] White's argument effectively started the field of "religion and ecology" which is quite robust 50-ish years later. Again, there were always minor traditions within Western cultures that decentered humans such as those found in pantheisms, panentheisms, American Pragmatism, and goddess-/Wiccan-/pagan-based traditions. Likewise, there were scientists who refused the reductive and productive model of modern Western Science.[28] But Merchant and White were critiquing the dominant narratives of Western monotheism and science, which make humans the apex of agency and value in the world.

The speculative Marvel Universe has also provided huge critiques of human exceptionalism and humans as the only agents of the worlds/universes in which they are found. Indeed, humans are not at the center, there are lots of space races and aliens. Flerkin's can swallow the infinity stone and/or a universe, in much the way that Hanuman from Indic traditions can swallow the sun. Time and space can be suspended (as mentioned above) and they are not fine-tuned to the scale of humans. Humans cannot solve the problems of the worlds in which they live, much less the universes in which they live because they are not the only agents (and often are minor one's at that) nor are they the only things that matter morally and ethically.

In this section, we want to look at Thanos, the Eternals, and the Kree to talk about how to speculatively imagine beyond humans as the crown of creation. In fact, such a "crown" depends upon a top and bottom, an up and down which we critiqued in the previous section in terms of our discussion of the multiverse. What is the "top"? what is the "bottom"? There is not one, rather there are multiple bottoms, multiple tops, multiple narratives. As part of this speculative distance, we can gain through thinking about our worlds in non-anthropocentric ways, we can also begin to see how religions (including those of monotheism) have traditions of the multiverse and human decentering as well. For example, in various religions, one finds: heaven and hell, deities, angels, ancestral spirits, animal spirits, and the list goes on. There is already an understanding of humanity that is not at the apex and not at the center. Most religious traditions, despite some of their more dominant interpretations, warn against the folly of human hubris. Humans are not in control. Dependent co-arising in Buddhism, trickster figures in indigenous traditions, angels and gods and divine agencies in monotheistic and polytheistic traditions, and ancestral and other spirits in African/Afro-Caribbean traditions: all of these traditions suggest that humans are not as powerful as they think. The scientific narratives of evolution and cosmology also do much to decenter human. How can the Marvel Universe help us recapture this fundamental understanding of the world as detailed in these religious and scientific traditions?

Finally, this section argues that both Modernity and postmodernity have removed agency from the rest of the natural world and placed it in the hands of humans (read wealthy, elite males). We have largely critiqued dominant Western modernity, but postmodernity, in its very effort to displace modernity, smuggles in some of the assumptions it is trying to distinguish itself from. In this case, postmodern thought has largely been concerned with diversity and multiplicity of the human world and not so much with the rest of the natural world. In fact, there has often been a fear of the category of nature, for it can always be a place to find ideas of what is "natural." Thus at the end of this chapter, we argue that Marvel's multiverse, and the hybrid humans therein, might suggest more of a critical interplanetary romanticism. A critical planetary romanticism places humans within the rest of the natural world, as part of that world. As part of that world, there is a bit of Romantic mystery and attachment that can never be fully explained, because we are in, and not above the rest of the planetary community. However, the interpretation of this embeddedness cannot be housed in uncritical oneness or unity. Rather, it must be a critical planetary romanticism that acknowledges different bodies are affected differently depending upon the ways in which worlds are constructed (see the previous section of this chapter). An interplanetary critical romanticism begins to extend this to the possibilities of the multiverse. Now that "space" has become the next frontier and there is already talk of privatization and ownership of materials and planets outside of Earth, it is necessary to discuss some sort of interplanetary critical romanticism.

There are beings, for instance, in the MCU as well as the comic universe that would make the intellect of humans seem incredibly simple and limited. One of the most amazing things that the Marvel Universe has done is to open up our world to the idea that humans aren't the only beings of intellect in the cosmos, rather there are celestial beings with capabilities far beyond any human. The Sovereign, the Shi'ar, the Celestials, the Eternals/Deviants (Thanos is a notable son of the Eternals but has the Deviants gene), the Skrull, and the Kree are all examples of this decentering.

The Eternals were created by the Celestials, who had experimented on proto-humans on earth and have godlike powers and prolonged life. The Celestials themselves were forged from the First Firmament (the first being in the universe) and ventured to create universes of their own (thus experimenting on races such as proto-humans) for the universe to evolve with them. The Kree are the race that would ultimately become the militant power in the cosmos. They too have super strength and intellect and a class system of their very own. The Blue Kree are the pure-blooded ancestors of the Pink Kree (more humanlike in appearance) that ultimately rule the Kree Empire which is composed of thousands of planets in the northwest lobe of the Great Mellaganic Cloud: well beyond the mere one planet earth that humans inhabit.

The Skrull located in the Andromeda Galaxy are shapeshifters who are the primary adversaries of the Kree. The Skrulls originate from the planet of Skrullos, and were originally a mercantile civilization, primarily interested in free trade and willing to share their technology with all races they deemed worthy. When they encountered a new race, they simply transformed themselves to resemble that race. The Skrull empire that resulted from these contacts was based on free trade and mutual cooperation: a quite different approach to difference than has been assumed for much of human colonial history.

Finally, take the Shi'ar who are cold-blooded humanoids of avian descent; they resemble humans with feathered crests atop their heads in lieu of hair. Two different styles are common: most Shi'ar, particularly those of the aristocracy, have feathers sprouting in a triangular shape away from the face, one peak on the top of the head and one peak on each side slightly over the shoulder; the other commonly seen "hairstyle" is bushy on both sides and very flat on the top. The Shi'ar Empire is one of the most advanced and expansive civilizations in the universe, spanning entire galaxies. It is mainly an economic co-operative, where trade with other galactic powers is its driving force. Not all races have the same rights in the Imperium, as the Shi'ar appear to have a disproportionate influence on its governance. It is nominally ruled over by a high council, which has representatives from a large majority of the alien races that exist within the Imperium. However, in practice, the head of the council (the Majestor or Majestrix) exercises strong executive control and can institute policy virtually by decree. Even the colonial mindset and empires that exist elsewhere and that we would call problematic to say the least, far outstrip the might and power of the one planet of humans (who can't even seem to figure out how to live on that one planet). In contrast, the mutants on earth and the superheroes on earth, for the most part don't see beyond the planet. Iron Man is actually just a normal guy with a super-intellect and a whole lot of technology on his side. None of these earthly originations can take on the Eternals or Thanos by themselves, in fact. But as a coordinated part of a larger movement, they have a shot. Is that in and of itself an argument for cooperation? Coordination on such a grand scale that without it such an existential interstellar threat would never be able to be taken on? Again, going back to what Leguinn is asking of us: Is the Marvel Universe teaching us something? Have we had the key all along but haven't acted on it in a meaningful way? Should we not use our differences, our superpowers to work together to address planetary ills like pandemics and climate change? If we don't, we fear our fate will be decided by the snapping fingers of a Thanos, a Fate, or a Telos. Instead, might we be able to think together across disciplines, with our differences to imagine a radically different planetary community in which difference flourishes? If we can do this, we might be able to forge interplanetary alliances in the worlds to come.

NOTES

1. Ursula K. Le Guin, November 19, 2014: http://www.sfcenter.ku.edu/LeGuin-NBA-Medalist-Speech.htm.
2. Hannah Arendt, *Men in Dark Times* (Oralndo, FL: Harcourt Brace, 1955).
3. Lisa Stenmark describes this well in terms of the Science and Religion Discourse in: *Religion, Science and Democracy: A Disputational Friendship* (Lanham, MD: Lexington Books, 2013).
4. Fred Moten and Stefano Harney, *The Undercommons: Fugitive Planning and Black Study* (New York, NY: Minor Compositions, 2013).
5. Teresa Brennan, *Globalization and its Terrors* (New York, NY: Routledge, 2003).
6. Donna Haraway, *Staying with the Trouble: Making Kin in the Chthulucene* (Durham, NC: Duke University Press, 2016), 49.
7. Walter Mignolo, *The Darker Side of Western Modernity: Global Futures, Decolonial Options* (Durham, NC: Duke University Press, 2011).
8. Haraway, *Staying with the Trouble*, 33.
9. See e.g.: Walter Mignolo, *Darker Side of the Renaissance: Literacy, Territoriality, and Colonization* (Ann Arbor, MI: University of Michigan Press, 1997); Mignolo, *Darker Side of Western Modernity*; Edward Said, *Culture and Imperialism* (New York, NY: Vintage, 1993); Homi Bhabha, *The Location of Culture* (New York, NY: Routledge, 1994); and Gayatri Spivak, *A Critique of Postcolonial Reason: Toward a History of the Vanishing Present* (Cambridge, MA: Harvard University Press, 1999).
10. Haraway, *Staying with The Trouble*.

11. Donald Crosby, *Living with Ambiguity: Religious Naturalism and the Menace of Evil* (Albany, NY: SUNY Press, 2008), 67–68.

12. Mary Jane Rubenstein, *Worlds Without End: The Many Lives of the Multiverse* (New York, NY: Columbia University Press, 2014).

13. See Clara Moskowitz, "In a 'Rainbow' Universe, Time May Have No Beginning," *Scientific American*, December 9, 2013, http://www.scientificamerican.com/article/rainbow-gravity-universe-beginning/.

14. Mignolo, *The Darker Side of Western Modernity*, 54.

15. Rubenstein, *Worlds Without End*, 142–176.

16. Latour, *Politics of Nature*, 187.

17. Trish Ferguson, ed., *Victorian Time: Technologies, Standardization, and Catastrophes* (New York, NY: Palgrave, 2013).

18. Eduardo De Castro, "Cosmological Deixis and Amerindian Perspectivism," in *The Journal of the Royal Anthropological Institute*. 4.3 (Sept. 1998): 469–488: 469.

19. On the pace of progress vs. the pace of ambiguity see: Whitney Bauman and Kevin O'Brien, *Environmental Ethics and Uncertainty: Wrestling with Wicked Problems* (New York, NY: Routledge, 2019).

20. This is one way of dealing with difference: they all lead to the same reality. See, e.g.: Huston Smith, *The World's Religions* (New York, NY: HarperCollins, 1958).

21. Whitney Bauman, *Religion and Ecology: Developing A Planetary Ethic* (New York, NY: Columbia University Press, 2016), 63–84.

22. Mignolo, *Darker Side of Western Modernity*, 234.

23. Timothy Morton, *HyperObjects: Philosophy and Ecology After the End of the World* (Minneapolis, MN: University of Minnesota Press, 2013), Location: 2972.

24. Carolyn Merchant, *The Death of Nature: Women, Ecology and the Scientific Revolution* (New York, NY: HarperCollins, 1980).

25. Kocku von Stuckrad, *Die Seele im 20. Jahrhundert* (Leiden, The Netherlands: William Fink, 2019).

26. Anna Peterson, *Being Human: Ethics, Environment and our Place in the World* (Berkeley, CA: University of California Press, 2001).

27. Lynn White, "The Historical Roots of Our Ecological Crisis," in *Science*. 155(3767) (March 10, 1967): 1203–1207.

28. Rachel Carson, Barbara McKlintock, Marjory Stoneman Douglas, to name a few.

REFERENCES

Arendt, Hannah. 1955. *Men in Dark Times*. Orlando, FL: Harcourt Brace.

Bauman, Whitney. 2019. *Environmental Ethics and Uncertainty: Wrestling with Wicked Problems*. New York, NY: Routledge.

———. 2016. *Religion and Ecology: Developing a Planetary Ethic*. New York, NY: Columbia University Press.

Bhabha, Homi. 1994. *The Location of Culture*. New York, NY: Routledge.
Brennan, Teresa. 2003. *Globalization and its Terrors*. New York, NY: Routledge.
Crosby, Donald. 2008. *Living with Ambiguity: Religious Naturalism and the Menace of Evil*. Albany, NY: SUNY Press.
De Castro, Eduardo. 1998. "Cosmological Deixis and Amerindian Perspectivism," in *The Journal of the Royal Anthroplogical Institute*. 4.3 (September): 469–488.
Ferguson, Trish. Ed. 2013. *Victorian Time: Technologies, Standardization, and Catastrophes*. New York, NY: Palgrave.
Haraway, Donna. 2016. *Staying with the Trouble: Making Kin in the Chthulucene*. Durham, NC: Duke University Press.
Latour, Bruno. 1999. *The Politics of Nature: How to Bring the Sciences into Democracy*. Cambridge, MA: Harvard University Press.
Le Guin, Ursula K. 2014. "NBA Medalist Speech." November 19: https://www.youtube.com/watch?v=s2v7RDyo7os. Last Accessed April 1, 2021.
Merchant, Carolyn. 1980. *The Death of Nature: Women, Ecology and the Scientific Revolution*. New York, NY: HarperCollins.
Mignolo, Watler. 2011. *The Darker Side of Western Modernity: Global Futures, Decolonial Options*. Durham, NC: Duke University Press.
———. 1997. *Darker Side of the Renaissance: Literacy, Territoriality, and Colonization*. Ann Arbor, MI: University of Michigan Press.
Morton, Timothy. 2013. *HyperObjects: Philosophy and Ecology After the End of the World*. Minneapolis, MN: University Minnesota Press.
Moskowitz, Clara. 2013. "In a Rainbow Universe, Time May Have no Beginning." *Scientific America*, December 9: http://www.scientificamerican.com/article/rainbow-gravity-universe-beginning/. Last Accessed April 1, 2021.
Moten, Fred, and Stefano Harney. 2013. *The Undercommons: Fugitive Planning and Black Study*. New York, NY: Minor Compositions.
Peterson, Anna. 2001. *Being Human: Ethics, Environmental and Our Place in the World*. Berkeley, CA: University of California Press.
Rubenstein, Mary Jane. 2014. *Worlds Without End: The Many Lives of the Multiverse*. New York, NY: Columbia University Press.
Said, Edward. 1993. *Culture and Imperialism*. New York, NY: Vintage.
Smith, Huston. 1958. *The World's Religions*. New York, NY: HarperCollins.
Spivak, Gayatri. 1999. *A Critique of Postcolonial Reason: Toward a History of the Vanishing Present*. Cambridge, MA: Harvard University Press.
Stenmark, Lisa. 2013. *Religion, Science and Democracy: A Disputational Friendship*. Lanham, MD: Lexington Books.
Von Stuckrad, Kocku. 2019. *Die Seele im 20. Jahrhundert*. Leiden, The Netherlands: William Fink.
White, Lynn. 1967. "The Historical Roots of our Ecological Crisis," in *Science*. 155.3767 (March 10): 1203–1207.

Chapter 11

"Open Your Eye"

Psychedelics, Spirituality, and Trauma Resolution

Jennifer Baldwin

LOOKING THROUGH A KEY HOLE

What makes a person a superhero? Is it luck? Gamma rays? Spider bites? A ton of money, resources, and technical prowess? Is it an experience that fundamentally disrupts your way of existing in the world and prompts you to question, down to your core, who you are and who you want to be? Regardless of the means of superpower acquisition, most superheroes encounter experiences of profound threat or trauma prior to the emergence of their super. Within the bounds of the Marvel Cinematic Universe, the origin stories of our heroes/heroines often depict some form of trauma stimulus: for Iron Man, it was his capture and realization of the role of his weapons technology in the hands of the "bad guys"; for Captain America, incessant childhood bullying due to his size; for Thor, the emotional weight of failing to meet his father's expectations and subsequent banishment; for Wanda and Pietro Maximoff, fearing for their lives for days as they were stuck in the rubble of an exploded bomb with one that was unexploded; for Captain Marvel, the chronic experiences of seen as less than and harassed due to her sex and gender; Loki, the genocide of his people and subsequent adoption by those who enacted the genocide; and, for Star-Lord/Peter Quill, the death of his mother from cancer. Each of these lived experiences that threaten to completely overwhelm also provide the fuel and guide for growth into the super.

How we respond to experiences of crisis, threat, or trauma depends a lot on the resources we have available to us during and post-crisis. When we have "sufficient" interpersonal and supportive resources, we are more apt to move through traumatic response, recover our resiliency, and even move toward traumatic growth[1] (one lens through which to consider the "super" among in-real-life humans). If we do not have interpersonal or communal support, experiences of traumatic overwhelm are more inclined to slip into posttraumatic stress symptoms with risks of becoming a "villain" if you exist in universes depicted in comics or movies.[2] While encountering a significant adversary is an apparent given in the lives of superheroes, one's disposition prior to a traumatic crisis and the resources available during and after the crisis can have a definitive impact on resiliency and hero/villain status.

Though the intersection of traumatic crisis and superheroes is a rich a fascinating intersection deserving of a full text, Dr. Stephen Strange, as viewed through the film *Dr. Strange* (2016), provides a fascinating keyhole through which to explore themes of trauma, spirituality, and the growing role of psychedelics in trauma care.[3] The film invites us to explore concepts and experiences of profound injury, crisis of identity, hopelessness, spaces of altered consciousness, spirit as transformative, and moral responsibility. One of the core themes of the film is the journey of trauma, healing, and new life. This chapter will explore these themes through the lens of threat, trauma, and trauma-related altered states of consciousness (TRASC), psychedelics as a reliable means of entering into safety-dependent altered states of consciousness (SDASC), ritual as a pathway of transformation, mystical experiences as a form of religious experience, and integration as the practice of moving from the before, through altered spaces, and into the living of the new.

TO SHOW YOU JUST HOW MUCH YOU DON'T KNOW

At the start of the movie, Dr. Stephen Strange is a highly accomplished and competent neurosurgeon. With his skill and renown comes an arrogance that values and privileges his reputation of success over potential good and patient welfare that comes with a greater risk. He values prestige, money, and being the best in his area of practice. Of course, everything comes crashing down when his arrogance turns to recklessness causing him to drive off the road. The crash results in profound and irreparable medical trauma to his hands that creeps into financial depletion, and desperation. After exhausting all of the medical knowledge, resources, and collegial connections available to him, Strange takes a "hail Mary" trip to Kamar-Taj in search of "bleeding edge therapy"; instead, he finds an opening into the world and realm of knowledge utterly outside of his imagination. A door to altered states of consciousness, time, and space where our capacity to open our awareness, welcome spirit, and embody mystical energy generates embodied magic and supernatural powers.[4] Mr. Strange's journey from neurosurgeon to the Sorcerer Supreme can provide an interpretative lens for the journey from "before," through traumatic wounding, and into a new, fulfilling identity.

Experiences of threat are a fundamental and largely inescapable reality of existence on the planet; however, not all experiences of threat or crisis reach the threshold of trauma. Threats result in the activation of our human/mammalian mobilization systems and generate behaviors of protection and defense, that is, fawn/appease, flight, fight, or freeze.[5] Experiences cross over into the realm of trauma when the threat overwhelms our capacity to cope and our resources for resiliency in the moment and the immediate aftermath. Like the switches in the electrical panels in our homes "trip" or disconnect when the circuit is overloaded by too much power running to or from an outlet, trauma responses are most likely to occur when the circuit of our body's protective system is overloaded. For Dr. Stephen, the injuries to his hands in the car wreck and corresponding loss of identity and power in his inability to mobilize his connections, expertise, and wealth to restore what was lost are traumatic and destabilizing. When threat crosses the threshold and moves into trauma, strategies of protection and defense are overwhelmed and our neurophysiology fails to completely integrate and process the discrete components of sensory, narrative, and relational input. Consequently, the components of experience that are left out of our normative processing often correspond to the specific symptoms and manifestations of posttraumatic stress.[6]

Experiences of threat that reach the intensity to induce trauma responses frequently result in alterations of one's sense of time, embodiment, affect, or thought. While our body-mind has a cohesive process for integrating experiences of safety within states of normal consciousness, experiences of traumatic overwhelm have the potential to shift our physiology into varying degrees of altered states of consciousness. The altered states of consciousness that occur as a survival response to profound threat occur within a physiological "soup" of hormonal threat response, including increases in cortisol and adrenalin during fight and flight and increases in endogenous opioids in freeze states. These "trauma-related altered states of consciousness" (TRASC)[7] can range in intensity based on the frequency of occurrence, degree of compartmentalization, degree of dissociation, and prevalence of repetition during developmental periods. In other words, an overwhelm of the threat survival system that occurs once, within a cohesive narrative of life experience, with little psychological or physiological dissociation, during adulthood (Dr. Strange) will result in a lower intensity of TRASC than multiple types of overwhelm, occurring repeatedly during development with high psychological or physiological dissociation, and high compartmentalization of the experience/s (Jane, *Doom Patrol*).

Ruth Lanius and Paul Frewen offer a rich assessment of the neurophenomenology of TRASC integrating fMRI brain scans with phenomenological methodologies. In their work, they highlight and deeply explore alterations of time, thought, body, and affect subsequent to traumatic overwhelm. Alterations of time span from "intrusive recall and reminder of distress" to "flashbacks, reliving, and fragmentation" of one's experience and perception of the direction, pacing, and movement of time; alterations of thought move from "negative self-other referential thinking" to "hearing voices" that are critical; alterations of body can vary from "physiological hyperarousal" or anxious activation to "depersonalization"/feeling as if your body or parts of your body are not real or not accessible to your felt sense; and alterations of emotion can be experienced as "general negative affective" up to "emotional numbing or the compartmentalization of emotion" in which some emotions are no longer available or safe to express.[8] In the film, Stephen Strange (and the viewer) experience disruptions in the cohesive flow of time when the narrative becomes dislodged from the calendar. (How long was he unconscious after the accident? How much time passed as he was desperately seeking a successful treatment option? How long was he a student of the Ancient One before Kaecilius began attacking the Sanctums?) Strange also displays posttraumatic body dysphoria and, utilizing another map, a disruption in his chi as well as general negative affect and bouts of rage when his emotions broke through the freeze of compartmentalization (e.g., his treatment of Christine in his home).

WHAT'S IN THAT TEA?

After his car wreck, Dr. Stephen Strange mobilized all of his professional and financial resources to mend the damage to his hands; however, at its root, the issue wasn't really a matter of hand function. Dr. Strange's more pressing and essential issue is one of identity and purpose. If he could no longer be a cutting-edge surgeon, who is he? These questions of identity, purpose, and how to cope with traumatic experiences are at the heart of spirituality and (when they fail) theodicy. The tools and therapies that are well suited to meet the needs of distress within the realm of apparently normal experiences in which the standard functioning of threat responses and neurophysical processing are capable of integration too often fail with the threat turning to overwhelming trauma and our ordinary processes are altered. In other words, where do we turn when "cutting edge" isn't enough? What do we do when all the things that normally work fail? To whom do we turn when we are out of answers? When science isn't enough, what next? How do we see more clearly when we are blinded by how much we do not know?

For Strange, these questions of identity and purpose represent the unmooring of his medicalized, allopathic, Western worldview that is arguably as overwhelming as the physical trauma of the car wreck. This loss prompts him to venture beyond—geographically, ideologically, spiritually, and physically—and point to the decentering of his being—or in Tillichian terms, his crisis of faith.[9] Faith, for Tillich, is a dynamic centering our being in a manner that provides cohesion, direction, and clarity. For Strange, medicine and success had provided this centering and his faith in the superiority of allopathic medicine, science, and spirituality over Eastern orientations of being and health, "magic," and spirit. With the last threads of his rope frayed and his resources for resiliency quickly evaporating, Dr. Strange makes one final attempt to pursue a treatment course and travels to Kamar-Taj for "bleeding edge" treatment outside of the jurisdiction of medical authorities. Fully expecting to find a medical solution that aligns with his view of the world and how it works, Strange seeks consultation with the Ancient One. While their first encounter is rich with opportunities for a critical discourse on gender, power, race, Euro-centrism, and Christian centrism, the dynamic most relevant to our current discussion is his experience of awakening to realms beyond his prior awareness.

The path Strange as yet unknowingly seeks to explore is one that will require a recentering of his being, awareness, and will test the limits of his existing frames of knowledge. In the immediate and ongoing aftermath of traumatic disruption, the frames of reference that guided life pre-trauma lose their potency. Much of the important work in psychotherapy for trauma recovery and resiliency is not only to recall and remember elements of experience and process the package of elements of the experience as a unit but also to create a new way of being that integrates the past, threat, survival, and co-creation of the new. For Strange and survivors of traumatizing experiences, moving forward often requires courageously stepping into unknown spaces. As Mordo wisely advises as they enter Kamar-Taj, "Forget everything you think you know."

Upon entering the sanctuary of the Ancient One, Strange attempts to assert his prior identity and power by embodying the role of the surgeon quizzing his colleagues. The Ancient One, all too familiar with this form of engagement, refuses to engage on his terms unveiling her knowledge of his medical history and offers a reorientation from the keyhole of Westernized medicine to the expanse of the mystical arts. She offers an awareness of the organic intelligence of cellular regeneration, life, energy, and spirit and begins to assess his potential to be open to that which lies beyond his medical knowledge. Assuming that the maps of the chakra system, acupuncture, and

MRIs are all she has to offer, Strange indignantly rejects anything outside of his prior understanding. In response to his escalating aggression, the Ancient One, with profound ease, pushes his astral form out of his physical form generating disbelief and the confusion that can become a catalyst for new learning. Upon reentry to his bodily form, Strange asks, "What's in that tea? Psilocybin? LSD?" To which, she responds, "Just tea with a little honey." While Dr. Strange should know that neither substance acts quickly enough in the body to produce that experience only a few minutes after consumption (psilocybin takes at least 20 minutes or more and LSD takes at least an hour to be felt), his instinct to link altered states with these substances is reasonable.

Practices that induce or facilitate altered states of consciousness are a robust resource for gaining a new perspective, opening curiosity to new maps of experience and being, and exploring new conceptualizations of identity and self. It is important to note that not all altered states of consciousness facilitate growth and healing (e.g., trauma-related altered states of consciousness as a survival strategy and trace of overwhelming threat); however, altered states of consciousness can be a powerful antidote to TRASC when they are entered into with intention, consent, volition, and in physiological and psychological contexts of secure safety as SDASC. There are many practices that utilize the body's innate resources to induce altered states including ecstatic dance, forms of pranayama, concerts, drum circles, sweat lodges, meditation, contemplative prayer, and so on. These practices are often incorporated in spiritual disciplines and utilize the infrastructures of the body to enter into altered forms of conscious awareness—some of these practices are effective because they induce the release or activation of many of the endogenous substances that are involved in medicine-induced altered states (i.e., body-made DMT, cannabinoids, oxytocin, opioids, etc.) While spiritual practices like the ones referred to above have the capacity to induce altered states and/or mystical experiences, these states are not always predictably achieved. Another route to states of altered consciousness is plant medicines or classic psychedelics.

"Psychedelics" most generally means mind/soul clearing or manifesting. These medicines, in a variety of ways, induce altered states of consciousness with high reliability through a variety of routes. Mind-manifesting medicines interact with varying receptors in the brain including serotonin (psilocybin, MDMA, LSD, mescaline), opioid (ibogaine, salvia), glutamate (ketamine), sigma-1 (DMT/ayahuasca)[10], oxytocin (MDMA), and endocannabinoids (cannabis) and have shown to have clinical benefit for a variety of mental and spiritual health challenges. Many of these medicines have a long history of use in religious and spiritual ceremonies throughout the planet and derive from plants in different ecosystems including the use and presence of salvia in Mexico, ayahuasca in Central and South America, peyote in North America, iboga in West Africa, cannabis in Central Asia and India, and psilocybin on all continents except Antarctica.

While psychedelics have been utilized across cultures for spiritual rituals and healing through the journeys of the shamans, research into their therapeutic benefits is reemerging in the Westernized medical arena after being shut down and moved underground in the United States during the Nixon era via the Controlled Substances Act of 1970. Organizations such as MAPS,[11] Heffter Research Initiative,[12] and Compass[13] are currently spearheading FDA research trials on the use of MDMA and psilocybin for the treatment of PTSD, treatment-resistant depression, and end of life anxiety. Many of these studies utilize "psychedelic" medicines, entheogens, or enpathogen/entactogens to catalyze a psychotherapeutic process. In other words, the medicines open channels of trust between a therapist/guide and the patient/client as well as new avenues of awareness on the part of the client. In many studies, individuals report experiences of profound connection, intra- and interpersonal awareness, and a greater awakening to God or the divine.[14] For instance, in a study done at Johns Hopkins, "when administered under supportive conditions, psilocybin occasioned experiences similar to spontaneously occurring mystical experiences that, at 14-month follow-up, were considered by volunteers to be among the most personally meaningful and spiritually significant of their lives."[15]

Above ground, psychedelic-assisted psychotherapy has varying availability based on the medicine assisting the work. Ketamine is legally available with a prescription in all areas of the United States. Cannabis has limited legal availability. MDMA, psilocybin, DMT, and LSD are currently only legal in the United States in the context of FDA-approved research. Other countries have different legal boundaries based on the substance that allows for legal work to occur with ibogaine, ayahuasca, and psilocybin. While the intra- and interpersonal quality of the assisted psychotherapy work depends significantly on the substance offing assistance, all of these forms of therapy share a commitment to physical and psychological safety, set (intention for the work), and setting (the location of the work). Careful attention to the neuroceptive assessment of safety, set, and setting is essential for promoting a therapeutic experience that is primed for an opening of awareness that is healing while limiting the potential risk of an adverse experience. Subjectively, psychedelic healing work (therapy, ceremonies, personal work) has the profound potential to reliably open up SDASC or liminal spaces to explore new perspectives, vantage points, or vistas of awareness. The opening of psychological and spiritual space is both an apocalypse (uncovering) and revelation (disclosure of something that was previously unknown).

WIDENING THE KEYHOLE

SDASC are liminal spaces where the norms and structures that ordinarily hold life in a semi-predictable rhythm and flow are released increasing the potential for transformation. For survivors of trauma who continue to experience posttraumatic responses, the structures that often hold life are ghosts from overwhelming threat and their corresponding survival reflexes and strategies. Trauma-induced liminal spaces often present as symptoms of dissociation and dissociative disorders and manifest many of the features described and tracked by Frewen and Lanius as TRASC. However, in the context of safe, consensual, volitional, and intentional induction, SDASC's, including psychedelic-assisted therapy and spiritual ceremonies, can offer rites of passage from dis-ease into states of clarity, curiosity, compassion, and courage.

Ritual theory offers a helpful framework for tracking the phases of transformation. Arnold van Gennep[16] and Victor Turner[17] have offered a highly utilized framework for understanding ritual processes. Van Gennep discusses the three phases of ritual: separation, liminality, and incorporation. The rites of separation mark the movement from ordinary states and activities of life into the realm of the ritual. The liminal phase is the space of transition in which the social markers of the "before" and of the "after" are suspended—time, space, awareness, perspective, and identity take on a sense of malleability. The rites of incorporation welcome the reintegration of the person into the social community in a new way or with a new status. After the rite, things are different. Psychedelic-induced altered states of consciousness have the potent potential to instigate a form of van Gennep's rites of passage. In both ceremony and psychotherapy settings, there are rites of separation that can include physical, psychological, and spiritual preparation for the experience. These rites can include intentional meditation or prayer, changes in diet, or intake and preparation appointments. For Strange, the rites of separation included his trip to Kathmandu and Kamar-Taj. Rites of incorporation are also present in ceremonial and psychotherapeutic uses of medicine and can include various rituals of integration of the experience and open curiosity about the potential of the experience to catalyze meaningful change. For Strange, the rites of incorporation include his plea to learn, integration into the community, and journey of learning and practice. The liminal phase of the rites is the in-between in which social markers are suspended. In TRASC, the liminal phase aligns with episodes of dissociation and are maladaptive precisely because they do not potentiate a new way of being distinct from the prior state. In SDASC, the liminal phase can align with the "trip" experience if/when the experience opens new psycho-spiritual learning or awareness that can move us toward more clarity, connection, and compassion.

Experiences of liminality are vital for social, personal, and neurophysiological changes to occur. They provide both a "time-out" from the established norms and default patterns of being and a different vantage point and perspective. The "time-out" is important for disrupting the entrenched patterns of behavior, thought, or awareness that perpetuates the status quo or the default. In nontraumatized daily life, our habituated "doing" takes on a form of perpetual motion leaving little room to take stock of our internal, external, societal, and global patterns. In the context of post-trauma, our "doing" is often marked by incomplete survival reflexes and strategies that can keep us in a time loop akin to the time prison Dr. Strange generated to alter Doromamu's plans. Psychedelic medicines currently under study provide a reliable means of initiating a "time out." In addition to a "time out," we also need an opportunity for a new vision or perspective. This second component is essential for prolonged benefit from the experience. Perspective can include receiving a new awareness or vision from the experience itself, a new understanding of existing concerns that allows for a different response, or a release of existing burdens or hurts that facilitate renewed vitality or peace. A shift in perspective is not an alteration of the facts of an experience but a renewal in the ways we interpret the meaning of an event in light of broader information, values, or considerations. It is not a generation of "alternative facts"; it is a seeing more, a widening our keyhole.

Neurologically, we can think of widening the keyhole as a metaphor for neuroplasticity. One of the most promising discoveries emerging from psychedelic-assisted therapy is its potential for catalyzing windows of neuroplasticity.[18] The popularized version of Hebb's law from neuroscience states that "neurons that fire together, wire together." Most simply, neuroplasticity points to our brain's capacity to generate new neural connections and pathways that allow us to think, feel, and move in novel ways. In cases of chronic traumatization, TRASC, and the replaying of trauma responses, there is a tendency for the keyhole to narrow further cementing threat responses and survival strategies. While this biological phenomenon is helpful for ensuring survival by keeping us away from the watering hole with the alligator, it is less helpful for societies that depend on social engagement and connections to ensure safety. The resulting rigidity of learning and erosion of trust limits the options we have available to us. Some of these limitations may be external; others are driven by internal limitations of what we can imagine within a safe enough context. When we feel safe enough in our physiology (neuroception), emotional life, and relational life, we are more inclined to seek out novel experiences and enjoyment. When we perceive and experience threat, we hunker down and limit novelty that could open space for threat. Consequently, TRASC narrows our possibilities of experience while SDASC has the potential to widen our options. Hebb's law provides a theoretical framework for both why it is challenging to get out of established patterns and as well as a way out of those same patterns. In the aftermath of experiences of traumatizing overwhelm provides a sense of perspective that is often eclipsed by our patterns of suffering. Often the patterns that keep us anchored in our threat or trauma responses are ill-equipped to move us toward resiliency. However, if and when we are able to induce experiences that support neuroplasticity in the context of safety and opportunities for learning and new perspective, new possibilities open, novel perspectives emerge, and our keyhole widens beyond what we previously thought possible.

REORIENTING THE SPIRIT: INTO THE MYSTICAL ARTS

The question of what extends beyond the reach of our perception enters into the realm of spirituality, mysticism, magic, theology, and the numinous. It is the realm both within and beyond the bounds of our material-derived existence that grants meaning, awe, and mystery. All of the world's spiritual traditions have means of accessing and honoring this dimension of life and reality—the gift and power of life force, spirit, and the divine that lies beyond the keyhole in the liminal space/s. How people, communities, and traditions navigate the opening of our awareness to divine life varies considerably based on factors internal to the spiritual tradition and external cultural factors. Most avenues move through some form of ritual structure. Rituals can be used with altered state-inducing substances to either open us up to the internal dimensions of life we have buried or to the expanse of connection that exists beyond our individual embodied form. They can be used with practices of movement, elements of our natural world, vocal intonations, or instrumental guides to join us together as a community in worship or sacred journeys. Rituals also mark our personal journeys of spiritual growth or of daily practice. In all of the various ways in which human beings seek connection with divine presence and wisdom, there is a centralized intuition that there is a deeper pool of awareness available just outside the limits of our day to day going one—a call to connect with the holy, however, one encounters it.

Encounters with the holy that utterly transform our existence in the world have a mystical quality. William James offers four marks of the mystical form of religious experience. First, mystical experiences have an "ineffability" rendering them difficult to fully describe using ordinary means of communication. Their profundity transcends linguistic efficacy—there are simply no words capable of describing the experience. Second, they have a "noetic quality" imparting a clear message to the experiencer to benefit their life journey. These experiences teach us something. "They are states of insight into depths of truth unplumbed by the discursive intellect. They are illuminations, revelations, full of significance and importance, all inarticulate though they remain; and as a rule they carry with them a curious sense of authority for aftertime."[19] Third, mystical forms of religious experience are "transiency" and rarely last more than an hour unless supported by soul manifesting medicines. Fourth, while they can be induced through prescribed actions, the experience itself involves a form of "passivity" on behalf of the experiencer.[20] As Job learned in his experience with YHWH in the whirlwind (Job 38), when divine presence opens to our awareness, we are not in a position to make demands or set the agenda.

Of course, simply having a mystical experience does not always translate into a religious or spiritual life any more than having a traumatizing experience leads to an existentially ruined life. Profound experiences that open up mystical or dissociative spaces are like seeds that can either be cultivated or ignored. When spaces of trauma-related dissociation split open, we can either ignore or avoid the harm thereby fostering posttrauma symptoms of distress or we can wisely attend to the harm and foster resiliency and posttraumatic growth. Likewise, when we encounter mystical experiences through whatever means, the opening of our consciousness to the connections and compassion that infuse cosmic life force, can either be cultivated and formed into a more spiritual and loving life or it can just be an intense experience that doesn't transform how one lives in the world. In both forms, the experience itself does not necessarily determine its long-term influence; the impact is determined by how we respond and what we choose to do next.

Steven Strange's life had already been completely upended by the trauma of the car wreck and debilitating injuries to his hands. This rupture of the normal rhythms of his life, vocation, and identity into the liminal space of multiple surgeries served to close the possibilities of the life he knew. Without this traumatic disruption, there is no reason to imagine that he would have had cause to venture onto a new path. Profound trauma does have a way to concluding whatever chapter of our life we are currently on and often prevents a return to the before. For some, this closure is itself overwhelming and fosters chronic despair or hopelessness that can lead down a life-destroying path. For others with subjectively enough resources for resiliency, the closure can lead through the darkness onto a new path and become an origin story. For Strange, the ending of his life as a practitioner of the medical arts opens a path to his study of the mystic arts.

Strange's initiation into this wider realm of mystical experience begins with the Ancient One's twofold intervention: first, pushing his astral form out of his physical form and second, his journey to "open your eye," which pushed him out of his body and through multiple dimensions. The first mystical intervention functions to quickly disrupt his self-righteous tirade and get his attention effectively communicating that there is more in this multiverse than he is aware. When the first intervention gets his attention but fails to fully move past his Westernized medical explanations the Ancient One aims "to show you just how much you don't know," touching his forehead at the location of the third eye, Ajna, the sixth chakra sending him on a "trip." The "trip" proceeds from the opening of the eye of the sixth chakra, out of his body through the crown chakra, and into alternative dimensions and spaces of consciousness and has visual resonance with psychedelic trips initiated via various substances.

Both the voice-over by the Ancient One and the visual imagery of his journey, helpfully point to qualities of mystic experience. Totaling less than 2.5 minutes, Strange's mystical trip experience encompasses James's four criteria: ineffability, noetic quality, transiency, and passivity. Strange is catapulted out of the sanctum and into space as he freaks out, uttering "oh shit, oh god, oh god, no, no, no, no, what's happening, this isn't real, this isn't," as his body flails through space. Upon seeing a butterfly, he pauses, touches it, and is catapulted around the curvature of the planet and through something akin to a wormhole. As his heart rate increases (heart rate or blood pressure elevations are two of the medical concerns to monitor with psychedelic-assisted therapy), he is pulled back to the sanctum, assessed as medically cleared to continue, and jettisoned back into his journey. As his trip unfolds, the voice-over offers a "whirlwind"-esque direction. The Ancient One via a voice-over provides noetic teaching:

> You think you know how the world works
> You think this material universe is all there is
> What is real?
> What mysteries lie beyond the reach of your senses?
> At the root of existence
> Mind and matter meet
> Thoughts shape reality
> This universe is only one of an infinite number—worlds without end
> Some benevolent and life giving
> Others filled with malice and hunger
> Dark places where powers older than time lie ravenous and waiting
> Who are you in this vast multiverse, Mr. Strange?[21]

Visually, Strange moves from panic to proprioceptive orientation as he travels along a path of the sanctum, Earth's orbit, a wormhole/Einstein- Rosen bridge moved forward by a ball of light or fire that splits into colors emanating from his limbs, fracturing his image into multiples as he is pulled into a portal moving him into a space of the birthing of dimensions and galaxies, through something resembling a Mandelbrot fractal, into a realm containing the hands of his trauma that threatens to consume him. As his journey continues, the hands morph into his facial image as he goes into his physical right eye, breaking into a mirrored dimensions with countless reflections and choices of identity and path, exploring places of life and those of malice, including our first look at Doramamu, and into silence and rest/passivity/death before being pulled back into the sanctum. Strange's mystical journey does, in fact, open all of his eyes as he asks "teach me."

The journey itself is rich with noetic qualities. It moves from the familiar, through trauma, into possibility, and concludes with a question of chosen identity. "Who are you in this vast multiverse?" Who will you choose to be? How wide will your courage allow your awareness to be? Are you open to exploring that which lies beyond the material universe you thought you knew? Are you ready to learn and do the work to step into the new? These are questions that often follow mystical experiences whether supported by physical practices or plant medicines. They are questions that call us to attention and require a choice. Who will we grow into?

OPEN THE DOOR

The doors of our perception, awareness, and attunement can be opened via mystical or psychedelic experiences; however, an experience is not a crafted life of meaning and purpose. Opening a door beyond traumatic response and the limitations of our prior awareness is merely the first step. We also have to walk through it and into the new—this is the work of integration (either of trauma experiences or of psychedelic journeys). Integration is a component of psychedelic ceremony or therapy (as distinct from purely recreational use). It often includes three components: (1) the return from altered spaces and into connection with a trusted individual or community, (2) identification of the type of experiences that emerged and lessons given, and (3) devising concrete steps to implement the wisdom gained from the experience.[22] These three components of psychedelic integration have helpful parallels to the broad strokes of trauma care—returned awareness to the present with a connection to a sense of safety in this moment with a safe enough other; re/collection of the components of sensory experience, and the skilled movement of experience from past into the present along the functional path of the limbic system,[23] cultivating the courage to live more fully and authentically posttrauma recovery.

In their first lesson, Strange asks the Ancient One how he gets from where he is to where she is. Her response points him back to his journey of becoming a surgeon: "through study and practice . . . years of it." Likewise, the path of recovery from profound traumatic wounding also requires diligent and informed therapeutic support. There is no magic treatment. The best things in life require clear-eyed vision, courageous tenacity, and an open heart. Love, at first sight, may happen in a flash but a loving relationship is built over decades. Clarity of one's work calling may occur suddenly but the knowledge and skill to become an expert evolves over time. Mystical awareness of the profound interconnections of all life may happen in a single prayerful sitting or ceremony but living a life reflecting that awareness is crafted. Trauma may happen in a moment but resiliency is built over time and often with the support of the community. As in life, Strange's moments of awakening are not the climax and conclusion of the film. Rather they occur in the first quarter of the movie as the bulk of the film explores the process of learning and transforming from the arrogant neurosurgeon into the Sorcerer Supreme. Stepping into who we authentically are is a life-long process full of twists and turns, ruptures and repairs, dark nights, and vivid awakenings. Altered states of consciousness can occur as survival strategies in times of trauma, wondrous moments of mystical awakening, or through the intentional use of medicines in the context of therapy or ceremony. The distinction between altered states that mark profound hurt and those that offer avenues of healing is whether or not they occur in the context of threat or the context of safety and if we have the support needed to properly integrate them for the benefit of our life path. For Dr. Strange, his encounter with mystical awakening catalyzed his entry into the mystical arts and his path to become a protector of the galaxy. What potential exists just beyond the bounds of our awareness? Who are we in this vast multiverse?

NOTES

1. David Feldman and Lee Daniel Kravetz, *Supersurvivors: The Surprising Link Between Suffering and Success*, New York: HarperWave, 2015.

2. Wanda and Pietro Maximoff are prime examples of the importance of appropriate support and connection post-trauma as it predisposes one toward becoming a hero or villain. Loki demonstrates the change that can occur with ongoing care and support.

3. *Black Panther* could also serve as a rich catalyst for this discussion due to the role of the heart-shaped herb in the ritual transition into the Kingship.

4. Sallie McFague, *Super, Natural Christians: How We Should Love Nature*, Minneapolis: Fortress Press, 2000.

5. Jennifer Baldwin, *Through Dangerous Terrain: A Guide for Trauma-Sensitive Pastoral Leadership in Times of Threat*, Eugene: Cascade Books, 2020.

6. Baldwin, *Through Dangerous Terrain*; and Bessel van der Kolk, *The Body Keeps the Score: Brain, Mind, and Body in the Healing of Trauma*, New York: Viking, 2014.

7. Paul Frewen and Ruth Lanius, *Healing the Traumatized Self: Consciousness, Neuroscience, Treatment*, New York: W. W. Norton, 2015.

8. Ibid., 29.

9. Paul Tillich, *Dynamics of Faith*, New York: Harper and Row, 1957.

10. Steven Barker, "N, N-Dimethyltryptamine (DMT), an Endogenous Hallucinogen: Past, Present, and Future Research to Determine Its Role and Function," *Frontiers in Neuroscience* 12, 2018. https://www.ncbi.nlm.nih.gov/pmc/articles/PMC6088236/ Site accessed October 10, 2020.

11. MAPS, the Multidisciplinary Association for Psychedelic Studies, is nearing completion of Phase 3 studies with hopes of having MDMA reclassified as a drug for treatment of PTSD. www.maps.org Site accessed August 8, 2020.

12. www.heffter.org Site accessed October 11, 2020.

13. Compass Pathways is conducting research on the benefits of psilocybin as a therapy for treatment-resistant depression. www.compasspathways.com Site accessed August 8, 2020.

14. Thomas Roberts, editor, *Psychedelics and Spirituality: The Sacred Use of LSD, Psilocybin, and MDMA for Human Transformation*, Rochester: Park Street Press, 2020; William Richards, *Sacred Knowledge: Psychedelics and Religious Experiences*, New York: Columbia University Press, 2016; Douglas Osto, *Altered States: Buddhism and Psychedelic Spirituality in America*, New York: Columbia University Press, 2016.

15. Roland Griffiths, Wa Richards, et al., "Mystical-type Experiences Occasioned by Psilocybin Mediate the Attribution of Personal Meaning and Spiritual Significance 14 Months Later," *Journal of Psychopharmacology* 22.6, 2008: 621–632.

16. Arnold van Gennep, *The Rites of Passage*, London: Routledge, 1909.

17. Victor Turner, *The Ritual Process: Structure and Anti-Structure*, Piscataway: AldineTransaction, 1969, 2007.

18. Calvin Ly, Alexandra Greb, and Lindsay Cameron, "Psychedelics Promote Structural and Functional Neural Plasticity," *Cell Reports* 23.11, 2018: 3170–3182; Frederick Barrett, Manoj Doss, et al., "Emotions and Brain Function are Altered Up to One Month after a Single High Dose of Philocybin," *Scientific Reports* 10, 2020: 2214; Romain Nardou, Eastman Lewis, et al., "Oxytocin-dependent Reopening of a Social Reward Learning Critical Period with MDMA," *Nature* 569, 2019: 116–120; Ginetta Collo, and Emilio Pich, "Ketamine Enhances Structural Plasticity in Human Dopaminergic Neurons: Possible Relevance for Treatment-resistant Depression," *Neural Regeneration Research* 13.4, 2018: 645–646.

19. William James, *The Varieties of Religious Experience*, New York: New American Library, 1958, 319.

20. Ibid.

21. *Dr. Strange* (2016).

22. Francoise Bourzat, *Consciousness Medicine: Indigenous Wisdom, Entheogens, and Expanded States of Consciousness for Healing and Growth*, Berkeley: North Atlantic Books, 2019, 182.

23. See Baldwin, *Through Dangerous Terrain* or van der Kolk, *The Body Keeps the Score*.

REFERENCES

Baldwin, Jennifer. *Through Dangerous Terrain: A Guide for Trauma-Sensitive Pastoral Leadership in Times of Threat.* Eugene: Cascade Books, 2020.

Barker, Steven. "N, N-Dimethyltryptamine (DMT), an Endogenous Hallucinogen: Past, Present, and Future Research to Determine Its Role and Function." *Frontiers in Neuroscience* 12, 2018. https://www.ncbi.nlm.nih.gov/pmc/articles/PMC6088236/ Site accessed October 10, 2020.

Barrett, Frederick, Manoj Doss, et al. "Emotions and Brain Function are Altered Up to One Month after a Single High Dose of Philocybin." *Scientific Reports* 10, 2020: 2214.

Bourzat, Francoise. *Consciousness Medicine: Indigenous Wisdom, Entheogens, and Expanded States of Consciousness for Healing and Growth.* Berkeley: North Atlantic Books, 2019.

Collo, Ginetta, and Emilio Pich. "Ketamine Enhances Structural Plasticity in Human Dopaminergic Neurons: Possible Relevance for Treatment-resistant Depression." *Neural Regeneration Research* 13.4, 2018: 645–646.

Feldman, David, and Lee Daniel Kravetz. *Supersurvivors: The Surprising Link Between Suffering and Success.* New York: HarperWave, 2015.

Frewen, Paul, and Ruth Lanius. *Healing the Traumatized Self: Consciousness, Neuroscience, Treatment.* New York: W. W. Norton, 2015.

Griffiths, Roland, W. Richards, et al. "Mystical-type Experiences Occasioned by Psilocybin Mediate the Attribution of Personal Meaning and Spiritual Significance 14 Months Later." *Journal of Psychopharmacology* 22.6, 2008: 621–632.

James, William. *The Varieties of Religious Experience.* New York: New American Library, 1958.

Ly, Calvin, Alexandra Greb, and Lindsay Cameron. "Psychedelics Promote Structural and Functional Neural Plasticity." *Cell Reports* 23.11, 2018: 3170–3182.

McFague, Sallie. *Super, Natural Christians: How We Should Love Nature.* Minneapolis: Fortress Press, 2000.

Nardou, Romain, Eastman Lewis, et al. "Oxytocin-dependent Reopening of a Social Reward Learning Critical Period with MDMA." *Nature* 569, 2019: 116–120.

Osto, Douglas. *Altered States: Buddhism and Psychedelic Spirituality in America.* New York: Columbia University Press, 2016.

Richards, William. *Sacred Knowledge: Psychedelics and Religious Experiences.* New York: Columbia University Press, 2016.

Roberts, Thomas, editor. *Psychedelics and Spirituality: The Sacred Use of LSD, Psilocybin, and MDMA for Human Transformation.* Rochester: Park Street Press, 2020.

Tillich, Paul. *Dynamics of Faith.* New York: Harper and Row, 1957.

Turner, Victor. *The Ritual Process: Structure and Anti-Structure.* Piscataway: AldineTransaction, 1969, 2007.

van der Kolk, Bessel. *The Body Keeps the Score: Brain, Mind, and Body in the Healing of Trauma.* New York: Viking, 2014.

Part IV

FORMING IDENTITY

Chapter 12

Marveling at Captain Danvers, Or, What Is So Super about Our Heroes?

Contesting the Identity Politics of Self-Other

John C. McDowell

When preaching on Luke 23:34, Martin Luther King Jr. raises issues regarding relations of inequity and violence in a system of injustice.[1] In a challenge to moral sloth, he proclaims that "sincerity and conscientiousness in themselves are not enough. History has proven that these noble virtues may degenerate into tragic vices. Nothing in the world is more dangerous than sincere ignorance and conscientious stupidity."[2] Spending time reflecting on the "tragic blindness" of Jesus's executors allows King to exhort his audience toward developing insightful and honest moral self-examination, what he refers to as "enlightenment."[3] In fact, they, as members of the church, are to remind everyone "that they have a moral responsibility to be intelligent."[4]

Theodor Adorno's work on the culture industry is an effort to cultivate in his audience prudential insight. Jointly with Max Horkheimer, he argues that the Hollywood entertainment machine produces, at worst, the kind of moral blindness that King derided, or, at best, conditions that distract the masses from the ills of modern life. The market economy's regulation of the screened production reduces the shape and content of art to a form of "candy-floss entertainment" that contributes to "mass deception."[5] This, then, involves processes of production that, in the words of Henry Giroux, "render the workings of its own ideology indiscernible."[6] As Giroux observes, "Audiences are consistently bombarded with messages that suggest that one function of such films is to entertain rather than educate."[7] However, even "Storytelling . . . is never [politically] innocent."[8] Popular cultural texts, such as those of cinema, contribute to the manufacture of social expectations and codes of understanding, of "dominant social reading formations that often limit the range of meanings that can be taken up by readers in addressing films and other media texts."[9] That means, first, that popular film expresses a range of cultural understandings so that we should be looking first to popular culture as a barometer of social change and as a source for identifying the key issues that inform the culture we are becoming.[10] In the second place, however, it more importantly entails that cinema contributes to the manufacture of subject positions, to plausibility structures, and to the understanding of the options for moral and political judgment.

SUPERHEROES IN KAIROTIC TIME POST 9/11

The connection between the reflection, conservation, and perpetuation of hegemonic values has frequently been noticed by commentators on the superhero genre. Christian Steinmetz, for instance, speaks of "Comic books' tendency to promote nationalism," and proclaims that "Superhero narratives reveal that their ideology is mostly a conservative one that never allows the characters to establish a Utopia; thus, their fantastic fisticuffs can continue forever, protecting the status quo from change (Wolf-Meyer)."[11] The difficulty, it would seem, is largely one of providing macho "power-fantasies" for adolescent males.[12] However, as Matthew Costello observes, something more interesting has particularly occurred over the past two decades. "The twenty-first century brought a revival of direct political commentary to comic books."[13] While political references had not been entirely absent from the genre since the 1970s, recent years have nonetheless returned to providing intensively explicit attention to political matters Moreover, the material was surprisingly subtle, even if it was confronting. "Without a clear definition of national mission," Costello maintains, "and with a continued questioning of American virtue, there was no clear sense of how the nation should approach the War on Terror."[14] In fact, "Within two years of the attacks of 9/11 comics were questioning U.S. culpability. Americans could no longer define themselves as a virtuous nation in pursuit of a progressive global mission."[15] Even the superheroes, "frequently offered as morally superior to politicians and therefore capable of bearing the national burden with more virtue, are rendered morally problematic themselves, and they are thus unable to save America from itself."[16]

Much of the catalog of the Marvel Cinematic Universe (MCU; in particular the four *Avengers* movies) takes its shape from the kind of "post 9/11 cinema" that deals with "resounding cultural trauma" through cathartic compensation.[17] Susan Sontag names this process a "reflect[ion of] world-wide anxieties" through offering a mechanism that "serve[s] to allay them."[18] The term "9/11," after all, has not functioned merely as a temporal reference to a moment in history. Rather, it has been discursively exaggerated to have the character of something the kairotic.[19] As Kevin Wetmore explains, "Politicians, pundits and media figures use 'pre-9/11' and 'post-9/11' to categorize ways of viewing the world and the subsequent necessary actions we must individually and collectively take. . . . The phrase thus refers to a day, an event, a period, a mindset and a cultural shift."[20] Nevertheless, the handling of this context and the subsequent 'War on Terror' has been less politically sophisticated and nuanced than in, for example, the massive comic book tie-in, *Civil War*. As an event of "rupture," 9/11 is addressed by superhero cinema in a way that is informed by a "globalized need to comprehend, to explain and to restore."[21] In this way, Terence McSweeney argues in his study of the MCU, on the whole, "the genre continues to replay and perpetuate deeply embedded mythological values which have become formative aspects of American identity."[22]

CAPTAIN MARVEL AND A POLITICS OF HOSPITALITY

Social media conversations around the launch of *Captain Marvel* tended to focus on the piece's feminist potential. Largely this was predicated on having a female lead rather than on any explicit offering of a feminist analysis of structures of patriarchal power in the film itself. The casting is certainly noteworthy given the masculine-normativity of the genre, and particularly the MCU's tactical focal choices up until this point. Apart from Black Widow, the sole female member of the Avengers team until Scarlet Witch, the MCU's women function as supporting cast. There are a few interesting nods in *Captain Marvel* toward contesting female domesticity and reduction to the male sexualized gaze. For instance, at one point a biker urges Vers to "lighten up honey" and to give him a "smile." This could allude to the possibilities of sexual abuse and male domination. On another occasion, Talos patronizingly addresses Maria Rambeau as a "young lady," and the result is the latter's vigorous response: "Call me 'young lady' again and I'm gonna put my foot into a place it's not supposed to be." Finally, the reference in a scene on a plane to "Goose" (the "cat" is later revealed to be a Flerkin) is a reference to the macho airforce picture *Top Gun*. Certainly, these moments provide a subtlety beyond the scene during the battle with Thanos in *Avengers Endgame* whenever a number of women step forward together, looking particularly heroic, in order to offer resistance to the threat. Cristina Lucia Stasia's observation about the girl-power hero of many movies since the 1990s is only partly well-placed, however: "This new female action hero not only manifests anxieties about changing gender roles, but indicates a lack of anxiety as popular culture fulfils the prophecy of the term postfeminism: convincing women they live in a post-patriarchy. This model resonates with the female action film and the triumph of the fittest body/mind—a body which is almost exclusively white and middle-class and a mind which is free of political concerns."[23] *Captain Marvel*, it will be argued, does indeed attempt to open up a space that can contest any cultural evasion of political concerns within a post-9/11 context.

There are several broadly shared features of post-9/11 cinema. First, the terror threat is intensified by portraying its global significance. This can occur in two main ways. In the first place, the *range* of the threat is itself a global one, as is evident in a significant proportion of blockbuster movies made since 9/11 that depicts the situation at issue as world-changing and world-threatening. Of course, while this has intensified it is certainly not new given the American world-power of Superman to the world-saving British spy James Bond. In the second place, the global threat is portrayed as a threat to global *life itself*. Wetmore depicts "The media, politicians, and the media at large" as having shifted the significance of terrorism from being a local threat to "an existential threat . . . to all life and human existence itself."[24] One mechanism for this has been the use of an apocalyptic catastrophism. Some time ago, Frank Kermode declared that "The paradigms of apocalypse continue to lie under our ways of making sense of the world."[25] However, several cultural commentators regard an accentuation of this regulative trope in contemporary cinema. For instance, Elizabeth Ford and Deborah Mitchell observe that "filmmakers of all genres now employ the language systems of disaster as if they are the *lingua franca* of every cinematic conversation."[26] Here, one only needs to observe the global catastrophism associated with the Chitauri invasion of New York, and the galactic reach of Thanos's death-dealing purge, to recognize the MCU's propensity to play into the hands of what Wheeler Winston Dixon describes as "the romance of Armageddon," but which is just as easily an expression of fear as "romance."[27]

While the threat in *Captain Marvel*, in the end, is revealed to be less the threat to the Earth and its inhabitants than the threat to the survival of the Skrulls, nonetheless, the initial cosmic setting of the drama incorporates the Earth through Vers's landing and the subsequent conflict. This would certainly appear to imperil the Earth, the planet the Kree refer to as C53. After all, Yon-Rogg early on explains that the Skrulls "have invaded yet another border planet." With their accidental discovery of earth in pursuit of Vers, the Skrulls might be imagined to have Earth next on their imperial hit list.

A second feature of post 9/11 cinema is that it pre-eminently projects healing action onto powerful agencies that take responsibility for acting. According to cultural anthropologist Ernest Becker, the hero is of supreme importance because he or she allows society to be "delivered . . . from the evil of the termination of life."[28] Speaking more specifically of superheroes, Robin Rosenberg observes that "Collectively, we began to yearn for larger-than-life heroes—to be inspired by them and to be rescued by them."[29] Yet, it is almost as if we have lost faith in our ability to envisage a peaceably cooperative and common life, plan prudently for our flourishing, and trust in our ability to foster productively just social arrangements. "It is almost as if people no longer believe that heroes of sterling character can be produced by society, and that goodness can transpire only by a freak of technology (such as electrocution or *radioactive poisoning*)."[30] Two further things are at issue here: the form of vigilante violence which has been detected by several commentators as having shaped the American imagination through the influence of Westerns in particular; and the superhero as an American representative, so that what is displayed is the fantasized depiction of America as the global superheroic power acting to offset the crisis in the world's interests.[31] The cultural turn to the superhero genre, with all its trappings of heroic self-sacrificing but indestructible power and individualized capacity to take on the burden of social advocacy and responsibility, then, is not incidental to the culturally therapeutic process of offering social catharsis resistant meaning from within disaster. In this regard, within the conflictual geopolitical reality of contemporaneity, it is hardly insignificant that Carol Danvers is part of the American military-industrial complex. According to Jason Dittmer, the marked contrast between the exceptionalist undertones of construing "the 'American-ness' of the superhero genre" is actually intensified when one considers "the origins of the superhero genre [that] transcend national borders."[32]

A third mark of American cinema in the wake of the so-called "War on Terror" is what might be described as a self-depiction within a politics of purity. According to Paul Petrovic, "The ideologies embedded in mainstream American film often privilege stories of America's national victimhood in the wake of 9/11, but victimhood is a status that is sanctioned only under certain conditions. . . . In turn, this master narrative of 9/11 remained codified."[33] That *Captain Marvel* has a post-9/11 political setting (even if the narrative itself is set many years earlier) is suggested by Ronan's speaking of the Skrulls as a "terrorist threat," and that they are a clear and present danger to national security since "Skrulls anywhere is a threat to Kree everywhere." Danvers herself later announces to Talos that his people are "terrorists." The sense of American/earthly innocence is suggested through the imperial picture the Skrulls had been painted in. It is clear the Earth (with the action occurring on United States soil, and involving American citizens) is only accidentally, and unwittingly, drawn into, and consequently imperiled by, the longstanding and highly destructive Kree-Skrull conflict. Therefore, Slavoj Žižek argues, "the shattering experience of September 11 ultimately served as a device which enabled the hegemonic American ideology to 'go back to its basics', to reassert its basic ideological co-ordinates against the antiglobalist and other critical temptations."[34]

Yet, as Žižek admits, "there is nothing 'innocent' about this rediscovery of American [or any other peoples' sheer] innocence, about getting rid of the sense of historical guilt or irony which prevented many Americans from fully assuming their national identity."[35] The suggestion is that the politics of purity is deeply simplifying. First, it reduces subjects to the constitution of being national subjects committed passionately to a "zealous cult" of the nation-state.[36] Second, it "enacts a nostalgia for absolute values, values and virtues that are then associated with the nation itself."[37] And, third, it purifies the national memory. In this way, McSweeney argues, post-9/11 cinema functions as a discursively audience-insulating "cinema of proselytisation, one that is content to perpetuate the master narrative of 9/11 instead of asking troubling questions."[38] This entails the production of "an uncritical and unreflective narrative of American victimisation, a pronounced disconnection from the complexities of the geopolitical arena, and, in some cases, an elaborate erasure of political and historical context."[39] What is rendered invisible, then, are things like complexity, deep and complicated causes, the social grounds of individual experience, and the role of collective action for change and the responsibility for it.

A fourth mark of post-9/11 cinema emerges as the concomitant flipside of this politics of purity. This is the politics of blame. Cinema's narrative conventions may well indicate vulnerability and victimhood, but they result in the reassertion of dominance and control. The way this happens through a form of 'othering' is a telling reflection of the purity-blame schema. Those who are declared to be guilty of manufacturing the threat are depicted in terms that define them as outsiders, strangers, pure other, alien, and monstrous. Douglas Kellner regards this as a "Manichean mentality [that] projects evil onto its 'other', denying its own violent and aggressive tendencies."[40] What then occurs is a process of imaginative reduction of those classified as "them" to dehumanizing subject categories of the unrecognizable sub-person so that their very humanity is refused intelligibility. "[T]he dialectics of othering" renders that other "unable to speak."[41] Accordingly, the "others" become exposed to a particular vulnerability: that of the brutal survivalist logic of the "us" against the now precarious bare life of the disposable "them." Discursive conditions refract, produce, and condition otherness through the particularizing lens of nationalist politics in such a way that the presence, role, importance, and even subjectivity are marginalized and erased. "When a life that does not figure as normatively human is violated," Athena Athanasiou argues, "this violation remains as unrecognized, misrecognized, or recognized in an injurious way, through terms that enable a derealizing violence."[42] This means that the one who is othered is conventionally positioned in a particular way that dehumanizes by virtue of being denied a human face on which human vulnerability and intelligible motivation become in any way perceptible. The visual construct, the literal human de-facing or effacing of the human visage, reinforces a binary with a strict border, and as a result, the violent purge of monstrous otherness is conducted as a moment of ontological hygiene and social therapy. In fact, the political *pharmakon* thereby complacently justifies the otherwise morally illegitimate and reprehensible actions such as brutal torture, unilateral action, pre-emptive strike, and the ungrieving for civilian collateral damage within the undifferentiated massification of monstrousness.

It is important to recognize *Captain Marvel*'s use of cinematic conventions to design a process of self-other that involves the alienating of the other who now is reduced to becoming a pure threat. (As we will see later, however, it does this only to crucially subvert it.) In a telling moment, Vers questions Fury with the purpose of determining whether he was an impersonating Skrull or not, and the reference to his previous work includes the antagonistic politics of the friend/enemy contrast during the Cold War, even his operation as a spy in the Irish Troubles when stationed in Belfast. Following that Fury admits that he has been "trying to figure out where our future enemies are coming from. It never occurred to me they'd be coming from above." The threat arrives from outside agencies as an alien threat, and audiences will, of course, recall the threatening alien used to prominent effect in *The Avengers* with the invasion of the Chitauri and the subsequent Battle of New York. At another point, Yon-Rogg warns Vers, "Remember your training. Know your enemy. Don't let your emotions override your judgment." She is not to let her emotional sympathies overrule her violently death-dealing duty to the Kree against the Skrulls. Žižek recognizes that "The majority needs to be 'anaesthetized' against its elementary sensitivity to the suffering of others."[43] Moments early in the movie provide the conditions for understanding the Skrulls as the enemy. For instance, they use what appears to be a torture-like machine to extract information from Vers's memory. Moreover, when Vers first meets Agent Nick Fury a Skrull unsuccessfully attempts an assassination shot at her. Talos dishes out a beating to Nick Fury, in a way that further intensifies the impression that the Skrulls are being cast as the enemy "other." Fury requires Vers (now beginning to regain her memories of having been Carol Danvers) to rescue him from potential death.

Following a science fiction cinema convention, the movie depicts those portrayed initially as the enemy in monstrous terms. In this regard, the film's opening is ominous. In what turns out to be a slow-motion dream sequence, the woman we know from the movie advertising posters will be revealed to be Captain Marvel herself, is surrounded by flaming rubble. The visual reference is to the destruction caused by armed conflict, and the spectacle is one of catastrophe. Smoke pervades the scene and nothing but one human woman (later revealed to be Dr. Lawson/Mar-Vell from the Kree world Hala) holding a pistol is left living or untouched other than the woman watching her. The younger woman surveys the devastation with seeming shock, and even initially with blue blood flowing from her nose. A moment later a silhouetted figure emerges from the smolders and raises a weapon in her direction. Although the image is a little indistinct, one has just about visual clues as to recognize her impending assailant as a Skrull soldier. The Skrulls come to be depicted as reptilian in appearance in a way that resonates with the television mini-series *V*, the Lizard in *The Amazing Spider-Man*, and even the Chitauri in *The Avengers*. Fury, a character the audience has learned to trust and love in the MCU, is later heard to call the dead Skrull on the autopsy table a "lizard," a racist term of "othering" not unlike the reference to the Nexus 6s in *Blade Runner* as "skin jobs." "Wow," Fury exclaims, "they're ugly bastards, aren't they?" The response is "Yeah, well, they're no Brad Pitt, sir." Keller then addresses the corpse. His claim "I will finish what we started" sounds distinctly menacing, particularly so given that a similar line has been used in *Star Wars. Episode VII: The Force Awakens* by Kylo Ren, when addressing the charred remains of the distorted helmet of Darth Vader. It is also not insignificant for building audience expectation that the Australian actor Ben Mendelsohn played the role of the Skrull commander, General Talos, and he has become familiar particularly through recent depictions of the treacherous Director Orson Krennic in *Rogue 1* and the self-serving corporate tyrant Nolan Sorrento in *Ready Player One*. Once the Caucasian-skinned Kree, Yon-Rogg (played by the likeable Jude Law), is introduced as Vers's mentor and supervisor, the scene is set for duping the audience into the evil physically alien Skrulls versus the more human-like Kree.

What is more chilling, however, is the nature of the enemy's chameleon-like ability. If Vers is to "Know your enemy," it is not obvious where the enemy is given the Skrulls's ability to shapeshift. As *X-Men* and *X2* demonstrated so convincingly, the ability to infiltrate or to hide by assuming another's identity; this is a powerful skill. In *Captain Marvel*, a Skrull takes the form of an innocuous-looking elderly lady on the train, and later impersonates Agent Colson and is therefore able to draw his weapon on Nick Fury in the car. Another Skrull even assumes the form of Fury's S.H.I.E.L.D. boss Keller. The political resonance of this is significant since this too provides something of a nod back to the height of the kind of claustrophobic Cold War paranoia that generated the horror of films like *Invasion of the Body Snatchers* and *Stepford Wives*. "We can't trust anyone, not even our own men," Director Keller admits. Referring to Carl Schmitt's friend/enemy duality, Žižek warns that the "political struggle is providing/constructing a recognizable *image* of the enemy."[44] Otherwise, "the enemy is by definition, always—up to a point, at least—*invisible*; he looks like one of us; he cannot be directly recognized."⁴⁵ Accordingly, in exposing the enemy's true visage, Žižek, continues, "one has to 'schematize' the logical figure of the Enemy, providing it with concrete tangible features which make it an appropriate target of hatred and struggle."⁴⁶

The fifth and final mark of post-9/11 cinema is a consequence of the logic of each of the progression of the other marks. As a conflict from within a discursively conceived politics of self-other, good "us" versus evil "them," innocence-blame, the threat is invariably dealt with through the kind of necessarily resistant action that now has the character of "redemptive" action, a form of violence conducive to what Terry Eagleton calls "holy terror."⁴⁷ According to Kellner, "the depiction of violence as a mode of solving problems and empowering males is . . . a standard trope of media culture."⁴⁸ Lawrence and Jewett argue that the binaristic political imagination "gives Americans a fantasy land without ambiguities to cloud the moral vision, where the evil empire of enemies is readily discernible, and where they can vicariously (through identification with the superhero) smite evil before it overtakes them."⁴⁹ Yet, the matter of "the myth of a Good War" is more destructive than the retaliatory biblical language of "smiting" here would suggest.⁵⁰ When the enemy behaves in a way "worse than murder," Sontag explains, the disciplinary restraints are actually removed. Accordingly, even the most brutal forms of retribution are justified since the situation poses "no moral problems and offers no moral qualifications."⁵¹ Dittmer, then, speaks of "America's simplistic moralistic framing of its foreign policy with its near-limitless capacity to inflict violence on others" in a muscular assertiveness that appears in dominant superhero narratives, and recognizably so "as a discourse *through which* the world becomes understandable."⁵²

This problem, Žižek claims, is that "The conflict cannot be resolved in its own terms: the only way to break out of the vicious struggle is through an act which would change the very co-ordinates of the conflict."⁵³ What is suggestive is that this admission comes in a chapter entitled "From *Homo Sacer* to the Neighbour."⁵⁴ Here is where *Captain Marvel* begins to subvert its own representational binary coding and therefore offers an interrogation of audience expectation.

Of course, anyone paying attention to the MCU series up until that point will have been sensitive to the odd way the Kree had been portrayed as victims seeking only to protect their national security. They will recognize the reappearance of the politically powerful and fanatical Ronan the Accuser who had been the chief menace in *Guardians of the Galaxy*. He had led a genocidal campaign against the Xandarians, and in *Captain Marvel* he appears with Starforce in order to hunt down the galactically scattered Skrulls. Those familiar with the comic books will be aware of the Kree's experimentation on ancient humans (this produced the superpowered Inhumans), their valuation of genetic purity (which even resulted in the criminalizing of interspecies relationships, and the persecution of the genetically impure interbred "white" Kree), their intensive militarized society that is imperialistically ambitious, and their worship of the military dictator—the Supreme Intelligence (the minority practice of pacifism is outlawed). Moreover, the comic book backstory of the Kree-Skrull war depicts the former's aggressive expansion into the latter's more peaceful trade-operated empire. Equally worth mentioning involves the incorporation of the Avengers into these hostilities. Captain Marvel revealed that the Kree had been planning genocidal action against humanity. On the other hand, comic book aficionados will undoubtedly be familiar with the Skrulls's role as an enemy of the superheroic teams. According to Costello, in the 1990s' rebooted Captain America series, Hydra's leader was a Skrull who used the American public's paranoia regarding the shape-shifting aliens to induce panic and produce violent action against "their neighbors, friends, and even family, attacking anyone who seems different as a potential Skrull."[55]

For those un- or under-initiated into the Marvel universe, the turning point begins around exactly mid-way through the movie. Talos appears uninvited in Maria Rambeau's house by the backdoor. He is, initially at least, an intruder, an unwelcome "guest," and the anticipation is that he will be a threat, hostile to Maria as "host." His opening remark is significant: "You know, you really should be kinder to your neighbours. You never know when you're going to need to borrow some sugar." The second sentence here is slightly lighthearted, but the first one sets the tone for what the second half of the movie will now offer: a refusal of neighborliness by the "peaceable" Kree to the supposedly colonizing militaristic machine of the repressive Skrulls.

While unarmed, and ready to tell his people's story in the hope of persuading Danvers of the role of her people in the injustice of his people's plight, he has a precaution in place with one of his troop's holding of Maria's daughter, Monica. Only this threat of paedocide provides the condition for him to exercise his voice and to be recognized. An injured Mar-Vell had asked Danvers to "Remember what I said about our work here, what it's for?" Danvers repeats what she had learned: "To end wars." To that Mar-Vell had explained that "But the wars are bigger than you know." She had admitted that "I spent half her life fighting a shameful war." After recounting this story, and with Danvers's memories slowly returning, Talos is able to announce that Mar-Vell recognized that she had been "on the wrong side of an unjust war." "Everything I knew was a lie," Danvers confesses. The ideological mask is coming apart in her hands, and her fog of memory-loss begins to clear. But she is not quite ready to relinquish everything she has learned just yet. "Your people are terrorists! They kill innocents. I saw the ruins on Torfa." Terrorist, and even the term "war" to depict state action against terrorism, are themselves ideological constructs. As Slavoj Žižek argues, "today, all the main terms we use to designate the present conflict—'war on terrorism', 'democracy and freedom', 'human rights', and so on—are false terms, mystifying our perception of the situation instead of allowing us to think it. In this precise sense, our freedoms themselves serve to mask and sustain our deeper unfreedom."[56] Terry Eagleton observes that language of "evil" functions in this way as well. "In the so-called war against terror, 'evil' is used to foreclose the possibility of historical explanation."[57] The upshot is, Žižek claims, that "In this paranoiac perspective, the terrorists are turned into an irrational abstract agency. . . . Every explanation which evokes social circumstances is dismissed as covert justification of terror."[58]

The connection between war and terrorism is significant in a post-9/11 context, as is the alien's admission that it was "unjust." Talos deflects the criticism by accusing the Kree of being responsible for the atrocities. They "are ruins that the Accusers are responsible for." His people had "lived as refugees on Torfa, homeless ever since we resisted Kree rule and they destroyed our planet," a status of radical displacement generated by the imperial Kree's own expansionistic activities. Their violent resistance was the product of Kree oppression, of domineering hegemony. Of course, the story being propagated by the Kree is fundamentally the opposite. As Žižek recognizes regarding the post-9/11 geopolitical scene, "enacting the punishment of those responsible [for the terror attacks] is a sad duty, not an exhilarating retaliation—what we are getting instead is the forceful reassertion of the exceptional role of the USA as a global policeman, as if what causes resentment against the USA is not its excess of power, but its lack of it."[59]

Even the Skrull's status as refugees, as survivors on the run, is distinctly precarious. The Kree are then the ones depicted as genocidal: "And the handful of us that are left will be slaughtered next unless you help me finish what Mar-Vell started." This certainly resonates with Ronan's assertion that "Skrulls anywhere is a threat to Kree everywhere." At least Yon-Rogg refuses "to bomb them out of the galaxy," and he insists that the mission can and should be accomplished instead by his team. Yet, later, Ronan equates the Skrulls with a virus, so that healing would involve their termination. "For the good of all Kree, the infestation [of the Skrulls] will be eradicated." In the light of this, Yon-Rogg's language of the "collective" and his citation of the Kree warrior phrase "For the good of all Kree" has distinctly ominous overtones for the Kree's enemies.

The movie adds further humanization to Talos and his people with a touching scene in Mar-Vell's lab involving a reunion between him and his partner and child. When his partner winces on seeing the earthlings, Talos insists they are "friends." The contrast with the arrival of Yon-Rogg and his team is stark. The Kree's first words are an indictment of Danvers and a dehumanizing reduction of the Skrulls to a generalizing category,

"Fraternising with the enemy." On the other hand, that scene reveals a further point about hospitality: moral action of responsibility for the wellbeing of the Skrulls can occur through *empathetic* action. They can be recognized as the objects of sympathy because, in so many ways, they are just like us.

CONCLUSION

Given the formative role popular culture plays in the disciplinary technologies of the self, it is evident that political use of violence does not arise from a vacuum. Post 9/11 cinema is memorably described by McSweeney as "a cinema of proselytization," so that film not merely visually indexes cultural anxieties but produces, prolongs, and shapes them, regulates how meaning is given to them, and codifies the limitation of the range of possible responses.[60] On the other hand, McSweeney reads *Iron Man* "as something of a contestory mythopoetic fantasy of how America sees itself in both its rejection *and* perpetuation of hegemonic master narratives of American identity."[61]

Captain Marvel has shown significant signs of itself offering a contestation of hegemonic values that have asserted themselves geopolitically and culturally after 9/11. Not only does it subvert the dominant masculine code of the mythic hero, but, when aligned with the second and third features in the *Captain America* series, it challenges, at least up to a point, dominant political issues of power that result in the neat racialized exclusion of "the other." Here, it can be conducive to a politics of hospitality for "unlearning the inherent dominative mode" that alienates and excludes otherness.[62] Vers herself endures a crisis of subjectivity, with the decoupling of consciousness from the intelligibility of the disciplining world of what has been learned. But her relearning involves something of a reparative restoration of who she was in a way that challenges her own way of being with others. Moreover, it depicts the refugees as the production of the Kree's imperial advance. As Žižek argues regarding the "new empire" of the global market, "the true threat to our common way of life does not come in the shape of refugees but lies in the dynamic of global capitalism."[63] With "the production of 'redundant people'," "refugees are [then,] the price humanity is paying for the global economy."[64]

On the other hand, there are several cautions that are required before the film is politically positioned as a *radically anti-hegmonic* one. First, given the superheroic genre, the movie requires intensive acts of violence to even begin to subvert a central binarism. This devolves, then, into the legitimation of violence and planning for violence as a political act—the only political act. Second, *Captain Marvel* adds to the burgeoning material depicting woman's role in the violence, entailing that women no less than men are the subjects of national violence as well as objects of sacrificial death in commitment to the belligerent demands of their nation-state. Third, even though the movie subverts racial binarisms at one point, and thereby rescues the refugees, it continues to perpetuate another binarism by casting the Kree, instead, as villainous. True, Mar-Vell is Kree, but the species is summed up in her description of the attackers on the aircraft as "the bad guys." This suggests that while the film is attentive to the differences of cultural reception of the "War Against Terror" and the array of political decisions taken in its light, particularly with the ease of the Manichaean-like binarisms of the innocent-us-versus-evil-them, it nonetheless succumbs to the nostalgic inhospitality that the MCU has staged with the ominous appearance of the Kree. According to Henry Giroux, "Violence has become so normalized that it no longer has a history. . . . [V]iolence in America is fed by a culture of fear shaped, in part, by a preoccupation with surveillance, incarceration, and the personal security industry. Fear not only undermines trust, it also breeds a hatred of the other and undermines any sense of compassion."[65] *Captain Marvel* does not undo the fear, even if it attempts to invoke compassion for the Skrull refugee community—it merely changes the object of the fear. Fourthly, the film remains complicit in the culture industry's politically conservative fascination with the American subject as exceptional global saviors and the desire for morally unambiguous certitude. It remains, in other words, trapped by cinematic superhero conventionality. There is, then, no distinctive contestation of the popular presentation of "'the official story of American benevolent tolerance' . . . that posit the nation as comprised of good and tolerant subjects."[66] Fifthly, the depiction of hospitality is a limited one: the Skrulls are not given an earthly home. Of course, the narrative explanation is that Earth would not be a safe haven for them given the Kree's knowledge of, and access to, it. Nonetheless, as Talos explains, their only hope is in a "lightspeed ship capable of carrying us to safety . . . [to] where the Kree can't reach us . . . We just want a home." By forcing the persecuted Skrulls to voyage in search of a homeland, the film perpetuates a sympathy for them while continuing to keep them on the margins—literally forcing them back onto the margins. There can be no integration, no alliance, no day-to-day mutuality, only a difference between those possessing their own distant homelands. Finally, the talk of a homeland echoes post-WWII Israel, but it does nothing to consider the possibility that this may result in the displacement of indigenous or settler peoples.

Terry Eagleton argues, "What may persuade us that certain human bodies lack all claim on our compassion is culture. Regarding some of our fellow humans as inhuman requires a fair degree of cultural sophistication."[67] While *Captain Marvel* does attempt to disrupt this pattern of dehumanizing perspective, it is not entirely evident, in the end, how far it can successfully contribute to Richard Kearney's urgent challenge against "the polarization between Us and Them," or Martin Luther King's exhortation to moral intelligence.[68]

NOTES

1. Martin Luther King, *Strength to Love* (London and Glasgow: Collins, 1963), ch. 4.
2. King, *Strength to Love*, 43.
3. King, *Strength to Love*, 40.
4. King, *Strength to Love*, 44.
5. Theodor W. Adorno and Max Horkheimer, *The Dialectic of Enlightenment*, trans. John Cumming (London and New York: Verso, 1979), xv, 120. Cf. Walter Benjamin, *Illuminations*, Harry Zohn (New York: Schocken Books, 1968), 224, 234.
6. Henry A. Giroux, *Breaking into the Movies: Film and the Culture of Politics* (Malden and Oxford: Blackwell, 2002), 75.
7. Giroux, *Breaking into the Movies*, 79.
8. Richard Kearney, *On Stories* (London and New York: Routledge, 2001), 155.
9. Giroux, *Breaking into the Movies*, 79.
10. Andrew Schopp and Matthew B. Hill, "Introduction: The Curious Knot," in Andrew Schopp and Matthew B. Hill (eds.), *The War on Terror and American Popular Culture* (Madison, NJ: Farleigh Dickinson University Press, 2009), 11–42 (16).
11. Christian Steinmetz, "A Genealogy of Evil: Captain America vs. the Shadows of the National Imagined Community," in Robert G. Werner (ed.), *Captain America and the Struggle of the Superhero: Critical Essays* (Jefferson and London: McFarland, 2009), 190–203 (191).
12. Citation from Marc DiPaolo, *War, Politics and Superheroes: Ethics and Propaganda in Comics and Film* (Jefferson, NC: McFarland, 2011), 22.
13. Matthew John Costello, in his *Secret Identity Crisis: Comic Books and the Unmasking of Cold War America* (New York: Continuum, 2009), 212.
14. Costello, *Secret Identity Crisis*, 213.
15. Costello, *Secret Identity Crisis*, 228.
16. Costello, *Secret Identity Crisis*, 219.
17. Terence McSweeney, *The 'War on Terror' and American Film: 9/11 Frames Per Second* (Edinburgh: Edinburgh University Press, 2014), 32, 11.
18. Susan Sontag, "Tuesday and After," *New Yorker* (21 September 2001), 395, cited in Elizabeth A. Ford and Deborah C. Mitchell, *Apocalyptic Visions in 21st Century Films* (Jefferson, NC: McFarland, 2018), 46.
19. Stephen Joyce provides a caution against rhetorical complacency: "It is tempting to assert that everything changed on 9/11; however, the narratives that influenced the American public in its aftermath were not born on that day but pre-written by the history of American exceptionalism and engraved in the popular imagination by Hollywood cinema of the 1990s." ["Foreshadows of the Fall:

Questioning 9/11's Impact on American Attitudes," in McSweeney, *American Cinema in the Shadow of 9/11*, 207–224 (222)].

20. Kevin J. Wetmore, *Post-9/11 Horror in American Cinema* (New York and London: Continuum, 2012), 4.

21. Kristiaan Versluys, *Out of the Blue: September 11 and the Novel* (New York: Columbia University Press, 2009), 4.

22. Terence McSweeney, *Avengers Assemble: Critical Perspectives on the Marvel Cinematic Universe* (London and New York: Wallflower Press, 2018), 188.

23. Cristina Lucia Stasia, "'My Guns are in the Fendi!' The Postfeminist Female Action Hero," in Stacy Gillis, Gillian Howie, and Rebecca Munford (eds.), *Third Wave Feminism: A Critical Exploration*, 2nd edn (Basingstoke and New York: Palgrave Macmillan, 2004), 237–249 (238).

24. Wetmore, *Post-9/11 Horror in American Cinema*, 11–12, citing Frank Furedi, *Invitation to Terror: The Expanding Empire of the Unknown* (New York: Continuum, 2007), 51.

25. Frank Kermode, *The Sense of an Ending: Studies in the Theory of Fiction* (London: Oxford University Press, 1967), 28.

26. Ford and Mitchell, *Apocalyptic Visions in 21st Century Films*, 4.

27. Wheeler Winston Dixon, *Visions of the Apocalypse: Spectacles of Destruction in American Cinema* (London: Wallflower Press, 2003), 97.

28. Ernest Becker, *Escape from Evil* (New York: Free Press, 1975), 150.

29. Robin S. Rosenberg, "Our Fascination with Superheroes," in Robin S. Rosenberg (ed.), *Our Superheroes, Ourselves* (Oxford and New York: Oxford University Press, 2013), 3–18 (16).

30. Walter Wink, *The Powers That Be: Theology for a New Millennium* (New York and London: Doubleday, 1998), 44.

31. See John Shelton Lawrence and Robert Jewett, *The Myth of the American Superhero* (Grand Rapids: William. B. Eerdmans, 2002); *Captain America and the Crusade Against Evil: The Dilemma of Zealous Nationalism* (Grand Rapids, MI: William B. Eerdmans, 2003).

32. Jason Dittmer, *Captain America and the Nationalist Superhero: Metaphors, Narratives, and Geopolitics* (Philadelphia, PA: Temple University Press, 2013), 15.

33. Paul Petrovic, "'You Be Very Mindful of How You Act': Post-9/11 Culture and Arab American Subjectivities in Joseph Castello's *The War Within* (2005) and Hesham Issawi's *AmericanEast* (2008)," in McSweeney (ed.), *American Cinema in the Shadow of 9/11* (Edinburgh: Edinburgh University Press), 89–108 (89).

34. Slavoj Žižek, *Welcome to the Desert of the Real: Five Essays on September 11 and Related Dates* (London and New York: Verso, 2002), 47. Cf. Susan Faludi, *The Terror Dream: Fear and Fantasy in Post-9/11 America* (New York: Henry Holt, 2007), 3–4.

35. Žižek, *Welcome to the Desert of the Real*, 45.

36. Jewett and Lawrence, *Captain America and the Crusade Against Evil*, xv.

37. Jewett and Lawrence, *Captain America and the Crusade Against Evil*, xv.

38. McSweeney, *The 'War on Terror' and American Film*, 12–13. Cf. Michael Alford, *Reel Power: Cinema and American Supremacy* (London and New York: Pluto Press, 2010), 3.

39. McSweeney, *The 'War on Terror' and American Film*, 11.

40. Douglas Kellner, *Cinema Wars: Hollywood Film and Politics in the Bush-Cheney Era* (Malden, Oxford, and Chichester: Wiley-Blackwell, 2010), 8.

41. Stuart Hall, "Subjects in History: Making Diasporic Identities," in W. Lubiano (ed.), *The House that Race Built: Black Americans, U.S. Terrain* (New York: Pantheon, 1997), 296, cited in Randy Cota, "'Real Americans': Inclusion, Difference, and Tolerance in Post 9/11 Nationalist Discourse," in Lisa M. Detora (ed.), *Heroes of Film, Comics and American Culture: Essays on Real and Fictional Defenders of Home* (Jefferson, NC: McFarland, 2009), 301–313 (306).

42. Athena Athanasiou, in Judith Butler and Athena Athanasiou, *Dispossession: The Performative in the Political* (Cambridge and Malden: Polity, 2013), 90.

43. Slavoj Žižek, *Living in the End Times* (London and New York: Verso, 2011), 97.

44. Žižek, *Welcome to the Desert of the Real*, 109.

45. Žižek, *Welcome to the Desert of the Real*, 109.

46. Žižek, *Welcome to the Desert of the Real*, 110.

47. Terry Eagleton, *Holy Terror* (Oxford and New York: Oxford University Press, 2005), title.

48. Kellner, *Cinema Wars*, 110.

49. Lawrence and Jewett, *The Myth of the American Superhero*, 48.

50. Citation from Trevor McCrisken and Andrew Pepper, *American History and Contemporary Hollywood Film* (Edinburgh: Edinburgh University Press, 2005), 123.

51. Susan Sontag, *Against Interpretation and Other Essays* (New York: Farrar, Straus & Giroux, 1966), 393, 391.

52. Dittmer, *Captain America and the Nationalist Superhero*, 2. Cf. Alford, *Reel Power*, 3.

53. Žižek, *Welcome to the Desert of the Real*, 128. Žižek is specifically here speaking of the Israeli-Palestinian struggle.

54. Žižek, *Welcome to the Desert of the Real*, 112.

55. Costello, *Secret Identity Crisis*, 204.

56. Žižek, *Welcome to the Desert of the Real*, 2.

57. Eagleton, *Holy Terror*, 106. Cf. Žižek, *Welcome to the Desert of the Real*, 142.

58. Žižek, *Welcome to the Desert of the Real*, 33.

59. Žižek, *Welcome to the Desert of the Real*, 49.

60. McSweeney, *The 'War on Terror' and American Film*, 13.

61. McSweeney, *Avengers Assemble*, 43.

62. Citation from Raymond Williams, *Culture and Society, 1780-1950* (London: Chatto & Windus, 1958), 376.

63. Slavoj Žižek, *Against the Double Blackmail: Refugees, Terror and Other Trouble with Neighbours* (Milton Keynes: Allen Lane, 2016), 19–20.

64. Citations from Zygmunt Bauman, *Strangers at Our Door* (Cambridge and Malden: Polity, 2016), 3; Žižek, *Against the Double Blackmail*, 101.

65. Henry Giroux, *Zombie Politics and Culture in the Age of Casino Capitalism*, 2nd edn (New York, et al.: Peter Lang, 2014), xiii.

66. Randy Cota, "'Real Americans': Inclusion, Difference, and Tolerance in Post 9/11 Nationalist Discourse," in Lisa M. Detora (ed.), *Heroes of Film, Comics and American Culture: Essays on Real and Fictional Defenders of Home* (Jefferson, NC: McFarland, 2009), 301–313 (303), citing Rey Chow, *The Protestant Ethnic and the Spirit of Capitalism* (New York: Columbia University Press, 2002), 12–13.

67. Terry Eagleton, *After Theory* (London and New York: Penguin Books, 2003), 156.

68. Citation from Richard Kearney, *Strangers, Monsters, and Gods: Interpreting Otherness* (London and New York: Routledge, 2003), 5.

REFERENCES

Adorno, Theodor W., and Max Horkheimer. *The Dialectic of Enlightenment*. Translated by John Cumming. London and New York: Verso, 1979.

Alford, Michael. *Reel Power: Cinema and American Supremacy*. London and New York: Pluto Press, 2010.

Bauman, Zygmunt. *Strangers at Our Door*. Cambridge and Malden: Polity, 2016.

Becker, Ernest. *Escape from Evil*. New York: Free Press, 1975.

Benjamin, Walter. *Illuminations*. Harry Zohn, New York: Schocken Books, 1968.

Butler, Judith, and Athena Athanasiou. *Dispossession: The Performative in the Political*. Cambridge and Malden: Polity, 2013.

Costello, Matthew John. *Secret Identity Crisis: Comic Books and the Unmasking of Cold War America*. New York: Continuum, 2009.

Cota, Randy. "'Real Americans': Inclusion, Difference, and Tolerance in Post 9/11 Nationalist Discourse," in Lisa M. Detora (ed.), *Heroes of Film, Comics and American Culture: Essays on Real and Fictional Defenders of Home*, Jefferson, NC: McFarland, 2009, 301–313.

DiPaolo, Marc. *War, Politics and Superheroes: Ethics and Propaganda in Comics and Film*. Jefferson, NC: McFarland, 2011.

Dittmer, Jason. *Captain America and the Nationalist Superhero: Metaphors, Narratives, and Geopolitics*. Philadelphia, PA: Temple University Press, 2013.

Dixon, Wheeler Winston. *Visions of the Apocalypse: Spectacles of Destruction in American Cinema*. London: Wallflower Press, 2003.

Eagleton, Terry. *After Theory*. London and New York: Penguin Books, 2003.

———. *Holy Terror*. Oxford and New York: Oxford University Press, 2005.

Faludi, Susan. *The Terror Dream: Fear and Fantasy in Post-9/11 America*. New York: Henry Holt, 2007.

Ford, Elizabeth A., and Deborah C. Mitchell. *Apocalyptic Visions in 21st Century Films*. Jefferson, NC: McFarland, 2018.

Giroux, Henry. *Zombie Politics and Culture in the Age of Casino Capitalism*. 2nd edn. New York, et al.: Peter Lang, 2014.

Giroux, Henry A. *Breaking into the Movies: Film and the Culture of Politics*. Malden and Oxford: Blackwell, 2002.

Joyce, Stephen. "Foreshadows of the Fall: Questioning 9/11's Impact on American Attitudes," in Terence McSweeney (ed.), *American Cinema in the Shadow of 9/11*, Edinburgh: Edinburgh University Press, 2017, 207–224.
Kearney, Richard. *On Stories*. London and New York: Routledge, 2001.
———. *Strangers, Monsters, and Gods: Interpreting Otherness*. London and New York: Routledge, 2003.
Kermode, Frank. *The Sense of an Ending: Studies in the Theory of Fiction*. London: Oxford University Press, 1967.
Kellner, Douglas. *Cinema Wars: Hollywood Film and Politics in the Bush-Cheney Era*. Malden, Oxford, and Chichester: Wiley-Blackwell, 2010.
King, Martin Luther, Jr. *Strength to Love*. London and Glasgow: Collins, 1963.
Lawrence, John Shelton, and Robert Jewett. *Captain America and the Crusade Against Evil: The Dilemma of Zealous Nationalism*. Grand Rapids, MI: William B. Eerdmans, 2003.
———. *The Myth of the American Superhero*. Grand Rapids, MI: William. B. Eerdmans, 2002.
McCrisken, Trevor, and Andrew Pepper. *American History and Contemporary Hollywood Film*. Edinburgh: Edinburgh University Press, 2005.
McSweeney, Terence. *Avengers Assemble: Critical Perspectives on the Marvel Cinematic Universe*. London and New York: Wallflower Press, 2018.
———. *The 'War on Terror' and American Film: 9/11 Frames Per Second*. Edinburgh: Edinburgh University Press, 2014.
McSweeney, Terence, ed. *American Cinema in the Shadow of 9/11*. Edinburgh: Edinburgh University Press, 2017.
Petrovic, Paul. "'You Be Very Mindful of How You Act': Post-9/11 Culture and Arab American Subjectivities in Joseph Castello's *The War Within* (2005) and Hesham Issawi's *AmericanEast* (2008)," in Terence McSweeney (ed.), *American Cinema in the Shadow of 9/11*, Edinburgh: Edinburgh University Press, 2017, 89–108.
Rosenberg, Robin S. "Our Fascination with Superheroes," in Robin S. Rosenberg (ed.), *Our Superheroes, Ourselves*, Oxford and New York: Oxford University Press, 2013, 3–18.
Schopp, Andrew, and Matthew B. Hill, eds. *The War on Terror and American Popular Culture*. Madison, NJ: Farleigh Dickinson University Press, 2009.
Sontag, Susan. *Against Interpretation and Other Essays*. New York: Farrar, Straus & Giroux, 1966.
Stasia, Cristina Lucia. "'My Guns are in the Fendi!' The Postfeminist Female Action Hero," in Stacy Gillis, Gillian Howie, and Rebecca Munford (eds.), *Third Wave Feminism: A Critical Exploration*, 2nd edn, Basingstoke and New York: Palgrave Macmillan, 2004, 237–249.
Steinmetz, Christian. "A Genealogy of Evil: Captain America vs. the Shadows of the National Imagined Community," in Robert G. Werner (ed.), *Captain America and the Struggle of the Superhero: Critical Essays*, Jefferson and London: McFarland, 2009, 190–203.
Versluys, Kristiaan. *Out of the Blue: September 11 and the Novel*. New York: Columbia University Press, 2009.

Wetmore, Kevin J. *Post-9/11 Horror in American Cinema*. New York and London: Continuum, 2012.
Williams, Raymond. *Culture and Society, 1780-1950*. London: Chatto & Windus, 1958.
Wink, Walter. *The Powers That Be: Theology for a New Millennium*. New York and London: Doubleday, 1998.
Žižek, Slavoj. *Against the Double Blackmail: Refugees, Terror and Other Trouble with Neighbours*. Milton Keynes: Allen Lane, 2016.
———. *Welcome to the Desert of the Real: Five Essays on September 11 and Related Dates*. London and New York: Verso, 2002.

Chapter 13

The Supermuslim and the Marvel Cinematic Universe

A Complicated Trajectory of Fantasy and Agency

Dilyana Mincheva

THE AGE OF THE SUPERHERO: POSITIONING ISLAM AND ISLAMIC FORMS OF IMAGINATION WITHIN AND BEYOND THE MARVEL UNIVERSE

Within the creative, sociological, pragmatic, and spiritual universe of Islam, the superhero symbolizes two distinct forms of imagination, both of which are complex, are interrelated, and warrant carefully crafted interdisciplinary examination. The two forms—easily discernible within the superhero genre—correspond to "the superhero as a force of good in the world" and the antagonistic "evildoer, the antihero-villain figure." I argue that examining the distinction between these two forms of imagination within the Islamic context (and perhaps, within any superhero monomyth) also requires analyzing their conceptual, pragmatic, and normative interdependency. The *Supermuslim*[1]—a term introduced by Benslama in his psychoanalytical model of the Islamic State warrior—exhibits an extraordinary amount of ethical and psychic ability in the implementation of justice, freedom, and retribution through magnificent feats of bravery, often accompanied by melancholia and self-doubt. The Marvel Cinematic Universe (MCU) appears to be an inspirational reservoir for the two imagination forms not only through its representational and narrative inclusion of Islamic symbolism and spirituality but also through its grandiose transmediation of narratives and images that inspire Islamic responses, agencies, and resistance.

The MCU encompasses all of the types of media, thereby creating the *ultimate* superhero experience—a complex transmedia matrix that is, in turn, influenced and transformed by Muslim agents. The Muslim superhero is either profoundly reimagined as a reincarnation of moral justice, as exemplified by such ultra-successful superheroes as *Burka Avenger*, *Qahera*, and *The 99* by Naif Al-Mutawa. Or, as the ultimate Muslim anti-superhero—the Islamic State warrior—digitally portrayed through events of spectacular violence, mediated on a portable device and amplified primarily by the Western media[2] as being representative of historical justice for the Muslim people. Weaving treacherous enemies, intergalactic battles, and magical superpowers with surreal action sequences and poetic pensiveness in a cosmic digital simulacrum, the Marvel movies create a "world beyond"—one that encompasses transcendence and enchantment as well as damnation and salvation. It is therefore not coincidental that for all their resistance to anything Western, Islamic State warriors draw inspiration for their own cinematic imagery from the Marvel universe. This was notable in the currently suspended Twitter accounts of enthusiastic Islamic State campaigners who were responsible for the viral #AllEyesOnISIS campaign (Arab. #حملة_المليار_مسلم_لنصرة_الدولة_الإسلامية). The defining moments in their campaign revealed not only their fascination with a just and superhero-esque fantasy world based on Islamic principles inspired by Western and Hollywood pop culture but also the visual references to *Iron Man*'s cave escape scene (2008) and the *Battle of New York* (2012), recreated in a *Clanging of the Swards*-style media productions.

In a genealogy that seeks to excavate the radical origin of superheroes, linking it to figures such as Robin Hood and Guy Fawkes, Chris Galaver ingeniously remarked, "When God retired from politics, Superman claimed the empty throne. . . . Even when the star-spangled warriors of World War II fought for democracy, they never represented it. Peel back Captain America's flag costume and you find Guy Fawkes and Oliver Cromwell, revolutionary radicals championing their own self-defined liberty. Today, we call them terrorists."[3]

One of the most unique features of the MCU is the way in which it fills the "God" void. This happens not only through the extension of the superhero fantasy to a subliminal state of heroism against subversive villains but also in its multiple embodiments of experiences—simultaneously larger-than-life and perfectly mundane—embedded in the banal, ubiquitous computer and smartphone screens. There is something unsettling as well as incredibly accurate in Martin Scorsese's seemingly dismissive evaluation of the MCU as a "theme park."[4] The excitement generated by a theme park, including its ability to create intense, ephemeral, and transformative emotions, is always coupled with what Scorsese calls a "lack of risk." In the present context, this is understood as a refurbishment of themes, tropes, and storylines that have existed and have been circulated before. The Supermuslim operates in a similar fashion. On the one hand, the Supermuslim acts to avenge the incredible colonial injustice inflicted upon the Islamic world since the nineteenth century by Western militarism and imperialism. On the other hand, the Supermuslim represents a network-based and highly reliable on social media and YouTube simulacrum. This simulacrum circulates around the world in ways that replicate the circulation and fluidity of global capital, images, and communication networks and creates radical politics as a citation. The Supermuslim's spectacular on-screen performance is marred by its impossibility to generate non-melancholic and radical new forms of lasting heroism. If Martin Scorsese has rightly evaluated the MCU as a "theme park," then the Islamic State's 2015 announcement regarding opening its own Islamic theme parks in Raqqa (Syria) and Fallujah (Iraq)[5] further extends the scope of comparison between them. Therefore, only by analyzing the ultimate heroism that is "without risk" can one understand the melancholy and perpetual unfulfillment that permeates the superhero fantasy in both the Islamic State heroism and the MCU.

THE SUPERHERO AS A POSITIVE MODEL, SAVIOR, AND FORCE OF GOOD IN THE WORLD

The 2018 New York City Comic Con witnessed the arrival of an inspiring group of Muslim women dressed in hijabs and Avengers costumes. Like other attendees, these women were dressed as some of their favorite superheroes— Thor, Captain America, and Iron Man—with the Islamic hijab incorporated in the costumes. Maliha Fairooz, one of these participants, even posted a picture of herself on Instagram, proudly announcing, "Hello Internet, I give you #HijabHeroes at #nycc2018."[6] Twitter was soon flooded with praise for this initiative, with many agreeing that the women brought a Muslim and female perspective to the superhero genre; moreover, the group of cheering young Muslim women on Twitter demonstrated the diversity of Marvel's audiences. Indeed, the upcoming Disney+ series *Ms Marvel*, scheduled to start filming in the summer of 2020, is the first Muslim superhero, Kamala Khan, also expected to make a grand appearance as Ms Marvel in the MCU.[7] Another viral Twitter discussion started by Maliha Fairooz in May 2019 that was retweeted over 20,000 times highlights that the plot of *Avengers: Endgame* suggests that a Muslim man—the Afghani Dr. Yinsen—saves the MCU in 2023 by implanting an electromagnetic device in Iron Man's chest in 2008. Dr. Yinsen is killed by an Afghani terrorist group, the Ten Rings, shortly afterward. Ms. Fairooz prefaced her discovery with a scriptural reference "And whoever saves one, it is as if he had saved mankind entirely" (Quran 5:32). In another Tweet, Ms Fairooz delved deeper into the relationship between Tony Stark and Dr. Yinsen by illuminating it theologically, stating that Dr. Yinsen is a "real Muslim" and "an embodiment of the Quran"; he is someone who does not boast a religious personality by wearing religious attire or preaching, but he is indeed the one person who recognizes the good in both Tony Stark and humanity, and forgives Tony Stark for his weapons and violence. "Hold to forgiveness; command what is right; But turn away from the ignorant (Quran 7:199)," tweeted Ms Fairooz.[8]

The introduction of Ms Marvel in the cinematic universe of superheroes and heroines is a necessary and welcome gesture that is welcome as a disruption of the monocultural and monolithic representations of superheroes.[9] Ms Marvel is a sixteen-year-old Pakistani-American girl named Kamala Khan who lives in New Jersey with her family and masterfully navigates a plethora of identities—Muslim, female, an American, and a superheroine. She is introduced to her powers by her mosque leader, Sheikh Abdullah, and effortlessly balances her school life with family and religion. Kamala Khan has been carefully crafted as a three-dimensional character by Sana Amanaat, G. Willow Wilson, and Adrian Alphonso who diversifies religious representation in the MCU while also projecting the fantasy of a tolerant post-9/11 world. The cinematic appearance of Ms Marvel is expected to provide an authentic depiction of Muslim female agency through one of the most powerful fictional universes in popular culture. The multifarious industry and creative approach to Ms Marvel has undoubtedly been prompted by the increased visibility of Islam in the Western media, which is generally populated with narratives of both vilification and victimization of Muslims.

Politically, Ms Marvel has been designed to counteract Islamophobic stereotypes that assume the oppression and invisibility of Muslim women. Her image even transcended the world of the comics in 2015—long before she was announced as a film heroine in the making—when it was painted by San Francisco street artists to cover Islamophobic ads in metropolitan public spaces.[10] The digital comic format of Ms Marvel reached audiences and sparked conversations that were locally generated but globally consumed.[11] Despite being a highly hybridized superhero, Kamala Khan's Islamic identity is not compromised. While saving another girl before she becomes aware of her own powers, she remembers a quote from the Qur'an—"Whoever saves one person, it is as if he has saved all mankind."[12] Moreover, in her journey as a superhero, Kamala is supported by Sheikh Abdullah, who recognizes and values the rebellious and creative sides of her.

Ms Marvel is one of the latest inventions in a genre that has a lengthy and variegated international history pre- as well as post-9/11. Muslim superheroes have appeared in American comics at least since the introduction of the Nazi-fighting Kismet in *Bomber Comic #1* in 1944. Some notable names among pre-9/11 Muslim superheroes are Archer of Arabia (*Adventure Comic #250*,

July 1958), Black Tiger (*Deadly Hands of Kung Fu #29*, October 1976), the first Arabian Knight (*Incredible Hulk #257*, March 1981), the Iraqi Superhero team Desert Sword (*New Mutants Annual #7*, August 1991), and Batal (*New Warriors #58*, April 1995).[13] In 1988, Salima Baranizar, an Iranian niqabi character, appeared in a DC Comics issue of *Millenium*. Baranizar is chosen by the Guardians of the Universe to be granted immortality, only to be killed shortly afterward by being stoned to death by her fellow countrymen (*Blue Beetle*, "*Iran Scam*," 1988). In 1991, Marvel Comics introduced Veil, a minor villain, in a limited appearance during the first Gulf War in *X-Men*.[14] Nameless and faceless, the Veil is burned to death by American X-Forces for using "chemical weaponry against civilian targets."[15] All of these characters either fit within a hegemonic scheme of representation that capitalized on stereotypes of exoticism and oppressive religion or, in a few cases (such as Kismet), by breaking away from them. It is notable, though, that due to audiences' lack of interest in these characters, they remained underdeveloped and disappeared quickly.

In the post-9/11 context, both American and international Muslim superheroes have appeared frequently and with more nuanced representation in popular culture. In December 2002, against the cultural backdrop of the aftermath of 9/11, Marvel introduced Sooraya Qadir in *New X-Men #133*. Codenamed Dust and donning a niqab that she chooses to wear to protect her modesty, this Muslim girl from Afghanistan has mutant powers that allow her to "transform into sand, and [she] can project herself with enough velocity to flay her skin off you."[16] A complex character with grand powers and abilities, Dust's representation nonetheless raised questions as she needed to be saved by a team of white X-Men who also destroy an entire Afghan village.[17] In a way, the importance of Dust lies not so much in being a stereotype breaker but as the beginning of a genealogy of Islamic characters in the Marvel universe, the culmination of which is Ms Marvel.

Despite comic book superheroes and films being an American creation, Muslim superheroes originating from Muslim-majority countries were a prominent response to regional politics and American popular culture after 9/11. The Egyptian publisher AK Comics started a series in 2004 with the objective of providing positive superhero models to Arab youth. Thereafter, in 2006, Naif Al-Mutawa introduced *The 99*. This title refers to the 99 attributes (names) of Allah—which include generosity, faith, and wisdom—to generate positive narratives of the Muslim superhero, and ultimately, "to reposition Islam not only to the West but to Muslims themselves as well."[18]

These superhero representations have also generated numerous questions—is it appropriate to represent Islamic divine virtues? Are the moral and spiritual agendas of the superheroes in *The 99* theologically accurate, and who is in a position to judge this? Are Muslim women accurately represented by Muslim creators such as Al-Mutawa? Batina the Hidden, a Muslimah from Yemen, is one of only five female characters who cover their heads in *The 99*. Some of the female superheroes, such as Sora, wear immodest tank tops; therefore, who is "more Muslim"—Batina the Hidden or Sora? Al-Mutawa responded to these questions as follows: "The question here is, is Islam measured by behaviour, which anyone can fake by praying and wearing a headscarf, or is it measured by values and faith?"[19] Later on, Al-Mutawa stated that his aim was to provide a Muslim and Qur'an-based version of the superheroes created by Marvel and DC Comics, both of which tend to emphasize Biblical ideals.

At present, the list of indigenous Muslim superheroes is lengthy as various Muslim-majority territories respond to global, local, historical, and cultural concerns regarding Islam. Nonetheless, these superheroes always existed as a variegated response that includes both resistance to and appropriation of pre-existing American archetypes of the genre. For example, the Burka Avenger, is an empowered and liberated Muslimah created by Aaron Haroon Rashid, who appeared in an animated 2013 Pakistani TV series, shortly after the cinematic release of Marvel's *The Avengers* in 2012. Burka Avenger is in no way an American avenger. She uses her modest Islamic clothing to represent her religiosity and values, and is determined "to fight for justice in the name of Islam"[20]; simultaneously, she actively dismantles the Western and Muslim expectations of female identity. Nonetheless, Burka Avenger has been imaginatively linked to the original genre conventions. Similar to most famous American superheroes, she is an orphan (references to Captain Marvel, Superman, and Spiderman), adopted (reference to Jessica Jones), and her powers reign over a decayed metropolis. Burka Avenger is a defender of the oppressed and, similar to the X-Men Marvel mutants of the 1960s and 1970s, her existence is a metaphor for those who are excluded today from both the liberal and Islamic mainstreams. *Qahera the Superhero*, a webcomic created in 2013 by the young Egyptian artist Deena Mohamed, also portrays the adventures of a burqa-clad superheroine. Like Burka Avenger, although Qahera is positioned somewhat locally, her engagement with injustice is global and universal—she fights misogynist Islamic practices, liberal Western feminists, and sexual predators in Cairo.

THE AMBIGUOUS MUSLIM VIGILANTE AS A FORCE OF JUSTICE AND REVENGE IN THE WORLD

Twitter also presents us with a different fascination with superheroes than Ms Fairooz's. One such example is that of Fasil Towalde, a 21-year-old convert to Islam from North London. Towalde aspired to be an actor and achieve

Hollywood stardom, and was a huge fan of the Avengers comics, Superman films, and Marvel and DC superhero universes. He decided to travel to Syria in 2013 to join the Islamic State and adopted the name Abu Abdullah Al-Habashi. Shortly before being killed fighting for ISIS, Towalde tweeted about the decapitation of a Syrian soldier, his own profile picture showing him sporting a fashionable Superman T-shirt.[21] The Islamic State propaganda comprised multi-channel, transmedia activity that targeted young people who were extremely familiar with Hollywood movies, video games, and social media.[22] In terms of media creation and dissemination, the Islamic State created a franchise of successful magazines and "Mujatweets" in multiple languages—*Dabiq* (in Arabic and English, 2014–2016), *Dar Al-Islam* (in French, 2014–2016), *Konstantiniyye* (in Turkish, 2015–2016), and *Rumiyah* (in Arabic and English, 2016–2017)—some of them even written in the style of Marvel and DC Comics.[23]

An uncanny link between the MCU and the Islamic State is crystalized in the actions of the American, Iraqi, and other vigilantes who are currently fighting the terrorist group, also through violence.[24] In April 2015, the peculiar skull symbol of the Punisher, was, curiously, seen printed on the backs of helmets of Iraqi security forces and Shi'ite militia fighters in Tikrit.[25] The Punisher is a Marvel villain originally conceived as a marginal character; however, due to the character's popularity, he was given depth and multiple story arcs. The Punisher is a Vietnam veteran, Frank Castle, who becomes a vigilante justice seeker upon not receiving retribution for the death of his family in a mob fight. In his search for justice, the Punisher demonstrates considerable brutality—he kidnaps, tortures, and kills with the conviction that justice can be served through extremism. The Punisher has also been turned into a Netflix Original series by Marvel. While some experts have remarked upon the irony of Iraqi forces adopting American pop culture insignia, considering the profound resentment and anti-Americanism of these fighters,[26] I believe that the merging of ambiguous symbols and sentiments is part of the global digital idiosyncrasy embodied by all superheroes. This is an example of how a universal symbol is hybridized and seemingly given its own life and agency in lands where multiple versions of Islam compete for the hearts and minds of the locals.

The directors of *Avengers: Endgame*, brothers Joe and Anthony Russo produced the 2019 war drama *Mosul* to represent the desperate and violent battle of Iraqi citizens against the Islamic State, particularly for reclaiming the city of Mosul (which was occupied by the Islamic State during 2014–2016). For the Russo brothers, who are probably MCU's most iconic directors, writers, and producers,[27] *Mosul* was inspired by an ethnographic report published in *The New Yorker* about the efforts of a motley group of over a hundred thousand people (the Nineveh SWAT Team)—comprising soldiers, policemen, militia members, and Kurdish fighters—to liberate Iraq's second-largest city.[28] To reinforce the Arabic perspective, the story is told entirely in the Iraqi dialect by an entirely indigenous cast; the creators aimed to make the movie as authentic as possible to the Iraqi fight for justice, which inevitably involves differentiation between Western colonial narratives and narratives originating on the local Iraqi ground.[29] Scripted and directed by Matthew Carnahan, *Mosul* shows the fight against terrorism in striking yet profoundly humane tones; the movie is sparse on dialogue, and casts the Islamic avengers as relentless fighters for justice in a world with seemingly permanent blurred boundaries between "right" and "wrong." The driving force for the Mosul avengers in the movie is grief—grief for lost loved ones; for the faux normalcy of the pre-2003 "war on terror"; for a lost homeland; for the fight against terrorism, which is easily politicized but rarely deeply perceived by "experts," pundits, and well-meaning but far-removed intellectuals; and for a religion that the Islamic State instrumentalized in order to mesmerize youthful and theologically illiterate desperados[30].

There is a structural similarity between all of these justice fighters. Although the Islamic State warriors, Nineveh SWAT Team, and the MCU's Avengers inhabit sociologically and fictionally different spaces, they are linked at the macro-level of mythological experience and affect by the passionate yet melancholic, insurgent yet mundane, radical yet morally ambiguous, and utopian drive toward justice. The story of heroism in all fictional and pragmatic contexts is also, inevitably, a story of grief and melancholy.

Olivier Roy reminds us that countless jihadi fighters, even those who volunteered to sacrifice themselves for the Islamic cause, are unable to provide specifics regarding their reasons to act violently.[31] They act on behind a universalized and abstract "Muslim ummah"; as the MCU Avengers act to save a universalized and abstract "humanity." Mohammad Siddique Khan, the leader of the group responsible for the 2005 London bombings, emphasized on the oppression of "the Muslim people" during his trial; he presented himself as, in the words of Roy, an "avenging hero" and as someone who experienced the weight of all Muslim oppression, whether historical or present, on his shoulders.[32] *The Avengers: Endgame* somewhat fictionally explores precisely this melancholic aspect of heroism. The movie opens with a flashback from the time when the villain Thanos, already in possession of the Infinity Stones, snaps his fingers and obliterates half of the universe's population. In the next scene, we encounter the familiar Marvel superheroes five years later dealing with grief individually—Thor is in denial, Hawkeye is angry, Steve tries to bargain, Natasha is depressed, and Hulk is at the point of reconciliation. The superheroes' personal trajectories in the movie invite a reflection on the tremendous and emotionally devastating cost of adventure and heroism.

Among other things, the superheroes are melancholic justice warriors carrying a ginormous cosmic burden.

WHAT IS A MUSLIM SUPERHERO? THE MODEL OF FETHI BENSLAMA

In *Un Furieux désir de sacrifice. Le surmusulman* (*A Furious Desire for Sacrifice: The Supermuslim*), Benslama largely ignores the cultural and religious variances of the Muslim superhero by proposing that there is a universal experience of trauma that influences young people to passionately embrace a version of Islam that brings them closer to a fantasy of being exemplary, pious, and more Muslim than any other followers of Islam.[33] This drives the aspiring jihadists to pursue a type of Muslim *Überman*, which is a combination of Nietzsche's superman and Freud's superego.[34] According to Benslama, the Supermuslim, signifying a generalized and integrated metaphor, becomes sociologically apprehensible when the young wannabe Muslim avengers accept "the jihadist offer."[35] Therefore, the Supermuslim is both a fictional and embodied, phantasmic and real, and localized and universal figure of cosmic redemption that turns the fighters into automatons that act on behalf of the wounded Muslim ideal. It is thus necessary to note that Benslama's methodological approach constructs a discursive matrix for understanding the psychic dimensions of the Supermuslim based on clinical evidence, the geopolitical positioning of Islam, popular culture, and historical knowledge of Islam's relationship with the political imaginations of its oppressors. Benslama insists that we cannot fully comprehend the Supermuslim without understanding the individual and collective traumas of young Maghrebi youths in France or recent converts to Islam, which often involve specific systemic exclusions such as police profiling, racism, and economic marginalization. Nonetheless, these traumas can be simultaneously extended to include historical suffering articulated in the theo-political and normative popular culture as the eternal battle between noble and evil forces. This explains the prominence of the superhero genre in the words, actions, and self-presentation of young individuals of the Islamic caliphate.[36] The "jihadist offer" provides disenfranchised young people (related to Islam either through origin or by choice) with a sense of belonging to a community of believers (the Muslim ummah), provides a higher purpose (passionate defense of Islam), and through the promise of martyrdom, gives hope for the future to those whose lives seem meaningless. All of these identitarian promises of the "jihadist offer," Benslama states, are particularly attractive during adolescence and early adulthood; therefore, it is not surprising that his psychoanalytical model is scaffolded predominantly with individuals aged 15–25 years.[37] Benslama treats their radicalization as a symptom of the personal narratives of belonging and exclusion, which coincide with macro-identitarian myths within Islam. He places these intersections within the individual psyche, while simultaneously raising the question of what might be an affordable means of resistance to those who have been pushed by a range of forces to embrace and embody the best and worst excesses of the superhero/supervillain figures.

Nouri Gana extends the description of the Supermuslim with an emphasis on melancholy.[38] In purely Freudian terms, melancholia refers to psychic state resulting from an experience of loss.[39] The affective world of the Supermuslim is characterized by the loss of "the Islamic utopia," sustained in the past by the perfection of the first Muslim community led by Prophet Muhammad. Melancholia exists in both the violent and nonviolent versions of the Supermuslim, and should not be mistaken with mourning, which signifies an irreversible loss of something or someone, and always has a negative connotation. Melancholia is a much more complex emotional state in which the reactive, violent engagement with loss accompanies the more critical and reflective experience of loss.[40] Therefore, the incarnation of the Supermuslim as both an Islamically specific avenger for justice on the one hand, and prone to visceral violence on the other, can also be viewed as two manifestations of melancholia within Islam that inevitably permeate psychic terrain of the superhero. The Islamic reception of one of Marvel's most iconic figures, Jessica Jones, provides some evidence regarding this observation.

THE MELANCHOLIA OF THE SUPERMUSLIM: THE MUSLIM RECEPTION OF *JESSICA JONES*

Two high-profile Muslim influencers have openly discussed the character of Jessica Jones. A social media star within American Islam—Imam Marc Manley—posted a 12-minute video rant on his blog, which bashes the "pornified and sexually obsessed" character of Jessica Jones in the Netflix series.[41] On the other hand, Mona Eltahawy, the Egyptian-American journalist, feminist, and activist who founded the #MosqueMeToo social media campaign has praised the series on Twitter.[42] My argument is that Jessica Jones receives attention from individuals who are influential within the global and mediatized Muslim community, as her character's melancholia shares affinities with the melancholic aspects of the Supermuslim. Jessica Jones' inability to come to terms with her past, move on from her obsessions, and her sometimes inadequacy as a superhero reveal a longing for a lost wholeness that cannot be recovered even through the most heroic acts. On a purely visual level, the neo-noir aesthetics of the series also reinforce its melancholic undertones.

Although Jessica Jones is not an indigenous Muslim character, she exhibits an agency and emotional range that attracts the attention of important stakeholders in Islam, along with debates regarding intimacy, body choices, violence, and the pursuit of vigilante justice. The Netflix series, which was recently made available in the Middle East, made this character easily accessible to audiences and commentators.[43] The Twitter handle @ArabicMarvel has hosted some discussions of this character; however, due to the relative novelty of Netflix in the Middle East, the localized resonance of Jessica Jones is yet to be examined.[44] Rather, I focus on the followers of Eltahawy and Manly, who are precisely the young men and women, who according to Benslama's demographic data and Roy's influential analysis, are the best candidates to pursue the Supermuslim ideal. Imam Manley addresses the Muslim millennials in his capacity as a spiritual authority, whereas Eltahawy tweets as a "feminist giant" with a Muslim background.

Marc Manley claims that Jessica Jones represents the "pornification" of a character, and therefore, betrayal of the superhero figure. He seems particularly enraged by the explicit sexualization of the character. Is this deliberate "pornification" not a kind of objectification? The show has been written and directed by feminist filmmakers to counter the historically prevalent "male gaze" in Hollywood. However, Manley insists that the show's writers and directors are equally guilty in presenting women as objects. Manley notes that the show is *haram* (Arab. prohibited), which in Islam refers to prohibited actions such as cursing, fornication, and murder. Jessica Jones is indeed guilty of all of these "sins." Manley states that in "old-school comics," "a hero is a hero," and further claims that the best thing about comics of the pre-1970's era is that they explored uncomplicated acts of heroism—heroes are "good," and villains are "bad." The power of comic books as fantasies therefore resides in their simplicity.

Manley next proceeds to comment on the objectification of the male body by highlighting specific scenes in the second season of *Jessica Jones*, in which a male character's genitalia are visible. Gradually, Manley's argument becomes less about Jessica Jones and more about what he calls "heterosexual porn," which is seemingly "ubiquitous" and, by implication, requires intervention by a Muslim authority. The public "homoeroticization" of the male body is linked to the present-day "gender ideology," which aims to collapse the distinctions between the sexes and needs to be resisted.[45] Finally, Manley states that homosexuality is sinful. Manley seems unconcerned with the character of Jeri, the controversial lawyer in the series who is openly gay and unfaithful to her partners. Rather, he appears to be obsessed with thrashing Jessica Jones' character. His final thoughts are about the ideological pairing of Jessica Jones, a hypersexualized superheroine, with Luke Cage. He mentions that Jessica's "pale body" pressed against the hypermasculine black body of Luke Cage is supposed "to do something to him," which he resists.

On the other spectrum of the Muslim reception of *Jessica Jones* is Mona Eltahawy. A journalist, writer, social media guru, and women's rights activist, Eltahawy is a deliberately angry Egyptian-American feminist who applauds the series. She tweeted: "A male friend in #Egypt—after I insisted he watch an episode @JessicaJones turned to me and said mid-episode "You just want to watch a woman beating up men" BINGO!"[46] In fact, Eltahawy started a viral Twitter campaign called #IBeatMyAssaulter after she was groped on a dancefloor in Montreal, as well as a #MosqueMeToo campaign as a Muslim feminist response to the #MeToo movement.[47] One of Eltahawy's favorite mottos is #FuckThePatriarchy, and her writing and public activism have given a Muslim dimension to the feminist rage we see portrayed in popular culture.[48] Jessica Jones' character embodies the feminist ideas that Eltahawy presents in her new book, *The Seven Necessary Sins for Women and Girls*, the central topic of which is feminist anger. Jones says: "I'm angry. And I'm not sure there's anything I won't do anymore. Especially to a prick like you who thinks you can take whatever and whoever he wants."[49]

As a feminist tool, rage certainly humanizes the superhero Jessica Jones, who has suffered rape, child abuse, family loss, and psychological torment by the twisted mind-control villain Kilgrave. In the show's second season, Jones undergoes anger management therapy. In the third season, her melancholia pushes her toward a profound self-reflection on the sacrifice and meaning of heroism through her character's juxtaposition with Trish, her adopted sister. Jessica Jones, at best, is a reluctant superhero. Dressed in her ripped jeans and sports leather jacket, she looks and acts more like an alcoholic than a superhero. Furthermore, even though it can be argued that her sex life is part of her character, Jessica Jones is not presented as eye candy for the average viewer. She is portrayed as a mess, both emotionally and physically. In a very radical rewriting of the camera gaze in this show, we actually witness the undoing of a superhero rather than her glamorous ascension. The quote, "Humanity sucks and they don't deserve saving,"[50] clearly defines Jessica's angry brand of superheroism. While she does "save the world" by ridding it of its Kilgraves and Salingers, she seems incapable of saving those who matter to her the most; for example, she betrays Luke Cage, is unable to save her sister from the superhero fantasy, and is unable to save both her real and adoptive mothers from being killed.

Jessica Jones, more than any other MCU character, symbolizes ethical crisis and melancholia. This internal conflict of the character is what links her to the Supermuslim of Benslama. On the one hand, Marc Manley's critique of the show reveals the patriarchal aspirations that a superhero must conform to, demonstrating visceral and ultra-masculine feats of heroism. Within such a scheme, the superhero (as one version of the Supermuslim) is indeed an automaton whose psychic life is defined by the search for *jouissance*. Manley's superhero expectations are disturbed by Jessica Jones' reluctance to take this leap without questioning it. It is unsurprising that Eltahawy, who has dedicated her activism to destroy patriarchal ideologies not only globally but also specifically within Muslim mentalities, praises Jessica Jones. There is a utopian and anarchist undertone to Eltahawy's activism, which is not defined by the loss of a "golden Islamic past" but rather by an almost eschatological vision of a better future. This vision involves the complete destruction of a world that has been, both historically and presently, particularly unjust for women, and more specifically women of color and Muslim women.[51] This grand transformative vision needs superheroines such as Jones, even if they are not Muslim, to fit within the unapologetic ideal of the feminist vindicator. Eltahawy's anticipation of the post-patriarchy world is also somewhat melancholic; it is immersed in rage but cannot escape reflection. The feminist liberation must progress alongside the creation of an Islamically just world. This world, however, is not ecstatic (unlike Manley's uber-masculinized superhero), even if it involves the pursuit of pleasure. The emergence of this happy post-patriarchy world is passionately anticipated, even though it remains unfulfilled. The promise of such a world is accompanied by the anxiety that it may never be realized. This ambiguous emotional economy of Jessica Jones is what fascinates both Islamic and feminist stakeholders.

THE MARVEL CINEMATIC UNIVERSE AND THE SUPERMUSLIM: A TRANSMEDIA WORLD

Speaking about the Muslim superhero in generalized terms always runs the risk of essentializing the enormous cultural, linguistic, and spiritual diversity of Islam. Both Muslim and non-Muslim creators work within various discursive understandings of authenticity, and their engagement with injustice is largely informed by their socio-historical positionings. Further, both the fictional and real-world protagonists inside the Supermuslim action-fantasy framework are diverse in nature. Ms Marvel is different from Qahera, even though both characters can be considered to belong to a superheroine branch of Islamic feminism. The German Lebanese woman who leaves behind her three kids in Germany, moves to Syria, and marries a jihadi fighter there is driven by considerably different forces than the Tunisian girl whose search for Islamic justice arose as a reaction to being bullied in school for wearing a hijab. However, these women demonstrate a common characteristic in their ability to articulate their agency in terms of seeking justice within Islam, which is one of the essential traits of the Supermuslim in Benslama's model. Benslama is interested in the intersection of macro-historical and individual narratives of injustice within the psychic landscape of the Supermuslim. The addition of a media dimension may, I believe, complicate Benslama's model.

The Supermuslim is also, among other things, a mediated event. It is neither purely fictional, nor fully embodied; the Supermuslim traverses the terrains of the real and symbolic in ethically complex disguises. The agency of the Supermuslim—whether it is understood as primarily a good force or a bad one—is traceable in print, cinema, TV, or videogames, and circulated in the vast and unchecked virtual environment. Often, the Supermuslim takes on a new life and meaning by encountering the transformative imaginations and agencies of its audiences that perceive the original image from a distance—either cultural, spiritual, or geographical. The Marvel universe, which is the ultimate transmedia world of heroism and villainy, is re-appropriated and reimagined in indigenous Islamic environments, either through direct engagement with the media or through the creation of novel characters and symbols in response to the Marvel superheroes. The encounter between the Marvel transmedia universe and the Supermuslim occurs within the techno-human infrastructure of networked technologies and engenders a twofold event. The extraordinary fantasy of the superhero becomes a performative ground that justifies the pursuit of goodness, justice, and/or violence in the real world. Simultaneously, this fantasy circulates ad infinitum as a constellation of dismembered images of hate and adoration, which are copied, re-used, downloaded and re-uploaded, turned into gifs and memes, and manipulated in various ways. The virality and spreadability of the superhero fantasy—arguably a sign of its success—is also a source of anxiety that the superhero is meaningless symbol of heroism, and incapable of improving the world.

NOTES

1. A complex psychoanalytical metaphor analyzed in this text, developed by the Franco-Tunisian psychoanalyst Fethi Benslama in *Un Furieux désir de sacrifice. Le Surmusulman*, Paris: Seul, 2016.

2. Della Rata, Donatella. "ISIS and Western Media: Accidental Allies?" in: *Al-Jazeera English*, September 25, 2014, https://www.aljazeera.com/indepth/opinion/2014/09/isil-western-media-allies-2014924121817329713.html, last checked March 5, 2020.

3. Galaver, Chris. *On the Origins of Superheroes: From Big Bang to Action Comic #1*, Iowa City: University of Iowa Press, 2015: p. 48.

4. Scorsese, Martin. "I Said Marvel Movies Aren't Cinema. Let Me Explain," in: *New York Times*, November 14, 2019, https://www.nytimes.com/2019/11/04/opinion/martin-scorsese-marvel.html?fbclid=IwAR3tE6u4paTJtZl00QTDHKzwQxAv_Ou6gjxh5-UPMie2z2X68EwyaN4j9kI, last checked March 2, 2020.

5. Batchelor, Tom. "PICTURED: Inside Brutal Islamic State's Bizzare Theme Park," in: *Express*, October 15, 2015, https://www.express.co.uk/news/world/609908/Islamic-State-theme-park-Syria-Iraq, last checked March 9, 2020.

6. Weiner, Zoe. "Hijabi Women Dressed Like the 'Avengers' at Comic Con," in: *Teen Vogue*, October 10, 2018, https://www.teenvogue.com/story/hijab-avengers-comic-con-cosplay?utm_campaign=falcon&mbid=social_facebook&utm_source=facebook&utm_medium=social&utm_brand=tv&utm_social-type=owned&fbclid=IwAR24Nmzb_rI4J0ode_Wt7qgxr043tL3J2lIN2X9nFMkLAOPQa9wn1qvHNFY.

7. Fidducia, Christopher. "Ms. Marvel Reportedly Films This Summer, Will Appear in First MCU Film Soon After," in: *Screen Rant*, February 4, 2020, https://screenrant.com/ms-marvel-tv-show-filming-dates-movie-future/.

8. The tweets are available on the profile of Twitter user @malihaness. I have kept the spelling and punctuation as they appear in the original Tweets; last checked Feb 6, 2020.

9. See: Jebreal, Rula. "Meet the Muslim Ms. Marvel: Kamala Khan's Fight Against Stereotypes," in: *The Daily Beast*, November 8, 2013, https://www.thedailybeast.com/meet-the-muslim-ms-marvel-kamala-khans-fight-against-stereotypes, last checked February 18, 2020.

10. Latamendi, Andrea. "Meet the Muslim superhero fighting bigotry on San Francisco buses," in: *The Guardian*, February 1, 2015, https://www.theguardian.com/books/2015/feb/01/meet-the-muslim-superhero-fighting-bigotry-on-san-francisco-buses, last checked Feb 18, 2020.

11. For the potential of the digital comic to mobilize large-scale trans-national conversations, see: Landis, Winona. "*Ms. Marvel, Qahera* and Superheroism in the Muslim Diaspora," in: *Continuum: Journal of Media and Cultural Studies 33* (2); 2019: pp. 185–200.

12. Cited in Berlatsky, Noah. "What Makes the Muslim *Ms. Marvel* Awesome: She's Just Like Everyone," in: *The Atlantic*, March 20, 2014, https://www.theatlantic.com/entertainment/archive/2014/03/what-makes-the-muslim-em-ms-marvel-em-awesome-shes-just-like-everyone/284517/, last checked March 10, 2020.

13. For a historical introduction and comment on the variety of Muslim superheroes, see: Martin Lund and David Lewis. "Whence the Muslim Superhero?," in: David Lewis and Martin Lund (edit.), *Muslim Superheroes: Comics, Islam and Representation*, Ilex Foundation, Boston, MA, 2017: pp. 1–20.

14. For history of female representation of Muslims in American comics, see: Karanukaran, Shamila. "Muslimahs in Comics and Graphic Novels: History and Representation," in: *The iJournal 3* (2); 2017: pp. 1–22.

15. Lynn, Madison Mahdiya. "Dust and the Veil: Muslim Marvel's Problematic Faves," in: *Muslim Girl*, 2016, https://muslimgirl.com/dust-veil-muslim-marvels-problematic-faves/, last checked February 19, 2020.

16. Morrison, Grant and Ethan van Sciver. *New X-Men 1* (133); New York, 2002.

17. Pumphrey, Nicholas. "*Niqab* Not *Burqa*: Reading the Veil in Marvel's Dust," in David Lewis and Martin Lund (edit.), *Muslim Superheroes: Comics, Islam and Representation*, Ilex Foundation, Boston, MA, 2017: pp. 20–40.

18. Cited in Sara Hamdam. "Comic Book Heroes Help Change Image of Islam," in: *New York Times*, July 27, 2011, https://www.nytimes.com/2011/07/28/world/middleeast/28iht-M28C-ISLAMIC-COMICS.html, last checked Feb 20, 2020.

19. Cited in Sara Hamdam. "Comic Book Heroes Help Change Image of Islam," in: *New York Times*, July 27, 2011, https://www.nytimes.com/2011/07/28/world/middleeast/28iht-M28C-ISLAMIC-COMICS.html, last checked February 20, 2020.

20. Arjana, Sophia Rose. "*Burqa Avenger* and the Subversive Veil," in: *Veiled Superheroes: Islam, Femininity and Popular Culture*, Lexington Books, 2018: p. 86.

21. The Twitter account of Fasil Towalde has been changed several times; however, as of today, his Superman T-shirt is still clearly visible on his profile picture: https://twitter.com/yungsmiley?lang=en, last checked February 19, 2020.

22. Monaci, Sara. "Explaining the Islamic State Online Media Strategy: A Transmedia Approach," in: *International Journal of Communication 11*; 2017: pp. 2842–2860; Abdelrahim, Yasser Abuelmakarem. "Visual Analysis of ISIS Discourse Strategies and Types in *Dabiq* and *Rumiyah* Online Magazines," in: *Visual Communication Quarterly 26* (2); 2019: pp. 63–78; Picart, Caroline Joan S. "Jihad Cool/Jihad Chic: The Roles of the Internet and Imagined Relations in the Self-Radicalization of Colleen LaRose," in: *Societies 5*; 2015: pp. 353–383.

23. Alejandro Beutel, Steven M. Weine, Aliya Saeed, Aida Mihajlovic, Andrew Stone, John Oakley Beahrs, and Stephen Shanfield propose that the Islamic State capitalizes on widely popular superhero narratives that define Western popular culture (Marvel and DC Comics are prominently featured), and which are reinterpreted through the Islamic lens of local cultural mythologies. See: "Field Principles for Countering and Displacing Extremist Narratives," in: *Journal of Terrorism Research 7* (3); September 2016: p. 41.

24. A report on the American volunteers in the fight against ISIS is found in New York Times, see Percy, Jennifer. "Meet the American Vigilantes Who Are Fighting ISIS," in: *New York Times*, September 30, 2015, https://www.nytimes.com/2015/10/04/magazine/meet-the-american-vigilantes-who-are-fighting-isis.html.

25. The adoption of the Punisher symbol by Iraqi anti-Islamic State forces became a Twitter sensation with multiple reports from Italian journalist Danielle Raineri in the Spring of 2015, see: https://twitter.com/DanieleRaineri/status/585691464010706945, https://twitter.com/DanieleRaineri/status/585691678469677057, https://twitter.com/DanieleRaineri/status/585692299973255168, https://twitter.com/DanieleRaineri/status/585692987172265985.

26. See Collard, Rebecca. "How A Marvel Comic Hero Became the Icon of the Fight Against ISIS," in: *Time*, April 13, 2015, https://time.com/3819227/punisher-iraq-isis/

27. The Russo brothers have directed four of the MCU movies: *Captain America: The Winter Soldier* (2014), *Captain America: Civil War* (2016), *Avengers: Infinity War* (2018), and *Avengers: Endgame* (2019).

28. Mogelson, Luke. "Desperate Battle to Destroy ISIS," in: *New Yorker*, January 30, 2017, https://www.newyorker.com/magazine/2017/02/06/the-desperate-battle-to-destroy-isis.

29. The Russo brothers have been criticized for failing to hire an Arab director and screenwriter for this project. They are accused of "falling prey to the white saviour complex." See Flint, Hanna. "With *Mosul* the Russo Brothers Fall Victim to White Saviour Syndrome," in: *The Guardian*, September 20, 2019, https://www.theguardian.com/film/2019/sep/20/with-mosul-the-russo-brothers-fallen-prey-to-white-saviour-syndrome.

30. Olivier Roy's argument is that jihadism is nihilistic denial of the world as it exists, but this denial is not Islamic in nature. The political and global positioning of Islam as the religion of the oppressed, stigmatized, and formerly colonized people, particularly in the aftermath of 9/11, is what attracts these young people who are otherwise theologically illiterate. While it is true that most of the Islamic State returnees have said that they went to fight in Syria and Iraq to live in a just Islamic society, many of the young fighters and converts have no knowledge of sharia law or even basic understanding of the sacred texts and Islamic traditions. See Roy, Olivier. *Jihad and Death: The Global Appeal of Islamic State*, Oxford: Oxford University Press, 2017.

31. Ibid, pp. 21–24.

32. Roy, Olivier. "Who Are the New Jihadis," in: *The Guardian*, April 13, 2017, https://www.theguardian.com/news/2017/apr/13/who-are-the-new-jihadis.

33. Benslama, Fethi. *Un furieux désir de sacrifice. Le surmusulman*. Paris: Seul, 2016.

34. The comparison between Nietzche's superman and Freud's supergo is pertinently provided in an article commentary on Benslama's work by Gana, Nouri. "Jihad On the Couch," in: *Psychoanalysis and History*, March 20, 2018, p. 371.

35. Benslama, Fethi. *Un furieux désir de sacrifice. Le surmusulman*. Paris: Seul, 2016, Ibid., p. 60.

36. Al-Qaeda's propaganda has also heavily relied on inspirational superhero tropes, particularly revealed in their propaganda magazine *Inspire* (2010-present). See: Sivek, Susan Curie. "Packaging Inspiration: Al-Qaeda's Digital Magazine *Inspire* the Self-Radicalisation Process," in: *International Journal of Communication* 7; 2013: pp. 584–606.

37. Benslama, Fethi. "The Subjective Impact of the Jihadist Offer," in: *Interdisciplinary Journal for Religion and Transformation in Contemporary Society* 2 (2); 2016: pp. 75–85, online, https://www.vr-elibrary.de/doi/abs/10.14220/jrat.2016.2.2.75.

38. Gana, Nouri. "Jihad on the Couch," in: *Psychoanalysis and History*, p. 378.

39. Freud, Sigmund. "Mourning and Melancholia," *The Standard Edition of the Complete Psychological Works of Sigmund Freud, Volume XIV (1914-1916): On the History of the Psycho-Analytic Movement, Papers on Metapsychology and Other Works*, pp. 237–258, http://www.arch.mcgill.ca/prof/bressani/arch653/winter2010/Freud_Mourningandmelancholia.pdf.

40. Gana, Nouri. "Jihad on the Couch," in: *Psychoanalysis and History*, p. 379.

41. Manley, Marc. "Jessica Jones and the Pornification of Superheroes?" March 15, 2018, http://www.marcmanley.com/tag/sexuality/. A quick look around the very well-maintained website of Marc Manley reveals that he is a highly active and well-recognized figure in the world of American Islam. There are links to numerous Quranic lectures, *tafsir* readings (Quranic exegesis), awards, and activism events provided on the website. The website points to a pious character who is technologically savvy, interested in the lives and minds of young people, and committed to the American version of Islam.

42. Eltahawy's posts are still available on her Twitter profile: https://twitter.com/monaeltahawy/status/968980714430574592.

43. Middle East Film and Comic Con praised the show on Facebook. Wired Magazine, the Middle East Section, recommended the show for binge watching in September 2019. The show triggered discussions in the United Arab Emirates, Lebanon, and Egypt. It has also been presented on the YouTube channel of Marvel Arabia. *IGN Middle East* curates careful presentation on all seasons of Jessica Jones, available here: https://me.ign.com/en/krysten-ritter. *Gulf News* reports on the show, see: Villarreal, Yvonne. "Krysten Ritter On Being a Marvel Superhero," June 11, 2016, https://gulfnews.com/entertainment/tv/krysten-ritter-on-being-a-marvel-superhero-1.1843712 *Emirates Woman* dedicates a special presentation to Kristen Ritter, see: Pudney, Harriet. "These Stars Show Doesn't End After the Oscars," March 11, 2020, https://emirateswoman.com/krysten-ritter-jennifer-lawrence-lebanese-designers/ For the popularity of the Marvel characters in the Middle East, see Fernando, Chris. "Meet Your Favourite Celebs at Middle East Film & Comic Con," in: *GadgetVoize Middle East*, March 13, 2019, https://www.gadgetvoize.com/2019/03/13/meet-your-favourite-celebs-at-middle-east-film-comic-con/.

44. Arabic Marvel on Twitter, which has over 18,000 followers, shows polarized engagement with the series: https://twitter.com/ArabicMarvel/status/1131620035431141376.

45. These particular comments are made at about the 8-minute mark in the rant, see: Manley, Marc. "Jessica Jones and the Pornification of Superheroes?" March 15, 2018, http://www.marcmanley.com/tag/sexuality/.

46. Eltahawy, Mona, https://twitter.com/monaeltahawy/status/968980714430574592.

47. Eltahawy, Mona, https://twitter.com/monaeltahawy/status/1091755836505014272.

48. Bernstein, Arielle. "Mad Women: How Angry Sisterhood Is Taking Over the Small Screen," in: *The Guardian*, March 7, 2018, https://www.theguardian.com/tv-and-radio/2018/mar/07/mad-women-angry-sisterhood-taking-over-tv.

49. *Jessica Jones*, Season 1, episode 4 "A.K.A God Help the Hobo." See also, Eltahawy, Mona. *The Seven Necessary Sins for Women and Girls*, Boston, MA: Beacon Press, 2019. Particularly, chapter 2 "Anger" (pp. 15–36) and chapter 6 "Violence," pp. 135–157.

50. *Jessica Jones*, season 1, episode 11, "A.K.A. I've Got the Blues."

51. Eltahawy, Mona. "Muslim Women Caught Between the Rock and the Hard Place," in: *New York Times*, November 19, 2017, https://www.nytimes.com/2017/11/19/opinion/muslim-women-sexism-violence.html.

REFERENCES

Abdelrahim, Yasser Abuelmakarem. "Visual Analysis of ISIS Discourse Strategies and Types in *Dabiq* and *Rumiyah* Online Magazines." *Visual Communication Quarterly 26* (2); 2019: 63–78.

Arjana, Sophia Rose. *Veiled Superheroes: Islam, Femininity and Popular Culture.* Lanham, MD: Lexington Books, 2018.

Batchelor, Tom. "PICTURED: Inside Brutal Islamic State's Bizzare Theme Park," in: *Express*, October 15, 2015, https://www.express.co.uk/news/world/609908/Islamic-State-theme-park-Syria-Iraq.

Beahrs, John Oakley, Stephen Shanfield, et al. "Field Principles for Countering and Displacing Extremist Narratives." *Journal of Terrorism Research 7* (3); September 2016, 35–49.

Benslama, Fethi. *Un Furieux désir de sacrifice. Le Surmusulman.* Paris: Seul, 2016.

———. "The Subjective Impact of the Jihadist Offer." *Interdisciplinary Journal for Religion and Transformation in Contemporary Society 2* (2); 2016, online, https://www.vr-elibrary.de/doi/abs/10.14220/jrat.2016.2.2.75.

Berlatsky, Noah. "What Makes the Muslim *Ms. Marvel* Awesome: She's Just Like Everyone," in: *The Atlantic*, March 20, 2014, https://www.theatlantic.com/entertainment/archive/2014/03/what-makes-the-muslim-em-ms-marvel-em-awesome-shes-just-like-everyone/284517/.

Bernstein, Arielle. "Mad Women: How Angry Sisterhood Is Taking Over the Small Screen," in: *The Guardian*, March 7, 2018, https://www.theguardian.com/tv-and-radio/2018/mar/07/mad-women-angry-sisterhood-taking-over-tv.

Beutel, Alejandro Steven M. Weine, Aliya Saeed, Aida Mihajlovic, Andrew Stone, John Oakley and Rebecca Collard. "How A Marvel Comic Hero Became the Icon of the Fight Against ISIS," in: *Time*, April 13, 2015, https://time.com/3819227/punisher-iraq-isis/.

Della Rata, Donatella. "ISIS and Western Media: Accidental Allies?" in: *Al-Jazeera English*, September 25, 2014, https://www.aljazeera.com/indepth/opinion/2014/09/isil-western-media-allies-2014924121817329713.html.

Eltahawy, Mona. "Muslim Women Caught Between the Rock and the Hard Place," in: *New York Times*, November 19, 2017, https://www.nytimes.com/2017/11/19/opinion/muslim-women-sexism-violence.html.

———. *The Seven Necessary Sins for Women and Girls.* Boston: Beacon Press, 2019.

Fernando, Chris. "Meet Your Favourite Celebs at Middle East Film & Comic Con," in: *GadgetVoize Middle East*, March 13, 2019, https://www.gadgetvoize.com/2019/03/13/meet-your-favourite-celebs-at-middle-east-film-comic-con/.

Fidducia, Christopher. "Ms. Marvel Reportedly Films This Summer, Will Appear in First MCU Film Soon After," in: *Screen Rant*, February 4, 2020, https://screenrant.com/ms-marvel-tv-show-filming-dates-movie-future/.

Flint, Hanna. "With *Mosul* the Russo Brothers Fall Victim to White Saviour Syndrome," in: *The Guardian*, September 20, 2019, https://www.theguardian.com

/film/2019/sep/20/with-mosul-the-russo-brothers-fallen-prey-to-white-saviour-syndrome.

Freud, Sigmund. *The Standard Edition of the Complete Psychological Works of Sigmund Freud, Volume XIV (1914-1916): On the History of the Psycho-Analytic Movement, Papers on Metapsychology and Other Works.* http://www.arch.mcgill.ca/prof/bressani/arch653/winter2010/Freud_Mourningandmelancholia.pdf.

Galaver, Chris. *On the Origins of Superheroes: From Big Bang to Action Comic #1.* Iowa City: University of Iowa Press, 2015.

Gana, Nouri. "Jihad on the Couch," in: *Psychoanalysis and History*, March 20, 2018.

Hamdam, Sara. "Comic Book Heroes Help Change Image of Islam," in: *New York Times*, July 27, 2011, https://www.nytimes.com/2011/07/28/world/middleeast/28iht-M28C-ISLAMIC-COMICS.html.

IGN Middle East: https://me.ign.com/en/krysten-ritter.

Jebreal, Rula. "Meet the Muslim Ms. Marvel: Kamala Khan's Fight Against Stereotypes," in: *The Daily Beast*, November 8, 2013, https://www.thedailybeast.com/meet-the-muslim-ms-marvel-kamala-khans-fight-against-stereotypes.

Karanukaran, Shamila. "Muslimahs in Comics and Graphic Novels: History and Representation." *The iJournal 3* (2); 2017: 1–22.

Landis, Winona. "*Ms. Marvel, Qahera* and Superheroism in the Muslim Diaspora." *Continuum: Journal of Media and Cultural Studies 33* (2); 2019: 185–200.

Latamendi, Andrea. "Meet the Muslim Superhero Fighting Bigotry on San Francisco Buses," in: *The Guardian*, February 1, 2015, https://www.theguardian.com/books/2015/feb/01/meet-the-muslim-superhero-fighting-bigotry-on-san-francisco-buses.

Lewis, David A., and Martin Lund. *Muslim Superheroes: Comics, Islam and Representation.* Boston, MA: Ilex Foundation, 2017.

Lynn, Madison Mahdiya. "Dust and the Veil: Muslim Marvel's Problematic Faves," in: *Muslim Girl*, 2016, https://muslimgirl.com/dust-veil-muslim-marvels-problematic-faves/.

Manley, Marc. "Jessica Jones and the Pornification of Superheroes?" March 15, 2018, http://www.marcmanley.com/tag/sexuality/.

Mogelson, Luke. "Desperate Battle to Destroy ISIS," in: *New Yorker*, January 30, 2017, https://www.newyorker.com/magazine/2017/02/06/the-desperate-battle-to-destroy-isis.

Monaci, Sara. "Explaining the Islamic State Online Media Strategy: A Transmedia Approach." *International Journal of Communication 11*; 2017: 2842–2860.

Morrison, Grant, and Ethan van Sciver. *New X-Men 1* (133). New York: Marvel Comics, 2002 ASIN: B000S2WQ0M 32 pages.

Percy, Jennifer. "Meet the American Vigilantes Who Are Fighting ISIS," in: *New York Times*, September 30, 2015, https://www.nytimes.com/2015/10/04/magazine/meet-the-american-vigilantes-who-are-fighting-isis.html.

Picart, Caroline Joan S. "Jihad Cool/Jihad Chic: The Roles of the Internet and Imagined Relations in the Self-Radicalization of Colleen LaRose." *Societies 5*; 2015: 353–383.

Pudney, Harriet. "These Stars Show Doesn't End After the Oscars," in *Emirates Woman*, March 11, 2020, https://emirateswoman.com/krysten-ritter-jennifer-lawrence-lebanese-designers/.

Pumphrey, Nicholas. "*Niqab* Not *Burqa*: Reading the Veil in Marvel's Dust," in David Lewis and Martin Lund (eds.), *Muslim Superheroes: Comics, Islam and Representation*. Boston, MA: Ilex Foundation, 2017: 20–40.

Roy, Olivier. *Jihad and Death: The Global Appeal of Islamic State*. Oxford: Oxford University Press, 2017.

———. "Who Are the New Jihadis," in: *The Guardian*, April 13, 2017, https://www.theguardian.com/news/2017/apr/13/who-are-the-new-jihadis.

Scorsese, Martin. "I Said Marvel Movies Aren't Cinema. Let Me Explain," in: *New York Times*, November 14, 2019, https://www.nytimes.com/2019/11/04/opinion/martin-scorsese-marvel.html.

Sivek, Susan Curie. "Packaging Inspiration: Al-Qaeda's Digital Magazine *Inspire* the Self-Radicalisation Process." *International Journal of Communication* 7; 2013: 584–606.

Villarreal, Yvonne. "Krysten Ritter On Being a Marvel Superhero," June 11, 2016, https://gulfnews.com/entertainment/tv/krysten-ritter-on-being-a-marvel-superhero-1.1843712.

Weiner, Zoe. "Hijabi Women Dressed Like the "Avengers" at Comic Con," in: *Teen Vogue*, October 10, 2018, https://www.teenvogue.com/story/hijab-avengers-comic-con-cosplay.

Chapter 14

Bad Girls Turned Superwomen

A Critical Appraisal of the MCU Archetype for Superheroines

Will Abney

This chapter will examine the common trope that has developed for strong female superheroes' origin stories in the Marvel Cinematic Universe (MCU). While other critical analyses of the MCU have discussed various issues around representation and agency of female characters, none have addressed the similarities of the origin stories of the six major superheroines introduced into the MCU films thus far: Natasha Romanoff, Wanda Maximoff, Hope van Dyne, Gamora, and Carol Danvers. Each of these women has (or will have by the time of publication) a film with their name in the title (*Ant-Man and the Wasp*, *Captain Marvel*, and *Black Widow*) or is part of the titular ensemble (the Avengers or the Guardians of the Galaxy). Each of these characters could be called "bad girls" before they are made to understand the error of their ways, consequently choosing to fight with the "good guys" and earn their place among the heroes and superheroes of the MCU.

This trend has been noted in the popular press, with commentators using it to lament the formulaic nature of MCU women. But none of these critiques offers more than surface-level attempts at discussing the issue. In this chapter, the problem will be addressed through the lens of feminist criticism, including discussions of the ways that postfeminism and the monomyth have limited expectations for female characters. Other issues to consider include the comic-book origins of these characters, laziness in the writing room, and financial incentives to "stick to what works."

While there appears to be a structural similarity to the archetype that has become the standard superheroine origin story, none of these female characters fits into the mold perfectly. Additionally, there appears to be a shift in the MCU beginning in Phase 3, where perhaps the filmmakers have started to address many of the postfeminist critiques, sometimes explicitly.

After diving into the general critical issues mentioned previously, it will be necessary to look at each of these female characters on a case-by-case basis. Tracing the character arcs of these women will allow the reader to see how the MCU developed the archetype to help create "strong female characters." It will also become evident how postfeminist beliefs were incorporated into the characterizations to set up false agency and choice for these women in Phases 1 and 2. Phase 3 represents a growing awareness of this trend within the MCU and an attempt to depart from it. But we will see how *Captain Marvel*, one of the final films in Phase 3, returns to the archetype, and how *Avengers: Endgame*, the culmination of Phase 3, still has problems with allowing some female characters true agency.

TROPES, THE MONOMYTH, AND POSTFEMINISM

After the release of *Captain Marvel* in March 2019, two articles appeared online that laid bare the similarities in origin stories among the five female superheroes that will be discussed in this article. Dani Di Placido was the first to offer this comparison, concluding that they all fit into the same "template."[1] In the second article, published four days later, Daisy Phillipson offered a bit more nuance: "They all started out as flawed characters—villains, really, before realising they were fighting for the bad guys, moving over to the good side and subsequently fitting into the 'powerful women with hearts of gold' trope."[2] Di Placido likewise commented that these women's "flaws stemmed from fighting for the wrong team, rather than personality issues." For strong characters, the audience expects flaws for the character to overcome. But if the trope for MCU superheroines is for their major character flaws to evaporate once they switch from the bad side to the good side, can these women truly be fully developed characters?

Karen Gillan, the actor who plays Nebula in the MCU, was much blunter about the topic in 2017. She praised the strong female character trope but put in a word of caution: "there are females in big action, sci-fi movies, but we were sort of in danger of them becoming stereotypical in the senses that they're 'badass' and 'super strong' and 'sexy'. It's like people think, 'Oh, we're going to do the right thing be making a female strong', when really, that's almost as bad in itself. There has to be a selection. There has to be more than one archetype."[3] What is the motivation behind filmmakers turning an archetype into a stereotype?

Many people may be familiar with Joseph Campbell's structuralist triumph, the monomyth, which has given the world its archetype for constructing legends of heroes and superheroes. In the monomythic tradition, the hero is male and must use his strength to overcome obstacles and improve the world from which he comes, which is under threat. He departs but returns with the sought-after boon, having gained experiences and stories to recount for ages to come. He may change himself along the way, but this is not a necessity. The same cannot be said of monomythic heroines.

When we look at heroines or superheroines, they do not face the same challenges as monomythic men. Though they may overcome outside obstacles, their demons are typically internal. Sandra J. Lindow has examined folktales with female protagonists and found that, instead of answering the "call to adventure" like their male counterparts, "young women were . . . driven out by extremes of drudgery, deprivation, neglect, and emotional and physical abuse."[4] Another contrast between male and female monomythic heroes lies in their expected outcomes. Men tended to be strong and ready for the fight; women were habitually innocent and weak when they were forced into their quest. Furthermore, "their journeys taught them strategies, patience, networking, resilience, and wisdom—psychologically killing the dragons in their psyches and creating characters worthy of their new and better homes."[5] Thus, it appears that women engaging in the monomythic struggle did not look to bring anything back to their points of origin; instead, their quest was to defeat their inner demons in order to fit into a new location. They had to reinvent themselves to conform to societal expectations.

This is a trope the MCU knows all too well. Mary Louise DeMarchi asserts that "tropes promote the consumption of hegemonic ideologies, like what it means to be a woman and society's expectations of them."[6] This is the way postfeminism infects the discourse. Put another way, this is the method by which postfeminism shuts down the discourse. Postfeminism "emphasizes the freedom of choice . . . [asserting that] women have choices . . . [and that] they are active agents in control of their own destiny, and they have autonomy. But . . . the only truly enlightened choice to make as a woman . . . is to become a 'mom' . . . It both draws from and repudiates feminism."[7] Thus, women can choose all these various paths toward self-actualization, but if they want to become real women, they will choose the options laid out by patriarchal society. To refuse this choice is to be branded selfish and evil. But if powerful women choose to be a real woman, they can return to society and be one of the good guys.

To acclimate to that prescribed role in society, the woman allows herself to be objectified. Postfeminism would assert that it is the woman's choice, but since this "male gaze" has its origins in a patriarchal order of things, it can hardly be that the woman is completely free in her choice. Along with becoming the object of men's stares, the woman must also defer to male leadership. Again, postfeminism frames this as the woman's choice.

While she may be a CEO or a superheroine, her primary power derives from her relationships with men. Male characters have the power and true agency; female characters may aid them, but for the postfeminist, it is more important for women to be seen as helpful team players. They may nudge the male characters toward a solution, but the female characters should never challenge the men's role outright.

Real women, then, won't choose aggression, which is a masculine trait, as evidenced by the fact that social tolerance for aggression is gendered.[8] Our rigid societal standards for gender, especially masculinity, reject the inclusion of women as inherently aggressive. According to Joffe, "violent women are seen neither as sane nor as women. Society needs to see violent women as different—either mad or bad—because otherwise we would need new discourses to understand that both men and women can be violent."[9] Thus, these bad girls only become women (and fit into a societal stereotype for women) when they consciously choose to reject their former aggression against the (male) heroes. Their supposed agency places them back into the hierarchy in a more diminished role. For the postfeminist, the superheroine's true strength comes in her ability to understand a woman's place in society and accept this lesser position. The outcome, then, is the containment of potential threats presented by the true female agency. But conforming to the "good" side means the character's flaws disappear.

THE SAFE AND EASY CHOICE

The issue of creating strong female characters is nothing new, especially in the world of the MCU. Joss Whedon (in)famously responded to questions about how and why he creates strong female characters with the quip, "Because you're still asking that question." Whether he has succeeded in breaking out of postfeminist stereotypes, however, is up for debate. But Karen Gillan's desire to offer a different archetype for strong female characters is one of the biggest critiques of the MCU. Marvel has many female characters from which to choose, with thousands of stories, so Gillan's criticism is germane to the issue. Why do they all have similar origin stories?

Can we blame the comics, from which all these movies find their source material? Partially, we can, since filmmakers frequently rely on those stories in developing their own take on the character(s). But this would be a simplistic conclusion. One can find sexist and objectifying elements in the comic tradition, but filmmakers are free to make their own adaptations. DeMarchi makes no bones about this process, laying the blame for "monolithic female representations on screen" squarely at the feet of the studio.[10] If the writers, directors, producers, and other studio executives have allowed this trend to continue, it is because they want it.

Whedon's retort about needing to write strong women likely also stems from a lack of women writers. There is a famous metaphor about allowing a lamp to stand in for any female character in a comic book—the point is that most female characters in comic books have had no personality. They were two dimensional because they had no flaws. Flaws and weaknesses provide motivations for character development. As we saw with postfeminism, though, the major flaw was that the women hadn't accepted their appropriate roles in society; once they made the switch, the supposed flaws no longer existed. Starting out your female character on the bad side, or with a backstory involving villainy, was an easy way to present them as both 'strong' and in need of containment by society. The archetype conformed well to the postfeminist aesthetic, and it became the standard method of writing the stereotypical strong female character.

But keeping the archetype of the bad girl turning to the good side may be more than laziness in the writing room. The studios want to make money, after all, and they know what sells. They are, therefore, risk avoidant. As Phillipson comments, "DC and the MCU tend to play it safe with the women at their core. But in their quest to reduce risk, the studios give us cookie cutter cape-wearers whose personalities are underdeveloped compared to their male counterparts." The MCU has found a formula that works, so why jeopardize that?

Let us examine the individual female superheroes in order. Doing so will allow us to see the continuation of an archetype-cum-stereotype but also the ways the MCU has attempted to overcome and perhaps even subvert the formulaic postfeminism endemic to this archetype in more recent films.

NATASHA ROMANOFF

Of all the superheroines of the MCU, Natasha Romanoff receives the most screen time in Phases 1–3. She is the first of the "strong female characters" that the audience encounters, going all the way back to *Iron Man 2*. She is also the only female member of the original Avengers team. When we first encounter her, she is undercover for SHIELD, which indicates that she has already made the "switch" from bad girl to good woman before we meet her. The development of her backstory is piecemeal, beginning in the first Avengers film and explored intermittently until her death in *Avengers: Endgame*. Despite her death, and after much lobbying by fans and by Scarlett Johansson herself (who plays the character), Black Widow will finally receive a standalone film in May 2021.

Black Widow is the alias of Natasha Romanoff, an ex-KGB agent who abandons that organization sometime before the events of *Iron Man 2*. Only in Avengers do we find out that Clint Barton, aka Hawkeye, spared Romanoff's life when he was sent to kill her for SHIELD. In spite of her turn to the "good side," Romanoff repeatedly claims she has "red in her ledger" and desires to erase it. Loki, the big baddie in Avengers, attempts to exploit her supposed guilty conscience but is, in turn, deceived by Romanoff, who uses her feminine vulnerability to induce Loki into revealing his plan.

If we stop with Phase 2 of the MCU, all we see is Romanoff falling into this archetypal postfeminist role: a bad girl shown the error of her ways by a white man, she changes sides and uses her femininity to aid the rest of the crew but never saves the day herself. The truly heroic activities are left to the men around her: Iron Man and Captain America in their respective franchises, and the male Avengers in the first two installments. Romanoff "is intellectually and physically able (she even bests Hawkeye in *The Avengers*), but in the course of her exploits she often needs to be saved in ways that her male counterparts do not."[11] We see this necessity specifically in *Avengers: Age of Ultron*, where she is saved twice—first by puny Bruce Banner (not the Hulk) after becoming the only Avenger captured by Ultron, and then at the end of the battle when the Hulk leaps from the rising city in Sokovia to deposit her on the helicarrier. None of the male Avengers need saving in such ways.

The damsel in distress is certainly one of the tropes of postfeminism, and Black Widow will not be the only female superhero subjected to this role, for her male counterparts to rescue. But this is not the only trope of postfeminism that Black Widow (either in her ridiculously tight-fitting black outfit or in her equally revealing street clothes as Natasha Romanoff) is forced to endure in Phases 1 and 2. We simply cannot discuss Black Widow without mentioning her sex appeal.

One of the fallacies of postfeminism is that women are free to choose their own roles, including the ways that they wish to be perceived. As we have seen, though, the best roles for women to choose are those that reinforce the patriarchal stereotypes of women. When it comes to physical beauty, we often refer to the "male gaze," which, once a woman has chosen to turn from the bad side to the good side, she often internalizes as the desired outcome. Not only has the female character had to give up her aggressive past, but she also must self-objectify, which leads women to "devalue their own subjective experiences in favor of conforming to societal standards of beauty."[12] Lindow found that this was the outcome of female protagonists in folktales, as well: "Most of the tales reinforced a tyranny of standards for youth, beauty, and modesty that most women found impossible . . . the myths of virginity."[13]

So, while the viewer may objectify Romanoff, she herself is chaste. She flirts with Tony Stark in *Iron Man 2*, and there's even speculation that she and Steve Rogers might develop a relationship in *Captain America: The Winter Soldier*. But not until *Avengers: Age of Ultron* do we get any hint that Romanoff might actually settle down with one of her male teammates, in a scene that drew the ire of many feminists across the internet.

As if drawing from the postfeminist playbook, the writers for *Age of Ultron* attempted to create a flaw or weakness for Romanoff to overcome by exploiting her sterilization in the Red Room during her KGB training days. After revealing her story to Bruce Banner, she asks, "Still think you're the only monster?" For the postfeminist, this is the ultimate monstrosity—the ideal woman should desire above anything else to be a mother. Since there was no flaw to overcome once she became an Avenger, this was the best they could do to give Black Widow a weakness. In essence, the writers took three tropes associated with postfeminism—woman as forgoing the bad side, woman as objectified by choice, and woman as a mother above all else—and rolled them into a single character. These choices were safe and relatively easy to make, given the currency of postfeminist thought in the American movie industry of the time. Throughout Phases 1 and 2, then, Black Widow was the posterwoman for postfeminism.

GAMORA

The next superheroine we are introduced to in the MCU comes from another ensemble: the Guardians of the Galaxy. Gamora is the only female in this group, which includes four other ostensibly male characters. Sounds a lot like the Avengers, doesn't it? Gamora fits into the archetype under discussion here, and like Natasha Romanoff, her post-bad girl existence fulfills many of the postfeminist criteria for a strong female character.

Unlike Romanoff, however, Gamora's change from the "bad side" does not begin after her life is spared by one of the "good guys." It's true that her full conversion will take place as she interacts with Quill and the other Guardians, but her initial departure from the side of Thanos is related to money. If we are to believe her motives in *The Guardians of the Galaxy*, she intends to sell the infinity stone to The Collector instead of handing it over to Thanos, because it will make her free of Thanos. In *Infinity War*, however, we learn that she has already determined that Thanos is too powerful, and her rationale behind keeping the stone from him (and from finding the one on Vormir) is because she sees his evilness for what it truly is.

In Phase 2 of the MCU, then, Gamora presents as an aggressive and greedy female character who is transformed as the result of the newfound family she experiences with the Guardians, not to mention the love of Quill. But in Phase 3, she appears to have already made the choice to abandon her evil ways, exhibiting kindness toward her sister, Nebula, in flashback scenes in *Endgame*. Thus, Phase 2 presents a mostly postfeminist approach to liberating Gamora from her bad-girl ways, but Phase 3 opens up other possible avenues for her to present her agency. That trajectory, though, is still convoluted.

Despite her reputation as the "fiercest woman in the galaxy"—an honor accorded her by her adoptive father Thanos—Gamora's femininity is always an issue. Upfront among this liability is her tendency to become a damsel in distress. In this way, her ferocity (and potentially her aggression, a male character trait) is tempered by her vulnerability. In *The Guardians of the Galaxy*, she must be rescued twice by male characters: the first time by Drax in the Kyln (and subsequently by Quill, who convinces Drax to keep her alive), when the inmates have taken her aside in the middle of the night to exact their revenge on her; and the second time, after Nebula destroys the necropod flown by Gamora, Quill exits his own pod to give her his breathing apparatus to save her life while expecting to sacrifice himself in the process. Gamora, then, becomes a vehicle by which the male characters around her can demonstrate their own powers and heroism. Finally, most of the Guardians' role in *Infinity War* (minus Rocket and Groot) is an elaborate scheme to retrieve Gamora from the clutches of Thanos, who captures her and preys upon her feminine weaknesses to extract the location of the soul stone.

According to Edmunds, "Male heroes are often seen as independent, capable of handling incredible odds on a 'lone wolf' basis.... Females, however, are often seen as more social than their male counterparts, preferring the company of others to being alone. By inference, then, female superheroes should prefer to operate as part of a team rather than independently."[14] This accords well with the transformation of Gamora in the first installment of *Guardians of the Galaxy*. In her first encounter with Quill, Rocket, and Groot, she holds her own and nearly succeeds in keeping the infinity stone for herself; it takes all three of them, though not operating in conjunction, to thwart her plans. But once Gamora accepts her role within the Guardians, we never see her operating in the "lone wolf" capacity. She is always part of the team, subsuming her identity in that group.

As part of the Guardians, she also warms up to the idea of romance with Quill. Not until *The Guardians of the Galaxy, Vol. 2* does that relationship become actualized. This component of the postfeminist ideology is essential, as it feminizes the woman and, in many ways, diminishes her agency. While she was working for Thanos, Gamora did not entertain notions of romance or family. Yet, when she becomes part of the Guardians, romance seems almost inevitable. And if she wanted to dismiss the issue—which she seems to do when Mantis attempts to touch her, after revealing that Quill is in love with

Gamora after touching him—the entire episode on Ego's planet involves parenting and children (specifically Ego's relationship with Quill's mother and with Quill himself). Gamora is inundated with notions of family life and motherhood, and even after the intervention of Nebula to inject some chaos into the storyline, the end of the film finds Gamora and Quill as romantic partners.

Her will is again violated in *Infinity War*, this time by her romantic partner. Thanos, of course, has a role to play in thwarting Gamora's plan, but the viewer can see that she has become 'softer' due to her time with the Guardians. She asks Quill to kill her if Thanos overcomes her, since she knows she will not be able to hold out against Thanos' power. Perhaps it is also implied that she won't be strong enough to take her own life.

WANDA MAXIMOFF

Scarlet Witch is the alias of Wanda Maximoff, one of the Sokovian twins who voluntarily undergo experiments with Baron von Strucker to enhance their abilities with the mind stone. Maximoff's conversion from bad girl into superheroine is clearly visible and explicitly done throughout *Avengers: Age of Ultron*. Her backstory involves nearly being killed by one of Stark Industries' missiles while a child in Sokovia. Her motivation, then, is simple: she and her twin brother Pietro desire revenge on Tony Stark (and the Avengers, by extension) for the suffering and loss he inflicted upon their family. The twins join forces with Ultron, the artificial intelligence that inhabits multiple incarnations of robots, to exact that revenge over various incidents from Sokovia to Africa and Korea. Maximoff's sudden glimpse into Ultron's "mind," however, causes her to understand the ultimate destructive goals that Ultron intends to accomplish; the image frightens her and leads to her defection, along with Pietro, to the Avengers.

As with most villains in the MCU, Maximoff's focus was single-minded: revenge on Tony Stark and those who support him. After her conversion, however, her focus slips. Even during the battle against Ultron, she becomes unable to deal with the conflict and has a mental breakdown. She is purported to be young, perhaps a teenager, so one might be tempted to blame her instability on her youth. Yet, her twin brother is able to join the ranks of the Avengers without any of the emotional problems. The postfeminist argument would say that Maximoff has rightfully abandoned her aggressive impulses, which were masculine, and should defer to the men for support and direction.

This type of diminution is typical of the "strong female character" of postfeminism. Maximoff had her time as a powerful character, but now her agency is limited to a support role for the male superheroes. Joffe offers an interesting commentary on this particular scene: "She is currently the most powerful superhero in the MCU, and yet she is the only one who panics in the midst of a climactic battle. She cowers in an abandoned building until Hawkeye, a straight, white male character with no actual superpowers gives her a pep-talk."[15] How ironic! But how expected in a postfeminist arc. The final part of that film involves Maximoff being carried off the battlefield by Vision, despite the fact that she just ripped out the "heart" from the primary Ultron robot; also despite the fact that Maximoff herself can fly.

This process of infantilization is most remarkable with Maximoff, and it continues through *Captain America: Civil War*. She is literally confined to the Avengers compound, treated like a child by nearly all of the Avengers with whom she has contact. This treatment ostensibly derives from her role in the destruction of a Nigerian apartment building at the beginning of the film; she had been on a mission with the good guys, but she was unable to control her power. Strangely, this had not been the case while she was a villain. This is no coincidence. As postfeminism mandates, her femininity is forced to the surface after her conversion to the good side; this includes physical and/or mental weakness. As Edmunds points out, "Heroines with great power are often shown to be unable to wield it responsibly and eventually cause great damage to those they love most. This feminine weakness—whether mental or emotional—allows these heroines to either be easily exploited by outside forces or to personally wield their power recklessly."[16] Maximoff thus falls under the "protection" of the male Avengers, and her infantilization is complete.

HOPE VAN DYNE

The Wasp is the alias of Hope van Dyne, daughter of Hank Pym, the man who invented the Ant-Man suit and its accompanying technology. Despite being the first female superhero mentioned in a movie title in the MCU (*Ant-Man and the Wasp*), the character takes a long time to develop. In fact, only in the post-credits scene to *Ant-Man* does she encounter the Wasp suit for the first time. So for the first Ant-Man film, she remains simply Hope van Dyne, not the Wasp.

Similar to Natasha Romanoff, van Dyne's villainous backstory is already in the past by the time we meet her for the first time. A careless viewer might even wonder why she is on this list of "bad girls" who become superheroes. The resentment that she directs toward her father, whom she blames for the loss of her mother, is a primary driving force in *Ant-Man*. In fact, the viewer is led to believe for a good chunk of this film that she is still actively trying to thwart Hank Pym's plans. Once we find out that she is actually in league with her father to try and uncover the diabolical plans of her boss, Darren Cross, a former protégé of Hank Pym, we might think that it was all simply a ploy; but a quick reference by Pym uncovers the truth: that van Dyne had indeed sided with Cross to ensure Pym's ouster from the company. In fact, she worked to help Cross develop much of the weapons technology before she comprehended the evil direction Cross was taking the company.

Nevertheless, Hope van Dyne is a postfeminist's dream character: ambitious, smart, sexy, and physically strong. While she is unmarried and childless, we see her prioritize family not only with the great loss she feels regarding her own mother but also how she softens to Scott Lang (the new Ant-Man) once she finds out that he has a daughter. Before the advent of *Ant-Man and the Wasp*, one critic even offered this harsh critique of the character: "[S]he has every attribute that might make her a suitable candidate for being a superhero, were she not a woman. She is intelligent, determined, strong, and is even shown to be physically able to beat Lang in a fight."[17] Yet, the writers of *Ant-Man* infantilize her by subordinating her desires to those of her father, presumably out of his desire to protect her from suffering the same fate as her mother, his wife. The comparison between Lang's six-year-old daughter Cassie is even made explicit when Pym compares his and Lang's desires to provide a good future for "them."

Ant-Man and the Wasp is squarely in Phase 3 of the MCU, yet van Dyne is still conforming to the mentality that female superheroes work well in teams but not on their own. She is given a single scene where she demonstrates her ability with the Wasp suit, but she is thwarted by another female character, The Ghost, after which time Ant-Man becomes the hero of the film. Scott Lang, the new Ant-Man, helps Hope and Hank escape police custody; and then Hank, the former Ant-Man, goes subatomic to rescue his wife, Janet, from the quantum realm. At the end of this film, though van Dyne has a new superhero alias—The Wasp—she has no real agency on her own. This is also true of her part in the climactic battle in *Avengers: Endgame*—she is paired with Scott to try and restart the van containing the time machine and later aids the group of women who try to help Captain Marvel get the infinity gauntlet to the time machine.

What of van Dyne's character flaws? Other than the aforementioned brief association with the diabolical Darren Cross, she hardly has any flaws. In a tongue-in-cheek appraisal of her character, Dani di Placido says, "Her biggest flaw is . . . being kind of unfriendly? I'm not sure she even has a flaw." This is problematic for a superhero, either male or female. This was the reason many of the writers stuck to the archetype of the bad girl who needed to turn good; it was an easy way to create a character arc and give the character any semblance of dramatic tension. But after discovering that her father was not to blame for her mother's death, van Dyne seems to be out of problems to overcome. While she is no longer being infantilized by her father (or Scott) at the end of Phase 3, the post-battle scene in *Avengers: Endgame* sees her fulfilling that postfeminist dream: she is now cast in the role of mother as she enjoys the fireworks with Scott and Cassie in a very family oriented pose.

CAROL DANVERS

Carol Danvers, alias Captain Marvel, is the first female superhero in the MCU to get a solo film. This was the cause of much rejoicing in feminist circles, and for good reason. It took eleven years and eighteen movies before Marvel was comfortable making a standalone superheroine flick. That being said, many were still unimpressed with the treatment of Captain Marvel, most notably for this chapter the formulaic turn from bad girl to superheroine.

As a former captain in the U.S. Air Force who had her memories suppressed, it is easy to forgive Danvers for fighting for the wrong side. She was brainwashed, probably in the same way Natasha Romanoff had been in the Red Room. As far as she knew, she was fighting the good fight with the Kree Empire. This goes on for six years until she comes to Earth after escaping from a Skrull ship in orbit. Her quest to find the Skrulls leads her to a journey of self-discovery, where she is able to recall her true identity with the help of Talos, the Skrull general, and her friend from her previous life, Maria Rambeau. Nick Fury also happens to tag along, and after their adventure, he is led to create the Avengers Initiative in the mid-1990s.

Danvers's arrival and development are completely within Phase 3 of the MCU. Why, then, would the studio continue to use the archetype stereotype for the "strong female character"? After all, we don't need a villainous backstory to alert us to the fact that she can be aggressive. It's true that one of her character traits on Hala, when shown training with Yon-Rogg, is that she cannot control her powers when she gets angry. Nevertheless, her memories from childhood demonstrate that her aggression stems from the fact that she was frequently discounted because of her gender. Her time as a pilot with the top-secret Pegasus project also indicates that she is driven to perform as well as, or even better than, her male colleagues.

It could very well be that the studio decided to use the same trope to show that the "strong female character" need not be so monolithic. We have seen that characters like Gamora and Scarlet Witch were single-minded and powerful while they were on the bad side, but their powers diminished with the introduction of feminine characteristics in their "good" phase. By contrast, Vers (the Kree name of Carol Danvers) is hardly single minded; in fact, she is easily distracted, as we see in her sparring sessions with Yon-Rogg. Furthermore, her identity is important to her, and this quest to discover who she truly is occupies as much of her time as does becoming a good Kree soldier; conversely, the other female superheroes introduced so far are fixated on their respective missions while they are on the "bad" side. Carol Danvers shows that female characters can have more going on than just being mission oriented.

Once she does turn to the "good" side, though, none of the postfeminist tropes seem to apply to Danvers. She is never the damsel, and thus far no romantic relationship appears to be in the works. Her femininity is not a liability; in fact, once she demonstrates how powerful she is, her gender is never even an issue. Mizco reports a research study that concluded two things regarding superhero gender and the objectification of superheroines: "Superhero behavior . . . seems to be defined as masculine, regardless of the gender of the hero performing it . . . . The results of the study suggest that objectification can be overcome if competence, rather than appearance, is emphasized."[18] This appears to be the tack that the studio has taken with *Captain Marvel*. Once her powers are unleashed, she quickly learns to wield them effectively. There's no waffling or uncertainty, no mental breakdown or victimization. Her suit is not skin-tight, though it is form-fitting, but it covers her entire body. Thus, she is neither sexualized nor made to play the victim, two of the more common tropes associated with postfeminist superheroines. Captain Marvel survives the transition from "bad girl" to superheroine without falling into those traps, though we still are waiting to see what her flaws might be.

CONCLUSION: SOME NEW DIRECTIONS IN PHASE 3

This shift in characterization would be in line with the treatment of other female superheroes in Phase 3. Perhaps, we could call Phase 3 the beginning of the redemption of the MCU postfeminist superheroine. Maja Bajac-Carter asks in the introduction to her anthology whether "a female superhero can stand alone, and reach her potential, without having her femininity become a liability."[19] *Captain Marvel* appears to have overcome this hurdle.

But Carol Danvers and Wanda Maximoff aren't allowed the spotlight in *Avengers: Endgame*. Maximoff only appears at the blip, after Thanos's snap is reversed, but her motivation is out of rage and revenge for the loss of her lover, Vision, whom Thanos murdered at the end of *Avengers: Infinity War*. Her climactic scene involves a one-on-one with Thanos, and just when it appears that she will be the one to triumph over him, Thanos brings in the heavy artillery from his ship to distract her focus. The same is true of Carol Danvers's one-on-one encounter with Thanos in the battle. Once Thanos realizes her power, he removes a single infinity stone from his gauntlet and punches her, sending her flying off and unable to continue the fight. These are arguably the two strongest characters—not just the strongest female characters—in the entire MCU at this point. Yet, their heroic activity is limited. Perhaps the story arc demands that it be Iron Man who defeats Thanos. Nevertheless, these two women are contained by the male characters. But they survived the battle and will see future action. *Captain Marvel 2* is slated for release in 2022, and as of this writing, Wanda Maximoff is currently the focus of the first live-action series in the MCU, *WandaVision*.

Aside from the potential direction for Carol Danvers and Wanda Maximoff, Natasha Romanoff needs one final consideration for her role in *Avengers: Endgame*. We find out that the first-generation Avengers have all stopped their avenging in the wake of Thanos's seemingly irreversible snap. Romanoff is the lone exception, having in fact become the leader of the remaining Avengers team. She feels the responsibility, and she has taken the structural power that was denied her when she was the oversimplified postfeminist "honey pot" from Phases 1 and 2. We see her agency when she determines to sacrifice herself on Vormir, an act that she claims has been her goal from the moment she took over as the team leader. She won't be the only one to sacrifice herself in the movie, but Captain America and Iron Man have both acted in self-sacrificing ways in multiple previous films. Romanoff is the first one to suffer the ultimate fate, however.

We have already addressed the ways that Gamora and Hope van Dyne are still problematic in Phase 3 of the MCU, being treated as the damsel in distress and having limited agency. They work well in teams but don't ask them to do anything on their own, much less save the day. At least Gamora seems to have a weakness to overcome—her perplexing attachment to Thanos, which leads to her capture and eventual murder of Vormir. Of course, with her return at the end of *Endgame*, the studio has left open the possibility that all her postfeminist baggage might be erased with Gamora Prime. Phase 4 may show us how Gamora's repudiation of her "bad girl" ways could have gone in a less formulaic direction.

McSweeney observes that "the characterisations of many of the heroes in the MCU are demonstrative of trends in contemporary American film that offer men a much wider range of complexities than were ever offered before, or have ever been offered to women."[20] Perhaps, the MCU is beginning to open the container for their female superheroes.

NOTES

1. Dani Di Placido, "'Captain Marvel' Shows That the MCU Is Still Struggling With Female Superheroes," *Forbes*, March 10, 2019, https://www.forbes.com/sites/danidiplacido/2019/03/10/captain-marvel-shows-that-the-mcu-is-still-struggling-with-female-superheroes/#5d28f1904645.
2. Daisy Phillipson, "Captain Marvel Highlights the Major Problem with Female Superheroes," *DigitalSpy*, March 14, 2019, https://www.digitalspy.com/movies/a26819388/captain-marvel-female-superheroes/.
3. Quoted in Kate Erbland, "'Avengers: Endgame' Needed More Than One Pandering 'Girl Power' Moment to Make Its Female Superheroes Soar," *Indiewire*, April 29, 2019, https://www.indiewire.com/2019/04/avengers-endgame-girl-power-scarlet-witch-1202129153/.
4. Sandra J. Lindow, "To Heck with the Village: Fantastic Heroines, Journey and Return," in *Heroines of Comic Books and Literature: Portrayals in Popular Culture*, eds. Maja Bajac-Carter, Norma Jones, and Bob Batchelor (Lanham: Rowman & Littlefield, 2014), 53.
5. Ibid.
6. Mary Louise DeMarchi, "Avenging Women: An Analysis of Postfeminist Female Representation in the Cinematic Marvel's Avengers Series" (PhD diss., DePaul University, 2014), 56.
7. Robyn Joffe, "Holding Out for a Hero(ine): An Examination of the Presentation and Treatment of Female Superheroes in Marvel Movies," *Panic at the Discourse: An Interdisciplinary Journal* 1, no. 1 (April 2019): 14.
8. Ibid., 13.
9. Ibid.
10. DeMarchi, "Avenging Women," 77.
11. Terence McSweeney, *Avengers Assemble!: Critical Perspectives on the Marvel Cinematic Universe* (London: Wallflower Press, 2018), 34.
12. Nathan Miczo, "Punching Holes in the Sky: Carol Danvers and the Potential of Superheroinism," in *Heroines of Comic Books and Literature: Portrayals in Popular Culture*, eds. Maja Bajac-Carter, Norma Jones, and Bob Batchelor (Lanham: Rowman & Littlefield, 2014), 177.
13. Lindow, "To Heck with the Village," 4.
14. T. Keith Edmunds, "Heroines Aplenty, but None My Mother Would Know: Marvel's Lack of an Iconic Superheroine," in *Heroines of Comic Books and Literature: Portrayals in Popular Culture*, eds. Maja Bajac-Carter, Norma Jones, and Bob Batchelor (Lanham: Rowman & Littlefield, 2014), 217.
15. Joffe, "Holding Out for a Hero(ine)," 10.
16. Edmunds, "Heroines Aplenty, but None My Mother Would Know," 213.
17. McSweeney, Avengers Assemble, 182.
18. Miczo, "Punching Holes in the Sky," 180–181.
19. Maja Bajac-Carter, Norma Jones, and Bob Batchelor, eds., *Heroines of Comic Books and Literature: Portrayals in Popular Culture* (Lanham: Rowman & Littlefield, 2014), xiii.
20. McSweeney, Avengers Assemble, 169.

REFERENCES

Bajac-Carter, Maja, Norma Jones, and Bob Batchelor, eds. *Heroines of Comic Books and Literature: Portrayals in Popular Culture*. Lanham: Rowman & Littlefield, 2014.

Brown, Jeffrey A. *Beyond Bombshells: The New Action Heroine in Popular Culture*. Jackson, MS: University Press of Mississippi, 2015.

Cocca, Carolyn. *Superwomen: Gender, Power, and Representation*. New York: Bloomsbury Academic, 2016.

DeMarchi, Mary Louise. "Avenging Women: An Analysis of Postfeminist Female Representation in the Cinematic Marvel's Avengers Series." PhD diss., DePaul University, 2014. https://via.library.depaul.edy/etd/167.

Di Placido, Dani. "'Captain Marvel' Shows That the MCU Is Still Struggling With Female Superheroes." *Forbes*, March 10, 2019. https://www.forbes.com/sites/danidiplacido/2019/03/10/captain-marvel-shows-that-the-mcu-is-still-struggling-with-female-superheroes/#5d28f1904645.

Edmunds, T. Keith. "Heroines Aplenty, but None My Mother Would Know: Marvel's Lack of an Iconic Superheroine," in *Heroines of Comic Books and Literature: Portrayals in Popular Culture*, edited by Maja Bajac-Carter, Norma Jones, and Bob Batchelor, 211–219. Lanham: Rowman & Littlefield, 2014.

Erbland, Kate. "'Avengers: Endgame' Needed More Than One Pandering 'Girl Power' Moment to Make Its Female Superheroes Soar." *Indiewire*, April 29, 2019. https://www.indiewire.com/2019/04/avengers-endgame-girl-power-scarlet-witch-1202129153/.

Goodrum, Michael, Tara Prescott, and Philip Smith, eds. *Gender and the Superhero Narrative*. Jackson: University Press of Mississippi, 2018.

Hightower, Hannah. "Damsels, Babes, and Heroes: The Evolution of the Female Avengers from *Avengers* #1 to A-Force." Student paper, Collin College, 2016.

Joffe, Robyn. "Holding Out for a Hero(ine): An Examination of the Presentation and Treatment of Female Superheroes in Marvel Movies." *Panic at the Discourse: An Interdisciplinary Journal* 1, no. 1 (April 2019): 5–19.

Lindow, Sandra J. "To Heck with the Village: Fantastic Heroines, Journey and Return," in *Heroines of Comic Books and Literature: Portrayals in Popular Culture*, edited by Maja Bajac-Carter, Norma Jones, and Bob Batchelor, 3–15. Lanham: Rowman & Littlefield, 2014.

McSweeney, Terence. *Avengers Assemble!: Critical Perspectives on the Marvel Cinematic Universe*. London: Wallflower Press, 2018.

Miczo, Nathan. "Punching Holes in the Sky: Carol Danvers and the Potential of Superheroinism," in *Heroines of Comic Books and Literature: Portrayals in Popular Culture*, edited by Maja Bajac-Carter, Norma Jones, and Bob Batchelor, 171–183. Lanham: Rowman & Littlefield, 2014.

Mottram, James. "Wonder Woman 'Not a Feminist Hero', Says Groundbreaking Movie's Female Director." *South China Morning Post*, May 22, 2017.

Nadkarni, Samira. "'I Was Never the Hero That You Wanted Me to Be': Feminism and Resistance to Militarism in Marvel's Jessica Jones," in *Gender and the*

Superhero Narrative, edited by Michael Goodrum, Tara Prescott, and Philip Smith, 78–95. Jackson: University of Mississippi Press, 2018.

Phillipson, Daisy. "Captain Marvel Highlights the Major Problem with Female Superheroes." *DigitalSpy*, March 14, 2019. https://www.digitalspy.com/movies/a26819388/captain-marvel-female-superheroes/.

Sadri, Houman. "The Super-Heroine's Journey: Comics, Gender and the Monomyth." Paper presented at the 3rd Global Conference of the Graphic Novel, Oxford University, Oxford, September 3–5, 2014. https://gup.ub.gu.se/file/158908.

Zechowski, Sharon, and Caryn E. Neumann. "The Mother of All Superheroes: Idealizations of Femininity in *Wonder Woman*," in *Heroines of Comic Books and Literature: Portrayals in Popular Culture*, edited by Maja Bajac-Carter, Norma Jones, and Bob Batchelor, 133–143. Lanham: Rowman & Littlefield, 2014.

Index

The 99, 218, 221, 222

afrofuturism, 16, 68, 81, 85, 145, 149, 153, 157, 158
Al-Mutawa, Naif, 218, 221, 222
altered states of consciousness, 180–84, 192; Safety dependent (SDASC), 180, 184–87; Trauma related (TRASC), 180–87
antichrist, 127–37
appropriation, 61, 71, 73, 74, 77, 79, 80, 222
archetype, 6, 34, 222, 239, 240, 242, 243, 245, 249, 250

Bacon, Francis, 11, 12, 15, 17n10
Benslama, Fethi, 217, 225, 227, 229, 230
Black Lives Matter, 34, 50, 52, 56, 162
Buddhism, 68, 70, 74, 173
Burqa Avenger, 232

center-periphery thinking, 143, 162
characters: Ancient One, 68, 71, 72, 74, 81n3, 151, 153, 154, 182, 183, 189–91; Avengers, 3–5, 8, 16, 17, 22, 33, 70, 82, 83n22, 90, 91, 113–15, 120, 122, 123, 127, 131, 132, 135, 146–49, 162, 163, 166, 170, 171, 198, 199, 203, 204, 206, 219, 222–25, 239, 240, 243–45, 247–52; Bruce Banner/Hulk, 3, 75–77, 82n9, 117, 123, 146, 221, 224, 244, 245; Carol Danvers/Captain Marvel, 163, 171, 179, 199–201, 203, 206, 208, 209, 240, 249; Clint Barton/Hawkeye, 17, 123, 147, 224, 244, 248; Eternals, 81n6, 172, 174, 175; Jessica Jones, 46, 64, 222, 226, 229, 234n41, 234n43; Kamala Khan/Ms. Marvel, 219, 220; Loki, 3, 72, 73, 75, 77, 88, 90, 115, 179, 192n2, 244; Luke Cage, 33, 42, 44, 47, 49, 56, 57n11, 58n13, 59n32, 60n40, 228; Magneto, 163; Mjolnir, 75, 87, 88, 90–92, 95–97, 115, 151; N'Jadaka/Killmonger, 19, 20, 22–27, 68, 69, 72, 79, 80, 106, 108, 109, 111; Natasha Romanoff/Black Widow, 17, 156n11, 224, 239, 243–45, 248, 250, 252; Nick Fury, 96, 131, 135, 138n36, 203, 250; Odin, 69, 72, 73, 75–77, 87–97, 115; Peter Parker/Spider-Man, 17, 127, 131–35, 137, 138n25, 222; Peter Quill/Star Lord, 179; Pietro Maximoff/Quicksilver, 166, 169, 192n2; Punisher, 223, 232n25; Quentin Beck/Mysterio,

127, 131, 132, 134, 136, 138n36; Steven Strange/Dr. Strange, 145, 149, 151, 153, 154, 167, 180–84, 187, 189, 192; Steve Rogers/Captain America, 3, 4, 10, 22, 68, 69, 88, 97, 101, 123, 144, 146–49, 156n11, 162, 163, 179, 206, 208, 218, 219, 244, 245, 248, 252; T'Challa/Black Panther, 19–24, 27, 28, 67–72, 77, 78, 80–82n8, 101–5, 149, 153, 157n23, 161, 163–65, 192n3; Thanos, 4–7, 16, 33, 97, 113–15, 120, 123, 163, 164, 171, 172, 174, 175, 199, 200, 224, 245–47, 251, 252; Thor Odinson, 69, 70, 73–77, 82n8, 87–97, 102, 113–15, 117, 120, 122, 123, 123n1, 224; Tony Stark/Iron Man, 3, 5, 7–17, 69, 123, 127, 131–35, 144, 146–49, 155n2, 162, 171, 175, 208, 218–20, 243–45, 247, 252; Ultron, 3–6, 8, 13, 148, 244, 245, 247, 248; Vision, 88, 92, 248, 252; Wanda Maximoff/Scarlet Witch, 4, 239, 247, 251, 252
Christ, 38–40, 55, 58nn14–15, 58n24, 87–91, 104, 105, 107, 109, 116, 117, 119, 121, 122, 127–30, 132–37
chronological, 165, 168–69
colonization, 69, 76, 77, 82n12
community, 6, 24, 26, 27, 33, 35, 37–47, 52, 56, 58n13, 71, 106, 160–61, 167–69, 173, 186, 188, 191, 192, 209, 225, 226

deception, 128–37, 197
Descartes, Rene, 11–12, 15
divine: attributes, 117–18; command, 92–93; impassibility, 118; right of kings, 69, 72, 77, 82
Du Bois, W.E.B., 107–09

Egyptian, 78, 221, 222, 226, 228
Ellul, Jacques, 4
Eltahawy, Mona, 226–29
entertainment, 8, 9, 55
envy, 103–04

euchronia, 145, 148

freedom, 15–17, 40, 47, 50–52, 77, 118, 119, 147, 207, 241

gender, 44, 46, 49, 73–75, 179, 183, 199, 227, 242, 250, 251
Girard, Rene, 19–27, 102–11
Grant, George Parkin, 14

hate, 46, 49, 93, 103, 230
Heidegger, Martin, 4, 7–10, 13
hermeneutics, 35, 122
hip hop, 40–43, 59n37
Holocaust, 113, 114, 117
Ho Yinsen, 5, 17, 219, 220
hubris, 5, 6, 12, 92, 148, 172, 173
humility, 90, 131, 134–36
hybridity, 160–61, 163, 167, 171

ideology, 143–44, 146, 149, 154, 164, 197, 201, 227, 246
integration, 162, 163, 180, 182, 186, 191, 209

jealousy, 103–4

kingship, 25, 69, 72, 73, 77, 79, 80, 89
Kree, 172, 174, 200, 201, 203–9, 250, 251

liminal, 185–89
love, 13–14, 17, 24, 26, 35, 42, 49, 75, 93, 96, 97, 117–20, 122, 147, 246, 248

magic, 70, 91, 92, 121, 145, 149–54, 168, 181, 183, 188
Manley, Marc, 226, 227, 234n41
mediation, 104–5, 107–8, 110
Messiah, 40, 129, 131, 134–36
Metz, Johann Baptist, 114, 116, 117, 123
mimetic, 19–28, 102–11, 226
Moltmann, Jürgen, 114, 116–21
monomyth, 217, 239
multiplicity, 52–54, 165, 169, 173, 176

multiverse, 145, 147, 149, 153, 154, 160, 162, 165–67, 170–73, 190
mystical, 75, 122, 151, 155, 167, 180–85, 188–92
myth, 20–22, 26–28, 205

nationalism, 37, 38, 40, 198

Okorafor, Nnedi, 154, 155
othering, 202, 204

peace, 3, 21, 27, 37, 89, 96, 147, 187
planetary, 155, 160–62, 164, 167–69, 173, 175
Plato, 93–95
political Theology, 120
Pope Francis, 4, 6, 12, 15
popular culture, 34, 57n2, 198, 208, 218, 220, 223, 225, 228
post-9/11 cinema, 200, 202, 205
postcolonial, 69, 144, 149, 162
postfeminism, 199, 240, 242–52
posttraumatic, 115, 180–83, 186, 189
profane, 41–43
psychedelic, 185–87, 190–91

Qahera, 218, 222, 229
queer, 45, 145, 151, 153, 162, 163, 169

race/racial, 23, 35, 44, 52, 73, 74, 90, 107, 118, 153, 170, 174, 183, 209
rainbow, 75, 151–52, 165
refugees, 82n5, 207–09
representation, 68, 110, 133, 220, 221, 239
Revelation, 47, 59n26, 127–30, 185, 187
ritual, 21, 25, 42, 72, 108, 180, 186, 188

sacred, 4, 13, 41–43, 79, 89, 188, 233n30
sacrifice, 3, 5, 19, 20, 28, 39, 88–91, 97, 106, 131, 224, 225, 228, 246, 252
scapegoat, 19–22, 27, 106, 107
scientific triumphalism, 143, 149
secular, 41–43, 54
Sölle, Dorothee, 114, 120
speculative fiction, 144, 149, 153, 155n4
spirituality, 15, 41, 180, 182, 183, 188, 217
standing reserve, 4, 10–14
suffering, 90, 109, 114, 116–23, 188, 203, 225, 247, 249
superheroine, 220, 222, 228, 229, 239, 242, 245, 247
supermuslim, 217–19, 221, 223, 225–26, 229–30
SWAT Team, 223, 224

theodicy, 15, 182
theomusicology, 41, 59n37
tragedy, 45, 113
trauma, 115, 116, 123n2, 179–84, 186–92, 198, 225
twins, 20, 26, 27, 247

utopia, 145, 148, 198, 203

vengeance, 20, 22, 24, 25, 87
virtue, 91, 123, 135, 137, 198, 203

War on Terror, 198, 199, 201, 207
warrior spirit, 87, 91, 92
whiteness, 68, 75

About the Contributors

Jennifer Baldwin is director of Grounding Flight Wellness Center, Woodstock, Georgia. Her primary area of scholarship is the intersection of traumatology and systematic theology. Rev. Dr. Baldwin's publications include four edited volumes and two monographs, *Trauma Sensitive Theology: Thinking Theologically in the Era of Trauma* (2018) and *Through Dangerous Terrain: A Guide for Trauma-Sensitive Pastoral Leadership in Times of Threat* (2020).

Daniel White Hodge is a recognized Hip Hop culture expert and cultural literacy communications scholar with 21 years of academic work experience. Dr. Hodge is professor of Intercultural Communications, department chair of the Communication Arts Department, and research lead on the Catalyst_ _ 606 program. His research interests are at the intersections of faith, Hip Hop culture, race/ethnicity, and young adult ethnic-minority emerging generations. Dr. Hodge has worked in the young adult and Hip Hop context for over 25 years and continues to focus on justice and disparity issues as it concerns ethnic-minority populations. His seven books are *Heaven Has A Ghetto: The Missiological Gospel & Theology of Tupac Amaru Shakur* (2009), *The Soul Of Hip Hop: Rimbs, Timbs, & A Cultural Theology* (2010), *Hip Hop's Hostile Gospel: A Post Soul Theological Exploration* (2017) *Homeland Insecurity: A Hip Hop Missiology for the Post-Civil Rights Context* (2018), *Baptized In Dirty Water: Reimagining the Gospel According to Tupac Amaru* Shakur (2019), *Intercultural Communication: A Societal Approach to Developing Intercultural Competencies* (2020), and *Hip-Hop and Dismantling the School-to-Prison Pipeline* (2021).

Will Abney has been on the faculty at Athens Technical College in Athens, Georgia, since 2016, teaching courses in literature and essay writing. He is a doctoral candidate in comparative literature from the University of Georgia, specializing in medieval literature and personifications of evil. He is also a candidate for the MFA degree in creative nonfiction writing at Bay Path University. He previously taught comparative literature courses at the University of Georgia, as well as courses in Greek and Hebrew exegesis at the McAfee School of Theology at Mercer University in Atlanta. In his spare time, Will enjoys attending college football games, re-watching Marvel movies, and collecting master's degrees from various universities across the United States. The current tally is five of them, going on seven. He also travels whenever possible, and his travel blog is easy to find online.

Adam Barkman received his PhD from the Free University of Amsterdam and is professor and chair of the Philosophy Department at Redeemer University (Canada), and is co-series editor of Lexington Books' Critical Companion to Contemporary Directors. He has authored or edited over a dozen books and has written many articles on the intersection between philosophy, religion, and superheroes.

Whitney Bauman is associate professor of religious studies at Florida International University in Miami. He is also co-founder and co-director of *Counterpoint: Navigating Knowledge,* a non-profit based in Berlin, Germany that holds public discussions over social and ecological issues related to globalization and climate change. His areas of research interest fall under the theme of "religion, science, and globalization." He is the recipient of a Fulbright Fellowship and a Humboldt Fellowship. His publications include *Religion and Ecology: Developing a Planetary Ethic* (2014), and co-authored with Kevin O'Brien, *Environmental Ethics and Uncertainty: Tackling Wicked Problems* (2019). He is currently working on a manuscript about the nineteenth-century German, Romantic scientist, Ernst Haeckel.

Matthew Brake is the creator and founder of the *Pop Culture and Theology* blog. He has a master's degree in interdisciplinary studies and philosophy from George Mason University. He also has a master of divinity from Regent University. He is the series editor of the *Theology and Pop Culture* series from Lexington/Fortress Academic, and the series co-editor (with A. David Lewis) of the forthcoming *Religion and Comics* series from Claremont Press.

George A. Dunn has taught philosophy and religion in both the United States and China. He is currently a special research fellow with the Institute for Globalizing Civilization in Hangzhou, China and serves on the board of the Global Council for Religious Research. He has edited or co-edited several volumes of essays dealing with philosophy, film, and popular culture, including *The Philosophy of Christopher Nolan*, co-edited with Jason T. Eberl. His latest book is *A New Politics for Philosophy: Essays on Plato, Nietzsche, and Strauss*, due to appear in 2021. He is also editing a volume of essays on René Girard and philosophy.

Jason T. Eberl, PhD, is professor of health-care ethics and philosophy and director of the Albert Gnaegi Center for Health Care Ethics at Saint Louis University. His research interests include the philosophy of human nature and its application to issues at the margins of life; ethical issues related to end-of-life care, genetics, and healthcare allocation; and the philosophical thought of Thomas Aquinas. He is the author of *Thomistic Principles and Bioethics*, *The Routledge Guidebook to Aquinas' Summa Theologiae*, and *The Nature of Human Persons: Metaphysics and Bioethics*, as well as the editor of *Contemporary Controversies in Catholic Bioethics*. Additionally, he has edited volumes on philosophical themes in *Star Wars*, *Star Trek*, *Sons of Anarchy*, *Battlestar Galactica*, and the films of Christopher Nolan. He has also written essays for similar volumes on *Terminator*, *Avatar*, *Harry Potter*, *The Big Lebowski*, *The Hunger Games*, Stanley Kubrick, J.J. Abrams, Metallica, *Hamilton*, and *Westworld*.

Rhiannon Grant works in the Center for Research in Quaker Studies at Woodbrooke, in partnership with the University of Birmingham and Lancaster University. Her main interests are religious language, the relationship of theology to practice, and understanding religion better as a category; her previous publications include work on Wittgenstein, *Star Wars*, Quaker ways of talking about God, *LEGO*, and multiple religious belonging, *Deadpool*, and cultural appropriation. Her most recent books are *Theology from Listening* (2020), and *Hearing the Light* (2021). Future projects are likely to include a new Wittgensteinian approach to the study of religions, theological analysis of the ways Quaker worship changed when moving online, and an intense period of watching *The Falcon and the Winter Soldier*.

Jo Henderson-Merrygold is based at the University of Sheffield where she recently completed a PhD in interdisciplinary biblical studies. Entitled "Gender Diversity in the Ancestral Narratives: Encountering Sarah & Esau through a Hermeneutics of Cispicion," Jo's research addresses the way cisnormative presuppositions impact our understanding of biblical characters. She is particularly interested in how insights from trans and queer theories can help make sense of quirks and idiosyncrasies in the narratives. Beyond her doctoral research, Jo is in the interplay between biblical and religious imagery in contemporary society, especially popular culture.

Imran Khan is responsible for the development of the production slate for Joerg Winger's new label, Big Window Productions, a subsidiary of UFA Fiction GmbH. Prior to his current role, he has worked in media for over 13 years at CBS Television, Warner Bros., and Turner Broadcasting in various roles including scripted series development and sponsorship marketing. He then launched his own media startup, The Snack Content Network™. After successfully exiting his startup, Imran was then recruited by Google where he spent the next eight years working across three different continents as a marketing consultant tasked with collaborating with creative agencies to develop brand initiatives for advertisers by capitalizing on dynamic opportunities in the digital world. He has been recognized for his efforts with prestigious Cannes Lion awards for his work on P&G Secret's Mean Stinks anti-bullying campaign and for P&G Always' #LikeAGirl campaign. Imran has two diametrically opposite degrees in Biochemical Engineering and Musical Theatre from Northwestern University in Chicago. In addition, he holds an MBA from Columbia Business School in NYC.

John C. McDowell is the academic dean at St. Athanasius College and professor of philosophy, theology, and ethics. Prior to his time as the institution's director of research, he was the Morpeth Chair of Theology & Religion at the University of Newcastle, NSW; the Meldrum Lecturer in Systematic Theology at the University of Edinburgh; and doctoral student at Cambridge University. He has authored several books and over seventy articles and book chapters in theology, philosophy, and ethics, including the studies in popular culture: *The Politics of Big Fantasy: Studies in Cultural Suspicion* (2014); *The Ideology of Identity Politics in George Lucas* (2016); and *The Gospel According to Star Wars: Faith, Hope and the Force*, 2nd edn. (2017). He has contributed to a number of volumes in a Theology & Pop Culture series: *Theology and Star Wars, René Girard and Pop Culture, Theology and Batman, Theology and Spider-Man, Theology and the DC Universe*, and *Theology and Tolkien*.

Dilyana Mincheva is assistant professor in critical media in the Department of Communication Studies and Multimedia at McMaster University, Canada. Her most recent research is engaged with the culturological study of Islamic feminism, the politics of image in cinematic feminism and utopia. She is the bearer of two international awards for research excellence (2012 and 2015) granted by the *Journal of Religion and Spirituality in Society* and the author of the monograph *The Politics of Western Muslim Intellectual Discourse in the West: The Emergence of a Western-Islamic Public Sphere*, Sussex Academic Press, 2016. Mincheva is currently at work on a second monograph focused on socially and cinematically mediated forms of Islamic feminism.

Ryan Smock has taught higher education philosophy, composition, and literature classes for eleven years. During this time, he has consistently received awards for "Effective or Highly Effective" teaching from the Department of Education despite being legally blind and hard of hearing. He currently teaches at Mesa Community College, where his unfathomable love for philosophy and pop culture infuses and invigorates every lesson. His current projects include developing a podcast series for special needs parenting, constructing a blog that explores Girard's mimetics as they appear in video games, and writing for his first novel.

Bennet Soenen is a graduate student in the philosophy department at McMaster University. He is the author of three recent book chapters and articles, including a chapter on forgiveness for Vernon Press' Philosophy of Forgiveness series and an article on David Chappelle's critique of racism for Open Court. He is also a reserve for the Canadian Armed Forces.

Lisa Stenmark teaches humanities and comparative religious studies at a San Jose State University. She is the author of *Religion, Science and Democracy: A Disputational Friendship*, on scientific and religious authority in public life, and is active in the American Academy of Religion and the Arendt Circle. She has written numerous articles on the relationship between religion and science particularly in the context of democratic discourse and within the broader culture. She earned an MDiv/MA from Pacific Lutheran Theological Seminary/the Graduate Theological Union, and a PhD in religious studies from Vanderbilt University. In her spare time, she runs, practices Aikido, and reads too much science fiction.

George Tsakiridis is senior lecturer of philosophy & religion at South Dakota State University. His published research includes the topics of guilt and forgiveness which are featured in journals such as *Theology and Science* and *Zygon: Journal of Religion and Science*. He is also the author of *Evagrius Ponticus and Cognitive Science: A Look at Moral Evil and the Thoughts* (2010). Currently, Dr. Tsakiridis is editing the volume *Theology and Spider-Man* in the Theology and Pop Culture series for Lexington Books/Fortress Academic. For the past several years, he has served as the assistant director of the Pappas Patristic Institute Summer Program where he has also taught. He holds a PhD in religion and science/theology from the Lutheran School of Theology at Chicago.

Andrew T. Vink is a PhD candidate in the Theology Department at Boston College. Andrew hails from Baltimore and has studied at universities on the East Coast and in the Midwest. His research interests concern Latin

American liberation theology, political theology, Catholic social teaching, and the thought of Bernard Lonergan. Andrew has had articles accepted by *The Heythrop Journal* and *Irish Theological Quarterly* and has presented both nationally and internationally. Outside of theology, Andrew's interests include baseball, fantasy novels, comic books, American music, and the intersection of philosophy and pop culture. He currently resides outside of Boston with his wife and son.

www.ingramcontent.com/pod-product-compliance
Lightning Source LLC
Chambersburg PA
CBHW020112010526
44115CB00008B/796